Crime and Justice

Crime and Justice

A Review of Research

Edited by Michael Tonry
and Norval Morris

with the Support of The National Institute of Justice

VOLUME 10

The University of Chicago Press, Chicago and London

This volume was prepared under grant number 86-IJ-CX-0016 awarded to the Castine Research Corporation by the National Institute of Justice, U.S. Department of Justice, under the Omnibus Crime Control and Safe Streets Act of 1968 as amended. Points of view or opinions expressed in this volume are those of the editors or authors and do not necessarily represent the official position or policies of the U.S. Department of Justice.

The University of Chicago Press, Chicago 60637
The University of Chicago Press, Ltd., London

© 1988 by The University of Chicago
All rights reserved. Published 1988
Printed in the United States of America
93 92 91 90 89 88   5 4 3 2 1

ISSN: 0192-3234
ISBN: 0-226-80804-1

LCN: 80-642217

The paper used in this publication meets the minimum requirements of American National Standard for Information Sciences—Permanence of Paper for Printed Library Materials, ANSI Z39.48-1984. ∞

Contents

Introduction   vii

Theme and Variation in Community Policing   1
Jerome H. Skolnick and David H. Bayley

Community Organizations and Crime   39
Wesley G. Skogan

The British Gas Suicide Story
and Its Criminological Implications   79
Ronald V. Clarke and Pat Mayhew

Co-offending and Criminal Careers   117
Albert J. Reiss, Jr.

The Law and Criminology of Drunk Driving   171
James B. Jacobs

Prison Populations: A System Out of Control?   231
Alfred Blumstein

Structuring Sentencing   267
Michael Tonry

Author Index—Volumes 1–10   339
Title Index—Volumes 1–10   341

Introduction

This is the tenth in a series of volumes of commissioned essays on research in crime and justice, designed to survey the contours of knowledge of crime and of society's methods to understand and deal with it.

Knowledge in criminology, as in other fields of research, grows by artificial isolation of a segment of a topic for close analysis and by the deliberate juxtaposition of insights gained from the study of other segments. We must both specialize and look across the borders of our own specialties. No one can see all the problems whole. No one can keep abreast of the major literature, for it far exceeds time and energy; but some effort at a broad overview is essential if only to lend direction to one's own specialty. Such an overview of research and knowledge in crime and justice is the ambitious purpose of this series.

Crime and Justice is necessarily interdisciplinary. At this early stage of criminological knowledge, what we have is a variety of scholars in the social and biological sciences turning their attention to problems of crime, justice, and juvenile delinquency. Around a core concern for measuring, understanding, and influencing our efforts to contain and control crime, there revolves a wide diversity of professional and scholarly interests.

Essays are of several types. The staple is a summary by a leading scholar of the state of the art on a defined topic, together with his or her views on the policy and research implications of that knowledge. Others are more speculative and idiosyncratic and report on analytical, conceptual, or empirical developments, or consider promising but novel lines of inquiry.

We are in no doubt of the need for a series like this; whether this enterprise can build bridges between the islands of parochialism that characterize research in and knowledge of crime and criminal justice is, of course, more speculative.

The preceding five paragraphs, with only minor differences, began the introduction to volume 1 of *Crime and Justice*. For us, volume 10 is a milestone; the double digits raise our confidence that *Crime and Justice* will endure and enhance our gratitude to those who have helped us lay the foundations of this series.

Whether the series has attained all that it set out to do is for others to decide. We have adhered to our aim to publish mostly state-of-the-art reviews of knowledge on specific subjects with a leavening of more speculative or conceptual essays. As we look at the cumulative lists of authors and topics at the back of this volume, we are struck by the number and diversity of writers whose work we have published and the breadth and comprehensiveness of the subjects on which they have written.

Crime and Justice was initially conceived, and titled, as an annual review of research. The aim for the annual volume each year is to commission twelve to fifteen essays on important research developments relating to crime, its causes, and control, and to the social institutions that administer the criminal law. The resulting drafts are read by the editors, members of the editorial board, and expert independent reviewers; roughly half of those commissioned are eventually published.

The only major change in *Crime and Justice* since it began has been the development of a number of volumes commissioned around a single core theme. *Communities and Crime* and *Prediction and Classification* appeared as volumes 8 and 9; volume 11 will center on the theme of "family violence as a criminal law problem," and volume 13 will be on drugs and crime. Albert J. Reiss, Jr., Don M. Gottfredson, Lloyd Ohlin, and James Q. Wilson have served as guest co-editors of these thematic volumes.

The process of development of a thematic volume is substantially the same as for the regular volumes. Our editorial board—a real working board, not merely a list of names on an inside front page—selects topics and authors; each essay is commissioned from a leading scholar; all of the writers, and other scholars and practitioners, later assemble at a research conference to discuss first drafts; each draft is sent to reviewers and board members; publication decisions are in large part based on those peer reviews. If time permits, new writers are commissioned on topics on which the originally commissioned essays are rejected; if time does not so permit, we publish the book with a gap, or persuade another writer to expand his or her coverage. So far, the thematic volumes seem to have been well received.

Before turning to the contents of this volume, we want to note our gratitude to the National Institute of Justice, its directors over the last ten years, and the civil servants who make it work. The institute has stayed the course since 1977 when the series began. All of the directors and acting directors during that period—Blair Ewing, Harry Bratt, Bob Burkhart, James Underwood, and James K. Stewart—have provided support and encouragement, and all have respected and protected the series' editorial independence. James K. Stewart has served the longest of these and permitted and supported the series' expansion to include thematic volumes. Paul Cascarano, assistant director of the institute, first proposed creation of the series and has nurtured and sustained it ever since. Ten years is a long run in the world of federal grantsmanship, and we thank all of those in the government who have worked to keep *Crime and Justice* alive and healthy.

This volume contains seven essays. Five—on drunk driving, co-offending, sentencing reform, community organizations and crime, and prison crowding—are of our staple genre: empirically informed reviews of research and policy. The other two may warrant fuller introduction.

Skolnick and Bayley's excellent book, *The New Blue Line*, led us to suggest to them that they relate their observations of policing in the six American cities they studied for that book to similar developments elsewhere in the world, and further to tease out the practical implications of these experiments in community-based policing for American policing generally.

Clarke and Mayhew's essay on the "British Gas Suicide Story," was the product of a dinner-table conversation between Ron Clarke and one of us, with no idea of an essay for *Crime and Justice* in mind. At first blush, suicide by putting one's head in a gas oven does not seem to have much to do with crime as it is generally understood. But there is an important linkage. The whole question of displacement of highly motivated human actions, if means be denied—displacement of crime by target hardening and by opportunity denying—is at issue, at least by powerful analogy. Those who decide to kill themselves this way would seem appreciably motivated; why, then, when this means ceases to be available, do they apparently often not seek other means—and they apparently do not. It is a question bearing importantly on many aspects of the study of human motivations and their expression, sometimes in crime, sometimes not. If the would-be suicide lacking lethal gas does not otherwise kill himself, or even try to, what does that suggest for the determined inhibition of crime?

On to volume 20.

Jerome H. Skolnick and David H. Bayley

Theme and Variation in Community Policing

ABSTRACT

Community policing appears to be increasingly popular around the globe. Recent research in the United States, Europe, Asia, and Australia indicates that community policing is a coherent concept grounded on the notion that, together, police and public are more effective and more humane coproducers of safety and public order than are the police alone. Programmatic elements constituting community policing include community-based crime prevention, reorientation of patrol to stress nonemergency service, increased accountability to the public, decentralization of command, and sometimes, civilianization. "Community policing" does not always achieve these unifying elements. Impediments to the development of community policing include norms grounded in traditional notions of the police role, police needs to react to emergencies, resource limitations, traditional assumptions about patrol strategies, assessment problems, customary public expectations of the police role, and bureaucratic isolation of community programs within the police department. Despite the obstacles, the community-policing movement is likely to grow because of benefits to the public from enhanced crime prevention and police accountability and to the police from increased legitimation through consensus building with the public, increased morale, and enhanced career opportunities.

A growing and extraordinary consensus has arisen among selected police executives around the globe that the movement toward commu-

David H. Bayley is professor of criminal justice at the State University of New York at Albany, and Jerome H. Skolnick is professor of law, jurisprudence, and social policy at the University of California, Berkeley. We are indebted to the National Institute of Justice and its director, James K. Stewart, for their generous support. We are grateful to police chiefs all over the world and to their officers for their warm cooperation. Hans Klette of Lund University was enormously helpful in Scandinavia. Without his efforts, the research could not have been completed.

1

nity policing is a positive development. At first thought, this is quite surprising. Why should police leaders in places as different as London, Oslo, California, and Singapore be attracted to a concept that challenges established conceptions of the role of the police in society?

The answer has to be this: with respect to crime—and perhaps more importantly, to perceptions and fear of crime—there is almost an international language, a virtually predictable set of public responses to rises in crime and fear of crime. One part of the response is to seek to punish criminals more severely and to fill prisons to capacity and overcapacity. Another part is to look to the police to prevent crime from occurring in the first place. The question then becomes, is it possible for police to prevent crime? Or, put another way, are there policies, allocative strategies, or techniques that, when adopted and carried out, lower crime rates? To that question, there is no simple answer. At best, we can offer a firm "maybe."

Modern police managers have come to understand the limits of police activity in fighting crime. In particular, they comprehend how unsuccessful crime-prevention strategies have been over the previous two decades. As we discovered in research for our book, *The New Blue Line: Police Innovation in Six American Cities*, they have learned that solutions to the crime problem are scarcely met by conducting business as usual. They comprehended the realities of what research findings were demonstrating.

First, increasing the numbers of police does not necessarily reduce crime rates, nor does it raise the proportion of crimes solved. Neither does "throwing money" at police departments by boosting police budgets and manpower. Certainly, if there were no police, there would be more crime. But, once a certain threshold has been reached, neither more police nor more money seem to help very much. Such crime-control measures do have an effect, but they constitute a minor part of the equation. Such social conditions as income, unemployment, population, and social heterogeneity are far more important predictors of variation in crime and clearance rates (Morris and Heal 1981).

Second, randomized motorized patrolling neither reduces crime nor improves the chances of catching criminals. Such randomized patrols do not reassure citizens enough to affect their fear of crime, and they do not generate greater trust in the police. Regular foot patrols, by contrast, have been shown to reduce citizens' fear of crime, although they do not appear to affect crime rates (Kelling 1981).

Third, two-person cars neither reduce crime nor catch criminals more effectively than one-person cars. Further, police are no more likely to be injured in one-person cars (Boydstun, Sherry, and Moelter 1977).

Fourth, although saturation patrolling does reduce crime, it does so at the cost of displacing it to other areas (Kelling et al. 1974).

Fifth, the legendary "good collar" is a rare event. Even more rarely do patrol police confront a crime in progress. Only "Dirty Harry" encounters an armed robbery with his morning coffee. Most of the time, cops passively patrol and provide emergency services (Skolnick and Bayley 1986).

Sixth, response time does not much matter. If even one minute elapses from the time the crime is committed, there is less than a 10 percent chance that police will apprehend the criminal. Even instantaneous reaction would not be effective. Since citizens delay an average of four to five and one-half minutes before calling the police, speed of response makes little difference. Citizens seem to want a predictable response. Crime victims recognize that the perpetrator will usually have left the scene by the time the police arrive. Citizens want a police response they can count on. They prefer, research has shown, a less rapid but assured response to a sometimes rapid but unpredictable response (Percey 1980).

Seventh, criminal investigations are not very effective in solving crimes. Generally, crimes are solved because offenders are immediately apprehended or because someone identifies them with a name, an address, or a license plate number. Holmes and Watson worked effectively from subtle clues to apprehension of criminals. Real-life detectives work from known suspects to corroborating evidence. This means that, in order to solve crimes, the police must obtain information from residents of the communities in which crimes occur. But, if residents are hostile and suspicious of police, citizens are less likely to provide information (Greenwood and Petersilia 1976).

To the thoughtful police administrator, such findings suggest that traditional strategies are neither reducing crime nor reassuring its potential victims. In effect, thinking police professionals have had to develop some new ideas. The key reformulation has been that the police and the communities they are policing must try to become coproducers of crime prevention. Roughly speaking, this concept of coproduction, of increased cooperation between police and the community, is what has taken hold as "community policing."

In 1986 we undertook international research in Europe and Asia to try to gain a better understanding of the potential, limits, and meaning of the community-policing idea. Specifically, we compared the community-policing movement in Europe and Asia—in Scandinavia, Singapore, Australia, and London—with what we had discovered in our sample of six American cities. This essay is about that comparison. We describe community policing's key programmatic components and provide illustrations from our field research in Section I. Section II describes some of the potential obstacles that can constrain the development of community policing. Section III discusses the enduring benefits of community policing for the public and the police. Conclusions are offered in Section IV.

I. The Programs of Community Policing

Listening to police executives in Western Europe, North America, Australia-New Zealand, and the Far East, one might conclude that community policing was already an established organizing concept of police operations and that examples of it abound. The reality is that, while everyone talks about it, there is little agreement on meaning. Community policing has been embraced as a buzzword, and the variety of activities associated with it seem to have little in common: Neighborhood Watch, revised departmental orders allowing junior officers to speak to the media, local consultative committees, specialized attention to the problems of women and families, liaison with gay communities, diversified recruitment, establishment of shop-front police stations, unsolicited visits by police to residences, and public-relations campaigns. One police chief created community policing by declaring every patrol officer to be a community police officer.

Many readers of this essay will think they already know what community policing is. They will expect pet programs to be discussed that they think are valuable. The point is that community policing is not a single program or even an accepted core of programs. If one goes to police departments and says, "Show me an example of community policing," one will be shown different activities in different places. This lack of programmatic clarity is cause for concern. Because community policing is an increasingly popular phenomenon in modern policing, it is easy to conclude that it is only rhetoric or merely a clever phrase coined to make policing appear more humane. Is this the case? We think not. We argue that community policing is a coherent concept and that it has identifiable programmatic elements.

The central premise of community policing is that the public should play a more active part in enhancing public safety. Neither the police nor the criminal justice system can bear the responsibility alone. In an apt phrase, the public should be seen along with the police as "co-producers" of safety and order. Community policing thus imposes a new responsibility on the police to devise appropriate ways for associating the public with law enforcement and the maintenance of order.

This unexceptional formulation of community policing does not really narrow the concept very much. Hard-bitten older officers recognize full well that their job is made easier if the public cooperates and supports the police. They spend much of their professional life asking for assistance from the public. What is new, they growl, about that? Nothing at all. It follows, therefore, that, if community policing is to mean something distinctive, it must refer to programs that change the customary interaction between police and public. New phrases are empty and misleading if they do not describe a new reality.

Accordingly, we propose that community policing should be said to exist only when new programs are implemented that raise the level of public participation in the maintenance of public order. The police can take credit for community policing only when such programs are of their own devising.

Community policing in this substantial sense is very much alive around the world and appears to be growing rapidly. Examining experience on four continents, we have found four programmatic elements occurring again and again under the banner of community policing: (1) community-based crime prevention, (2) reorientation of patrol activities to emphasize nonemergency servicing, (3) increased accountability to the public, and (4) decentralization of command, including, under certain circumstances, civilianization. These are the forms community policing takes when rhetoric becomes reality. These are the forms we describe, drawing on international experience.

Let us be clear on one point. All that is valuable in policing is not community policing. Hallowing every innovation by calling it community policing empties the phrase. Representative recruitment of minorities and participatory management, for example, are changes in policing that may benefit communities enormously, but they do not necessarily change the terms of police-public interaction. The same may or may not be true of civilianization, which we found to be an important initiative in American cities, particularly in Santa Ana, California. Civilianization does not, per se, qualify as community policing. Civilian employees of police departments are not the public. Hiring civilians to perform work previously handled by sworn officers, such as secretarial services, radio dispatching, or forensic analysis, does not enhance the role of the public. Police officers, too, were civilians before they were hired. But, if a program of civilianization is introduced, as in Santa Ana, for the explicit purpose of community involvement in crime prevention, then civilianization does qualify. In Santa Ana, civilians were employed alongside sworn police as community service officers. Their explicit tasks varied, but their overall assignment was clear—to reach out to citizens and to involve them in the department's crime-prevention programs. Thus, we distinguish between civilianization in Houston, designed primarily to put more uniforms on the street, and civilianization in Santa Ana, where a substantial number of civilians were hired to assist in community liaison (Skolnick and Bayley 1986).

It is not civilianization, per se, that makes the difference, but rather the theory behind its introduction. If civilianization is merely a substitution of nonsworn for sworn, primarily for economic reasons, then that scarcely qualifies as community policing. But, if civilianization is introduced to enhance community mobilization for crime prevention, it should qualify. In actuality, we did not find, in Europe or in Asia, the kind of considered civilianization that we did encounter in Santa Ana. For that reason, we do not discuss it further in this essay. At the same time, if thoughtfully introduced by an imaginative police executive, civilianization can provide an important undergirding for community policing.

We now describe the four recurring programmatic elements in community policing that we found internationally, giving examples from accessible countries of the free world.

A. Community-based Crime Prevention

The words "community" and "communicate" share a common origin. Community-based policing suggests active communication with the public. The police should demonstrate a presence in the community. They should be visible, accessible, and caring, with the goal of reducing fear and deterring crime (Goldstein 1987).

The centerpiece of community-based crime prevention is Neighborhood Watch, which encompasses organizing and training people to report criminal activity, engraving valuables with marks of identification, and having police officers make security surveys of premises. Signs are then posted, warning that particular areas and premises are covered by Neighborhood Watch. With great pride, police departments collect and publish statistics on the number of persons, blocks, families, and residences covered by Neighborhood Watch. They create specialized units to encourage its development.

Although Neighborhood Watch is an American invention of the early 1970s, it varies considerably throughout the world and sometimes even within the same country (Bayley 1986; Rosenbaum 1987; Weatheritt 1987). These programs vary with respect to whether the initiative comes from the police or the public; whether costs are borne by participants, government, or charitable organizations; the size of areas organized; the manner in which leaders are selected; the amount of effort devoted to maintaining high levels of activity and involvement; the kind of provision made for organizing neighborhood units into larger associations; and the level of ongoing support provided by the police.

The most ambitious and extensive neighborhood crime-prevention program is found in Japan, though it is not called Neighborhood Watch and does not owe its inspiration to the United States (Bayley 1976). From time immemorial, Japanese neighborhoods have had the rudiments of informal government—the creation of custom rather than statute. Membership was automatic and participation compelled by social pressure. Its leaders mediated disputes, lobbied for municipal services, organized neighborhood-improvement campaigns, communicated information about local concerns, and sponsored festivals. As an outgrowth of this tradition, most neighborhoods in Japan now have crime-prevention associations that distribute information, sell security hardware, publish newsletters, maintain a close liaison with local police, and occasionally patrol the streets. All neighborhood organizations belong to provincial and national crime-prevention associations.

Although closely watched by the police and often discouraged elsewhere, civilian street patrols are not unique to Japan. In the United States, citizen's band (CB) radio patrols are common. Although designed to increase the police surveillance capacity, CB personnel are cautioned against taking any action except notifying the police about emergencies or suspicious circumstances (Skolnick and Bayley 1986, chap. 3).

The police are also assisted by efforts of particular groups of people to protect themselves more successfully by developing education programs. A vast literature now exists in many languages with advice to the elderly, school children, working women, commuters, vending machine operators, taxicab drivers, and vacationers. In addition to developing brochures, police crime-prevention specialists, usually based in central headquarters, give lectures, organize meetings, conduct classes, publish newsletters, and coordinate media campaigns. There are now national and even international networks of crime-prevention personnel that trade material, exchange experts, and generally encourage one another to bear up against the ridicule and skepticism of the rest of the force.

B. Reorientation of Patrol Activities

In the past fifteen years, serious questions have been raised about whether traditional police strategies provide effective protection. These strategies have been based on the assumption that criminal and disorderly activity would be deterred if the police were a visible presence on the streets and promptly arrested people who broke the law. Accordingly, approximately 60 percent of personnel in police forces have been assigned to patrolling and the bulk of the remainder to criminal investigation (Bayley 1985, chap. 5). Over the course of several decades, patrol work has been handled increasingly from motor vehicles and prompted by telephone solicitation and radio dispatch.

Although misleadingly described as the crime-fighting model of policing, the purpose of this system, in fact, was crime prevention. It is a source of confusion and ill feeling that proponents of community policing sometimes speak as if they had a monopoly on concern with prevention. What community policing questions is not the goal of policing but the means.

Buttressed by research that has shown that random motorized patrolling and rapid response may not effectively deter crime or lead to the more certain apprehension of criminals, community-police reformers contend that patrol operations should encourage a deeper involvement with the community, an involvement not instigated predominantly by emergency calls for service (Kelling et al. 1974; Percey 1980; Morris and Heal 1981). Rather than being deployed as an ambulance service, patrol officers should get to know the community by talking to people in all walks of life, by encouraging requests for nonemergency services, and by becoming a visible but unremarkable part of the community scene. This is not merely an equation with foot patrol—that would be a gross oversimplification—but rather an attempt to overcome the psychological barriers to communication that the roving and reactive squad car often presents (Goldstein 1987). In this way, patrol officers will be able to assist individual as well as collective self-protection, to intervene at earlier stages and prevent problems from arising, to develop a heightened appreciation of the community's problems, to explain police services more accurately, and to solicit information that leads to arrests and prosecution. Police would still handle genuine emergencies, but with a much reduced force. The point, in effect, is to unhook a large portion of patrol personnel from the emergency-response system so they can engage in proactive crime prevention.

This kind of reorientation of patrol, practiced in the name of community policing, is being accomplished in a variety of ways. The most dramatic change is the redeployment of patrol officers from motor vehicles into small, decentralized police posts. They are called ministations in Detroit, shop-fronts in Australia, neighborhood police posts in Singapore, and *koban* in Japan. The Japanese, Norwegian, and Singaporean posts are miniature police stations, responsible for all aspects of policing except criminal investigation: they receive complaints, respond to calls for service, provide information and advice, patrol on foot or bicycle, organize community crime prevention, and develop personal contacts. Detroit's ministations, however, like those in Stockholm and like Melbourne's Broadmeadows shop-front, do not do general police work but are responsible only for community crime prevention. Their personnel organize Neighborhood Watch, give lectures on self-protection, and serve as a liaison between the police force and institutions with special security needs. In Copenhagen, they teach schoolchildren the rudiments of public safety. Like community policing itself, fixed posts are not cut to a single pattern; there are operational differences in purpose and performance.

An intensive form of community involvement is the house visit, in which officers go door to door asking about security problems, offering service, soliciting suggestions about police activity, and sometimes collecting information about residents. *Koban* officers in Japan and Singapore are expected to call at every residence and business in their areas at least twice a year. House visits are also made by community service officers in Santa Ana and in Oslo, although not as routinely as in Japan. Detroit and Houston police have also made house visits and, contrary to some expectations, were welcomed with enthusiasm rather than being thrown off the porches (Police Foundation 1986; Skolnick and Bayley 1986).

Foot patrols and horse patrols, both traditional strategies of policing, are coming back everywhere. In Singapore and Japan, foot patrols are the mainstay of patrol coverage. Singapore stresses "vertical patrols," in which officers walk through the connecting corridors of the vast multi-storied public housing estates in which 80 percent of the population lives. These open-air corridors are located on the outside of buildings and are screened only by a waist-high railing. Furthermore, because of the year-round warm climate, apartments are rarely closed. Home life is readily on view, and officers can easily strike up conversations. Singapore patrol officers are still a visible presence, therefore, from building to building as well as within buildings. Singapore's foot patrolling, which seems so intensive, is a practical adaptation to the need to establish an accessible police presence in three dimensions rather than in two.

Foot patrol officers in Stockholm, Copenhagen, and Santa Ana work in conjunction with neighborhood ministations. Scandinavian ministations are especially attractive, warmly furnished, inviting places, where neighborhood residents talk to police about a variety of problems—such as a husband's excessive drinking or a child's failure to meet school obligations—that may not bear directly on crime.

In most countries, however, foot patrols are used selectively, in areas of high pedestrian traffic such as malls, shopping centers, entertainment "strips," and public transportation facilities. Some police forces have ordered mobile personnel to park their vehicles regularly and walk targeted foot beats. Others have put foot patrol officers in cars with instructions to cover several dispersed areas during a single tour of duty.

Foot beats also serve to unhook police from the emergency system, allowing them to mingle with the public outside of a context of demands. Foot beats may not, of course, lessen the volume of services requested, but they extend, deepen, and personalize interaction.

C. *Increased Police Accountability*

Community policing in practice involves not only listening sympathetically but also creating new opportunities to do so. This is a big step for most police forces, who are afraid to open the floodgates to unfair criticism. It also clashes with their cherished belief that they are professionals who know better than anyone else what must be done in order to protect the community and enforce the law. Yet police have discovered that, if they want to enlist public support and cooperation, they must be prepared to listen to what the populace has to say, even if it may be unpleasant. Neighborhood Watch and getting to know people will not work if police insist on one-way communication. Unless police are willing, at the very least, to tolerate public feedback, community policing will be perceived as public relations, and the chasm between police and public will grow wider once again.

In England, *The Scarman Report*, an inquiry into police-minority conflict in Brixton in 1981, has been notably influential in developing the idea of liaison. Scarman's report concluded that the riots represented an "outburst of anger and resentment by young black people against the police." The report attributed the riots, at least in part, to the failure of police to maintain a formal liaison with the black community of this inner London borough, concluding that "a police force which does not consult locally will fail to be efficient" (Scarman 1981, pp. 110, 62).

Police forces are establishing an array of liaison officers and councils with groups whose relations with the police have been troubled, such as blacks in the United States, Aborigines in Australia, Koreans in Japan, Indians and Afro-Caribbeans in Britain, and gays in many places. Melbourne even has a liaison committee with lawyers. Naturally enough, liaison officers spend much of their time fighting fires—for police encounters with these groups sometimes generate an uprush of anger, confusion, and violence. They also try to cultivate contacts in those communities and develop programs to meet special needs, and they are frequently asked to create educational programs that will increase the knowledge and sensitivity of their colleagues in dealing with nonmainstream groups.

Police are also trying to cooperate more closely with established groups and institutions that have a working interest in crime and order. It is common, for example, for commanders of all ranks in Britain, Sweden, Japan, and Singapore to meet with crime-prevention organizations..So, too, do the police in Houston, Santa Ana, and Detroit. In London, some heads of local police stations are more receptive than others to meeting with local groups. Those in charge of stations in areas where riots have occurred are particularly sensitive to this need. An inspector in charge of a neighborhood police station in Singapore estimated that he participated in regular meetings with nine permanent organizations in the area, such as the residents' committees of housing estates, community center management committees, senior citizens' recreation center committees, and sports clubs. Ministation and shop-front police-station officers in the United States and Australia act as informal security advisers to halfway houses for the mentally disturbed, homes for battered women, schools, and hospitals.

Even more far reaching, police are creating new formal committees and councils to advise them about security needs and operations. Such consultative committees exist throughout Great Britain and Scandinavia. They take a variety of forms but generally are a mix of elected officials and community representatives. In Britain, for example, despite the fact that each police force is responsible to a police authority, whose membership is one-third judicial magistrates and two-thirds elected local council politicians, the police in various cities have recently set up special consultative committees at the police-station level. Their purpose is to mobilize public participation, assess consumer opinion about police services, and communicate information that will help the police carry out their duties more effectively (Morgan 1985). Detroit created similar groups in its precincts. Australia has no tradition of local control over its police, who, apart from the federal force, are responsible to the seven state governments. As a result, the commissioner of police of New South Wales, John Avery, and the Victoria Police Commission have strongly advocated the creation of consultative committees for every police station.

The role consultative committees are actually to play is more problematic. Morgan, in his study of police community-consultation arrangements in England and Wales, distinguishes three models (not mutually exclusive) of the role that consultative groups can play. One is the *steward* or *auditing* model, requiring the chief constable to publish an annual report—rather like that of a publicly traded corporation—that gives an account of policing in his area for his police authority. But, in this model, policy and practice are the sole responsibility of the police.

The *partner* model is much akin to what we are defining as community policing. It stresses the importance of police being in touch with citizen views and emphasizes "the desirability of the police jointly engaging with citizens and other agencies in crime prevention and detection initiatives." In sum, policing is supposed to be congruent with community priorities and inviting of public cooperation "to know about and solve most crime."

Finally, the *directive* model puts police policy in control of democratically elected authorities, either Parliament or elected local committees. Morgan lists as "core problems of this approach" that local political groups may disagree with the law, ignore minority interests or rights, and be susceptible to corruption (Morgan 1985, p. 8).

Striking at a sometimes even more sensitive nerve, efforts are expanding to allow civilians to observe police operations in order to ensure that they are conducted fairly and legally. Britain, for example, now allows "lay visitors" to inspect police stations, with particular attention to the holding cells; so does Sweden. Many American forces, despite a tradition of reflexive hostility to civilian review, allow civilians to go on patrol, provided a serious educational purpose is served. Police complaints tribunals have recently been established in all Australian states, contrary to the most sanguine predictions even eight years ago. Several American cities, such as Miami, Washington, D.C., Detroit, and Los Angeles, have quietly created various models of civilian oversight in the last decade.

In short, community policing embraces the expansion of civilian input in policing. Reciprocity of communication is not only accepted but encouraged. Under community policing, the public is allowed to speak and to be informed about strategic priorities, tactical approaches, and even the behavior of individual officers.

D. Decentralization of Command

Although police operations are always decentralized geographically to some relatively small precinct or station-house jurisdiction, local commanders have usually had limited ability to shape the character of police operations. They have followed forcewide blueprints drawn up by headquarters staff—administering them "by the numbers." A key assumption of community policing, however, is that communities have different policing priorities and problems. Policing must be adaptable. To accomplish this, subordinate commanders must be given freedom to act according to their own readings of local conditions. Decentralization of command is necessary in order to take advantage of the particular knowledge that can come through greater police involvement in the community and feedback from it.

In some places, as in London, the sheer size of the force—nearly 27,000 sworn officers and over 13,000 civilians—constitutes a problem. The London Metropolitan Police report directly to the Home Secretary and, through him, to Parliament. There is considerable sentiment, particularly in the Labour party, to decentralize the metropolitan police and to make them accountable to local borough authorities. The typical London borough, after all, has a population of around one-quarter of a million residents. Moreover, the current size of the force makes it a vast bureaucracy. Vested interests have developed within Scotland Yard, with some duplication and confusion in lines of command. Innovative community relations programs developed in Scotland Yard may lose something in the translation to the local Brixton station.

On the whole, then, community policing implies that smaller and more local is better. Some of the cities we studied in *The New Blue Line* were similarly disaggregated. Santa Ana was divided into four areas into which entire teams of police and associated community-service officers would be assigned for substantial time periods, usually two or more years. The first step in community police reform in Adelaide, Australia, was a redrawing of subdivisional boundaries to make them coincide with smaller, more organic communities. Officers-in-charge were urged to develop their own plans for area policing, changing them as circumstances warranted. In Denver, computer terminals were installed and data collators assigned to assist district commanders in shaping patrol operations to counter emerging crime patterns. Lee P. Brown, chief of police in Houston, started a program on a pilot basis in 1984 that he hoped would transform patrol operations and command responsibilities throughout the city. Patrol beats were reduced in size and covered by teams of patrol officers and detectives. The commanders of the Directed Area Response Teams, as they were called, were given authority to determine how resources were to be used to meet area problems. Operational planning was to be collective, using the insights, knowledge, and suggestions of field personnel. Commanders could change deployment, shuffle personnel between uniformed and undercover assignments, and concentrate on emergent problems as needed.

The enhancement of decision-making responsibility under community policing extends beyond subordinate commanders. It involves the rank and file as well. In addition to their traditional duties, community police constables and patrol officers must be able to organize community groups, suggest solutions to neighborhood problems, listen unflappably to critical comment, enlist the cooperation of people who are fearful or resentful, participate intelligently in command conferences, and speak with poise before public audiences. Such duties require new aptitudes. Officers must have the capacity to think on their feet and be able to translate general mandates into appropriate words and actions. A new breed of officer is needed, as well as a new command ethos. Community policing transforms the responsibilities of all ranks: subordinate ranks are to become more self-directing; senior ranks are to encourage disciplined initiative while developing coherent plans responsive to local conditions.

Having reviewed the programmatic components that recur when more than lip-service is paid to the ideal of community policing, we can now address concerns about its reality and coherence.

E. Community Policing in Practice

The major programmatic elements of community policing—community-based crime prevention, reorientation of patrol, increased accountability, and command decentralization—dovetail to form a coherent package. Civilianization may be employed to enhance these elements. Accepting that the purpose of community policing is to involve the public in its own defense, sharing the burden of protection with the thin blue line, then the program components follow logically. Community-based crime prevention is the objective that the police set out to achieve. In order to do this, they must find resources, especially personnel, to mobilize communities and to point them in the right direction. This requires using patrol personnel, the largest reservoir of police talent, more effectively. Hands-on interaction is essential if the public is to be coaxed, prodded, and encouraged to assist in preventing crime and apprehending criminals. Furthermore, this cannot be done extensively enough by specialized headquarters details; every frontline police officer must be involved.

Expanded accountability follows inevitably from outreach. One reason the public is mobilized for crime prevention is to provide a richer amount of information to the police. The public is unlikely to be willingly passive in this relationship, especially when they meet in groups with the police. Accountability, in the sense of enhanced knowledge of collective and individual police activities and the opportunity to comment on them, is the price that the police pay for more wholehearted community cooperation.

Finally, command decentralization is the organizational adaptation that must occur to take advantage of the particularities of communities that become apparent. Increased interaction cannot be managed or increased information assimilated unless command centers are multiplied. The older system of management from the top down would simply be overwhelmed.

Thus, the four elements fit together theoretically. Moreover, police forces will find that if they embark seriously on community-based crime prevention, they will be led by the very process of interaction to the other three.

How real is community policing internationally? The answer is that it is often more rhetoric than substance. Movement toward community policing is very uneven. For example, almost all the programs are being tried somewhere in Great Britain. Variation in both commitment and form, however, is enormous. There are also now serious second thoughts developing because community policing has not prevented violence either among ethnic groups or toward the police in several places where it seemingly was tried with much fanfare. But as Rosenbaum concludes in his critical review of evaluation research on community crime prevention, it is often hard to tell whether the ineffectiveness of a program is attributable to a misguided theory or to a miscarriage of implementation (Rosenbaum 1987).

As a model, Japanese policing seems to conform best to the tenets of community policing. This might surprise the Japanese, who forged their system immediately after World War II out of a combination of traditional culture and American democratic ideals, long before community policing became popular. Singapore, prompted by Japanese success, is in the process of totally transforming its system in the direction of community policing. In the United States, on the other hand, community policing is often more aspiration than implementation. Although notable experiments are succeeding against great odds, as in Detroit, Houston, and Santa Ana, most police forces are using community policing to embellish rather than transform traditional strategies. Scandinavia, too, is making gestures toward community policing, but with considerable resistance from rank-and-file officers, and, in some instances, with little push from executives.

There seems to be a close connection between the substantiality of community policing from place to place and the reasons police leaders find it attractive. Some senior managers jump on the community-police bandwagon simply because to do so is progressive. Community policing is like motherhood: it cannot be denied. Such leaders talk a good game, but they rarely follow through. They are more concerned with appearances than reality. Others recognize that community policing has tremendous emotional appeal to the public. It provides a rationale for urging the public to support the police. Without necessarily being consciously cynical, such leaders tend to develop one-directional outreach programs. They form specialized media-relations units, undertake much-publicized programs in community education, and organize Neighborhood Watch. But these programs are tacked onto existing operations; community policing rarely touches operational practices, and it does not open the force to outside scrutiny and direction. The old concept of professionalism is maintained, with the police firmly in charge and the public kept at arm's length until needed.

Community policing becomes most substantial when leaders see in it solutions to the defects in customary practice and when it becomes part of a broader vision implying a change of values as well as programs. Innovation is most likely to follow analysis of failure. Diagnosis of shortcomings is the prerequisite to meaningful change. It is not an accident that three of the most ambitious experiments in community policing have taken place where there was a sense of strategic need. Great Britain's recent controversial but wide-ranging innovations under the rubric of community policing derive from the racial turmoil of the late seventies and early eighties. Although some voices called for the stern application of force, more advocated a wholehearted, conciliatory attempt to bridge the gap between the police and minorities. While it is too early to say that community police practices will persist in Britain in the long run, its police should be credited with being creative under fire and replying to violence with some measure of imagination rather than exclusively with a fist.

Detroit, too, constructed community policing out of the evidence of failure. Seared by devastating rioting and well-founded charges of racism, the city's predominantly white police force entered the 1970s facing an angry, largely black population. In 1974 Coleman Young, the city's first black mayor, appointed the city's first black chief of police, Bill Hart. Together they established police ministations, while at the same time strenuously recruiting blacks and women to the force. But Detroit's failure was also in crime control. Its crime rates were among the highest in the nation, and it had earned the ugly title of "murder capital of the United States." Furthermore, because of a revenue crisis stemming from recession in the automobile industry, the police were forced to lay off (in 1978–79) nearly one-third of the sworn officers on the force. With tremendous courage and resolve, Detroit's leadership responded by increasing the number of ministations, by upgrading their operation, by clarifying their purpose, and by starting neighborhood crime-prevention programs across the city. Stark necessity, therefore, produced strategic reform in the direction of community policing.

Finally, Singapore is using community policing to accomplish bold goals of nation building. Enjoying one of the highest standards of living in Asia, its leaders have been worried that prosperity would erode traditional moral values and, more fearful yet, would exacerbate tensions within the city's multiethnic population. Since neither Europe nor America appeared to have an answer to rising crime, incivility, and drug abuse, Lee Kuan Yew, Singapore's prime minister, announced that Singapore would henceforth "learn from the East." For the police, this meant Japan. After careful planning and training, five neighborhood police posts were established in 1983, modeled exactly on the Japanese *koban*. At the end of a trial year, the Singapore police decided to expand the system to the entire island by 1989. Singapore's leaders believed that a neighborhood police presence would help to draw together diverse ethnic groups into genuine communities. This was especially difficult since most of the population had been resettled during the previous ten years into large multistoried public housing estates. Since crime was already falling, the primary purpose of redeployment was not crime prevention, but the inculcation of lessons of citizenship. Police were to be an instrument in the creation of the "new Singapore man." As in Britain and Detroit, customary policing, derived in this case from British experience, was found wanting.

II. Potential Obstacles to Community Policing

However positively police executives may regard community policing, it is also true that identifiable and persistent constraints impede its development. We could identify twelve such obstacles.

1. *The Culture of Policing.*   How police officers learn to see the world around them and their role in it has come to be acknowledged by all scholars of police as an indispensable key to understanding the behavior and attitudes of police. "It is a commonplace of the now voluminous sociological literature on police operations and discretion," writes Robert Reiner, "that the rank-and-file officer is the primary determinant of policing where it really counts—on the street" (1985, p. 85). Moreover, after reviewing an increasingly broad and cross-national literature on police culture, he finds what those of us who have studied police across cities and nations have also discovered: that there are identifiable commonalities in police culture. Some of these commonalities, we believe, are especially salient to our understanding of the resistance of police to the introduction of community policing.

First is the perception of *danger*, which, although real, is typically magnified. Police officers are sometimes shot at and killed, of course. But the first line of defense against anticipated danger is *suspicion*, the development of a cognitive map of the social world to protect against signs of trouble, offense, and potential threat. Since community policing demands a degree of extroversion, the tendency toward suspicion and its concomitant tendency toward marked internal solidarity—the division of the world into we and they—must inhibit the degree of acceptance of ordinary citizens that is implicit in community policing.

2. *The Youth of Police.*   Students of police have frequently noted the *machismo* qualities in the world of policing (see Reiner 1985, p. 99). Men who are attracted to the occupation are often very young in chronological age as well as in maturity of temperament and judgment. England, for example, sets nineteen as the age of entry. Recruits typically have athletic backgrounds, are sports minded, and are trained in self-defense. It is not uncommon for trainees to build up the upper body (as football players do through weight lifting) so as to offer a more formidable appearance as a potential adversary in street encounters. They are also trained to handle a variety of offensive weapons, including deadly weapons. They are taught how to disable and kill people with their bare hands. No matter how many warnings may be offered by superiors about limitations on use of force, its possible use is a central feature of the police role and of policemen's perceptions of themselves.

Training in the use of force and authority to use it, combined with the youth of most police, can well inhibit the capacity of a police officer to empathize with the situation of those being policed in ethnically diverse and low-income neighborhoods. Community policing requires effective interaction between police and ordinary citizens. This implies a capacity to envision the world through the eyes of another, to develop a broader perspective, and to hone evaluative and communicative skills. In a word, community policing demands a degree of emotional *maturity* more likely to be present in somewhat older officers. Senior officers are not only less likely to be macho but are also more likely to feel comfortable in the problem-solving, almost parental role associated with community policing. Thus, the youth of police recruits—who can be veterans at twenty-four or twenty-six years of age—may disincline them to embrace the broader role encompassed by community policing.

3. *Street versus Management Cops.*   When scholars write about the culture of policing, they usually have in mind the streetwise cop who follows a blue code of solidarity with fellow officers. Streetwise officers are likely to be cynical, tough, and skeptical of innovation within management. By contrast, management cops tend to project a vision of policing that is more acceptable to the general public. This concept of two contrasting cultures of policing grew out of research conducted in New York City by Ianni and Ianni (1983), who developed a distinction between "street cops" and "management cops."

The streetwise cop is apt to approve of cutting corners, of throwing weight around on the street, and of expressing the qualities of in-group solidarity described above. Management cops tend to be more legalistic, rule-oriented, and rational. Management cops, on the whole, are thus more likely to be at least initially interested in the idea of community policing—as they are more generally interested in new ideas. By contrast, street cops are often hard-boiled cynics who deride innovations in policing as needless and unworkable incursions into the true and eternal role of the cop—the one they were socialized into as recruits by a sometimes venerated field training officer. Streetwise police are the young macho cops referred to above who, instead of maturing by developing a broader perspective—by taking advanced degrees in management, law, or criminal justice and so forth—reinforce their post-recruit identity. Unfortunately, this reinforcement can develop into a lifelong occupational vision rooted in an abiding, even growing bitterness that seems impervious to any sort of hope for change or new ideas.

The cynicism typifying the street cop may of course also be present at higher levels of management; after all, all police begin their careers as street cops, and the learning that takes place on the street is never outgrown by many. If community policing is to take hold, it requires a mature vision of a police executive to introduce it and to make it compelling to the working cops on the street. In our studies of police innovation in the United States, Europe, and Asia, we have found that in most places street-cop cynicism is a force undermining the potential introduction of community policing. The street cop tends to be resistant to all forms of innovation that are nontechnological. The management cop is not necessarily more accepting of the idea of policing as a broader social issue, but he is more likely to be receptive to a more expansive vision of the police role. The innovative management cop employs prior street experience to overcome the resistance of the street cop. By contrast, the self-conception of the traditional management cop remains firmly rooted in his earliest training experiences. In any case, a broader vision of the police role is a necessary but not sufficient condition for introducing community policing. Its absence is surely an obstacle.

4. *The Responsibility to Respond.*   Crime and fear of crime are international phenomena. All nations and many political subdivisions—states, cities, and regions—maintain crime statistics. However unreliable these might be, there is always some crime. Even among the most

peaceful cities in the world, such as Copenhagen, Oslo, and Stockholm, this is perceptibly true. Every modern police agency is an around-the-clock emergency service responsive to a three-digit number available to any citizen.

Many police executives now regard the emergency response system as a monster that is consuming the operational resources of the department. Calling the emergency number is so easy that police could spend all their time speeding in patrol cars to anonymously placed calls, often handling trivial matters that may not even involve law violations. (That someone has lost their keys and is locked out of their dwelling is not an uncommon call.)

This pressure to react insures the high priority of responsive ability and acts as an additional constraint on innovation involving relations with citizens. Under a response model, the patrol car—usually with two persons occupying it—is paramount. Insuring that the responsibilities of the emergency service system are met becomes the highest priority of the command staff, not community policing (see Sherman 1986).

The interpretation of amounts of crime depends much on subjective assessment. In 1986, Oakland, California counted 146 homicides. Copenhagen counted sixteen homicides in 1985. Objectively, Oakland has about nine times as many homicides as Copenhagen. Oakland officials and citizens perceive homicide and violent crime as a desperate problem. The chief judge of Oakland's superior court, Henry Ramsey, told us recently in an interview that some dramatic and innovative measures must be taken to keep Oakland residents from killing each other. He half-seriously suggested paying $1,000 annually to every Oakland family whose members stay clear of the criminal courts for a year.

That officials and citizens in Oakland should be concerned about crime is understandable. But crime is also seen as an increasingly serious problem in relatively peaceable Copenhagen. As one Scandinavian criminologist, Annika Snare, said in an interview, "Feelings about crime are not quantifiable. We feel that there should be no homicides, so sixteen seems like an enormous number." (In Oakland, officials and citizens would rejoice if the annual number of homicides was to fall to sixteen, or even to sixty.)

What is the point of this tale of two cities? It is this: The perception of crime and danger, whatever its comparative reality, puts increased pressure on police to respond. The more police feel this pressure, either through calls for service or through complaints by citizens groups about rises in crime, the more the immediacy of this pressure is likely to undermine the possibilities of redirecting police resources to innovative programs.

5. *Limitations of Resources.*   The perception of resource limitation is a constraining factor closely related to the responsibility to respond. In several locations, particularly in Scandinavia, we encountered a rhetorical acceptance of the idea of community policing that was scarcely met in practice. "Community policing is a good idea," we were told, "provided that we are given the additional manpower it demands." With such a stance on the part of police executives, community policing cannot develop without expanding the dimensions of an already sizable bureaucracy.

Is this a fair assessment? Are resources so limited that community policing cannot be undertaken without additional manpower? There is no clear-cut answer to this question. What is self-evident, however, is the subjectivity of the concept of "necessary resources." For example, we visited the radio dispatch room of the city of Stockholm on a Wednesday evening at 8:30 P.M. in June 1986. At this time, seventy two-person cars, including traffic-enforcement cars, and two ten-man vans were assigned to street patrol.

Stockholm's main control room is outfitted with strikingly modern equipment. A large illuminated map of the city dominates the room. Ten sworn officers occupy each of ten surveillance subscreens allocated to various parts of the city, with additional screens monitoring the central railroad station.

At 8:39 P.M. we counted not a single call for service. We noted that only one dispatcher was actually working. Some were watching ordinary TV programs; others were having dinner; others were reading newspapers. Our impression, based on riding in patrol cars over four Stockholm nights, was of manpower redundancy. This impression, of course, was based on limited observation at a particular time of year. Several Stockholm officials insisted that our impressions were wrong, that police are often busier, and that there is in fact a manpower shortage. Moreover, we were told that it was essential to have two persons in each of the seventy patrol cars because it would otherwise be too dangerous to be a policeman in this capital city. Whatever the reality, there is no question that a perception of lively demand, danger, and busyness pervades Stockholm's and other Scandinavian police departments and that this perception is a significant factor in constraining the development of community policing.

6. *The Inertia of Police Unions.* Police unions have become more powerful in the United States, Scandinavia, and Great Britain since the 1960s, and for fairly evident reasons. Mostly, the power of police unions has correlated with the rise in crime and the fear of crime over the past two decades. All over the United States, Great Britain, and parts of Scandinavia (with the exception of Norway) police are among the highest-paid public service workers, whereas they were among the lowest paid twenty years ago. The size of police salaries is not necessarily, as might be thought, correlated with dominant politics. Thus, police salaries have risen substantially under the Thatcher administration's promise of a greater commitment to law and order. At the same time, however, police salaries have risen substantially in Sweden and Denmark under socialist and welfare state governments.

By Scandinavian standards, Swedish police are especially well paid. The average policeman earns around $23,000 per year, which is roughly 20 percent higher than the salaries earned by Finnish or Norwegian rank and file and about the same as Danish. Another indicator of the power of Swedish police unions is that the head of the National Police Union earns the same salary (around $44,000) as the national chief of police, with whom he collectively bargains. Unions are generally strong in Scandinavia, and police unions are no exception.

Norwegian police salaries are not as high as those in Sweden, partly because of a troubled economy but mostly because of an unwritten norm, we were told, of a communitarian society that considers it unseemly for one part of the public sector work force to earn substantially more than other parts. This means that a rise in police salaries would have to be accompanied by increases in the salaries of nurses, doctors, and bus drivers. This is not to suggest that Norwegian police unions are weak. It is rather that they function under a different set of constraints.

Given their increasing power, what police unions think about community policing is important. Generally, they are less than enthusiastic, for reasons they state and for others that might be inferred.

For some union leaders, community policing is seen as a threat to the proper role of the police in a good society. In this vision, the police are supposed to provide the citizen with protection against crime. Neighborhood Watch is perceived as a substitute for the police, one that relieves the state of a moral responsibility to protect the citizen.

Similarly, community policing is seen as a threat to police professionalism. Police are the designated and appropriately trained personnel to handle crime, whether through prevention or apprehension. Citizens are neither needed nor wanted. Moreover, community policing implies a degree of police accountability to citizens, which is yet another hazard to police unions.

Finally, community policing appears threatening to police unions if it means or appears to mean that fewer police will be necessary. The unionization of police unquestionably encourages them to claim authority over crime-prevention activities, even when interaction with the citizenry might well reduce crime. For police unions, jobs and job benefits are primary concerns. The prevention of crime seems to merit a lower priority. This stance, of course, constrains the development of community policing.

7. *The Two-Officer Car.* The so-called personnel shortage is undoubtedly related to the apparently unyielding practice of assigning two officers to a patrol car. If one-officer cars were to become the norm (as in California police departments), there would no longer be a shortage of manpower for such community-policing strategies as foot patrol and ministations.

Those who advocate—indeed, insist on—two-officer cars say they are necessary, first of all, to protect against danger. But with modern communications technology, officers can obtain assistance quickly in virtually any dangerous situation. Studies have shown two-man cars to be no less dangerous or more effective than one-man cars (Boydstun, Sherry, and Moelter 1977).

In addition, two-officer patrol cars foster a sense of camaraderie or enjoyment in working with one's fellow officers: a special relationship with a partner is considered a prerogative of the job. Indeed, in Sweden, we were told, there is a law that nobody should work alone and that it is the right of working people to enjoy their work.

Whatever the validity of these reasons, they are contrary to the value of efficiency and, perhaps more importantly, the value of community. Although the two-officer patrol car may engender a sense of security and job enjoyment among those who are policing, it may also generate a sense of remoteness from the population being policed. Two officers riding together in a patrol car tend to become their own movable community distant from the people they are policing. In any event, the two-officer car, by claiming so much manpower, may prove to be the single most important resource constraint on the development of community policing.

8. *Command Accountability.* Police organizations are characteristically arranged in hierarchical form—they are, after all, paramilitary

institutions. Policy is made by the chief or commissioner and the command staff. Community policing, by contrast, implies a degree of decentralization of authority. In many police departments in which precinct systems prevail, authority is, in fact, decentralized. Thus, in Newark, which we reported on in *The New Blue Line*, the precinct commander was jokingly referred to as a "baron." The tension between hierarchical command accountability and the decentralization of authority is not exactly new or surprising. Nevertheless, the decentralization of command implied by adopting a neighborhood policing or ministation strategy, which are integral features of community policing, may not easily be adapted to departments with a strong centralized orientation. Thus, as a general proposition, we would conclude that the more centralized and hierarchical the accountability system of a police department, the more difficult it will be to introduce community policing.

9. *The Reward Structure.* Community policing not only creates a problem of restructuring the norms of hierarchical command; it also reconstitutes the norms of effective policing by which the higher command can judge the effectiveness of police. This is not to suggest that traditional police departments have worked out exemplary or widely accepted criteria for judging exactly who is the more proficient cop. On the contrary, the difficulty of developing a set of such criteria has bedeviled police administrators for generations. Arrests, felony arrests, clearances, convictions, street stops, traffic tickets—none of these is an entirely satisfactory indicator of police performance. Still, if police are playing the traditional role of criminal apprehension, it seems sensible to employ some of the above criteria.

But how do we evaluate the performance of the community-oriented police officer whose task is crime prevention as well as apprehension? Not only is it impossible to measure the amount of crime a particular police officer contributed to preventing; a community police officer's success also involves initiating subtle changes in community behavior and attitudes. Measuring these effects would mean asking questions such as, Is a neighborhood more enthusiastic about self-defense? Are people more willing to provide critical information to police? Are referral services more effectively engaged? Are victims able to reconstitute their shattered lives more quickly? Is the sense of citizen efficacy against crime enhanced? Is trust developed among neighbors? Does the fear of crime diminish? and Is there a greater sense of partnership with the police? Because police forces have not learned how to reward such performance systematically, they find it difficult to encourage rank-and-file officers to dedicate themselves to it.

In sum, community policing exaggerates the ambiguity of police performance and, by implication, of measures of evaluation and reward. Police executives recognize the problem even when they do not articulate it. We have come to believe that the ambiguity of evaluating and rewarding the quality of community police performance constitutes a factor, albeit not a dispositive one, in inhibiting the development of community policing.

10. *Public Expectations of Police.* Community policing is supposed to be more satisfying to the public than traditional policing, and it may be, if citizens experience a diminished fear of crime, a heightened sense of efficacy, and an increased trust in the police. At the same time, some citizens may prefer and demand more traditional modes of policing. In part, this is simply what they are used to; they do not want to deal with police service officers or community-service officers. They want their police to be "real," with appropriate badge and gun. Many such citizens, and there are such, may be especially discontented when they encounter female police.

There is, in addition, a more insidious reason for citizen mistrust of community policing. Citizens may come to believe that community policing is actually interfering with standard crime-fighting capabilities. This can occur if community policing is permitted to bear the responsibility within the police department for reductions in the patrol force, response time, and so forth. Such a message, if permitted to take hold within the department, will eventually make its way to the general public. Thus, community policing is easily maligned by traditional police who resent change and want to return to the old ways of preventive patrol in two-officer cars. If community policing is to succeed, administrative leadership must insure that unfairly attributing the crime problem to resource constraints caused by community policing is not allowed.

11. *Failure to Integrate with Crime Detection.* Departmental segregation has by now become an almost predictable problem of community policing. Community-policing activities are assigned to newly created, specialized units—crime-prevention branches, ministation commands, and community relations squads. Community police personnel may be attached to decentralized commands, but they "do their own thing" and are not integrated into traditional patrol or criminal investigation activities. Where community policing has been successful, however, one of

its most positive contributions has been to provide the department with information useful to preventing crime or apprehending criminals. But this can happen only if community policing is advertised, seen, and organized so as to facilitate crime control functions. Serious thinking and seriously monitored interpretation need to be undertaken to find out how to accomplish this goal successfully.

12. *The Ambiguity of Community*.   Community is an inherently ambiguous, almost elusive idea. It implies a commonality of interest, values, identities, demands, and expectations. When one considers how fragile a two-person relationship can be, it requires little imagination to comprehend the difficulties of expanding the notion of mutuality of interest to a larger group of human beings. Nevertheless, the quest for community seems an almost universal aspiration. Community is the apple pie and motherhood of social organization. As Raymond Williams has observed (1976, p. 65), unlike such similar terms as "state," "nation," and "society," "*community*" "seems never to be used unfavourably" (1976, p. 65). Moreover, as Morgan and Maggs have observed in their study of provincial police departments in England (1984, p. 3), every chief constable and local police authority affirms the import of community "consultation" and "liaison," but the terms are slippery and vague and mean significantly different things to different people.

Moreover, there can be quite a bleak side to the idea of community when some of its members become overprotective and threaten or engage in violence to perceived outsiders. The most notorious recent example of this occurred in the Howard Beach section of New York City, where a black youth was beaten and driven to run to a highway, where he was struck by an oncoming automobile and killed.

Police-community reciprocity can be achieved only when there is a genuine bonding of interests between the police and the served citizenry and among definable sections of the public. That may turn out to be progressively more difficult to accomplish in demographically complex urban areas, with their increasing ethnic diversity. Moreover, contiguous ethnic variation prevails in parts of many major cities throughout the world. London offers perhaps one of the most striking examples of the phenomenon. The city experienced the most destructive riot in its history on October 5, 1985, a riot that Metropolitan Police Commissioner Sir Kenneth Newman described as "violence on an unprecedented scale." One police officer was hacked to death with machetes; 248 were injured by rocks, other missiles, and petrol bombs; and seven were injured by gunshot wounds. The Broadwater Farm

Estate—which is a high-rise urban low-income housing project—is located in Haringay, a mostly working-class borough. A tour of the area surrounding the estate, however, reveals blocks of solidly middle-class housing. This neighborhood's residents had comfortably formed a watch group—evidently to protect against potential burglaries that might be committed by unemployed Estate youths. During the riot itself, police lines were drawn on the theory that the rioters were intent on looting what might be considered another community of interests—adjacent small businesses.

Nevertheless, the London Metropolitan Police have drawn some positive lessons from the riot. During the summer of 1986, efforts were being made to develop a strong liaison with groups within the Broadwater Farm Estate to stress commonalities of interest between Estate residents, other residents of Haringay, and the local police. This is a tense and difficult business because police are in the paradoxical—some might argue paternalistic—position of reaching out to residents, particularly young men, while retaining the authority to discipline. It is a more difficult role to play after the bitter residues of riot than before.

Nevertheless, the Broadwater Farm Estate riot can offer an important lesson for the theory of community policing, which is to distinguish between the *process* of coproduction of crime prevention and the concept of the appropriate *territory* to be considered. Within various administrative boundaries—cities, boroughs—we do find neighborhoods. Suttles defines "the defended neighborhood" as "the smallest area which possesses a corporate identity known to both its members and outsiders . . . an area within which people retreat to avoid a quantum jump in the risks of insult or injury they must take in moving about outside that area" (1972, p. 57). Police can perhaps resolve the ambiguity of community by themselves conveying broader communal norms of decorum and safety to individual neighborhoods. Like the Japanese police, they can seek to move beyond being merely the law's enforcers; they can aspire to teach the community's moral values within self-defined and cohesive neighborhoods.

III. The Value of Community Policing

Given the ambiguities of the concept of community and the realities of police resistance, should we conclude that the idea of community policing is without substance and that the constraints we discussed above make it virtually impossible to achieve? We think not. The aspiration is central to policing in a democracy, but it is not enough to employ it as a slogan. It needs to be carefully considered, studied further in actual practice, and its constraints and limitations candidly discussed. We think that community policing has enduring value. If police forces encourage community-based crime prevention, emphasize nonemergency interaction with the public, increase public input into policy-making, and decentralize command, substantial benefits can accrue both to the community and to the police.

A number of major themes or lessons can be extracted from recent experience with community policing. These are set out below in sections that separately discuss benefits to the public and to the police.

A. Benefits to the Community

The possible public benefits of community policing are improved crime prevention, greater public scrutiny of police activity, greater police accountability to the community, and encouragement of efforts to recruit women and minorities into police work.

1. *Crime Prevention.* The most critical question that needs to be answered is whether community policing will produce safer communities. Protection, after all, is the traditional raison d'etre of police, and no one advocating community policing wants the police to abandon that responsibility. Unfortunately, we cannot answer this crucial question. Although there are strong a priori reasons for thinking that community policing will be at least as effective as past approaches, there is little hard evidence to support the point. Again and again, we found that the police could not supply convincing data on the effect of changes in operations. Often preoccupied with problems of implementation and strapped for funds, they plow ahead without careful analysis of effects.

Singapore is the outstanding exception. A one-year pilot project in five areas of central Singapore was carefully evaluated by the police department and a team of scholars from Singapore National University. A before-and-after survey of public opinion was included. Briefly, it was found that compared with the rest of Singapore, especially adjacent neighborhoods, serious crime declined while reports of minor crimes rose; support for police increased; and the public's sense of security, already high, also rose (Quah and Quah 1987). Only after the results of the evaluation were studied did the government of Singapore decide to expand the new system to the entire island.

Community policing is advancing because it seems to make sense, not because it has yet been shown to be demonstrably superior. This is dangerous because policymaking unsupported by facts is fickle. Good practices both old and new may be cast aside on the basis of seat-of-the-pants impressions.

Although free-world policing is in an unprecedented period of soul searching and experimentation, police forces are unable to learn from one another because careful evaluations of program outcomes are not being made, or, when they are, results are difficult to pin down or to generalize. For example, Rosenbaum, Lewis, and Grant undertook a major evaluation of multineighborhood crime-prevention programs in Chicago. They evaluated community crime-prevention programs established by volunteer community organizations and found that on seven measures—participation, feelings of efficacy, behavioral change, social integration, reduced crime and incivility, reduced fear, and attachment to neighborhood—there were no significant differences between "treated" and "untreated" areas.

Why? When they looked more closely, they found little evidence of successful implementation. By contrast, "the one neighborhood that initiated a number of block watches showed fewer of these unfavorable results and, in fact, showed some encouraging effects along the lines of reductions in victimization, as well as increases in surveillance and home protection behavior" (1986, p. 127).

Whatever the validity of *community organized* crime-prevention programs, these results cannot be generalized to what would happen if a committed police agency were to undertake similar programs. Thus, we still do not have adequate measures of what happens when such programs are implemented and closely monitored by police in cooperation with neighborhood groups.

It is unrealistic to expect the police simultaneously to devise and implement new strategies and to evaluate their effect. Their priorities are operational, and their expertise in evaluation is limited. It is enough that they be creative and open. The responsibility for evaluating program results should be shouldered by agencies outside the police. Governments especially should study the effects of the many natural experiments in policing that are occurring throughout the world. Without this, the future of strategic innovation, not just community policing, is problematic.

2. *Public Scrutiny.* Even when community policing is only rhetoric, an opportunity is created for legitimate public examination of police practices. If community policing minimally means greater involvement of the public in public safety, how can the police convincingly deflect public discussion of police strategies? Community policing is like a

Trojan horse that attacks the pretensions of professional insulation from within.

3. *Public Accountability.* Community policing increases effective public accountability over the police. There are three primary ways in which the public can constrain what the police do: (1) by providing, or not providing, a framework of laws and money for police action, (2) by participating in policy-making with respect to the means of achieving desired objectives, and (3) by examining and possibly punishing errors in performance. Historically, the police in most places have fared reasonably well with respect to legal and financial support. They are powerful politically. They have, however, adamantly resisted public participation in policy-making. Claims about professionalism have been used to gain autonomy and exclude laypersons, including politicians, from policy deliberations. With respect to civilian supervision of errors in implementation, the police have been fiercely opposed. Ad hoc civilian review has been unthinkable; civil and criminal liability has to be mediated through strict due process; the press is considered unfair and inflammatory. Such is the standard police view.

Now something almost unimaginable is happening wherever community policing is being meaningfully developed. The police themselves are inviting the public into policy-making because they realize that this is the surest way to obtain the kind of public cooperation that is essential to successful crime prevention and crime fighting. In order for outreach to be successful, the police must sit still for feedback. The myriad consultative committees, crime-prevention councils, and liaison groups are making suggestions about policy that the police cannot cavalierly dismiss because the police themselves instigated the dialogue. For the police, mobilizing the public for crime prevention, especially when enduring institutions are created, is like climbing on the tiger's back—it is hard to get off. Community policing makes public collaboration in policy-making acceptable because it occurs at police initiative.

Community policing also makes civilian oversight of implementation more acceptable. The same dynamic is apparent. How can the police solicit public input into community safety and cut off inconvenient questions about their own failure to follow through? Though it is too early to say, collaboration between the police and the public in crime fighting and crime prevention may eventually build the kind of mutual trust that lessens police objections to civilian oversight. The police may discover that they share with the vast majority of the populace an interest in assuring proper as well as effective performance.

Community policing is a backdoor into comprehensive accountability. What could not be achieved by public demand through political channels may occur because the police believe wider community participation is essential to the achievement of organizational objectives. Accountability may occur under police auspices, where it could not under political ones.

4. *Recruitment.* Community policing provides a double-barreled rationale for representative recruitment. It challenges the macho, martial model of policing. Traditional officers are being very acute when they distinguish "hard" from "soft" policing. The tactics of community policing are indeed soft, though the goal of deterring criminality is not. While both community and traditional policing use hard and soft tactics, the emphasis in community policing is toward soliciting, enlisting, inviting, and encouraging, while in traditional policing it is toward warning, threatening, forcing, and hurting. Community policing is less direct than traditional policing. It is a kind of policing that can be done as well by women as by men, by the short as by the tall, by the verbal as by the physical, and by the sympathetic as by the authoritarian.

Community policing also requires an ability to interact constructively with a differentiated public. The police know from experience that all people are not the same. Community policing justifies making particularistic appeals and adaptations. In order to do this successfully, people with diverse backgrounds are needed in the police. Community policing helps to demonstrate the value of heterogeneity; it makes heterogeneity professional.

B. Benefits to the Police

Community policing also offers potential benefits to the police. Seven of these are described below.

1. *Political Benefits.* Politically, community policing is a game the police cannot lose. If coproduction through community participation leads to lower crime rates and higher arrest rates, the police can take credit as foresighted agents of change. If community policing fails to increase public security, the police can argue for an intensification of traditional strategies. Given the current fear of crime, the public is hardly likely to reduce support for policing because a new gambit does not work.

2. *Grassroots Support.* Community policing offers a magnificent opportunity to build grassroots political support for the police. It embeds the police in the community, giving them an opportunity to explain themselves, associate themselves with community initiatives, and become highly visible as concerned defenders of public safety. Commu-

nity policing makes the population at large a "special interest group" supporting police-led programs.

3. *Consensus-building*. Community policing is a means for developing a consensus between the police and the public about the appropriate use of law and force. The police have an obligation not only to catch criminals but also to maintain order in public places. There are sound crime-prevention reasons for this, quite apart from enforcement of standards of decency and propriety. Research has shown that people are made fearful and insecure by disorder and incivility, not just by criminal activity. In fact, criminal victimization is rare; most people's knowledge of crime comes second-hand through the media. Inability to curb public disorder—such as loud music, vandalism, drunkenness, and uncouth behavior—generates further disorder, more serious crime, and diffuse feelings of insecurity (Wilson and Kelling 1982).

In order to maintain public decorum, the police use the authority of law and sometimes the reality of constraint or the threat of force. This is a delicate balance: if police underenforce, the "signs of crime" multiply, encouraging further depredations; if they overenforce, the public becomes mistrustful or, worse yet, hostile, and perhaps even violent. Community policing is a vehicle for undergirding police action with moral support. Through community liaison, the police can assimilate local standards of conduct and acceptable levels of enforcement. This is not meant to imply that the police should always be bound by community sentiment. Communities, too, can be too punitive, permissive, or have double standards. But the police are less likely to be regarded as an army of occupation in ethnic neighborhoods if they are able to act in accordance with the wishes of the respectable, law-abiding people who work and reside there.

4. *Police Morale*. Community policing probably raises the morale of the police involved because it multiplies the positive contacts they have with those supportive people in a community who welcome police presence and activity. Traditional deployment concentrates police contacts on "difficult" people—criminals and incorrigibles as well as deserving but demanding claimants for police service, such as victims, incompetents, and mental cases. For different reasons, all these people are difficult to satisfy. One set sees the police as the enemy; the other sees them as being ineffective or unsympathetic. As officers throughout the world ruefully note, police work does not bring them in contact with an improving group of people. More to the point, it does not bring them in contact with people who readily say "glad to have you here."

Community policing leads to unemotional, nonemergency interaction with citizens, increasing contact with people who want nothing more from the police than their reassuring presence. Community policing increases the likelihood that the public's quiet regard will be displayed to individual officers. This improves police officers' sense of self-worth, and makes being a police officer more satisfying.

5. *Satisfaction.*   Because effective community policing requires that subordinate ranks take more initiative and responsibility, it makes the police job more fun. Community policing cannot be managed in a quasi-military way, fulfilling easily measured norms and avoiding stipulated errors. Community policing may, in fact, be the operational strategy that is peculiarly fitted to the new breed of police recruit. Police managers report that today's more highly educated officers are less accepting of routine, more likely to question command, and more impatient with nonsolutions to recurrent problems. Community policing may be the best program the police have devised for maintaining zest for the job.

6. *Professional Stature.*   Community policing raises the professional standing of the police by broadening the range of skills required. To be successful at community policing, police must be more than large, physical, and tough; they must be analytic, empathetic, flexible, and communicative. Breaking the old template is threatening to some of the older, less educated officers. It helps to explain why community policing is resented by many. In the long run, however, community policing will make police less marginal as professionals.

7. *Career Development.*   By enriching the strategic paradigm of policing, community policing creates more lines for career development. Because community policing encompasses and expands on the traditional model, it provides more ways for personnel to be valuable. For community policing to work, police forces must reward a wider range of performance skills. This provides career opportunities to a more diversified group of officers.

IV. Conclusions

When its good intentions have been transformed into concrete programs, community policing displays impressive coherence and offers substantial benefits to communities as well as the police. Indeed, it represents the most dramatic change in strategic vision since the rise of "police professionalism" in the early twentieth century. For these reasons, community policing deserves to be as popular in professional circles as it has become.

At the same time, its promise has not yet been convincingly demonstrated in relation to the tremendous amount of hard work required to deliver on that promise. Community policing cuts across the grain of accepted police practice. For this reason, many officers will be attracted to it but daunted by the obstacles—intellectual, organizational, and political. They will talk but not act. Other officers will try seriously to innovate and will be bruisingly defeated. A few fortunate ones will succeed, as some have already done.

Finally, despite its attractions and importance, there is a concern that community policing will be oversold, both to police and to the wider political community. There are dangers in it. It could invite corruption. It could invite vigilantism, pitting the police and reputable residents against the disreputable. The best patrol officers could be attracted to community policing, with the resulting irony that the quality of the regular patrol force will be diluted. It could lead to de-emphasis of important law enforcement abilities (such as knowledge of search and seizure laws) in favor of interactional skills. It is not a crime-control panacea. The classical social and economic correlates of crime—high rates of youth unemployment, family breakdown, social dislocation, violence, gangs, drugs, illiteracy, and historical patterns of racial discrimination—will not be removed by community policing. Community policing is no substitute for social and economic change. As a crime-control measure, it must be understood in limited perspective, not as a long-run or keystone feature of a successful anticrime policy. Despite these caveats, if we view community policing as a set of practices featuring civilian participation in the provision of public safety services, it is appropriate to regard it as a positive and significant innovation for police and public alike.

REFERENCES

Bayley, David H. 1976. *Forces of Order: Police Behavior in Japan and the United States.* Berkeley: University of California Press.

———. 1985. *Patterns of Policing.* New Brunswick, N.J.: Rutgers University Press.

———. 1986. *Community Policing in Australia: An Appraisal.* Adelaide: National Policing Research Unit.

Boydstun, John E., Michael E. Sherry, and Nicholas P. Moelter. 1977. *Patrol Staffing in San Diego: One or Two Officer Units.* Washington, D.C.: Police Foundation.

Goldstein, Herman. 1987. "Toward Community-oriented Policing: Potential, Basic Requirements and Threshold Questions." *Crime and Delinquency* 33:6–30.

Greenwood, Peter W., and Joan Petersilia. 1976. *The Criminal Investigation Process*. Washington, D.C.: Law Enforcement Assistance Administration.

Ianni, Elisabeth R., and Francis Ianni. 1983. "Street Cops and Management Cops: The Two Cultures of Policing." In *Control in the Police Organization*, edited by M. Punch. Cambridge, Mass.: MIT Press.

Kelling, George L. 1981. *The Newark Foot Patrol Experiment*. Washington, D.C.: Police Foundation.

Kelling, George L., Tony Pate, Duane Dieckman, and Charles E. Brown. 1974. *The Kansas City Preventive Patrol Experiment: A Summary Report*. Washington, D.C.: Police Foundation.

Morgan, Rod. 1985. *Setting the P.A.C.E.: Police Consultation Arrangements in England and Wales*. Bath: University of Bath, Center for Analysis of Social Policy.

Morgan, Rod, and Christopher Maggs. 1984. *Following Scarman? A Survey of Formal Police/Community Consultation Arrangements in Provincial Police Authorities in England and Wales*. Bath: University of Bath, Center for Analysis of Social Policy.

Morris, Pauline, and Kevin Heal. 1981. *Crime Control and the Police: A Review of Research*. Home Office Research Study no. 67. London: H.M. Stationery Office.

Percey, Stephen L. 1980. "Response Time and Citizen Evaluation of Police." *Police Science and Administration* 8:75–86.

Police Foundation. 1986. *Reducing Fear of Crime in Houston and Newark: A Summary Report*. Washington, D.C.: Police Foundation.

Quah, Jon S. T., and Stella Quah. 1987. *Neighborhood Policing in Singapore*. Oxford: Oxford University Press.

Reiner, Robert. 1985. *The Politics of the Police*. Sussex: Wheatsheaf.

Rosenbaum, Dennis P. 1987. "The Theory and Research Behind Neighborhood Watch: Is It a Sound Fear and Crime Reduction Strategy?" *Crime and Delinquency* 33:103–34.

Rosenbaum, Dennis P., Dan A. Lewis, and Jane A. Grant. 1986. "Neighborhood-based Crime Prevention: Assessing the Efficacy of Community Organizing in Chicago." In *Community Crime Prevention: Does It Work?* edited by Dennis P. Rosenbaum. Beverly Hills, Calif.: Sage.

Scarman, Lord. 1981. *The Scarman Report: The Brixton Disorders*. London: H.M. Stationery Office.

Sherman, Lawrence W. 1986. "Policing Communities: What Works?" In *Communities and Crime*, edited by Albert J. Reiss, Jr., and Michael Tonry. Vol. 8 of *Crime and Justice: A Review of Research*, edited by Michael Tonry and Norval Morris. Chicago: University of Chicago Press.

Skolnick, Jerome H., and David H. Bayley. 1986. *The New Blue Line: Police Innovation in Six American Cities*. New York: Free Press.

Suttles, Gerald D. 1972. *The Social Construction of Communities*. Chicago: University of Chicago Press.

Weatheritt, Molly. 1987. "Community Policing: Rhetoric or Reality?" Paper presented at the International Conference on Community Policing, Temple University, May.

Williams, Raymond. 1976. *Keywords: A Vocabulary of Culture and Society.* New York: Oxford University Press.

Wilson, James Q., and George L. Kelling. 1982. "The Police and Neighborhood Safety: Broken Windows." *Atlantic Monthly* 249(3):29–38.

Wesley G. Skogan

Community Organizations and Crime

ABSTRACT

Community organizations that have crime problems on their agendas are common across the country. They originate as an anticipatory response to crime or as a consequence of local criminal activity; none endure, however, by focusing exclusively on crime problems. Participation in anticrime groups is based on awareness of local problems and is linked to socioeconomic status and class-linked attitudes. One approach to fighting crime is for community organizations to request more and better policing. Another is to focus on the fundamental social and economic issues that are root causes of crime. Individual measures often emphasize preventing victimization and minimizing losses, while collective action involves efforts to defend or reform neighborhoods. Evaluations have not produced clear-cut evidence that prevention programs are effective. Organizations also attempt to control crime and disorder through intervention and by changing people's social behavior. Crime-prevention organizations can be implanted in new areas either by encouraging existing organizations to add crime problems to their agendas or by encouraging the formation of such community organizations.

This essay examines the role of community organizations in crime prevention. During the 1980s, there has been increased interest in the role that voluntary efforts can play in dealing with crime problems. In earlier decades, hiring more police officers seemed the obvious answer to mounting crime, but by the late 1970s municipal and federal budget

Wesley G. Skogan is professor of political science and urban affairs at Northwestern University. The author thanks Susan Bennett, H. Paul Friesma, Robert Sampson, Lloyd Street, and Richard Titus for helpful comments on an earlier version of this essay. They all mourn the passing of their friend Fred DuBow, a central figure in research on community crime prevention.

constraints made that a less viable approach. The emergence of "community crime-prevention theory" at about this time presented an intellectual foundation for experimenting with a new, "off-budget" approach to crime control rooted in local voluntary organization (Lewis 1979; Lewis and Salem 1981; Lavrakas 1985). Unfortunately, it appears that such organizations can play only a limited role in crime prevention.

The community approach to crime prevention emphasizes collaboration between the criminal justice system and community organizations. It assumes that the police and other elements of the criminal justice system cannot effectively deal with crime and fear on their own. In this view, voluntary, organized community efforts to control crime and alleviate excessive levels of fear must parallel government action if safety is to be achieved within realistic budgetary constraints and without sacrificing civil liberties.

The community approach assumes that contemporary crime problems reflect the decline of the traditional structure of urban neighborhoods. While in the past people were poor and illiterate, and levels of cyclical unemployment were often extreme, crime rates remained low because the traditional agents of social control were strong: families, churches, schools, ethnic solidarity, and traditional values. Crime problems now are vastly worse because those agents have lost their hold on many of today's youths. Many urban neighborhoods are disorganized because the informal control they once exerted has largely disappeared. If disorganization is the root of the crime problem, organization is the solution. We are now more secular and individualistic and perhaps more skeptical about the capacities of government, so in today's world the best vehicle for neighborhood reorganizing sometimes seems to be community organizing around crime problems.

Those organizing efforts stress a number of different tactics for preventing crime. They range from narrow, technical approaches to prevention to broader, social change strategies for rebuilding communities. Some efforts involve collective action (activities carried out by groups), while others call for individual initiative, which can also be encouraged and facilitated by groups. Some programs aim at reducing opportunities for crime; they encourage people to install window bars and alarms and stronger doors and locks. Groups also offer escort services to senior citizens, and produce and distribute newsletters identifying actions that individuals can take to protect themselves from harm. Other programs focus on collective surveillance and crime reporting. Groups attempt to mobilize neighbors to watch one another's homes, to be alert for suspicious circumstances, and to call the police when problems arise. Thoroughgoing surveillance programs can also involve active citizen patrols, which are frequently tied together by citizen's band (CB) radios. Organizations also push for the sanctioning of offenders through crime-tip hotlines that help to identify troublemakers and by court watch programs that attempt to ensure that offenders get tough treatment from judges. Finally, organizations mount programs aimed at attacking the causes of crime. What these causes are perceived to be varies from area to area, but the programs frequently involve recreational activities for youths, antidrug and antigang efforts, and campaigns to improve neighborhood conditions and foster youth employment.

The focus of most of this effort is, of course, crime prevention. However, this approach to community problem solving promises a wider set of benefits. An additional target of these organizing efforts is fear of crime. A growing body of research suggests that fear and related concerns are overstated. This may have important consequences, for the same research indicates that fear is linked to despair rather than positive action, and to a desire to move out of troubled areas (Skogan and Maxfield 1981). It is often assumed that, through organized efforts, worry about neighborhood crime can be reduced to more realistic levels and harnessed to positive actions to prevent crime.

Following a decade of organizing, national surveys point to modest levels of participation in these efforts. In 1981, 12 percent of the adult population claimed membership in a neighborhood group or organization that was involved in crime prevention (O'Keefe and Mendelsohn 1984). A national survey conducted in 1984 found that 7 percent of adults had joined a Neighborhood Watch group, one of the most common forms of collective activity (Whitaker 1986). This kind of participation (but not individual or household prevention measures, which are more uniformly adopted) is about twice as high in central cities as in nonmetropolitan areas.

During the 1970s and early 1980s, community approaches to crime prevention attracted the attention of politicians, who found diverse reasons for supporting it. It emphasized voluntarism and had smaller budgetary implications than most alternatives for dealing with crime, and it diverted attention from what some thought to be the root causes of crime—poverty, functional illiteracy, and racism. This suited conservatives. On the other hand, it promised to support organizing efforts in poor neighborhoods and to provide money for established community organizations, which suited many liberals.

The community approach to crime prevention also attracted the attention of researchers. It emerged during a period of growing public militancy with respect to crime, yet it offered an alternative to hiring more police for researchers who were skeptical that affordable increases in the level of traditional policing would have much of an effect on crime. In addition, the concurrent political exhaustion of the rehabilitative ideal had created an intellectual vacuum which the notion of empowering people to solve their own problems easily filled.

Finally, community crime prevention attracted the attention of public and private agencies with money. During the 1970s, a succession of federal agencies stepped forward to support organizing efforts around crime problems, and in the early 1980s the Ford Foundation put private support behind them as well. During the same period, federal research agencies sponsored studies of many aspects of this new, nonpolicing approach to crime prevention, which further fueled the interest of the research community.

This research suggests that the relation between community organizations and neighborhood crime problems is an uneasy one and is fraught with irony. Rather than uniting the community in outrage or common purpose, crime appears to undermine the capacity of communities to organize. Anticrime organizations are most often successful in communities that need them least. Many established organizations studiously ignore burgeoning crime problems, while others vigorously attack *other* problems (e.g., blighted housing) and call what they are doing "crime prevention." Organized responses to crime may divide communities rather than pull them together. When they are effective, crime-prevention efforts may redistribute resources in favor of those who are better off and work to the detriment of the poor.

Many kinds of organizations are involved in anticrime activities. In addition to traditional community organizations, they include condominium associations and community development corporations, consortiums of shopping strip merchants, and "umbrella" organizations that serve other organizations rather than individuals or neighborhoods. This essay does not describe them all, and most of the quantitative research on crime-prevention groups that it summarizes does not differentiate between types of organizations. However, I do distinguish throughout between organizations that are "preservationist" (Lewis, Grant, and Rosenbaum 1985) and others that are "insurgent" in orientation. By "preservationist" I mean something other than the architectural or historical preservation groups that exist in many places; as I use the term here, preservationist groups are concerned more generally with maintenance of established local interests, customs, and values. Such groups typically arise in stable, better-off areas. They represent the interests of long-term residents, home owners, small businesses, and local institutions in preserving the status quo. Insurgent groups, by contrast, have a stake in upsetting the current distribution of status and property. Leaders of insurgent groups necessarily are critical of society's institutions.

This essay is organized in the following manner. Section I discusses why community organizations come into being, how they are distributed in geographical and social space, and how they can sustain interest in crime problems over time. Section II reviews what is known about patterns of individual participation in community organizations. Section III reviews what community organizations do in response to crime problems. Section IV examines a crucial policy-related question: Can anticrime organizations be transplanted to places where they have not emerged on their own? Section V, the conclusion, considers the question of whether community-organizing responses to crime can succeed in any meaningful way. It also suggests some important caveats regarding the potential generality of the conclusions.

I. The Origin and Maintenance of Organizations

Relatively little is known about the origins of community organizations involved in crime problems. The best documented efforts are attempts by government agencies or city-wide umbrella groups to implant organizations where none apparently existed. These efforts are considered later, in light of what is known about organizing around crime. Indigenous groups also often form in response to threats from outside the community, in the form of impending construction or demolition, or fear of racial succession (Taub et al. 1977; Emmons 1979). An important but often overlooked role is also played by big institutional actors with an investment to protect. Hospitals, universities, banks, utilities, churches, and other institutions with large and difficult-to-uproot stakes in deteriorating communities can often be found behind the scenes, supplying money and staff to support local organizing efforts (Taub et al. 1977; Taub, Taylor, and Dunham 1984).

It seems clear that groups do not form automatically in direct response to serious and pervasive problems with crime. Conklin (1975) and Lewis and Salem (1981) both juxtapose what they describe as the "Durkheimian" view—that crime draws communities together—with their own, which is that crime is a divisive force. Their capsule version of the argument Durkeim presents in *The Division of Labor in Society* (1933) is that crime performs a positive social function when it strengthens community bonds. In reacting with horror to criminal events, community members seem to draw more sharply defined boundaries between acceptable and unacceptable behavior, and those sharing conventional values are brought together as a result.

Durkheimian analyses are still popular. For example, in their description of the formation of Neighborhood Watch programs, Garofalo and McLeod (1986) describe the following typical developmental sequence: a rash of unusual crimes occurs in a brief period of time; residents of the afflicted area are concerned, hold a meeting, and call on the police for assistance; the local crime-prevention officer helps residents organize a Neighborhood Watch program. This vignette, though it describes an integrative reaction to crime, differs from Durkheim's story in a number of ways. One is the presence and role of the crime-prevention officer. Another (as Garofalo and McLeod note) is that this kind of reaction to crime characterizes middle-class jurisdictions inclined toward instrumental problem-solving efforts.

By contrast, modern studies of high-crime neighborhoods find that crime and fear undermine support for law enforcement, stimulate withdrawal from community life, and at best favor individualistic, self-protective actions (Conklin 1975; Skogan 1986). In the face of decades of serious, life-threatening crime problems, residents are more typically distrustful of one another and have a negative view of their community and its potential.

Early organization around nascent crime problems is probably most typical of preservationist groups and may be the most common pattern. Interviews with participants in anticrime groups in the Chicago area indicate that about two-thirds of the groups were formed in anticipation of crime problems rather than in reaction to them (Lavrakas and Herz 1982). Interviews indicated that groups that formed to anticipate crime problems were concentrated in better-off areas. Reactive reasons for group formation were more often reported by residents of higher-crime, low-income, densely populated, minority neighborhoods.

A. The Distribution of Organizations

There have been several systematic studies of the geographic distribution of community organizations. Some used surveys to identify groups and then found and interviewed their leaders (Podolefsky and

DuBow 1981) or mailed them questionnaires (Lavrakas, Herz, and Salem 1981; Garofalo and McLeod 1986). Others categorized and counted organizations on lists gleaned from official sources or from newspaper stories and telephone directories (Henig 1978, 1984; Kohfeld, Salert, and Schoenberg 1983). The general conclusion to be drawn from these studies is that community organizations, and especially those concerned with crime, are least common where they appear to be most needed—in low-income, heterogeneous, deteriorated, renting, high-turnover, high-crime areas.

Community organizations are more common in better-off urban neighborhoods. The working hypothesis, advanced by Podolefsky and DuBow (1981), is that the relation between the density of local voluntary associations and the indicators of social and economic stability is curvilinear. Local organizational life is at its low point in poor, crime-ridden areas.[1] Residents of these areas typically are deeply suspicious of one another, report only a weak sense of community, have low levels of personal influence on neighborhood events (which goes along with a typically high external locus of control), and feel that it is their neighbors, not outsiders, whom they must watch carefully (Greenberg 1983; Greenberg, Rohe, and Williams 1985). Crime-prevention activities that require frequent contact and cooperation are less likely to be found in poor areas and in areas with high levels of fear, fatalism, and despair (Greenberg and Rohe 1983; Garofalo and McLeod 1986).

Local organizations are also less frequently encountered in the most stable and tightly knit (usually working-class) areas. There, high-density, informal networks substitute for the more formalized channels of communication required in other areas. Residents know one another and are frequently linked by church and family to many others in the immediate neighborhood (Crenson 1978). Life in these areas can resemble an "urban village." This is not necessarily to the advantage of residents. In modern society, tight-knit, cohesive neighborhoods like those described by Gans (1962) can persist only in isolated nooks and crannies of the city, and are measured in size by blocks rather than miles. As their environment changes around them, they maintain their identity by shrinking their self-defined jurisdiction to a smaller and

[1] An exception is church participation, which has demographic correlates different from all other common forms of local community activity. In research on local voluntary associations and crime, however, there is no mention of church-based anticrime activity. Parish churches were active in Saul Alinsky's original community-organizing efforts in Chicago, and in many poor neighborhoods they are a significant political force.

smaller area (Lewis, Grant, and Rosenbaum 1985). The community in effect is redefined by the threat of invasion by others (Suttles 1972). Within a small area, residents may still be able to identify "strangers," and quasi-vigilante activity by local youths may preserve their isolation, but they remain very vulnerable to larger political and social forces (Emmons 1979).

It is moderately cohesive areas that need organizations to bring people together and that at the same time support participation in voluntary associations. They may be the most typical urban neighborhoods. They are stable working- and middle-class neighborhoods where relatively prosperous home-owning residents live, but few strong local social and familial ties exist. In the absence of close ties, residents of these areas require some mechanism to bring them together to deal with local problems. They may succeed, because they are familiar with using organizations for instrumental problem solving (Crenson 1983).

Another empirically based generalization is that successful neighborhood organizations are more common in homogeneous areas. Neighborhoods featuring a mix of life-styles may need organizations in order to identify residents' common interests, but more frequently they do not have them (Henig 1982; Greenberg, Rohe, and Williams 1985). As Podolefsky (1983, p. 136) noted in his description of an ethnically and economically heterogeneous area of Chicago, "While many community organizations and social service groups can be found in Wicker Park, there is no single cohesive organization with which the entire community can identify. Community groups are either almost exclusively white or almost exclusively Latino. None is composed of an ethnic mixture which replicates the population of the neighborhood. The concerns to which the white and Latino groups address themselves are frequently different." In heterogeneous areas, the best that often happens is that preservationists unite against "bad elements" of their own community and *their* organizations, and thus opportunities for participation remain fragmented and exclusionary.

The advantage of socioeconomically, racially, and culturally homogeneous areas is that residents share a definition of what their problems are and who is responsible for them. They share similar experiences and objective life conditions, and they have the same broad conception of their public and private responsibilities (Henig 1982). The empirical evidence (summarized in Rosenbaum [1987]) is that in homogeneous areas, residents exercise more informal control and are more likely to intervene when they see problems, more residents feel positively about their neighbors and feel personally responsible for events and conditions in the area, and there are more active crime-prevention programs.

In multicultural areas, by contrast, there often are conflicting views of both the causes of crime and the solutions to it. Where neighborhoods are divided by race and class, concern about crime can be an expression of conflict between groups. Preservationists will identify the problem as some of the residents around and among them. Watching for "suspicious people" easily becomes defined as watching for a particular race and aggressively monitoring the circumstances under which different races come into contact. Yin et al. (1976) found that civilian patrols were most common in racially mixed areas of cities. Rather than drawing the community together, preservationist groups in these areas may selectively recruit members on the basis of their values and backgrounds, and their efforts—including crime prevention—may be divisive rather than integrative (Emmons 1979; Rosenbaum 1987).

Gentrifying neighborhoods provide a case study of the process at work. In gentrifying areas, newcomers and real estate developers form groups to promote the area and establish a middle-class environment. New residents use neighborhood redevelopment strategies to push up housing values and rents to levels that longer-term residents cannot afford. Thus, "one group's solution is likely to become another group's problem" (Lewis and Salem 1986, p. 90). Part of the redevelopment push involves attacking "undesirable" land uses (such as rooming houses, saloons, and single-room-occupancy hotels) and provoking the police to crack down on "bad elements" in the area. The newcomers often form civilian patrols or block watch groups (Taub, Taylor, and Dunham 1984; McDonald 1986) and attempt to use political influence to persuade police and other public officials to act against undesirables (Bottoms and Wiles 1986). In a study of one Washington, D.C., area, Henig (1984) found block-by-block differences in block watch formation and participation that reflected the spread of gentrification. Participation levels were higher and organized efforts more sustained on blocks with more home owners, fewer blacks, fewer children, and fewer elderly residents. Interestingly, gentrification appears to reduce area personal crime rates, but it does not affect levels of property crime (McDonald 1986).

The pattern of homogeneity prospering over heterogeneity may hit black Americans the hardest. Whites, who have a wider range of residential location choices, are generally more able to congregate in patterns reflecting their class, life-style, and family organization. This leads to a wider range of shared values in many white communities and thus fewer problems concerning many forms of public misconduct, standards of property maintenance, and control of children (Taylor, Gottfredson, and Brower 1980; Greenberg, Rohe, and Williams 1982; Taub, Taylor, and Dunham 1984). Black neighborhoods, however, can have greater difficulty developing consensual norms because segregation in the housing market leads to greater diversity of classes, life-styles, and family organization in the same geographical areas (Erbe 1975). Faced with more limited residential choices, many blacks cannot avoid living in propinquity to others with conflicting life-styles, which redounds to their further disadvantage when nascent insurgent groups attempt to form.

B. How Do Groups Sustain Anticrime Activity?

Almost every study of local crime-prevention efforts points to a decline in participants' interest and enthusiasm over time, even in places where initial levels of program awareness and participation were high (Fowler and Mangione 1982; Garofalo and McLeod 1986; Lindsay and McGillis 1986; Rosenbaum 1987). The question of how these efforts can be kept in motion thus is an important one. Where successful organizations support crime-prevention efforts, the activity presumably is somehow institutionalized, but it is not foreordained that organizations will be interested in institutionalizing such crime-prevention efforts.

It is almost an article of faith among community organizers that crime is a no-win issue, and few would be willing to bet their organization's survival on its capacity to focus exclusively on crime, much less on its ability to succeed in doing anything about it. There are several reasons for this. First, criminals are a furtive, almost invisible enemy. One of the basic "rules for radicals" (Alinsky 1971) is that organizers should personalize their target. While groups can picket the office of a real estate developer or march on the home of a bad landlord, criminals usually remain faceless. Opportunities occasionally present themselves in the form of abandoned buildings where drug users congregate ("shooting galleries") or wherever concentrations of street prostitutes appear, and these provide organizers with targets for direct action. However, crime also is an atomizing force. Unlike a smelly landfill, it visits individuals on a house-by-house basis, and people can keep their heads down and hope to be passed over. It is also hard to win a visible victory over crime. A successful struggle over a dangerous intersection may result in a stop sign or crossing guard for all to see, but a victory over crime involves preventing dozens or hundreds of individual events, and keeping them from happening next year as well. This is difficult to document or point to with pride. Finally, concern about crime simply does not provide a basis for sustained individual participation. As the next section documents, fear of crime does not motivate people to get involved in community activities.

This does not mean that neighborhood organizations have avoided crime problems during the 1970s and 1980s. But in almost every case groups do something else as well. Community studies suggest that few groups initially form around crime, and those that attempt to get started by tackling crime problems have neither long lives nor much success at recruiting members; further, anticrime groups that survive do so by adopting other issues or changing their function entirely, and most strong community organizations have complex, multi-issue agendas (Podolefsky and DuBow 1981; Fowler and Mangione 1982; Taub, Taylor, and Dunham 1984).

Understanding the circumstances under which existing organizations decide to add crime prevention to their agendas is a research issue with important policy implications. Unfortunately, we have very little systematic knowledge about this process. It is not automatic, for in successful organizations crime has to compete with other issues for agenda status, staff, and volunteers. Many of those issues seem more tractable and are likely to produce benefits for the organization. In principle, the adoption of crime as an agenda item should have something to do with how organizations market themselves to generate the members and resources they need in order to grow in influence.

Insurgent groups representing poor neighborhoods are least likely to feature crime programs, even though the objective threat of victimization in their community may be substantially higher. Like all organizations, they need to articulate their members' concerns and win victories that generate benefits for their constituents. In poor neighborhoods, these concerns are numerous and deeply felt, and the problem of generating material benefits for distribution is acute. Surveys asking city residents about the most important problems facing their area reflect the situation—white and better-off respondents are more likely than blacks and the poor to indicate crime as their leading problem, probably because their list is shorter (Furstenberg 1971; Podolefsky 1983). As organizers have noted, it is difficult to persuade people in poor areas to become involved in project work "when most residents are worried about putting food on the table" (Cook and Roehl 1982, p. 7). The potential constituents of insurgent groups tend to rank crime low on their lists of pressing problems. Insurgent groups are under more pressure to produce jobs, clinics, and other material benefits.

Groups that can survive pursuing a crime-oriented agenda are likely to be preservationist in character. Crime may serve as convenient shorthand for the more limited set of problems that face them, including population turnover, a softening of the local real estate market, and problems in schools (Taub, Taylor, and Dunham 1984). These problems strike directly at their interests as home owners and racial dominants. These groups often employ exclusionary tactics, including citizen patrols to monitor outsiders and efforts to control the real estate market. Unlike insurgent groups, preservationist groups can also distribute symbolic benefits for their members—reaffirming their members' status, reinforcing a positive image of their community, and extending local friendship networks (Salisbury 1970).

Preservationist groups sometimes are found walking a fine line between adopting a crime-prevention agenda and continuing to serve as boosters for their area and its real estate. Reporting on the activities of the Back of the Yards Council, a classic preservationist group on Chicago's white Southwest Side, Podolefsky (1983) noted that the council's weekly newsletter studiously avoided mention of local crime stories. Despite offering almost every other imaginable service, this powerful and professionally staffed organization also avoided promoting household protective efforts, crime reporting, or any other clearly labeled anticrime activity. For the council, overt support of crime prevention would bring to the surface a public relations problem it would rather address indirectly.

Money is one source of organizational sustenance. Government agencies, private foundations, and commercial stakeholders have recognized that the potential for meaningful action is enhanced by getting established organizations to take on crime issues rather than nurturing the development of new groups, and they have fostered crime prevention by, in effect, paying groups to do it. They do so in the hope of grafting the organization's visibility, legitimacy, leadership, and membership to their own agenda of local problems. This is discussed in Section IV below, but it should be clear that access to funding could play a potentially important role in increasing the viability of organizations in poor areas. Paid staff appear to be critical to the persistence of local voluntary associations (Taub, Taylor, and Dunham 1984; Greenberg, Rohe, and Williams 1985; Garofalo and McLeod 1986) as much today as in earlier periods when settlement houses, the YMCA, and domestic missionaries were on the scene and working on behalf of the immigrant poor.

Provision of funding to encourage local organizations to address crime problems is both more available and in many ways more attractive for preservationist groups than it is for insurgent groups. First, preservationist groups are "safe" recipients of funds because their aims tend to be conservative and conventional. The political risks of supporting insurgent groups are often substantial, for their leadership and ideology are often critical of social institutions. Second, unlike preservationist groups, insurgent groups are unlikely to accept a narrow, technical definition of the crime problem for long.

II. Participation in Organized Anticrime Activity
Participation in community organizations is a form of constrained voluntarism (Emmons 1979). That is, individuals participate within a neighborhood context that defines their alternatives. With the exception of a few organizational entrepreneurs who themselves create groups that turn out to have observable structure and some longevity, people can participate only by affiliating with existing groups that have active agendas. The local distribution of groups of various persuasions thus describes the opportunity structure for individual participation in an area (Stinchcombe 1968). Who participates and in what capacity turns on what opportunities are available, and neighborhoods differ in the opportunities they present.

As a result, it is difficult to make much out of many studies of participation in community organizations. National or even city-wide surveys examining the correlates of participation confound individual and neighborhood factors. They typically find that participants are more likely to be better-off, more educated, longer-term residents of their community who are married, have children, and own homes (Greenberg, Rohe, and Williams 1985). But it is also more likely that those fitting this profile enjoy a richer range of local organizations in which they can participate. One study that examined the influence of both individual and neighborhood factors on participation found that area-level characteristics were at least as important. Controlling for individual factors, program awareness and participation were higher in racially homogeneous, higher-status areas (Bennett, Fisher, and Lavrakas 1986). Participation is not just a reflection of individual attributes;

potential participants are not isolated individuals making choices that assess only the costs and benefits of acting.

Surveys of participation have employed two ways to get around this problem. Podolefsky and DuBow (1981) and others first asked if respondents knew of any local community groups or organizations, and then asked whether they were involved in one of them. Those who were involved were then asked what the group did. Respondents who mentioned crime prevention were identified for analysis as participants in crime-related groups. This turns out to be the best approach for learning about citizen participation in anticrime efforts. An alternative approach is to begin by asking respondents if they are aware of organized anticrime efforts in their community. The correlates of awareness then are treated as indicators of the social distribution of opportunities to participate, and studies are conducted of the individual correlates of participation only among those who report that they are aware of such efforts. The only national study along these lines confirms other research on the distribution of those opportunities—that awareness of anticrime groups is more common among informants from better-off, home-owning, single-family households (Whitaker 1986). However, this approach does not identify both groups that do and groups that do not take action with respect to crime, and it does not reveal any differences between participation in community groups generally and participation in crime-related groups specifically. This is a serious flaw, for the critical factor in understanding individual involvement is whether local groups are involved in anticrime activities.

A factor further confounding participation studies is that many city dwellers face three choices, not two. In addition to participating (if they can) or remaining quiescent, some city dwellers can also move to the suburbs; in Hirschman's (1970) terms, they can "exit" as well as exercise "voice." Research on suburban flight indicates that it is the family-oriented and better-off residents of a neighborhood who are most likely to move away (Skogan and Maxfield 1981). But, although there have been several studies of suburban flight (e.g., Duncan and Newman 1976; Frey 1980), participation in community organizations as one among three choices is not well understood. Emmons (1979) speculates that those who choose to leave rather than participate in community organizations are overwhelmed by the range of problems that confront their old neighborhood, feel that outside help is unlikely to appear, and perceive that there are few opportunities to participate in saving the community. Hirschman (1970) ties flight to a pattern of past failures to achieve success via "voice." The existence of this tripartite choice may help explain an important factor documented by many surveys of participation: controlling for other factors, blacks report higher rates of participation in community organizations (Skogan and Maxfield 1981; Lavrakas and Herz 1982; Greenberg and Rohe 1983; Greenberg, Rohe, and Williams 1985). In one of the few three-choice studies, Orbell and Uno (1972) also found that blacks were most likely to exercise a voice. If white residents of city neighborhoods truly face a tripartite choice, while for most blacks the real choice is activism or nothing at all, then more limited residential mobility may be the source of the higher levels of local participation by blacks that is indicated by surveys.

Despite these problems, past studies provide a useful portrait of patterns of participation in community organizations that do something with regard to crime.[2] The general lesson is that participation in anticrime groups results from the same factors that stimulate general involvement in neighborhood affairs. Those factors are, above all, indicators of socioeconomic status and class-linked attitudes concerning personal and political efficacy, extent of political information, and civic-mindedness (Verba and Nie 1972; Greenberg, Rohe, and Williams 1985; Lavrakas 1985). In a national survey, Whitaker (1986) found that, among those aware that groups were active in their area, participants in Neighborhood Watch programs were more likely to be better-off home owners. In a three-city study, Podolefsky and DuBow (1981) found the same pattern of participation in groups that respondents identified as "doing something" with regard to crime; in addition, families with children and those who planned to stay in their neighborhood were more likely to report such group involvement. Where there are groups at work, general participation levels run between 10 and 20 percent, and participation in crime-linked groups between 7 and 20 percent (Skogan 1981; Greenberg, Rohe, and Williams 1985).

A great deal of attention has been paid to the relation between peoples' participation in anticrime groups and their fear of crime. This stems from long-standing interest in the question, Can we scare people into protecting themselves? As observers of smokers and seat belt nonusers might guess, the answer is not clearly "yes." Survey studies of the problem report mixed findings. The DuBow, McCabe, and Kaplan

---

[2] "Do something" is the appropriate phrase; all of these studies were confined to simple "yes-no" measures of participation. None assessed the type or intensity of that participation, and the referent "groups" were totally undifferentiated with regard to their mission, jurisdiction, organization, or effectiveness.

(1979) literature review concluded that participants evidence higher levels of fear, while Skogan and Maxfield (1981) and Podolefsky and DuBow (1981) found they have lower levels of fear, and Lavrakas, Herz, and Salem (1981) report that fear and participation are unrelated. None of this research spoke directly to a hypothesis they all shared— that impulses toward participation are maximal among those who are both aware of local crime problems and are *moderately* concerned about crime. High levels of fear are thought to be incapacitating, while people with no knowledge or concern about local crime are unmotivated. This is a complex hypothesis concerning nonlinear statistical interaction, and it has been suitably tested (and supported) only in England (Hope 1986).

That there are few unique factors directly driving participation in organizations involved in anticrime activities should not be surprising. Participation is a function of opportunity and individual impulse, while what the groups are doing is a function of group leadership and decision making. Where the alternative is available, some people participate in local voluntary associations; in a three-city study, Skogan and Maxfield (1981) found that 44 percent of adults knew of local groups, and 47 percent of those who did (in other words, 21 percent of all respondents) said they were involved in one of them. Joiners participate in much of what their group does, and if and when their group decides to do something about crime, researchers class them as anticrime activists. In the same three-city study, 67 percent of those involved in an organization—defined as a group with a name—said their group did something with regard to crime, and of that subset fully 77 percent (10 percent of all adults) participated in that activity. Participation levels thus stem mostly from the level of success of organizations that pursue multiple goals, which explains why programs organized on the premise that people join groups because of crime usually go astray.

What this shows is that individual decisions to participate in anticrime efforts are not critical to the survival of community crime-prevention initiatives. Rather, the critical factor is the decision by multipurpose organizations to add crime prevention to their agenda. Participation levels are high in areas where organizations are successful and attract members. Most successful organizations have complex agendas; few of them were originally organized around crime concerns, and people join them for a variety of reasons revolving around their stake in the community and their citizenly instincts. It is when these groups take on crime prevention that participation in anticrime activities is high.

III. How Can Community Organizations Affect Crime?

Evaluations of community crime-prevention programs typically take a narrow focus on local Neighborhood Watch, Operation ID, or similar programs. They examine how groups promote property marking or organize block watches. However, studies of what groups do when they confront neighborhood problems point to a much broader range of reactions to crime. This section considers these reactions briefly and summarizes research on their effectiveness.

A. Capture Problem-solving Resources

Community organizations' first instinct is to get others to help. They attempt to leverage their resources by obtaining outside assistance in dealing with local problems; even if those problems are not solved (and few usually are), success in gaining attention downtown and gaining outside resources can be a significant organizational victory.

When the problem is crime, the first resource to which organizations lay claim is policing. They demand more policing in the form of beefed-up patrols in local hot spots. They often want "better" policing, usually foot patrols, as well, and perhaps recognition in the form of a new or reactivated precinct station house or storefront office. This is what Henig (1978) dubbed "the cop-a-cop game." Obtaining more and better policing may sometimes work to reduce levels of crime and disorder, even if problems like street prostitution are displaced into the next neighborhood (which is highly probable; see Cohen 1980). More likely, more policing may make residents and local merchants feel better—perhaps more secure, or more likely to shop in the area after dark. Sophisticated organizers are unlikely to believe that crime is a "winnable" issue, or that police will make any serious inroads into their community's real problems, but an organization-building victory can be won by successfully capturing a visible resource.

However, there is little evidence that organizations can sustain such resources, or at least not for very long. A large body of research on the spatial distribution of urban services points to the clear conclusion that in major cities distribution is almost completely explainable by simple bureaucratic decision rules (Antunes and Mladenka 1976; Lineberry 1977; Jones 1980). Research on police services is confusing because police pursue two somewhat contradictory goals at the same time: equalizing population coverage and equalizing crime coverage. The former tends to favor better-off areas with low crime, the latter worse-off neighborhoods with high crime. However, one rule or the other seems to explain most of the interneighborhood variance in the distribution of manpower, beat cars, or response time (Mladenka and Hill 1978; Jones 1982). In San Francisco, Henig (1978) found no relation between the spatial distribution of community organizations and police allocation of beat cars or foot patrol officers.

However, most resource-capturing efforts involve higher stakes. While promoters of crime prevention usually advance a relatively narrow view of what that entails, the instinctual reaction at the grass roots often is that more fundamental issues are involved. What those issues are depends on whether the groups are preservationist or insurgent in orientation.

Insurgent organizations typically pursue a broad agenda. Their relations with the police are often more antagonistic than those enjoyed by preservationist groups, and they approach the cop-a-cop game warily. Their constituents often fear the police and resent the way they exercise their authority, so the groups may be as interested in monitoring police misconduct and pressing for police accountability as they are in increasing police presence on the streets. Their constituents typically are concerned about a host of pressing problems, including unemployment, housing, health care, and discrimination. Podolefsky (1985) reports how organizations representing a poor, multicultural area in San Francisco rejected participation in a city-wide crime-prevention program because it took a narrow approach to the problem rather than addressing what residents perceived to be the real causes of crime.

Preservationist groups are more likely to pursue a narrower range of issues, and law enforcement may be central to their immediate concerns. This may include, in addition to more police, court-watch and victim-witness programs that promote sanctions for offenders. It often includes the formation of civilian patrols and Neighborhood Watch groups and posting signs indicating their new watchfulness, for they are trying to promote the image that theirs is a "defended" area. The same program that was rejected by a poor neighborhood in San Francisco was the object of intense lobbying by an organization representing a middle-class, home-owning area in the city. They wanted to be included, for there it was perceived that residents of a nearby public housing project were the major source of problems in the area (Podolefsky 1983, 1985).

B. Confront External Enemies

A second task facing local organizations is to identify the forces and actors outside the community that lie at the heart of their difficulties.

This provides an agenda for political action. In this regard, preservationist and insurgent groups usually have few interests in common.

In white neighborhoods, preservationist groups almost inevitably fix on racial transition. In a recent study of community responses to crime in Chicago, Taub, Taylor, and Dunham (1984) report that every successful preservationist organization they encountered defined its central task as controlling neighborhood population turnover and freezing the racial distribution at its current point. At the most elemental level, that was crime control.

Racial transition was also intimately related to the innermost interest of preservationist groups—protecting the value of their property. In all but one of the white neighborhoods Taub and his colleagues studied (except the area enjoying rapidly appreciating real estate prices), the major community organization focused on stabilizing the real estate market. This led organizations to develop political agendas of some complexity. One was to attack real estate sales practices by discouraging "panic peddling" and "block busting." They also challenged institutional decisions shaping the local real estate market, realizing that when mortgaging institutions and insurance companies refuse to make reasonable loans or to issue policies in certain neighborhoods (when they "redline" it), this effectively condemns those areas to decline (Bradford and Rubinowitz 1975). There are federal and state regulations against redlining, so its informal manifestations are more difficult to document now than in the past. In preservationist areas, groups also opposed efforts to locate subsidized housing and drug or mental health treatment centers in the neighborhoods, which are services likely to attract outsiders (Taub, Taylor, and Dunham 1984).

Insurgent organizations develop a broader agenda because problems in their area are more numerous and solutions to them are more clearly rooted in actions and resources outside of the community. They do not fix on controlling population turnover; insurgent groups typically represent already poor, deteriorated areas. They want subsidized housing and clinics. It is insurgent groups that talk about attacking the root causes of crime. They sometimes reject the narrowly defined programs advanced by crime-prevention specialists as diversionary, preferring instead to focus on what they see as more fundamental social and economic issues (Lewis, Grant, and Rosenbaum 1985; Podolefsky 1985). This also is more likely to generate material benefits for the area and political benefits for the organizations that succeed at redistribution. Crime problems for insurgent groups may be locally generated, but to focus on anything but root causes would instead legitimate the role of the police.

C. Push Crime Prevention

It is difficult to tell how many or what proportion of community organizations pursue crime prevention as it is more narrowly defined. Henig (1978) consulted San Francisco planning officials, and they identified 25 percent of the community organizations on his list as active on crime issues. By contrast, Podolefsky and DuBow (1981) found that two-thirds of survey respondents involved in any organization said the organization did something with regard to crime (using a survey estimate essentially weights groups by their size). The list of prevention activities these groups could promote is very long, but it is useful to group them into two categories: actions taken by individuals, and actions that can only be done collectively.

Most individual actions are aimed at preventing victimization and reducing losses. While these ultimately are pursued (or not) by individuals or households, they do not take place in a vacuum, and organizations sometimes devote a great deal of attention to encouraging and facilitating their adoption. Household prevention includes target hardening efforts (better locks, bars, and doors), which often are facilitated by home security surveys conducted by police or trained volunteers. Newsletters frequently describe personal precautions ("street smarts") that individuals can take to protect themselves from victimization and explain the benefits of theft insurance for renters. Police departments and organizations also actively promote property marking (Operation ID) and prompt crime reporting.

Studies of the spread of such efforts have found that, with one major exception, they are more common in better-off areas of cities. Home ownership, income, and length of residence best predict who has had a home security survey, has tried household target hardening, has marked property, and possesses insurance against theft (Lavrakas 1981). However, personal precautions (never walking alone, taking care to avoid strangers, staying home after dark) are more commonly taken by people living in poorer, higher-crime areas. Research on the effectiveness of these victimization-reduction activities is not very convincing because of the poor research designs that are typically used to evaluate them. The prevention programs being evaluated often involve a complex package of activities, so it is difficult to judge what may have worked, and few evaluations have gauged the actual extent to which those activities were carried out. Many evaluations have involved samples too small to demonstrate reliable statistical effects, and they are plagued by poor measurement and statistical analysis. They often employ no control groups or other research design features that would lend credibility to their conclusions. In a review of 102 evaluations claiming that Neighborhood Watch programs were a success, Lurigio and Rosenbaum (1986) found that 92 percent of them were fatally flawed.

Collective prevention efforts are similarly varied but require some degree of organization to pull them off successfully. In one category are efforts to defend the neighborhood, which are actions typical of preservationist groups. These include citizen patrols, whistle-stop campaigns, and block or Neighborhood Watch programs. They have in common the assumption that most local problems are caused by strangers who can be identified and made to feel unwelcome, and that by and large "insiders" can be trusted to watch out for each other's interests. Police crime-prevention officers may help them get started, but these activities typically are unfunded and conducted by volunteers. They probably are viable only in homogeneous, low-turnover areas where residents easily recognize their shared interests (DuBow and Emmons 1981; Garofalo and McLeod 1986; Rosenbaum 1987).

The second set of collective efforts are aimed at reforming the neighborhood and are more typical of insurgent groups. Actions in this category include drug prevention and treatment projects, antigang programs, efforts to control disorder in schools, job programs for youths, and a variety of social programs that are described as attacks on the root causes of crime in the area. In contrast to defensive efforts, these typically require trained staff and significant outside funding. While many defensive activities can operate autonomously, these require political connections, skills in acquiring grants, and professional organizers.

Along the road to success, insurgent groups can find themselves transformed. To manage these programs they may reorganize as nonprofit service organizations or neighborhood development corporations in order to receive grants and contracts. Their former constituents become their "clients"; the neighborhood becomes their "catchment area." There is a danger in this for the independence of these groups, of course. As they join the fabric of local government, there is pressure to swing their interests into line with those of politically dominant groups. But as a result, as long as there is a steady cash flow they may be a reliable mechanism for the delivery of crime prevention and other services (Mollenkopf 1983). For example, Podolefsky (1983) observed:

> The Woodlawn Organization (TWO) . . . has set aside the adversary approach which characterized its earlier years, and devotes most of its energies to developing local economic institutions and to assisting area residents in their dealings with city and federal agencies. Over the years, TWO has become a neighborhood institution and is probably the largest employer in the community. It has developed its own housing projects and retail outlets. It also provides many services which in other areas would be delivered by private or public agencies. There are roughly 230 people on the TWO payroll, not including those paid by other agencies but who work for TWO. . . . There is some controversy within the community about the direction that TWO is taking. Both staff and outsiders claim that the emphasis on economic development has forced attention away from the severe social problems still plaguing the community. [Pp. 164–65]

There is little solid evidence concerning the effects of any of these efforts on changes in neighborhood crime. McGahey's (1986) review of research on neighborhood development concludes that positive effects of programs attacking the economic roots of crime have yet to be demonstrated. Mostly this seems to be the fault of the programs themselves, which typically have only a marginal effect on the employability of participants, involve only a small percentage of those in need, do not remove potential offenders from a peer environment that encourages misbehavior, and are based on assumptions about the "rationality" of criminal behavior that are themselves unproven.

Garofalo and McLeod (1986) and Greenberg, Rohe, and Williams (1985) conclude that target hardening, Neighborhood Watch, and other tactics pursued by local organizations *probably* can have an effect on crime. This conclusion is suggested by the sheer weight of dozens of studies (usually lacking even a control area) showing declines in official crime counts, testimonials by activists, the enthusiasm of grant proposal writers, and a few statistical studies suggesting that crime is lower in organized areas even when numerous demographic and economic factors are taken into account. However, more sophisticated evaluations of community crime-prevention efforts do not support this optimistic assessment. The best evaluations carefully monitor the actual implementation of the planned program, measure its consequences using observational and survey data (not just official crime statistics), gather those data both before and after the program goes into action, and contrast what happened in the program area to matched control areas. Evaluations that meet these standards by and large have failed to find clear-cut evidence of the effectiveness of community crime-prevention programs. Well-documented quasi-experimental evaluations of programs in Minneapolis (Silloway and McPherson 1985; see below), Hartford (Fowler and Mangione 1982), and Chicago (Rosenbaum, Lewis, and Grant 1985) found no real evidence of program success. Only a burglary prevention program in Seattle showed positive results, although even there fear of crime went up, not down, in the program area, and the program's effects had disappeared eighteen months later (Cirel et al. 1977; Lindsay and McGillis 1986).

D. Activate Informal Internal Control

In addition to pushing prevention programs of one kind or another, organizations hope to control crime and disorder by initiating and supporting activities that will enhance residents' feelings of efficacy about individual and collective action as well as increase their sense of personal responsibility for these actions; they hope to stimulate attempts to regulate social behavior in the neighborhood by enhancing residents' feelings of territoriality and willingness to intervene in suspicious circumstances, and they hope to facilitate neighboring, social interaction, and mutual helpfulness to enhance solidarity and build commitment to the community. These ideas are as old as the Chicago School of Sociology. They assume (and this is supported by a great deal of evidence) that qualities such as efficacy, responsibility, territoriality, and commitment are undermined by the destabilizing forces of urbanization. Trouble-ridden communities are disorganized as a result, and the way to put them right is to organize them. Since delinquency and crime, in this view, are themselves the product of social disorganization, organizing forces can defeat them as well.

Research on the linkages between organizing efforts, the social processes summarized above, and crime suggests that community crime-control theory contains a nugget of wisdom but may also point in some wrong directions. For example, a great deal of correlational and experimental evidence (summarized by Goodstein and Shotland 1980; Shotland and Goodstein 1984; Greenberg, Rohe, and Williams 1985) stresses the importance of residents' territorial perceptions and willingness to intervene. Intervention is a two-step process: area residents must be alert for suspicious persons and activities, and they must be willing either to call the police or to challenge those up to no good. To do this effectively, they must know when and where to watch, and what is suspicious and what is not. Block or Neighborhood Watch programs are designed to build the familiarity and exchange of information (who lives where; when they will be away; who the troublemakers are) necessary to make this work. Survey studies of intervention behaviors or (more frequently) predispositions to intervene also point in the same direction—intervention is less frequent in central cities (Boggs 1971), poor neighborhoods (Hackler, Ho, and Urquhart-Ross 1974), heterogeneous communities (Greenberg, Rohe, and Williams 1985), and disorganized areas (Maccoby, Johnson, and Church 1958).

This leaves two unresolved questions: Can organizing efforts turn this around by stimulating higher levels of intervention, and (because we have already seen how such activities are less frequent in less well-off areas) can the necessary organizations be transplanted to places where intervention is currently low? The second question is considered in Section IV. The evidence concerning the first issue is affirmative. Survey studies typically find that participants in community organizations are more likely to take protective measures than are nonparticipants (Schneider and Schneider 1977; Pennell 1978; Lavrakas 1981; Skogan and Maxfield 1981) and report being predisposed to intervene (Lavrakas and Herz 1982; Rosenbaum, Lewis, and Grant 1985). There is less evidence that organizing efforts have much effect on nonparticipants, however. This is very important, for informal control can work only when large proportions of area residents can be counted on to watch and act, probably many more (no one knows what the threshold value is) than can be counted on to join organizations or show up at meetings. A quasi-experimental evaluation of several major organizing efforts in Chicago concluded there were no "rub-off" effects on nonparticipants (Rosenbaum, Lewis, and Grant 1985), while a more modest one-time study of forty-three blocks in New York City concluded there were general effects on participation, individual protection, and informal social activity (Perkins et al. 1986). A two-wave panel design like that employed in Chicago is critical for establishing the causal effects of individual or area participation, however. Activists are self-starters with many distinctive attributes, and block groups form more readily where trust and informal social activity are already high (Unger and Wandersman 1983). Because individual activists or active blocks usually differ from their quiescent cousins in many ways other than just their level of participation, it is important at a minimum to take readings of the supposed effects of participation before they begin as well as afterward and to include some unaffected individuals or neighborhoods in the study as a control group as well. Few studies of the effects of anticrime participation have employed even these minimal research standards, however (Lurigio and Rosenbaum 1986).

Individual efficacy and responsibility may be enhanced by what goes on when organizing efforts succeed in getting people together. Reports on these meetings indicate that organizers attempt to lead discussions of local problems, identify the common interests of the participants, emphasize their interdependence, and foster support for the organization's political agenda, including opposition to external forces contributing to the neighborhood's plight. Organizers also stress the efficacy of specific actions such as target hardening, property marking, and setting up "phone trees" so neighbors can contact one another (McPherson and Silloway 1980; Podolefsky and DuBow 1981; Cook and Roehl 1982). The most descriptive reports (e.g., Lewis, Grant, and Rosenbaum 1985) also reveal there is a great deal of confusion, uncertainty of purpose, and poor leadership at meetings and a great deal of frustration among people who have few "meeting" skills and no familiarity with Roberts's Rules of Order. The effects of all this are not clear. In a major review, Rosenbaum (1987) concludes that such meetings may magnify perceptions of area problems, stimulate fear of crime, exaggerate the individual racial fears of participants, and lead participants to feel more helpless as a result of attending. This issue is a critical one and clearly calls for more research.

Research suggests that neighboring, informal interaction, and helpfulness may not be very important aspects of the theory. The assumption is that these rather ordinary aspects of social life are "the precursors of social control" (Fisher 1977). Through them, area residents become familiar with one another, exchange information, develop a sense of community, and define the range of territory for which they feel responsible (Hunter 1974). These behaviors may be facilitated by local organizations (Unger and Wandersman 1983). However, those classified by researchers as active in groups typically attend just one or a few meetings and are often only peripherally involved in group programs (Podolefsky and DuBow 1981; Rosenbaum, Lewis, and Grant 1985). It is asking a lot to expect that attending a few meetings or receiving a newsletter will change day-to-day behavior that is rooted in people's life-styles (and the "dosage" that would be required is unknown). These social behaviors are powerfully affected by many other factors, including the typical family organization of the community, the age of the residents, and the physical layout of the neighborhood. Moreover, there is only a very tenuous link between the frequency of these behaviors and levels of area crime and disorder, and it runs in the wrong direction (Skogan 1987). These behaviors activate very subtle social processes. They exert control by spreading norms about appropriate behavior and teaching new residents how to behave; their sanctions are gossip, social exclusion, and, at most, embarrassing threats. Finally, these aspects of social life are perhaps too causally distant and difficult to measure for researchers to link them with measures of crime. Whatever the reason, research does not suggest that theories emphasizing the role of social processes in informal crime control will steer organizing efforts in the right direction.

IV. Can Crime-prevention Organizations be Transplanted?

The transplant hypothesis is that collective anticrime activities can be implanted in neighborhoods where they do not currently exist (Rosenbaum 1987). Two strategies have been employed in implant efforts. The first involves identifying existing organizations and encouraging them to make a greater commitment to crime prevention. The money behind this has come from private foundations (Lewis, Grant, and Rosenbaum 1985), real estate developers and private or not-for-profit institutions (Taub, Taylor, and Dunham 1984), and the federal government (Lavrakas 1985). Subsection A of this section describes two federal efforts of this sort.

The second strategy is to encourage the formation of organizations in communities that lack them. This is a far riskier strategy, albeit one more likely to assist poor communities without an existing infrastructure of successful organizations. The fates of two attempts to create organizations from scratch are described in subsection B below.

A. Reshaping Existing Organizations

Pursuing the implant hypothesis, the federal government mounted two programs during the 1970s designed to spark the interest of existing organizations in anticrime programs. The Community Anti-Crime Program (CACP) was a $30 million effort spawned by the Law Enforcement Assistance Administration (LEAA) during its peak budget year of 1976. Bypassing state and local government, it involved the direct transfer of federal funds to established community organizations.

It turned into an administrative quagmire; groups were given no assistance either in applying for the money or in spending it, and the whole effort was poorly implemented (McPherson and Silloway 1981; Lavrakas 1985). The Community Anti-Crime Program was followed by the Urban Crime Prevention Program (UCPP). This was a joint effort by LEAA and ACTION (ACTION is the successor agency to the old Peace Corps and domestic VISTA programs). It funded eighty-five organizations in nine cities over a seventeen-month period beginning in 1981 (Lavrakas 1985). Getting the money was not without cost; while the UCPP funding process was much more orderly than CACP, and technical assistance was available to organizations in applying for the money, it took an umbrella organization in Chicago a full year to prepare a $400,000 proposal and lobby for its acceptance (Lewis, Grant, and Rosenbaum 1985).

Federal guidelines and funding procedures for these programs clearly favored making awards to preservationist rather than insurgent groups. The process rewarded conventional, narrowly defined activities. Most of the funded projects were oriented toward burglary prevention through Neighborhood Watch, target hardening, or property marking; only a small percentage were youth programs or claimed to attack the causes or conditions underlying neighborhood crime problems. Both programs called for guarantees of cooperation with local criminal justice agencies, so organizations solicited letters of support from police and prosecutors. The result was that the bulk of the money went to noncontroversial organizations with uncontroversial proposals (DuBow and Emmons 1981; McPherson and Silloway 1981; Greenberg, Rohe, and Williams 1985). In Chicago, the one organization under the local UCPP umbrella that represented a poor, black neighborhood gave up its share of the money and dropped out of the program in frustration: "Auburn-Gresham wanted to mobilize its community and develop new elites that could articulate the interests of the black community. They were not comfortable with the more limited goals of [the umbrella organization] and what appeared to them to be the patronizing attitude of the latter group's leadership. Participation . . . meant the assertion of black interests and demands" (Lewis, Grant, and Rosenbaum 1985, pp. XI–9).

Despite everyone's cautious stance, it was still necessary to ensure that the funded activities actually were carried out. Critics of the UCPP contended that accepting the money and modifying their organization's agenda in a serious way was only one adaptation groups could make in response to the program; another was to take the money, do something else with it, and call that "crime prevention."[3] Since the successful applicants were all established organizations with a well-developed view of what their neighborhoods' real problems were, and had staffs committed to taking those problems on, someone should have wondered why they were not committed to crime prevention already.

A process evaluation of the UCPP attempted to monitor this possibility by reviewing the proposals and conducting a telephone survey to catalog what the funded groups were doing before the award, and updates of this list of staff activities and meeting counts were occasionally conducted. The idea was that unexplained shifts in organizational activity could reveal, for example, that groups were spending anticrime money on housing rehabilitation. Of course, this represented the unstated assumption of the funding agencies that housing renewal is not an anticrime activity, and it revealed their commitment to a narrow view of crime prevention that characterized UCPP because of the artificial realities of the funding process. There was a great gulf between LEAA's understanding of the nature of crime problems and that which was operative at the grass roots. Groups could pursue such tactics in good conscience because they did not really see crime problems as distinct from the other ills facing their communities, and they did not think much could be accomplished if they were to see them as distinct (Podolefsky and DuBow 1981).

B. Nurturing New Organizations

To implant collective anticrime efforts in poorer, high-crime areas plagued by fear and other severe social problems will take a great deal of effort. Organizing those areas requires professional staff, material incentives for early distribution to participants, and vigorous support from the police (Garofalo and McLeod 1986). Someone has to make hundreds of door-to-door contacts, distribute fliers, identify and train block captains, organize meetings, and find some way to get people to attend those meetings. Two process evaluations of attempts to do this in Minneapolis and Hartford illustrate how difficult the task can be.

The most recent of these implant experiments took place in Minneapolis in the early 1980s. In brief, professional organizers were hired by the city to identify neighborhoods ripe for organizing around crime

---

[3] In the grant game this is known as "Robin-Hooding"; it is not "stealing" the money, it is making "better use" of it.

issues and then plan and implement a program. Their efforts were carefully monitored (see Silloway and McPherson 1985). The program involved all of the grass-roots organizing efforts described above, plus the assignment of uniformed police officers to assist block groups in a random half of the treatment areas. Every household on every block in the program areas was contacted, and there were an average of four visits or mailings to each (Pate, McPherson, and Silloway 1987). The Minneapolis project, in effect, created an attractive opportunity structure for participation by neighborhood residents.

People did turn out in substantial numbers, but only in better-off target areas. The lack of any response by residents of poor and minority areas led organizers to increase their efforts, but there still was virtually no response. Systematic counts were made, by block, of organizing activities and the number of people who came to meetings and participated in program activities. They indicated that where block socioeconomic status (SES) was low, measures of organizing effort were high, but that citizen participation was low. As a consequence, there was a strong inverse relation between organizing effort and citizen participation.

An evaluation of a comprehensive, neighborhood-based crime-prevention program in Hartford, Connecticut, illustrates a second obstacle to the implant process—keeping anticrime efforts alive over time (see Fowler and Mangione 1982). The project was conducted by a not-for-profit corporation (the Hartford Institute of Criminal and Social Justice) with the support of an LEAA grant. The program involved more than just community organizing. The intervention involved a modest effort to reshape the flow of vehicular and pedestrian traffic through the target area, and a special police team was assigned to the neighborhood. New community organizations were formed to participate in planning the traffic control program and to advise the police district commander about neighborhood problems, and an existing but moribund organization was rejuvenated to tackle crime problems.

After five years, none of the groups activated in the area was still doing what was planned. The only preexisting organization in the area had become sophisticated and professional and more effective than ever before, but it could not sustain its block watch program. Crime had been its catalyst for rebirth, but the group shifted its attention to housing rehabilitation and was successfully raising money. The organizers of the Hartford project succeeded in setting up a second organization that focused exclusively on crime. It grew to forty members, basically on the strength of the enthusiasm of the organizers, then wasted away for lack of any successful projects. A number of older residents of an area of apartment buildings were organized into a block watch group. They were trained by the police, and the institute bought them CB radios. A few years later the evaluators found them still in business, but they did not do much patrolling; rather, they transformed themselves into a senior citizen's social group.

Another group was a committee composed of representatives of the other three. They met regularly with the district police commander to discuss neighborhood problems. The committee persisted even though their sponsoring groups drifted away from crime problems because the commander continued to meet with them. This gave them a bit of influence, which they later capitalized on. The final organization in the area was a nonprofit local development corporation set up by area business leaders to do something about housing. It failed to do anything, was unable to establish any relation with area residents, and was virtually moribund, when suddenly the citizen's committee meeting with the district commander needed a corporate shell to receive an LEAA grant. The nonprofit housing corporation became the vehicle for hiring a professional staff to organize new crime-prevention efforts in the area, but the evaluators were not sanguine about the future of this new activity after the money ran out again.

V. Conclusions

Attempts to create new opportunities for participation and to manipulate the agendas of successful local community organizations provide a test of the transplant hypothesis. They also test earlier conclusions concerning the relation between community organizations and crime, conclusions that were based on studies of "naturally occurring" groups. This section summarizes the implications of these two streams of evidence and then offers a few caveats concerning how generalizable they may be.

A. Implications of Past Research

First, voluntary participation cannot easily be initiated or sustained in poorer, higher-crime areas. Studies of where organizations arise find they are disproportionately concentrated in homogeneous, better-off areas of cities. Surveys indicate that better-off city residents more frequently know of opportunities to participate and are more likely to participate when they have the opportunity. Attempts to transplant organized anticrime efforts are more likely to succeed in better-off target areas. This does not mean that organizing areas that are more in need is impossible, but it will not be easy. Government, in particular, must find relatively simple and direct mechanisms for effectuating social change if it is going to engineer change across many areas and among many kinds of people, using relatively blunt policy instruments.

Second, voluntary organizations do not of their own accord narrowly focus on crime if they have anything else to do. Many, perhaps a slim majority of them, do not feature crime-prevention activities. Organizers think crime is a no-win problem. Insurgent organizations representing worse-off areas have few reasons to focus intensively on local crime problems. If organizations are formed that do not have anything else to do, they will perish.

Third, what voluntary organizations prefer to do about crime on their own accord varies but rarely resembles the narrow, technical view favored by funding agencies, law enforcement agencies, and evaluators. This is most true in the highest crime areas. There, insurgent groups push for redistributive social and economic policies that will bring outside resources into their community. If it is necessary to do so, they will dub this an attack on crime's root causes. Preservationist groups, by contrast, battle social change and the mounting crime rate they see that is sweeping it into their neighborhoods.

Fourth, outside funding can purchase traditional crime-prevention efforts for a while. Evaluations of federally and foundation-funded attempts to steer existing organizations in that direction find they do succeed, albeit in the face of strong centripetal forces. Established organizations have entrenched agendas that are based on their analysis of their external enemies and internal strengths, and they will want to bend the program to support those agendas. Insurgent organizations will press for more broadly focused efforts to meet both their constituents' and their own organization's needs, which are real and pressing. Preservationist groups link crime problems to their own economic interests and focus on the real estate market.

Fifth, however, since the 1960s, it has been difficult for insurgent groups to succeed at pushing their own agenda under the rubric of crime prevention. Current arrangements favor preservationists. The LEAA and ACTION programs described above favored narrow, technical approaches to crime. Since those big organizing experiments, federal activity with respect to community crime prevention has changed. While previously money was distributed directly to organizations without being filtered through local criminal justice agencies, the federal government has adopted a much more modest role. It now just sponsors a resource center that distributes pamphlets and recommends model programs. The government and foundation funds that are available for community mobilization efforts are now more scarce and are scooped up by a few more aggressive and already well-organized neighborhoods, while most languish without support (Henig 1982).

Sixth, several observers have noted that crime-focused groups begin and persist more easily when they operate in cooperation with the police (Garofalo and McLeod 1986; Yin 1986). Garofalo and McLeod's (1986) study of 550 Neighborhood Watch programs found that only 6 percent received no help from the police. The police provided training, information, technical support, and equipment. They also can lend visibility and apparent legitimacy to organizing efforts, which can be important in neighborhoods starting out with lower levels of mutual trust (see Skolnick and Bayley in this volume). The Minneapolis organizing experiment described above included a "cop-on-the-block" component that was to graft these advantages onto the program, but it proved to be a logistical failure (Silloway and McPherson 1985). On the other hand, an attempt by the Houston police to organize a community and spawn a viable group concerned with both crime and other neighborhood issues appears to have been a substantial success (Pate et al. 1986). Unfortunately, securing this cooperation is likely to be difficult in poor and minority communities in which relationships with the police are often strained, and it will not be the first impulse of insurgent groups to attempt to borrow legitimacy from the police.

Seventh, the more successful groups are, the less transferable their programs will be. The more precise the analysis of their community's real problems, the more fully articulated their programmatic response; and the more accurately both the analysis and the action plan reflect the interests of their community, the less transferable it will be to other settings.

Eighth, troubled communities need organizations, notwithstanding all the difficulties involved in forming and sustaining them. Serious neighborhood problem solving admits to few avenues for autonomous action. However, social change at the end of the twentieth century is working in the opposite direction. The bulk of the demographic correlates of opportunities for participation and levels of actual participation (income, ownership, education, family status, length of residence) are trending in the wrong direction in cities. Demographic projections of these factors predict declining activism in the future. To a certain extent, theories that stress the importance of resurrecting informal social control reflect nostalgia for a village life that is long gone from cities and that certainly does not look like what life will be like in them in the twenty-first century.

Ninth, even if extensive organizing efforts are mounted, it is not clear that they will have their intended effect. Two recent quasi-experimental evaluations—in Chicago (Rosenbaum, Lewis, and Grant 1985) and Minneapolis (Pate, McPherson, and Silloway 1987)—found that sophisticated, professional organizing campaigns increased both the awareness of target area residents of prevention measures and stimulated participation in organizing meetings. However, in neither case (and both projects involved several target areas) was there any evidence of the hypothesized *effects* of this on such presumed consequences of participation as exercising informal control, intervention behavior, feelings of community solidarity, the perceived efficacy of prevention, neighborhood satisfaction, or fear of crime. These findings raise the issue of whether "program failure" or "theory failure" was at work in the two experiments. It may be the former—that the programs were too weak, that their "dosage" levels were too low, or that they were not correctly targeted at neighborhood problems. However, in both cases there was a documented program of some magnitude, and it was reflected in measures of resident awareness and participation. An alternate explanation is that community crime-prevention theory may be wrong, or misdirected in terms of what it presumes can be accomplished by organizing neighborhoods against crime.

Last, much of this works to the disadvantage of the poor. Group formation succeeds more easily in better-off and white neighborhoods, and these groups appear to be preponderately preservationist in character. They want to freeze the current race and class distribution of desirable real estate. Residents of those areas find it much easier to work in conjunction with the police, and their programs frequently can function autonomously and without external funding. To the extent that organizations make a difference with regard to crime, the differential distribution of opportunities to participate also has distributional implications. Assigning voluntary local organizations a major role in achieving public safety "places lower-class communities at a disadvantage relative to middle-class groups" (Rich 1980, p. 590).

B. Caveats

This essay paints a broad picture of the relation between neighbor-hood characteristics and leadership orientations on the one hand, and the manner and extent to which local voluntary organizations partici-pate in crime-prevention efforts on the other. The generality of the portrait may be open to debate. First, most of the research reviewed here was conducted in particular neighborhoods and cities during the late 1970s and the early 1980s. Events in other places (e.g., in ideologi-cally politicized environments or in largely minority-controlled cities) and at other times (during the politically charged 1960s, or in the retrenching 1980s) might look different. The poor are far from incapa-ble of organizing; there is considerable variation in the extent of organi-zation within categories of neighborhoods, and not all middle-class communities have proven capable of responding collectively to external threat (Henig 1982). Further, the changing complexion of some great cities (involving both large numbers of newly enfranchised Hispanics and a significant influx of new immigrants from Asia, the Middle East, and elsewhere) may foretell changes in the structure of their turf-based politics in the future. There is no reason for the agendas of community organizations or the motives of individual participants to remain static either in time or space. However, I would judge that the period that spawned most of this research probably involved maximal participation in crime prevention by established neighborhood organizations, which both earlier and later had different ideological and budgetary battles to fight.

A second question involves the generality of my conclusions regard-ing the strength and persistence of local organizing efforts. In preparing this essay, I focused on the crime-related activities of neighborhood organizations. It turns out that one of the most interesting aspects of this topic is that the very definition of what crime prevention *is* hinges on the political outlook of the beholder, which I in turn related to the preservationist or insurgent neighborhood base for specific politics. However, the evidence also suggests that what most groups do most of the time is *not* really focused narrowly on crime (for good reasons), and I have tried *not* to speak generically on the potential for their success in other endeavors. Astute local groups are forever attempting to capture control over resources and the way community problems are to be solved. As I noted, crime problems may sometimes be their weapon of choice for pursuing power. However, their success or failure at dealing with crime problems, or at using crime problems for leverage on other issues, does not necessarily speak to their potential for success in gaining that power. Reports on many powerful groups pursuing other economic and social agendas doubtless never entered my field of search at all. From the point of view of criminal justice practitioners interested in using neighborhood organizations to deliver narrowly defined crime-prevention services, this may be another "nothing works" paper; from the point of view of community residents trying to capture control of their lives, it may be a "crime doesn't work" paper; but it is not a "community organizations don't work" paper.

REFERENCES

Alinsky, Saul. 1971. *Rules for Radicals*. New York: Random House.

Antunes, George E., and Kenneth Mladenka. 1976. "The Politics of Local Services and Service Distribution." In *Toward New Urban Politics*, edited by Louis Masotti and Robert Lineberry. Cambridge, Mass.: Ballinger.

Bennett, Susan F., Bonnie S. Fisher, and Paul J. Lavrakas. 1986. "Awareness and Participation in the Eisenhower Neighborhood Program." Paper presented at the Annual Meeting of the American Society of Criminology, Atlanta, November.

Boggs, Sarah. 1971. "Formal and Informal Crime Control." *Sociological Quarterly* 12:319–27.

Bottoms, Anthony E., and Paul Wiles. 1986. "Housing Tenure and Residential Community Crime Careers in Britain." In *Communities and Crime*, edited by Albert J. Reiss, Jr., and Michael Tonry. Vol. 8 of *Crime and Justice: A Review of Research*, edited by Michael Tonry and Norval Morris. Chicago: University of Chicago Press.

Bradford, Calvin P., and Leonard S. Rubinowitz. 1975. "The Urban-Suburban Investment-Disinvestment Process: Consequences for Older Neighborhoods." *Annals of the American Academy of Political and Social Sciences* 422:77–86.

Cirel, Paul, Patricia Evans, Daniel McGillis, and Debra Whitcomb. 1977. *Community Crime Prevention Program: Seattle Washington*. Washington, D.C.: U.S. Department of Justice, National Institute of Justice.

Cohen, Bernard. 1980. *Deviant Street Networks: Prostitution in New York City*. Lexington, Mass.: Lexington Books.

Conklin, John E. 1975. *The Impact of Crime*. New York: Macmillan.

Cook, Royer F., and Janice A. Roehl. 1982. "The Urban Crime Prevention Program: Interim Findings and Central Issues." Paper presented at the Annual Meeting of the Law and Society Association, Toronto, June.

Crenson, Matthew A. 1978. "Social Networks and Political Process in Urban Neighborhoods." *American Journal of Political Science* 11:578–694.

————. 1983. *Neighborhood Politics.* Cambridge, Mass.: Harvard University Press.

DuBow, Fred, and David Emmons. 1981. "The Community Hypothesis." In *Reactions to Crime,* edited by Dan A. Lewis. Beverly Hills, Calif.: Sage.

DuBow, Fred, Edward McCabe, and Gail Kaplan. 1979. *Reactions to Crime: A Critical Review of the Literature.* Washington, D.C.: U.S. Department of Justice, National Institute of Justice.

Duncan, George, and Sandra Newman. 1976. "Expected and Actual Residential Moves." *Journal of the American Institute of Planners* 42:174–86.

Durkheim, Emil. 1933. *The Division of Labor in Society.* Translated by G. Simpson. New York: Macmillan.

Emmons, David. 1979. "Neighborhood Activists and Community Organizations." Unpublished manuscript. Evanston, Ill.: Northwestern University, Center for Urban Affairs and Policy Research.

Erbe, Brigitte M. 1975. "Race and Socioeconomic Segregation." *American Sociological Review* 40:801–12.

Fisher, Claude S. 1977. *Networks and Places: Social Relations in the Urban Setting.* New York: Free Press.

Fowler, Floyd J., and Thomas Mangione. 1982. *Neighborhood Crime, Fear, and Social Control: A Second Look at the Hartford Program.* Washington, D.C.: U.S. Department of Justice, National Institute of Justice.

Frey, William H. 1980. "Lifecourse Migration of Metropolitan Whites and Blacks and the Structure of Demographic Change in Large Central Cities." *American Sociological Review* 49:803–27.

Furstenberg, Frank F., Jr. 1971. "Public Reactions to Crime in the Streets." *American Scholar* 40:601–10.

Gans, Herbert. 1962. *The Urban Villagers.* New York: Free Press.

Garofalo, James, and Maureen McLeod. 1986. "Improving the Effectiveness and Utilization of Neighborhood Watch Programs." Unpublished report to the National Institute of Justice from the State University of New York at Albany, Hindelang Criminal Justice Research Center.

Goodstein, Lynne, and R. Lance Shotland. 1980. "The Crime Causes Crime Model: A Critical Review of the Relationships between Fear of Crime, Bystander Surveillance, and Changes in the Crime Rate." *Victimology* 5:133–51.

Greenberg, Stephanie. 1983. "External Solutions to Neighborhood-based Problems: The Case of Community Crime Prevention." Paper presented at the Annual Meeting of the Law and Society Association, Denver, June.

Greenberg, Stephanie, and William M. Rohe. 1983. "Secondary Analysis of the Relationship between Responses to Crime and Informal Social Control." Grant report from the Research Triangle Institute, Research Triangle Park, North Carolina, to the U.S. Department of Justice, National Institute of Justice, Washington, D.C.

Greenberg, Stephanie, William M. Rohe, and Jay R. Williams. 1982. *Safe and Secure Neighborhoods: Physical Characteristics and Informal Territorial Control in High and Low Crime Neighborhoods.* Washington, D.C.: U.S. Department of Justice, National Institute of Justice.

————. 1985. *Informal Citizen Action and Crime Prevention at the Neighborhood Level: Synthesis and Assessment of the Research*. Washington, D.C.: U.S. Department of Justice, National Institute of Justice.

Hackler, James C., Kwai-Yiu Ho, and Carol Urquhart-Ross. 1974. "The Willingness to Intervene: Differing Community Characteristics." *Social Problems* 21:328–44.

Henig, Jeffrey R. 1978. "Copping a Cop: Neighborhood Organizations and Police Patrol Allocation." *Journal of Voluntary Action Research* 7:75–84.

————. 1982. *Neighborhood Mobilization*. New Brunswick, N.J.: Rutgers University Press.

————. 1984. "Citizens against Crime: An Assessment of the Neighborhood Watch Program in Washington, D.C." Unpublished manuscript. Washington, D.C.: George Washington University, Center for Washington Area Studies.

Hirschman, Albert O. 1970. *Exit, Voice and Loyalty*. Cambridge, Mass.: Harvard University Press.

Hope, Tim. 1986. "Support for Neighborhood Watch: A British Crime Survey Analysis." Paper presented at the Home Office Workshop on Communities and Crime Reduction, Cambridge University, July.

Hunter, Albert. 1974. *Symbolic Communities*. Chicago: University of Chicago Press.

Jones, Bryan D. 1980. *Service Delivery in the City: Citizen Demand and Bureaucratic Rules*. New York: Longman.

Jones, E. Terrence. 1982. "The Distribution of Urban Services in a Declining City." In *The Politics of Urban Public Services*, edited by Richard C. Rich. Lexington, Mass.: Lexington Books.

Kohfeld, Carol W., Barbara Salert, and Sandra Schoenberg. 1983. "Neighborhood Associations and Urban Crime." In *Community Crime Prevention*. St. Louis: Center for Responsive Government.

Lavrakas, Paul J. 1981. "On Households." In *Reactions to Crime*, edited by Dan A. Lewis. Beverly Hills, Calif.: Sage.

————. 1985. "Citizen Self-Help and Neighborhood Crime Prevention Policy." In *American Violence and Public Policy*, edited by Lynn A. Curtis. New Haven, Conn.: Yale University Press.

Lavrakas, Paul J., and Lisa Herz. 1982. "Citizen Participation in Neighborhood Crime Prevention." *Criminology* 20:479–98.

Lavrakas, Paul J., Lisa Herz, and Greta Salem. 1981. "Community Organization, Citizen Participation, and Neighborhood Crime Prevention." Paper presented at the Annual Meeting of the American Psychological Association, Los Angeles, August.

Lewis, Dan A. 1979. "Design Problems in Public Policy Development." *Criminology* 17:172–83.

Lewis, Dan A., and Greta Salem. 1981. "Community Crime Prevention: An Analysis of a Developing Perspective." *Crime and Delinquency* 27:405–21.

————. 1986. *Fear of Crime: Incivility and the Production of a Social Problem*. New Brunswick, N.J.: Transaction.

Lewis, Dan A., Jane A. Grant, and Dennis P. Rosenbaum. 1985. *The Social*

Construction of Reform: Crime Prevention and Community Organizations. Evanston, Ill.: Northwestern University, Center for Urban Affairs and Policy Research.

Lindsay, Betsy, and Daniel McGillis. 1986. "Citywide Community Crime Prevention: An Assessment of the Seattle Program." In *Community Crime Prevention: Does It Work?* edited by Dennis P. Rosenbaum. Beverly Hills, Calif.: Sage.

Lineberry, Robert. 1977. *Equality and Urban Policy: The Distribution of Municipal Public Services.* Beverly Hills, Calif.: Sage.

Lurigio, Arthur J., and Dennis P. Rosenbaum. 1986. "Evaluation Research in Community Crime Prevention: A Critical Look at the Field." In *Community Crime Prevention: Does It Work?* edited by Dennis P. Rosenbaum. Beverly Hills, Calif.: Sage.

Maccoby, Eleanor, Joseph P. Johnson, and Russell Church. 1958. "Community Integration and the Social Control of Juvenile Delinquency." *Journal of Social Issues* 14:38–51.

McDonald, Scott C. 1986. "Does Gentrification Affect Crime Rates?" In *Communities and Crime*, edited by Albert J. Reiss, Jr., and Michael Tonry. Vol. 8 of *Crime and Justice: A Review of Research*, edited by Michael Tonry and Norval Morris. Chicago: University of Chicago Press.

McGahey, Richard M. 1986. "Economic Conditions, Neighborhood Organization, and Urban Crime." In *Communities and Crime*, edited by Albert J. Reiss, Jr., and Michael Tonry. Vol. 8 of *Crime and Justice: A Review of Research*, edited by Michael Tonry and Norval Morris. Chicago: University of Chicago Press.

McPherson, Marlys, and Glenn Silloway. 1980. *Planning Community Crime Prevention Programs.* Minneapolis: Minnesota Crime Prevention Center.

———. 1981. "Planning to Prevent Crime." In *Reactions to Crime*, edited by Dan A. Lewis. Beverly Hills, Calif.: Sage.

Mladenka, Kenneth, and Kim Quaile Hill. 1978. "The Distribution of Urban Police Services." *Journal of Politics* 40:112–33.

Mollenkopf, John H. 1983. *The Contested City.* Princeton, N.J.: Princeton University Press.

O'Keefe, Garrett J., and Harold Mendelsohn. 1984. *"Taking a Bite out of Crime": The Impact of a Mass Media Crime Prevention Campaign.* Washington, D.C.: U.S. Department of Justice, National Institute of Justice.

Orbell, John M., and Toru Uno. 1972. "A Theory of Neighborhood Problem Solving." *American Political Science Review* 66:471–89.

Pate, Antony, Marlys McPherson, and Glenn Silloway. 1987. *The Minneapolis Community Crime Prevention Experiment: Draft Evaluation Report.* Washington, D.C.: Police Foundation.

Pate, Antony, Mary Ann Wycoff, Wesley G. Skogan, and Lawrence Sherman. 1986. *Reducing Fear of Crime in Houston and Newark.* Washington, D.C.: Police Foundation.

Pennell, Francine E. 1978. "Collective versus Private Strategies for Coping with Crime." *Journal of Voluntary Action Research* 7:59–74.

Perkins, Douglas D., Richard C. Rich, David M. Chavis, Abraham Wandersman, and Paul Florin. 1986. "The Limited Role of Community Organization in Crime Prevention and the Promising Role of Crime Prevention in Community Organization." Paper presented at the Annual Meeting of the American Society of Criminology, Atlanta, November.

Podolefsky, Aaron M. 1983. *Case Studies in Community Crime Prevention.* Springfield, Ill.: Thomas.

———. 1985. "Rejecting Crime Prevention Programs: The Dynamics of Program Implementation in High Need Communities." *Human Organization* 44:33–40.

Podolefsky, Aaron, and Fred DuBow. 1981. *Strategies for Community Crime Prevention.* Springfield, Ill.: Thomas.

Rich, Richard. 1980. "A Political Economy Approach to the Study of Neighborhood Organizations." *American Journal of Political Science* 24:559–92.

Rosenbaum, Dennis P. 1987. "The Theory and Research behind Neighborhood Watch: Is It a Sound Fear and Crime Reduction Strategy?" *Crime and Delinquency* 33:103–34.

Rosenbaum, Dennis P., Dan A. Lewis, and Jane Grant. 1985. *The Impact of Community Crime Prevention Programs in Chicago: Can Neighborhood Organizations Make a Difference?* Evanston, Ill.: Northwestern University, Center for Urban Affairs and Policy Research.

Salisbury, Robert H. 1970. *Interest Group Politics in America.* New York: Harper & Row.

Schneider, Anne L., and Peter Schneider. 1977. *Private and Public-minded Citizen Responses to a Neighborhood-based Crime Prevention Strategy.* Eugene, Oreg.: Institute of Policy Analysis.

Shotland, R. Lance, and Lynne I. Goodstein. 1984. "The Role of Bystanders in Crime Control." *Journal of Social Issues* 40:9–26.

Silloway, Glenn, and Marlys McPherson. 1985. "The Limits to Citizen Participation in a Government-sponsored Community Crime Prevention Program." Paper presented at the Annual Meeting of the American Society of Criminology, San Diego, November.

Skogan, Wesley G. 1981. "On Attitudes and Behaviors." In *Reactions to Crime,* edited by Dan A. Lewis. Beverly Hills, Calif.: Sage.

———. 1986. "Fear of Crime and Neighborhood Change." In *Communities and Crime,* edited by Albert J. Reiss, Jr., and Michael Tonry. Vol. 8 of *Crime and Justice: A Review of Research,* edited by Michael Tonry and Norval Morris. Chicago: University of Chicago Press.

———. 1987. "Disorder and Community Decline." Grant report from the Center for Urban Affairs and Policy Research, Northwestern University, Evanston, Illinois, to the National Institute of Justice, Washington, D.C.

Skogan, Wesley G., and Michael G. Maxfield. 1981. *Coping with Crime: Individual and Neighborhood Reactions.* Beverly Hills, Calif.: Sage.

Skolnick, Jerome H., and David H. Bayley. In this volume. "Theme and Variation in Community Policing."

Stinchcombe, Arthur L. 1968. *Constructing Social Theories.* New York: Harcourt, Brace & World.

Suttles, Gerald D. 1972. *The Social Construction of Communities.* Chicago: University of Chicago Press.

Taub, Richard P., George P. Surgeon, Sara Lindholm, Phyllis B. Otti, and

Amy Bridges. 1977. "Urban Voluntary Associations, Locally Based and Externally Induced." *American Journal of Sociology* 83:425–42.

Taub, Richard P., D. Garth Taylor, and Jan Dunham. 1984. *Patterns of Neighborhood Change: Race and Crime in Urban America*. Chicago: University of Chicago Press.

Taylor, Ralph B., Stephen D. Gottfredson, and Sidney Brower. 1980. "The Defensibility of Defensible Space." In *Understanding Crime*, edited by Travis Hirschi and Michael Gottfredson. Beverly Hills, Calif.: Sage.

Unger, Donald G., and Abraham Wandersman. 1983. "Neighboring and Its Role in Block Organizations: An Exploratory Report." *American Journal of Community Psychology* 11:291–300.

Verba, Sidney, and Norman H. Nie. 1972. *Participation in America*. New York: Harper & Row.

Whitaker, Carol J. 1986. "Crime Prevention Measures." Bureau of Justice Statistics Special Report. Washington, D.C.: U.S. Department of Justice.

Yin, Robert K. 1986. "Community Crime Prevention: A Synthesis of Eleven Evaluations." In *Community Crime Prevention: Does It Work?* edited by Dennis P. Rosenbaum. Beverly Hills, Calif.: Sage.

Yin, Robert K., Mary E. Vogel, Jan M. Chaiken, and Deborah R. Both. 1976. *Patrolling the Neighborhood Beat: Residents and Residential Security*. Santa Monica, Calif.: Rand.

Ronald V. Clarke and Pat Mayhew

The British Gas Suicide Story and Its Criminological Implications

ABSTRACT

Between 1963 and 1975 the annual number of suicides in England and Wales showed a sudden, unexpected decline from 5,714 to 3,693 at a time when suicide continued to increase in most other European countries. This appears to be the result of the progressive removal of carbon monoxide from the public gas supply. Accounting for more than 40 percent of suicides in 1963, suicide by domestic gas was all but eliminated by 1975. Few of those prevented from using gas appear to have found some other way of killing themselves. These findings suggest that suicide is an intentional act designed to bring an end to deep, though sometimes transient, despair, chosen when moral restraints against the behavior are weakened and when the person has ready access to a means of death that is neither too difficult nor repugnant. This view of suicide has implications for its prevention and, by analogy, for the prevention of crime. That blocking opportunities, even for deeply motivated acts, does not inevitably result in displacement has not been so clearly shown before, and the demonstration considerably strengthens the case for opportunity-reducing or "situational" means of crime control.

A few years ago, a proposal to erect an antisuicide barrier on San Francisco's Golden Gate Bridge is said to have been defeated through the combined opposition of environmentalists and psychiatrists. The

Ronald V. Clarke is dean of the School of Criminal Justice, Rutgers University. Pat Mayhew is principal research officer at the Home Office Research and Planning Unit, London; during the time that this essay was written, she was a Visiting Fellow at the National Institute of Justice, Washington, D.C. Thanks are due to British Gas for their estimates of carbon monoxide concentrations in the public gas supply of England and Wales.

former objected to the barrier's unsightliness; the latter said that potential suicides would find other ways to kill themselves, with no net saving in lives. Whatever the merits of the environmental position, the recent 35 percent drop in Britain's national rate of suicide suggests that the psychiatric objections were misplaced. It is now clear that this remarkable decline in suicide was brought about by removal of carbon monoxide from the domestic gas supply during the period. This was a by-product of the search for cheaper forms of gas and resulted from two separate developments: first, the adoption of new manufacturing processes for so-called town gas and, later, the wholesale replacement (between 1968 and 1977) of town gas by natural gas from the North Sea. Natural gas is free of carbon monoxide, and some of the new town gases contained as little as 2–7 percent carbon monoxide, whereas older town gas contained around 8–16 percent carbon monoxide. This means that, after being at highly lethal levels until the beginning of the 1960s, carbon monoxide was almost eliminated from the domestic gas supply by 1975. The decline in toxicity was accompanied by a fall in the number of gas suicides. Although these accounted for almost half of all suicide deaths in England and Wales in 1960, gas suicides had virtually disappeared by 1975. Faced with fewer opportunities to use gas, few potential gas suicides found some other way of killing themselves.

These facts have important implications for the prevention of suicide and, as long as the analogy with crime holds, also for the prevention of crime. If opportunity determines not merely the time, place, and method but the very occurrence of a behavior that is usually seen to be the outcome of strong internal motives, the same is likely to be true of crime, most of which seems less deeply motivated. That few people found other ways of killing themselves is especially instructive in that similar evidence of lack of displacement is difficult to obtain in the criminological field. The gas suicide story therefore considerably strengthens the case for opportunity-reducing, or "situational" (Clarke 1983), measures of crime prevention. Moreover, it suggests that the common assumption that criminality has drive-like properties may be false, supporting the need for theory that takes due account of both the objective and the subjective components of opportunity. This need may be filled by the recently developed decision-making or rational choice theories of crime (for reviews, see Clarke and Cornish [1985], and Cornish and Clarke [1986]).

Section I briefly introduces the situational approach to understanding crime and designing preventive measures and discusses the empirical and theoretical importance of displacement. Section II tells the British gas suicide story. It presents the statistics for gas and other suicides for the relevant period in relation to the reduced levels of carbon monoxide in the gas supply and discusses alternative explanations for the decline in suicide and seeming inconsistencies in the evidence. Section III considers the apparent reluctance of many who study suicide to accept the gas detoxification hypothesis and develops the argument for a revised theory of suicide similar to rational choice theories of crime. Section III concludes with an examination of the scope for preventing suicide through physical reduction of opportunities. Section IV considers the criminological implications of the gas suicide story, in particular, those for situational prevention. Improved understanding of the limits of crime displacement should allow research to address some other impediments to the development of situational measures; these include practical and ideological objections as well as a lack of understanding concerning the relation between the criminal opportunity structure and offender decision making.

I. Situational Crime Prevention and the Displacement Hypothesis

Situational crime prevention consists of measures that are directed at highly specific forms of crime, that involve the management, design, or manipulation of the immediate environment in as systematic and permanent a way as possible, and that therefore reduce the opportunities for crime and increase its risks as they are perceived by a wide range of offenders (Clarke 1983). These measures include various forms of target hardening to make the objects of crime less vulnerable (e.g., vehicle steering column locks, passenger and baggage screening at airports, check guarantee cards, and entry phone systems for apartment blocks), defensible space architecture (which encourages residents in housing projects to exercise territorial surveillance of the public space outside their dwellings), community crime prevention initiatives (e.g., neighborhood watch and citizen patrol schemes), and a number of less easily categorized measures such as improved coordination of public transportation with pub closing times or more sensitive public housing allocation policies that avoid the concentration of children in particular housing developments. The conceptual underpinning for situational prevention is provided both by criminal opportunity theory (Cook 1986), which draws attention to the role of the nature and distribution of criminal opportunities in the genesis of crime, and by choice or decision models of crime, which seek to explain how the offender perceives, evaluates, and acts on the opportunities that exist (Clarke and Cornish 1985). The situational approach to prevention can be contrasted with "social prevention" that seeks—though with little demonstrated effect (Morris and Hawkins 1970; Wilson 1975)—to ameliorate the social, psychological, economic, and educational deficiencies that are thought to give rise to criminal dispositions.

Despite the successes in practice of situational crime prevention (e.g., Clarke 1983; Heal and Laycock 1986), it has proved vulnerable to theoretical criticism, particularly concerning the presumed inevitability of displacement: in response to blocked opportunities or increased risks with respect to a particular offense, it has been thought that an offender would simply commit it elsewhere, choose a different time, target, or victim, change his modus operandi, or turn to some completely different form of crime (e.g., Reppetto 1976; Gabor 1978). The concept of displacement is consistent not just with the view of offenders as generalists rather than specialists but also with the prevailing "hydraulic" (Gabor 1981) or "dispositional" (Clarke 1980) view of criminal motivation, whereby the offender is regarded as being driven to commit crime as a result of his biological inheritance, maladaptive personality, unfortunate upbringing, or unfavorable social environment. This view of crime has its conceptual roots in drive theories of motivation, such as those of Dollard et al. (1944), Freud (1955), and Lorenz (1966), which depict behavior as being largely governed by the necessity of reducing tensions created by the organism's internal needs. Parallel mechanisms are seen to undermine preventive or treatment efforts in some other fields: in psychiatry, the concept of "symptom substitution," which refers to the appearance of fresh symptoms of a neurotic disorder following on the eradication of earlier ones; in accident prevention, the concept of "risk homeostasis" or "danger compensation," under which, for example, the development of safer cars is said to lead to more reckless driving (Orr 1984; Adams 1985); and in the addictions field, the concept of "escalation," which refers to the supposed need of addicts to move on to more powerful drugs when those they are using no longer satisfy their cravings.

Displacement has often been demonstrated—for example, the introduction of steering column locks for new cars displaced theft to older, unprotected vehicles in Great Britain (Mayhew et al. 1976), while a police "crackdown" on subway robberies in New York City displaced robberies to the street (Chaiken, Lawless, and Stevenson

1974). But there are also many well-known examples of reductions in specific forms of crime apparently having been achieved through situational measures. For example, the fitting of steering column locks to all cars in West Germany in 1963 brought about a 60 percent reduction in car thefts (e.g., Mayhew et al. 1976), and a variety of security measures dramatically reduced airliner hijackings in the early 1970s (Wilkinson 1977). Unfortunately, in these and similar cases it is difficult to be sure that there was no displacement of offending to some other kind of crime because the reductions achieved were small and easily concealed within overall, and generally rising, crime statistics. It is the unambiguous nature of the evidence concerning the lack of displacement to other means of death following detoxification (and the fact that thousands of lives were thereby saved) that makes the gas suicide story so potentially important in evaluating the scope of situational preventive measures.

II. Domestic Gas and Suicide in England and Wales, 1968–83

The data presented below are limited to England and Wales. While gas detoxification also had its effect in Scotland, procedures for determining suicide are different there, the statistics are kept separately and not in quite the same form, and the changes in the gas supply took place at different rates and at slightly different times (Kreitman 1976; Clarke and Mayhew 1987).

A. General Features of Suicide in England and Wales

International comparisons are beset with difficulties, but the suicide rates of England and Wales have always appeared low compared with those of many other similar countries such as France, Germany, Austria, Switzerland, and Scandinavia (Stengel 1964). As in most countries, suicide in England and Wales is powerfully related to sex and age: there are three male for every two female deaths and about twice as many deaths of those aged 55–64 as of those aged 25–34 (Adelstein and Mardon 1975).

Until detoxification of gas at the beginning of the 1960s, the suicide rate for men had been relatively steady during this century, though with a peak in the depression years and troughs during the two world wars. These war-related declines are comparable in magnitude to the declines following detoxification of gas, though they may be recording artifacts (Farmer 1980). For women, the picture is one of a fairly steady increase in suicide during the period with less change in the Depression

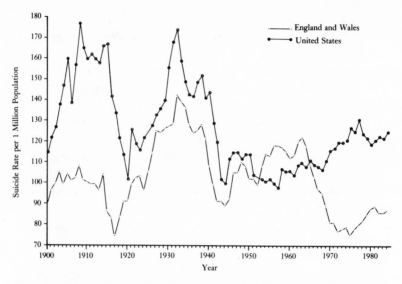

FIG. 1.—Crude suicide rates (per 1 million population) for England and Wales and the United States, 1900–84. Sources: Registrar General (1900–40); U.S. Department of Commerce (1901–85); Office of Population Censuses and Surveys (1985).

and war years. Figure 1 shows crude suicide rates (i.e., uncorrected for changes in population structure) during the twentieth century for England and Wales and, for purposes of comparison, for the United States.

From 1963, as will be shown in more detail below, rates of suicide for both men and women in England and Wales declined markedly until the mid-1970s. Only Scotland and Greece among eighteen European countries studied by Sainsbury, Jenkins, and Levey (1980) showed similar, though less pronounced, declines. Since the mid-1970s, female suicides in England and Wales have declined further, whereas those for males have risen, though not yet to the levels of the early 1960s (for commentary on long-term trends in suicide in Britain, see, e.g., Adelstein and Mardon [1975], Farmer [1979], and Low et al. [1981]).

Detoxification of gas has changed the distribution of different methods of suicide considerably, as figure 2 shows. For example, in 1960, suicides by domestic gas accounted for, respectively, just under and just over half of all male and female suicides; but by 1980, only 0.2 percent of all suicides were committed by this method. The most frequently used method of suicide in 1980 for men was hanging (including strangulation and suffocation), which accounted for nearly a third of deaths; hanging was followed by poisoning with solid and liquid sub-

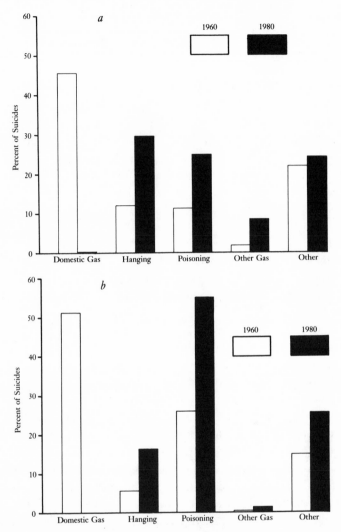

FIG. 2.—*a*, Changes in methods of suicide for males in England and Wales, 1960–80. *b*, Changes in methods of suicide for females in England and Wales, 1960–80. Source: Bulusu and Alderson (1984).

stances, which accounted for nearly one-quarter of deaths (fig. 2*a*). Poisoning by gases other than ones in domestic use (mostly car exhaust fumes) accounted for roughly a further 17 percent of the total male suicides. There was little change during the period, however, in the proportion of suicides using a variety of other methods such as cutting, shooting, drowning, and jumping.

The picture for female suicides in 1980 was quite different (fig. 2b). Women rarely used car exhaust gases (less than 3 percent of female suicides were by this method), while they used hanging and suffocation only about half as often as men. The commonest method of suicide for women in 1980 (54.3 percent of deaths) was poisoning by solid or liquid substances, most of which were painkillers, barbiturates, tranquilizers, and antidepressants (Bulusu and Alderson 1984).

In contrast to the situation in the United States, where gun suicides account for about 55 percent of the total (Lester 1984), firearms are much more rarely used in England and Wales (about 8.1 percent of male suicides and 0.4 percent of female suicides [Bulusu and Alderson 1984]).

B. Detoxification of Domestic Gas

Following nationalization of the British gas industry in 1949, an extensive program of modernization was begun: more than 600 of the old and inefficient local gas works were closed, and many of the larger works were extended and linked together by a new system of mains (Williams 1981). A program of research was also initiated to find more economical ways of manufacturing gas, which, at that time, was derived mainly from high-quality and increasingly scarce coal. These coal-based gases contained high concentrations of carbon monoxide (CO), and it was the search for economy that resulted in detoxification, the first stage of which began in the early 1950s. At that time, less toxic gases that were the fruits of the new production processes utilizing oil and petroleum as well as cheaper coals began to be mixed with the existing gas. The average CO content of the public gas supply in Great Britain gradually declined, with minor fluctuations, from a high of about 13 percent in the late 1950s to about 7 percent in 1968 (Kreitman 1976), the year the second major change began to take effect. This was the replacement of manufactured "town" gas by the then recently discovered natural gas from the North Sea. Natural gas consists largely of methane and is nonpoisonous. Because its combustion properties are different from those of manufactured gas, the two cannot be mixed, and natural gas had to be introduced area by area, as consumers' appliances were converted to burn natural gas. This massive conversion program, involving some 13.5 million consumers and 35 million appliances, took nine years and was completed in September 1977 (Elliott 1980).

While these changes were not motivated by the need to improve

safety, the side benefits of reduced toxicity were not wholly unantici-
pated. For example, an official government report (Morton 1970) on the
increased risks of undetected leaks and explosions associated with the
use of natural gas did comment favorably on the greatly reduced likelihood of "accidental" poisonings, though suicide was not mentioned.
The greater concern with accidents rather than suicides is ironic since
the latter outnumbered the former by more than three to one (in 1960,
e.g., there were 2,499 suicides and 744 accidental deaths due to domestic gas poisoning [Registrar General 1971]). Moreover, a proportion of
accidents were probably suicides, and some explosions were undoubtedly the result of suicide attempts. Indeed, one evening in 1970, one of
us was disturbed from his criminological studies (or perhaps it was
from changing his son's diaper) by an explosion that destroyed the roof
of a nearby apartment building: this turned out to be the result of
escaped gas resulting from a suicide attempt. The gas industry's inattention to the relation between toxicity and suicide seems to reflect a
general presumption: people who want to kill themselves will find a
way. Therefore, the authorities could hardly be held responsible for
people's intentional deaths in the way that they might for some accidents. As is suggested below, the presumption is ill founded, though
the gas authorities can hardly be criticized for being no wiser than
anybody else at the time, including most experts on suicide.

C. Detoxification and the Decline in Suicide: Statistics

Table 1 shows the numbers of suicides by gas and by other methods
in England and Wales for 1958–77, and figure 3 illustrates the relation
between numbers of gas suicides and the annual average proportion of
CO in the gas supply for England and Wales between 1960 and 1977
(figures for CO concentrations in 1958 and 1959 are available only for
Great Britain as a whole [e.g., Kreitman 1976]). The decline in gas
suicides closely matches reduced levels of toxicity. These suicides,
which numbered 2,499 in 1960, when CO concentrations were above
11 percent, declined to a mere twenty-three in 1975, when average CO
concentrations were less than 1 percent. Although CO concentrations
began to be reduced at the end of the 1950s (the peak year for gas
suicides was 1958), overall rates of suicide did not begin to decline until
1963 because the reduction in gas suicides before then was masked by a
general rise in other suicides.

The fit between toxicity and suicide could hardly have been any
closer. First, the measure of toxicity used is a relatively crude index

TABLE 1

Suicides by Domestic Gas, England and Wales, 1958–77

Year	Total Suicides	Suicides by Domestic Gas	Percent of Total
1958	5,298	2,637	49.8
1959	5,207	2,594	49.8
1960	5,112	2,499	48.9
1961	5,200	2,379	45.8
1962	5,588	2,469	44.2
1963	5,714	2,368	41.4
1964	5,566	2,088	37.5
1965	5,161	1,702	33.0
1966	4,994	1,593	31.9
1967	4,711	1,336	28.4
1968	4,584	988	21.6
1969	4,326	790	18.3
1970	3,940	511	13.0
1971	3,945	346	8.8
1972	3,770	197	5.2
1973	3,823	143	3.7
1974	3,899	50	1.3
1975	3,693	23	.6
1976	3,816	14	.4
1977	3,944	8	.2

SOURCE.—Office of Population Censuses and Surveys (1959–78).

because there were small daily, and larger regional, fluctuations in the actual toxicity of gas delivered to homes, depending on the contribution to the public supply of gas from different producing centers. Second, the measure of average CO concentration means somewhat different things before and after 1968, when conversion to natural gas began. Before 1968, the measure reflects the average toxicity of the gas in all homes. After 1968, an increasing proportion of homes—those that had been converted—had no CO in their gas supply; levels of CO in unconverted homes would therefore have been higher than is suggested by the graph. Third, certainty of death depends not just on the toxicity of the gas delivered but also on the rate at which it is absorbed into the bloodstream (e.g., Drinker 1938); this, in turn, depends on a range of other factors, including the size of the room, efforts to exclude fresh air, the amount of gas being released, and, possibly, the kind of appliance used (suicide may be easier with gas fires and ovens). Since the number of these appliances decreased during the period in question because of the widespread adoption of central heating and a general shift from gas

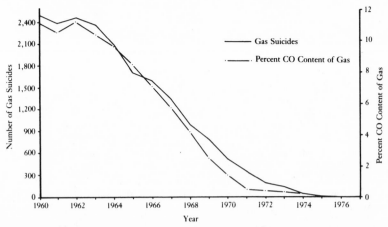

FIG. 3.—Relation between gas suicides in England and Wales and CO content of domestic gas, 1960–77. Sources: Registrar General (1959–73); Office of Population Censuses and Surveys (1974–85); unpublished estimates of CO content by British Gas.

to electric cooking, this, too, might have led to fewer suicide deaths in later years (Clarke and Mayhew 1987).

While there can be no doubt that detoxification of the gas supply caused the decline in gas suicides, the more important and interesting question concerns the effect of detoxification on the suicide rate as a whole. This question is pursued below. Because of the powerful relation with age and sex, data relating to suicide are presented in figure 4 for three age groups (twenty-four and younger, twenty-five to forty-four, and forty-five or older), and separately for men and women. In every case, rates are expressed per 1 million population in the various age groups. The top line for each age/sex group represents suicides by all methods, domestic gas included; the bottom line represents domestic gas suicides; and the middle line shows suicides by all other methods.

A number of conclusions can be drawn from inspection of these graphs.

1. The overall decline in male suicides between the early 1960s and the early 1970s is accounted for largely by the halving of suicides by the oldest age group—brought about by the elimination of gas suicides. There is no evidence that other suicides increased for this age group as gas suicides declined (fig. 4e).

2. The decline in gas suicides for the two younger groups of males during the same ten years is matched by increases in other kinds of suicide (fig. 4a, c). However, these other suicides had been increasing

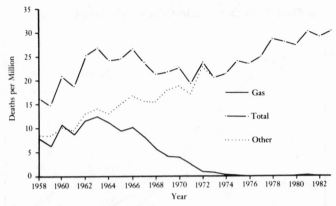

FIG. 4a.—Suicides in England and Wales by domestic gas and other methods for males under twenty-five years old. Sources for fig. 4, *a–f*: Registrar General (1959–73); Office of Population Censuses and Surveys (1974–85).

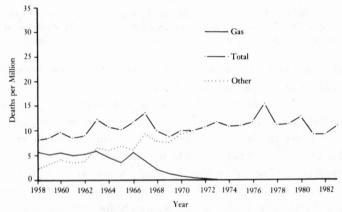

Fig. 4b.—Suicides in England and Wales by domestic gas and other methods for females under twenty-five years old.

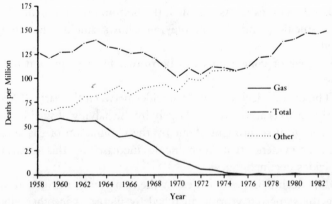

FIG. 4c.—Suicides in England and Wales by domestic gas and other methods for males twenty-five to forty-four years old.

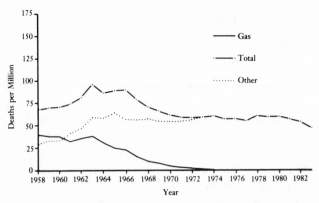

FIG. 4d.—Suicides in England and Wales by domestic gas and other methods for females twenty-five to forty-four years old.

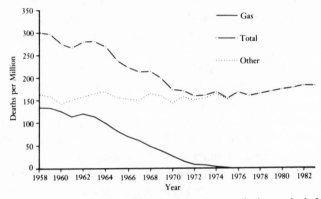

FIG. 4e.—Suicides in England and Wales by domestic gas and other methods for males forty-five years old or older.

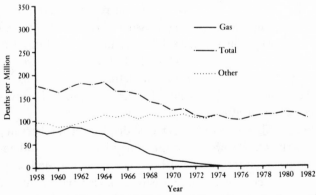

FIG. 4f.—Suicides in England and Wales by domestic gas and other methods for females forty-five years old or older.

before detoxification, which means that displacement from gas to other methods cannot wholly account for the observed pattern.

3. After 1975, when detoxification was all but complete, suicide rates for all three age groups of men show distinct rises (fig. 4a, c, e).

4. For women, the decline in gas suicides is not matched by increases in other kinds of suicide for the two older age groups, though this is the case for those under twenty-four years of age (fig. 4b, d, f).

5. Unlike the case for men, rates of suicide for women have shown very little increase since 1975.

While these facts indicate that, following detoxification, there was little displacement to other methods of suicide, especially by women and older men, and that thousands of lives were saved (6,700, according to the calculations made by Wells [1981]), some qualifications to both conclusions should be noted. Concerning displacement, one possibility is that some undetected displacement occurred in the form of *unsuccessful* attempts using less lethal methods such as drug overdoses. This would be difficult to test because records of attempted suicide are incomplete and also because attempts appear to outnumber completed suicides so greatly (by an estimated twenty to one [Wells 1981]), that, if all the latter were to be snatched from the jaws of death, the resulting increase in recorded attempts would be so small as to be barely detectable (Kreitman 1976). Moreover, it is widely believed that most attempts constitute a distinct behavioral syndrome—"parasuicide" (Kreitman et al. 1969)—motivated less by a wish to die than by an attempt to obtain help with personal problems. The increases in "attempts" that appear to have taken place in recent decades, especially among young people and women (Weissman 1974), cannot therefore be taken as evidence of displacement from gas unless—and this is a tragic possibility—some of those who died from gas were actually "parasuicides" who failed to realize its lethal nature. If this is so, as seems likely, detoxification achieved some of its effect by preventing such "accidental" deaths.

Another possible source of undetected displacement relates in particular to elderly suicides. Some of these may have poisoned themselves (e.g., with barbiturates) when gas became unavailable, and, as poisonings among the elderly are more easily confused with natural deaths than are gassings (Patel 1973), this may have artificially depressed the suicide statistics. However, concealment of such "displaced" poisonings will not have been complete, and it might be expected that, if the one method were readily substituted for the other, there would be an inverse relation between the number of older suicides using gas and those using poisons. This possibility has been checked by Richard Farmer (personal communication, 1986) using data reported in Low et al. (1981), but he found no significant relation.

On the savings in life, there is the possibility that some of the apparent gain might have been eliminated through "delayed" displacement, the suicide some years later of people prevented earlier from using gas. A disproportionate increase in suicides of older people throughout the 1980s would be consistent with, though not necessarily proof of, this. It is too early yet to observe any full effect of delayed displacement, though to date the greatest increases have been among younger rather than older age groups. Furthermore, it cannot be assumed that the savings of life achieved through detoxification will continue; the suicidal population may identify new ways of killing themselves that share some of the advantages of gas. Indeed, there may already be some evidence of this in the increasing use of car exhaust fumes in England and Wales; for example, there were almost three times as many male suicides by this method in 1980 as in 1970 (Bulusu and Alderson 1984).

D. Alternative Explanations for the Decline in Suicide

Detoxification was identified as the likely cause of the reduced suicide rate in Birmingham as long ago as 1972 (Hassall and Trethowan 1972). This was soon followed by the suggestion that reduced toxicity levels might account for the national decline in suicides (Malleson 1973) and a little later by two detailed studies (Adelstein and Mardon 1975; Kreitman 1976) that reached that conclusion. Similar declines in overall levels of suicide had also been observed following detoxification of gas in Vienna (Farberow and Simon 1969) and Brisbane (Whitlock 1975).

Nevertheless, not all students of suicide have accepted the detoxification hypothesis; many who have not are apparently influenced by Stengel (1964), who observed, though without presenting data, that the transient decline in suicides following detoxification of gas in Basel was soon followed by a compensatory increase in drownings. That such displacement has been seen as inevitable has meant that explanations other than detoxification have been sought for the decline in the British suicide rate.

The first such explanation was that the decline in suicides may have been due to a revision of the International Classification of Diseases (ICD) under which suicides are recorded (World Health Organization 1967). This revision introduced a new category in 1968 of "undetermined" cause of death, which could accommodate some of the marginal cases previously allocated to suicide. However, Kreitman (1976), Sainsbury (1983), and Bulusu and Alderson (1984) have concluded that, while a significant number of cases that previously would have been recorded as accidental poisonings began to be placed in the new "undetermined" category, the ICD revision seems to have had little effect on the recording of suicide. For example, Kreitman found that the decrement in suicides between 1967 and 1968 was no greater than that between other adjacent years in the period 1960–71 for all but two of fourteen sex-age subgroups. This result was repeated when CO suicides were examined alone.

A second hypothesis was that improvements in resuscitation and in treatment of poisoning, together with the establishment of more efficient ambulance services after World War II, should have resulted in the lives of some potential suicides being saved. While not an implausible idea, no supporting controlled study could be found by Brown (1979). Moreover, these improvements would be more likely to have achieved a reduction in suicides using less lethal methods (such as overdosing) than in those using gas, most of whom are discovered already dead.

Brown (1979) also investigated a third idea, that the improved treatment of suicidal patients—for example, through the wider use of antidepressants both in general practice and in the aftercare of mental hospital patients—may have brought about the drop in completed suicides (see also Barraclough 1972). Again, he was unable to find any supporting evidence, while Fox (1975) has pointed out that an unintended consequence of the wider prescribing of antidepressants would be to supply more people with the means of killing themselves.

A fourth explanation was that the declining suicide rates reflected the rapid development of the Samaritans, an organization that provides a lay crisis intervention service for depressed and suicidal people. Bagley (1968) compared changes in suicide rates in fifteen towns or cities that had Samaritans branches with those in two sets of fifteen control towns without such a service. He found that the Samaritans towns experienced a fall in their average suicide rates, while the other towns showed rises. As Brown (1979) points out, this study might show only that some third factor, such as social cohesiveness, could in the same town both increase the likelihood of the formation of a Samaritans branch and reduce the incidence of suicide. Nonetheless, Bagley's study was eagerly seized on by the Samaritans and their supporters (e.g., Fox

1975) and was called into serious question only nine years later by a replication study published by Barraclough, Jennings, and Moss (1977). Using a much larger sample of both Samaritans towns and controls and three different methods of matching, the new study could find no evidence of any preventive effect. Another major difficulty for the Samaritans hypothesis is that the decline in the suicide trend began to level off in 1971 while the numbers of Samaritans branches and their clients continued to increase until at least 1975 (Brown 1979).

A fifth hypothesis, that the suicide decline was due to improved social and economic conditions in Britain (Sainsbury, Jenkins, and Levey 1980), might appear somewhat perverse in that the Britain of the late 1960s and early 1970s is commonly thought to have been marked by "industrial unrest, rising unemployment and a constant state of economic crisis" (Fox 1975, p. 9). Indeed, it is clear that the 35 percent drop in the suicide rate between 1963 and 1975 occurred despite a 50 percent increase in the unemployment rate during the same period (Boor 1980; Kreitman and Platt 1984). Moreover, one other important social indicator, the rate of recorded crime, suggested a markedly deteriorating situation with a 60 percent increase between 1965 and 1974. The starting point of Sainsbury's study, however, was the observation that only Greece among eighteen other European countries had experienced a similar decline in suicide. Using a discriminant function analysis, it was shown that changes in the suicide rates in European countries between the periods 1961–63 and 1972–74 were correlated with socioeconomic changes as measured by such variables as the proportion of young people and working women in the population, the ownership of television receivers, rates of unemployment, divorce, and illegitimacy. Leaving aside whether suicide figures can be reliably used for international comparisons (in relation to Sainsbury's research, see Farmer and Rohde [1980]), the study is open to numerous technical criticisms. These concern the selection of socioeconomic variables and the rationale of their relation to suicide, the questionable division of countries into those with "high increases" in suicide and others with "low increases or decreases" for purposes of the discriminant function analysis, and the use of this analysis with fifteen variables but only eighteen cases. At best, the study demonstrates that socioeconomic change may be responsible for some changes in suicide rates. However, it does not provide an alternative explanation for the decline in the British suicide rate during the period in question: on the basis of the analysis presented, the suicide rate of England and Wales should have increased more than that of seven other countries, whereas in reality it showed the greatest decrease of all.

Besides these alternative explanations for the decline in suicide, some evidence apparently inconsistent with the gas detoxification hypothesis has also been produced. In particular, detoxification of the gas supply in Holland in the early 1960s seems to have had much less of an effect on the overall rate of suicide (World Health Organization 1982). Thus, in 1959, there were 807 suicides in Holland, of which 202 were attributed to domestic gas. Ten years later, in 1968, there was little change in the overall number of suicides—809 (because of population increases, this number represents a small decline of 0.8 per 100,000 in the rate of suicide). This was so even though domestic gas suicides, of which there were twelve, had been almost eliminated by 1968 (Centraal Bureau voor de Statistiek 1959–68). However, suicide by domestic gas never accounted for more than 25 percent of suicides in Holland, whereas in Britain the figure was closer to 50 percent. This may be due partly to the fact that fewer households in Holland than in England (in 1960, 60 and 80 percent, respectively) received a toxic gas supply (Clarke and Mayhew 1987). If gas suicides were less common in Holland, it may not be surprising that detoxification had a smaller effect on the overall rate of suicide.

Some other apparently inconsistent evidence relates to the claim that towns in England and Wales and provinces in Holland whose gas supplies were not detoxified until relatively late showed the same patterns of suicide as those whose supplies were detoxified earlier (Sainsbury 1986). Because of inadequate data, the claim cannot be evaluated with respect to Holland. As far as the British comparison is concerned, however, the claim does not appear to be well supported by the data. Only twelve towns (all of which had roughly the same levels of CO in their gas supplies in 1958, but five of which had lower levels by 1967) were included in the study, and between them these accounted for only a small number of suicides (135 in 1958 and 142 in 1967). Moreover, the study relates to a period before the conversion to natural gas, and the "detoxified" towns still had a small percentage (about 5 percent) of CO in their (manufactured) gas supplies. This level of CO is sufficient to kill, even though death may take longer; unfortunately, no data are presented about the number of suicides due to domestic gas in either group of towns.

To sum up so far, it is clear that substantial reductions in the CO content of the public gas supply in Britain led to the virtual disappearance of suicide by domestic gas. Because few people stopped from using gas found another way of killing themselves, a substantial decline in the overall number of suicides resulted. Since the mid-1970s, suicides have gradually increased and, for men, have now surpassed the levels that held prior to detoxification of the gas supply. In light of the evidence concerning a general rise in suicidal behavior, and also because of the increased use of some more novel means of suicide (such as car exhaust gases), it is not unreasonable to think that these increases might have occurred even without detoxification.

III. Implications for the Understanding and Prevention of Suicide

That the availability of a method can so significantly affect the incidence of suicide has important implications for both theory and prevention. Other evidence about the relation between suicide and the availability of different lethal methods is also reviewed in this section.

A. Why So Little Displacement to Other Lethal Methods?

Many, if not most, students of suicide found it difficult to accept that a reduction in opportunity could have such an important effect on the incidence of suicide—hence the strenuous search for what seem to have been unlikely alternative explanations, the sometimes acerbic correspondence on the issue (e.g., the exasperated tone of Malleson's [1973] letters to the *British Journal of Psychiatry*), and the guarded terms in which those (such as Adelstein and Mardon [1975], Farmer [1980], and Bulusu and Alderson [1984]) who otherwise seem persuaded by the evidence have drawn conclusions about the role of gas detoxification. It is not difficult to see, however, why the idea that the availability of a method could be an important determining factor in suicide has been so strongly resisted. It appears to demean the personal suffering that fuels most suicidal behavior and to call into question the role of the helping professions in effective prevention. It also fits uncomfortably with prevailing theories about the causes of suicide, which attach little importance to the availability of different methods.

These theories can be divided into two main groups, with a third overlapping category. First, sociological theories deriving from Durkheim (1957) locate the causes of suicide in social disorganization or disintegration. Studies in this tradition have demonstrated numerous correlations between social and economic indicators and regional and national variations in suicide. Second, psychological theories deriving from the early ideas of the psychoanalytic school see suicide as the outcome of personal disturbance, often associated with clinical depression. Related research has found suicides to be suffering from disturbed relations, ill health, financial or employment difficulties, bereavements or disappointments in love, or alcoholism and drug addiction. The third overlapping category, originating in Halbwachs's (1978) reinterpretation of Durkheim, stresses suicide's intentionality whether as the outcome of social or psychological pressures or of a rational assessment of the worth of current or future life (e.g., Brandt 1975).

Sociologists have often discussed variations in methods of death in relation to national and regional culture, and psychologists have routinely catalogued preferred methods by age, sex, and a variety of personal variables. Neither group, though—not even those who emphasize the rationality of suicide—seem prepared to regard availability of a method as a causal factor in itself. Rather, the assumption is that, once someone has reached the point of committing the act, how it is done is of limited importance: after all, there are surely just as many ways of killing oneself as of killing a cat.

To expose the questionable nature of this assumption requires some speculation about perceptions of gas as a method of death and how these might have changed with lessened toxicity. Much depends on how well informed people were in the first place about the highly lethal nature of gas. (As death could result in less than half an hour, gas would have been an unsuitable method for those primarily seeking attention— though some may not have known this.) Whatever the initial level of knowledge, few people would have known that gas was becoming less poisonous in the years before conversion, and many may not have known, at least initially, that natural gas was nontoxic—this was certainly not one of the benefits trumpeted by the media following the North Sea discoveries. This means, as Brown (1979, p. 1122) has commented, that many suicidal people must have continued through ignorance to do the traditional thing and "put their heads in the gas oven." Just how many is unknown because most would have suffered little worse than nausea or a headache (Kreitman 1976). What they did next would depend on their determination to die. Some of the less determined may have made a further unsuccessful attempt with one of the less lethal methods. Some will have decided, however, that they were "not meant to die"; others might have experienced a diminution in stress or might have obtained the help they needed.

Some of the more determined—though the statistics suggest not many—will have killed themselves in another way. It would not, however, always have been easy to identify an acceptable alternative because, prior to detoxification, gas had unique advantages as a lethal method. It was widely available (in about 80 percent of British homes) and required little preparation or specialist knowledge, making it an easy choice for less mobile people and for those coming under sudden, extreme stress. It was painless, did not result in disfigurement, and did not produce a mess (which women in particular will try to avoid [e.g., Marks 1977]). Because death was not as quick as with some other lethal methods, it had the advantage for the superstitious of allowing destiny some hand in the decision. Finally, it allowed dependents to conceal the suicide as an accident. Deaths by hanging, asphyxiation, or drowning all usually demand more planning, while more courage would be needed with the more violent methods of shooting, cutting, stabbing, crashing one's car, and jumping off high places or in front of trains or buses. These methods are also more likely to result in distress and danger to others and, in addition, could lead to physical disability were death not to result. Only CO poisoning by car exhaust gases possesses many of the same advantages as domestic gas poisoning, except that not everyone has a car, a garage, or, perhaps, the necessary knowledge.

To summarize, it would seem that there were two reasons for the drop in overall rates of suicide following detoxification of gas: some of the more determined individuals were unable to find an acceptable and equally lethal alternative, whereas some of the less determined may have been saved from making a lethal mistake. Which of these was more important is not known.

B. Suicide as a Decision

The above discussion suggests the need for a theory that takes proper account of the mental processes underlying and sustaining each act of suicide. These include the ways in which an individual predicament comes to be defined as hopeless, accompanying feelings of depression, the manner in which solutions are sought and evaluated, how suicide first comes to be entertained, and how plans are made and put into effect. The evaluation of life as no longer worth living, the decision to end it, and the choice of method may be interactive rather than sequential. For example, those for whom suicide is prohibited on religious grounds may gradually redefine their situations or find other solutions. Others may reinforce the idea with thoughts about people who have found it the only way out and may abandon the idea only when unable to find an acceptable method. Those who do succeed in identifying an acceptable method may go on to develop realistic plans, including a detailed scenario of the place and the time of death. The result of this mental preparation may be to reinforce feelings of hopelessness and the belief that there is "no other way out."

While elements of such a theory are scattered in the literature, they need pulling together under some framework such as is provided by the rational choice or decision perspective on crime (Clarke and Cornish 1985; Cornish and Clarke 1986). In this vein, suicide would be seen as an intentional act (Baechler 1975; Halbwachs 1978)—the outcome of a decision made with varying degrees of rationality and determination to end a life without hope (e.g., Farber 1968; Beck, Kovacs, and Weissman 1975). The decisions involved would need analyzing in terms not just of the sources of motivation and alternatives considered but also of the thought processes involved. Account would need to be taken of alcoholism—frequently encountered among suicides—and of depression, which, it has been suggested, leads to crude, "either/or" thinking and to pessimistic evaluations of alternative courses of action (Brandt 1975; Schneidman 1985). Extreme ambivalence and superstitious thinking associated with a "gamble with death" have also often been described. Finally, it would need to be recognized that a suicide decision may sometimes be fully rational (Battin and Mayo 1980).

Though the main focus of theoretical analysis would be the thinking and emotions underlying the suicidal decision, other important theoretical components would be the motivational and situational contexts of suicide. The former may not be especially problematic since almost any of the misfortunes and miseries of the human condition seem capable of providing the motivation. Rather, it is the method of dealing with these motivating factors that seems to be the issue. Contributing to thoughts and feelings, and ultimately to the choice of solution, will be aspects of the situation unrelated to the source of unhappiness or distress. Included among these will be features of the individual's daily life that could impede or facilitate suicide—such as the availability of an acceptable means of death.

This represents the merest sketch of a theory, but a number of features should be apparent. First, suicide is seen as the outcome of a dynamic interplay between objective motivating and facilitating conditions and the individual's thoughts and feelings. Second, it is apparent under this view that suicidal feelings could sometimes be quite transitory and may not be experienced again by a particular individual.

Third, nothing is implied about the pathology of the behavior: in many cases, the decision to commit suicide will be readily understandable, while, in others, the underlying reasoning may be greatly distorted (even leaving aside clearly psychotic suicides). Fourth, this view of suicide owes no allegiance to any single parent discipline: both psychological and sociological motivating variables have their place, while the decision perspective has antecedents in an economic analysis of suicide (Hamermesh and Soss 1974). Fifth, it provides a way of explaining some of the more puzzling features of suicide—for example, why religious beliefs sometimes protect their adherents from suicide, why newspaper accounts of suicides may stimulate imitative suicides (Phillips 1974, 1979), and why certain locations may serve as a magnet to the suicidally inclined. Finally, and most important in terms of the present discussion, it provides an understanding of the ways in which the characteristics of different methods play an important determining part in suicide and, in particular, of the reasons why wholesale displacement to other lethal methods of suicide did not take place in Britain following detoxification of gas.

C. Prevention of Suicide

The suicide literature is replete with examples of local or national variations in preferred methods of death, which are seen to reflect differences in the availability of methods or different traditions in their use. Thus, for example, the high rate of gun suicides in Australia and the United States (particularly the southern states) has been blamed on the more widespread ownership of firearms and the associated development of "gun cultures" (Farmer and Rohde 1980; Lester 1984). The commonest form of suicide in Holland until 1967 (when it was replaced by barbiturate deaths) was drowning: "The Dutchman knows about death, because he knows about the water" (Noomen 1975, p. 168). In India, "the common mode of attempting or committing suicide is by gulping down an insecticide (organophosphorous compound) preparation. They are cheap and easily available" (Rao 1975, p. 234). It used to be the case that more people in Upstate New York than in New York City killed themselves with car exhaust fumes, possibly because more upstate inhabitants had access to garages (Drinker 1938). Jumping from a high place—the Golden Gate Bridge—is a particularly common form of suicide in San Francisco (Seiden 1967), where the local byword is that, when stress gets too great, one can always "go off the bridge" (Seiden and Spence 1983–84, p. 206).

There are also many examples of changes in the frequency of particular forms of suicide that can easily be related to changing social or environmental conditions. For example, in Britain (Adelstein and Mardon 1975), Australia (Whitlock 1975), and elsewhere, suicides by overdosing with barbiturates became common with the increasing prescriptions of these drugs. Equally, reductions in these suicides came about with wider knowledge of the dangers of overprescribing and with the availability of safer alternatives. Lester and Murrell (1980, 1982) have shown for the United States that states with stiffened gun control laws experienced greater reductions in rates of suicide between 1960 and 1970 than other states, and Boor (1981) and Boyd (1983) have argued that a substantial rise in gun suicides in the United States since the early 1960s parallels the increase in the sales of guns. Finally, it has been claimed that suicide by jumping off tall buildings increased in both Helsinki (Achte and Lonnqvist 1975, p. 108) and Taiwan (Rin 1975, p. 251) as more of these were built.

One particularly revealing example concerns suicide by car exhaust gases. These suicides have become less common in the United States as a result of emission controls (Landers 1981; Hay and Bornstein 1984); for example, carbon monoxide concentrations in the exhaust gases of General Motors' cars declined from 8.5 percent in 1968 to 0.05 percent in 1980. In Britain, on the other hand, where emission controls have yet to be introduced, this form of suicide has substantially increased in recent years (Bulusu and Alderson 1984), presumably as a result of increased car ownership and more widespread knowledge about this means of death. (Additional factors may have been the construction of more houses with garages and the increased popularity of station wagons and "hatchbacks" with a rear door permitting the easier introduction into the passenger compartment of a hose to carry the exhaust fumes.)

Such observations have evoked relatively little interest because of the assumption that a genuinely suicidal individual will always find a method. However, the decline in suicide following detoxification of gas in Britain suggests that the variations in methods of suicide described above may just as much reflect differences in the incidence of the behavior as in its forms. This is easier to accept if suicide is seen not simply as the result of an inexorable drive to self-extinction. Rather, it may often be the combined result of deep but possibly temporary despair, the weakening of moral restraints against the behavior, *and* the availability of a method that is not too difficult or repugnant.

This has profound implications for prevention. Some of these relate to crisis intervention programs insofar as these—despite the generally negative evidence (pace Miller et al. 1984)—are able to reach those in temporary though lethal despair rather than, as often seems the case at present, less profoundly unhappy young women (Lester 1986). Others relate to the possibility that advertising suicide prevention services might in some way "legitimate" the option for those faced with a severe personal problem. The implications that most concern us here, however, relate to the reduction of opportunities for suicide—what Seiden (1977) calls the "public health/public policy" approach to prevention. Measures under this head would include stiffer gun control laws, elimination of carbon monoxide from public gas supplies and from car exhausts, barriers or reduced public access at notorious jump sites, restrictions on the sale of poisonous substances, and a range of measures designed to prevent overdosing, including not just tighter prescribing rules and the development of safer alternatives but also the supply of such drugs in "blister packs," in large capsule form, or—heaven forbid—only as suppositories.

The difficulty of thinking of realistic ways of reducing opportunities for traditional forms of suicide—such as cutting, hanging, or strangulation—makes the public health/public policy approach no panacea. Even when relatively certain gains are to be had, proposed measures will be resisted on various grounds, including ethical arguments about the desirability of preventing suicide, claims that fundamental causes of the behavior are being neglected, accusations that civil liberties are being eroded, and a range of arguments about the costs, impracticality, and inconvenience or unaesthetic qualities of the proposed measures.

Without undertaking a detailed discussion of these points, it should be noted that the failure to address underlying causes can be remedied in other preventive programs, though the availability of an easy method does of itself constitute a "cause." The ethical case for allowing individuals to take their own lives holds no less for other sorts of prevention, and the need to protect civil liberties has always to be tempered by a Benthamite calculus: for example, if costs and aesthetic considerations prohibit antisuicide hardware on the Golden Gate Bridge, then surely the long-term saving of lives would justify restricting pedestrian access? This is especially the case since Seiden and Spence (1983–84) have noted that the nearby Bay Bridge has many fewer suicides, partly because of restricted access, and that suicide deaths have been greatly reduced by limitations on access at some notorious sites, formerly accounting for hundreds of deaths, such as the Eiffel Tower and Mt. Mihara in Japan. Indeed, failure to take such precautions might, in this increasingly litigious age, become grounds for negligence suits.

IV. Criminological Implications

While both suicide and crime attract moral censure, the former is now treated in most countries as behavior requiring medical rather than legal intervention. This has led to a separation of the literatures relating to the problems, even though concepts and findings frequently overlap. Thus, both crime and suicide are seen to result from disturbed up-bringing, impaired relations, and alcoholism; Durkheim's (1957) concept of anomie was adopted largely unchanged to serve as the basis for Merton's (1938) influential sociological theory of crime; Menninger's (1938) psychoanalytic treatment of suicide sees its basis in aggressive impulses that could just as readily become homicidal as suicidal; and Henry and Short (1954) see both suicide and homicide as aggressive reactions to frustration induced by changes in the business cycle—suicide by higher-status individuals being more likely as their prosperity declines and homicide by lower-status individuals as the fortunes of others improve. However, both suicide and crime—especially violent or sexual crime—are commonly seen to derive from strong internal motivation, and it is this fact that permits criminological lessons to be drawn from the gas suicide story. In particular, it allows a more confident restatement of two themes previously developed in this series, concerning (1) the need to promote opportunity-reducing measures for crime, or "situational prevention" (Clarke 1983), and (2) the potential value of "choice" or "decision" models of crime in developing preventive and deterrent policy (Clarke and Cornish 1985).

A. The Lessons for Displacement

The gas suicide story is important precisely because it furnishes clear proof that the preventive gains of a reduction in opportunity were not merely dissipated through displacement. Even if some displacement occurred, particularly to less lethal methods, thousands of lives were still saved. This changes the balance of the argument about the value of situational measures. It is now more incumbent on the skeptic to show that displacement has defeated a crime prevention measure than for the advocate to prove beyond doubt that it has not. Adding further weight to the gas detoxification evidence is the fact that it relates to premeditated behavior for which it might be expected that opportunities would be sought or created rather than merely seized (e.g., Bennett and Wright 1984). The case for opportunity-reducing measures with respect to such behavior has been much more difficult to make than that for more trivial and, possibly, impulsive criminal acts. If the incidence of suicide can be so dramatically affected by reduced opportunity, there seems little reason why this should not also be true of deep-seated criminal acts of sex and violence or why situational prevention should not be effective in dealing with some self-destructive drug and alcohol offenses.

Despite this, there are some respects in which the gas suicide story permits only a limited commentary on the highly complex concept of displacement. In particular, it is concerned with just one of its forms—a change of method. More important, it leaves many questions unanswered about the *reasons* for the lack of displacement to other lethal methods following detoxification. For example, was it that many people who used gas were hoping to give fate a hand in the decision—something that would be more difficult with other lethal methods such as jumping off high places? Was it that, with the removal of this easy method, fewer people even began to think about killing themselves? Or did they give up the idea only after failing to kill themselves with gas?

While it may be hard to accept that people were put off killing themselves by the absence of an easy method, the means of death does seem of great importance to the potential suicide. Thus, women are more repulsed by violent and bloody methods (Marks 1977), and some people appear to rule out certain methods for symbolic reasons—for example, the suggestion (Seiden and Spence 1983–1984) that jumping off the Bay Bridge is seen as more "déclassé" than is jumping off the Golden Gate Bridge. It should not be surprising, therefore, that the absence of handguns does not simply lead to more people being strangled, beaten, and stabbed to death nor that increased bank security has not always resulted in an escalation of violence (Ball, Chester, and Perrott 1978). The methods of achieving a criminal end are not equivalent for the offender. For one, there are obvious differences in risk and effort that, for example, may give guns advantages over other murder weapons. There will also be important ethical distinctions to be drawn: not every bank robber is prepared to injure or kill to get the loot.

More research into offenders' decision making will be needed if these matters, and, thus, displacement itself, are to be properly understood. Indeed, the concept of displacement is consistent, not just with the

hydraulic model of offender motivation, but also with a rational perspective that sees crime as the outcome of choices and decisions made
by the offender in pursuit of his own interests (Cornish and Clarke
1986). Moreover, the contingent nature of displacement fits more comfortably with a choice perspective since this allows for the interplay of
criminal and noncriminal solutions to the offender's perceived needs. In
other words, the automatic response to blocked criminal opportunities
may not always be a crime displacement mechanism but a decision to
forgo crime in favor of some legal alternative action.

B. Practical Difficulties of Situational Prevention

The difficulty of thinking of ways of reducing the opportunity for
many violent crimes, particularly muggings, assaults, and rapes, is a
common objection. This is less true, however, of pub fights (Hope
1985a; Ramsay 1986) and of robberies of banks (Ball, Chester, and
Perrott 1978) and convenience stores (Castleman 1984). In our minds,
at least, there is little doubt that limiting the availability of firearms in
the United States would have a substantial effect on homicide and
probably also on other violent crimes. We draw this conclusion from
the fact that, for 1980–84, the nongun homicide rate in the United
States was only 3.7 times greater than that in England and Wales, while
the rate for gun homicides was 63 times and for handgun homicides 175
times greater (see table 2; other criminologists, however, differ and
question the linkage between gun availability and violent crime; see
Gates [1985]). We are also persuaded by the evidence that the presence
and nature of firearms play a substantial role in the characteristics and
outcome of violent crime (e.g., the finding that, among robberies, the
likelihood of victim injury is less when the assailant is armed with a
firearm because of the greater risks attendant on opposing the robber
and the related finding that, when injury occurs, victims of armed
robbers are more likely to be seriously injured or killed than are victims
of nonarmed robbers [e.g., Cook 1983]).

In the long run, however, the need to do something about the appall-
ing toll of violence (with black males presently having an estimated
lifetime risk of being murdered approaching one in twenty-one [Langan
and Innes 1985]) may promote more effective gun controls. This might
be more likely were homicide to be addressed—as we have suggested
suicide should be—from the more morally neutral perspective of a
public health problem. This would seem entirely appropriate given
that homicide is a leading cause of death for some important demo-

TABLE 2
Gun and Nongun Homicides in England and Wales and in the United States, 1980–84

Type of Murder	Homicides (N)		Average Annual Rate per 1m Population*		England and Wales/ United States Ratio
	England and Wales	United States	England and Wales	United States	
All gun†	213	63,218	.86	54.52	1:63.4
Handgun†	57	46,553	.23	40.15	1:174.6
Nongun†	2,416	41,354	9.75	35.67	1:3.7
Total‡	2,629	104,572	10.61	90.19	1:8.5

SOURCES.—Home Office (1981–85); Federal Bureau of Investigation (1981–85).
* Annual average population for 1980–84: United States, 231.9 million; England and Wales, 49.55 million.
† Figures for the United States involve some extrapolation from homicides for which weapon was known.
‡ Figures for England and Wales relate to offenses currently recorded as homicide.

graphic subgroups; for example, it is the leading cause of death for black American males, aged twenty to thirty-four (Baker, O'Neill, and Karpf 1984).

The difficulties facing gun control signify a more general problem of implementation: opportunity-reducing measures with respect to crime encounter the same objections concerning individual freedoms, costs, inconvenience, and so forth as they do with respect to suicide. In addition, prevention of crime is frequently seen as less important than its punishment. These obstacles have become more apparent with attempts to implement situational prevention (see, esp., Hope 1985a). Indeed, just as some of the theoretical objections to situational prevention—concerning its alleged neglect of fundamental causes and the dangers of displacement—begin to lose their force, so the practical impediments are assuming greater importance. This is somewhat ironic, as Hope (1985b) has pointed out, since the early advocacy of situational prevention (e.g., Mayhew et al. 1976; Clarke 1977) rested largely on its practicality, at least as compared with social prevention, which had been powerfully criticized as being impossible to implement (Morris and Hawkins 1970; Wilson 1975). The moral of this is not that there should be less investment in situational prevention since, unlike social prevention, there is much evidence that it works (Heal and Laycock 1986). Rather, it is that much more effort will have to be devoted to implementation and that the rate of progress is likely to be slower than originally anticipated. It takes time for the public to accept the need for change—to take an example from another field, it was long after the first convincing demonstration of the link between smoking and lung cancer that governments accepted the need to limit advertising of tobacco products and that people's smoking habits began to change.

C. The Opportunity Structure for Crime

The hydraulic model has also influenced ideas about crime at the societal level: societies tend to be seen as having their own "natural" levels of crime, determined by the collectivity of psychological and social pressures, while differences in crime patterns have been thought to reflect the comparatively unimportant effect of each society's criminal "opportunity structure." Similarly, unusual manifestations of crime (soccer hooliganism in Britain or violent student riots in Japan) are seen to represent weak points in a society's defenses or, if occurring in normally law-abiding countries, "safety valves" for pent-up aggression.

The gas suicide story suggests a different, stronger effect of the opportunity structure. Suicide by gas was common in Britain, not merely because it was the easiest way to act out suicidal despair, but because the existence of this method may have encouraged more unhappy people to pursue the idea of killing themselves. In other words, gas suicide may have been as much a product of the particular opportunity structure pertaining in Britain as it was of social and psychological malaise. This is as likely to be true of soccer hooliganism and violent student riots. Thus, soccer matches in Britain often bring together large crowds of working-class youths in a state of high, sometimes inebriated, excitement. They are herded in large uncomfortable stadia, under the expectant eyes of the media, to watch a fast-moving game in which fights may erupt among players and questionable decisions are made by referees. It is not difficult to understand how hooliganism might arise under these conditions or, in theory, how an attack on the opportunity structure could eliminate the behavior. Possible situational measures would include a ban on the sale of alcohol at the match, segregation of rival fans before, during, and after the game, provision of seating for all spectators, barriers to prevent fans from running onto the field, less sensationalized media coverage of hooliganism, and severe fines of players for unsportsmanlike behavior. More generally, rather than searching for general explanations and a panacea, it seems best to regard crime—and perhaps even suicide as well—as a set of diverse, loosely connected problems requiring specific, custom-made solutions.

The relation between opportunity structure and crime is, however, far from straightforward: many more opportunities for crime exist than are acted on (Clarke 1984), and, unquestionably, there are important intervening variables relating to the perception and evaluation of opportunities. For example, as certain material goods become more widely owned, there may come a point at which their social value declines and they are less sought after by thieves (Gould 1969), even if given less protection by their owners. A further example is provided by the fact that fewer people killed themselves with domestic gas in Holland than expected from measures of its toxicity and availability, possibly because suicide in Holland really is associated in the public consciousness with drowning rather than with gas.

Some useful lessons for criminology follow from speculating about the effect of detoxification on the opportunity structure for suicide in Britain. A likely consequence will be that new cohorts of potential suicides will identify novel methods, such as car exhaust poisoning, that then gradually become established in public knowledge. This process is similar to displacement except that the new methods are not necessarily identified and used by individuals prevented from using toxic gas: many of those now availing themselves of car exhaust fumes may not even have known that domestic gas was once an option. A crime example would be the rise in convenience store robbery that may have resulted from increased bank security: many of those now obtaining cash in such robberies may not have considered robbing banks— they may have been too young when this was a feasible option. Another change in the criminal opportunity structure producing displacement-like effects would be the move to the "cashless society." While reducing opportunities for theft, this has presented new possibilities for computer crime, for instance—possibilities exploited by offenders who may never have entertained the idea of mugging or committing other forms of personal theft.

The gas suicide story permits one further comment on the importance of the opportunity structure at the stage of first entertaining the idea of committing a deviant act. Doubt has been cast on the notion that much crime is impulsively committed, following the sudden perception of a criminal opportunity (Maguire 1980; Bennett and Wright 1984), and this, in turn, has been used to question the value of situational prevention. However, just as the existence of an easy method might have encouraged some people to think about suicide, so, for example, the recognition that residential burglary is now easier because of lower occupancy levels and a greater amount of "stealable" property might have tempted more individuals to try their hand at this crime (e.g., Cohen and Felson 1979). How this became recognized and how such knowledge about new criminal opportunities spreads would be a fruitful line of inquiry.

Finally, that crime and suicide rates are both importantly influenced by opportunity structure invites questions about their use as indicators of social malaise. For example, wartime declines in suicide are generally thought to result from an increased collective sense of belonging in response to an external threat (Durkeim 1957). However, aside from the possibility of less complete record keeping in time of war, other interpretations are possibly less favorable to a malaise hypothesis: despairing people during wartime (of whom there may be no fewer) may be more content to let fate take its course and perhaps be killed through enemy action; or they might postpone the suicide decision to the war's end (by which time despair may have evaporated). Likewise, the recent steady increases in suicide and attempted suicide for most age groups cannot be taken as clear evidence that people are becoming more alienated and despairing. Not only may there be more opportunities for suicide, but the increases may also reflect changes in ways of dealing with despair: as a result of wider knowledge and more stress on self-determination, more people might see suicide as an acceptable way of resolving their personal problems. This, too, would be difficult to interpret as evidence of social malaise.

Without wishing to push the analogy too far, rising crime rates might also indicate not just that the criminal justice system is becoming increasingly ineffective or that the population is now more callous, aggressive, and greedy. They may not even reflect simply more opportunities for theft, the increased numbers of adolescents, or less adult supervision (Felson and Gottfredson 1984). Rather, in the way that suicide may have become a more acceptable option as a result of improved education and higher levels of personal responsibility, so some of the increases in crime could be due to similar causes. More people have wider knowledge of the world and more role models to draw on, criminal as well noncriminal. They may also be making more complex judgments about the degree of harm caused by particular criminal acts. That so little is known about these matters further reinforces the need for major programs of research into the nature of criminal thinking and decision making.

REFERENCES

Achte, K. A., and J. Lonnqvist. 1975. "Suicide in Finnish Culture." In *Suicide in Different Cultures*, edited by Norman L. Farberow. Baltimore: University Park Press.

Adams, J. Q. U. 1985. *Risk and Freedom: The Record of Road Safety Regulation*. Cardiff: Cardiff Transport Publishing Projects.

Adelstein, A., and Christine Mardon. 1975. "Suicides, 1961–74." In *Population Trends*, vol. 2. London: H.M. Stationery Office.

Baechler, Jean. 1975. *Suicides*. New York: Basic.

Bagley, Christopher. 1968. "The Evaluation of a Suicide Prevention Scheme by an Ecological Method." *Social Science and Medicine* 3:1–14.

Baker, Susan P., Brian O'Neill, and Ronald S. Karpf. 1984. *The Injury Fact Book*. Lexington, Mass.: Heath.

Ball, John, L. Chester, and R. Perrott. 1978. *Cops and Robbers: An Investigation into Armed Robbery*. London: Deutsch.

Barraclough, Brian M. 1972. "Suicide Prevention, Recurrent Affective Disorder and Lithium." *British Journal of Psychiatry* 121:391–92.

Barraclough, Brian M., C. Jennings, and J. R. Moss. 1977. "Suicide Prevention by the Samaritans: A Controlled Study of Effectiveness." *Lancet* 2:237–39.

Battin, M. Pabst, and David J. Mayo. 1980. *Suicide: The Philosophical Issues*. London: Owen.

Beck, Aaron, M. Kovacs, and A. Weissman. 1975. "Hopelessness and Suicide Behavior." *Journal of American Medical Association* 234:1147–49.

Bennett, Trevor, and Richard Wright. 1984. *Burglars on Burglary*. Farnsborough: Gower.

Boor, Myron. 1980. "Relationships between Unemployment Rates and Suicide Rates in Eight Countries, 1962–1976." *Psychological Reports* 47:1095–1101.

———. 1981. "Methods of Suicide and Implications for Suicide Prevention." *Journal of Clinical Psychology* 37(1):70–75.

Boyd, Jeffrey H. 1983. "The Increasing Rate of Suicide by Firearms." *New England Journal of Medicine* 308(15):872–74.

Brandt, Richard B. 1975. "The Rationality of Suicide." In *A Handbook for the Study of Suicide*, edited by Seymour Perlin. Oxford and London: Oxford University Press.

Brown, James M. 1979. "Suicides in Britain: More Attempts, Fewer Deaths, Lessons for Public Policy." *Archives of General Psychiatry* 36:1119–24.

Bulusu, Luk, and Michael Alderson. 1984. "Suicides, 1950–82." In *Population Trends*, vol. 35. London: H.M. Stationery Office.

Castleman, Michael. 1984. *Crime Free*. New York: Simon & Schuster.

Centraal Bureau voor de Statistiek. 1959–68. *Overledenen Naar Doodsoorzaak, Leeftijd en Geslacht in Hetjaar*. Voorburg: Centraal Bureau voor de Statistiek.

Chaiken, Jan M., Michael W. Lawless, and Keith A. Stevenson. 1974. *Impact of Police Activity on Crime: Robberies on the New York City Subway System*. Report no. R-1424-N.Y.C. Santa Monica, Calif.: Rand.

Clarke, Ronald V. G. 1977. "Psychology and Crime." *Bulletin of the British Psychological Society* 30:280–83.

———. 1980. "Situational Crime Prevention: Theory and Practice." *British Journal of Criminology* 20:136–47.

———. 1983. "Situational Crime Prevention: Its Theoretical Basis and Practical Scope." In *Crime and Justice: An Annual Review of Research*, vol. 4, edited by Michael Tonry and Norval Morris. Chicago: University of Chicago Press.

———. 1984. "Opportunity-based Crime Rates: The Difficulties of Further Refinement." *British Journal of Criminology* 24:74–83.

Clarke, Ronald V., and Derek B. Cornish. 1985. "Modeling Offenders' Decisions: A Framework for Policy and Research." In *Crime and Justice: An Annual Review of Research*, vol. 6, edited by Michael Tonry and Norval Morris. Chicago: University of Chicago Press.

Clarke, Ronald V., and Pat Mayhew. 1987. "Crime as Opportunity: A Note on Domestic Gas Suicide in Great Britain and the Netherlands." Unpublished manuscript, School of Criminal Justice, Rutgers University.

Cohen, Lawrence E., and Marcus Felson. 1979. "Social Change and Crime Rate Trends: A Routine Activity Approach." *American Sociological Review* 44:588–608.

Cook, Philip J. 1983. "The Influence of Gun Availability on Violent Crime Patterns." In *Crime and Justice: An Annual Review of Research*, vol. 4, edited by Michael Tonry and Norval Morris. Chicago: University of Chicago Press.

———. 1986. "The Demand and Supply of Criminal Opportunities." In *Crime and Justice: An Annual Review of Research*, vol. 7, edited by Michael Tonry and Norval Morris. Chicago: University of Chicago Press.

Cornish, Derek B., and Ronald V. Clarke. 1986. *The Reasoning Criminal*. New York: Springer-Verlag.

Dollard, J., N. E. Miller, L. W. Doob, O. H. Mowrer, and R. R. Sears. 1944. *Frustration and Aggression*. London: Kegan Paul, Trench, Trubner.

Drinker, Cecil W. 1938. *Carbon Monoxide Asphyxia*. New York: Oxford University Press.

Durkheim, Emil. 1957. *Suicide*. Translated by J. A. Spaulding and G. Simpson. London: Routledge & Kegan Paul. (Originally published 1897.)

Elliott, Charles. 1980. *The History of Natural Gas Conversion in Great Britain*. Royston and Cambridge: Cambridge Information and Research Services in association with the British Gas Corp.

Farber, Maurice L. 1968. *Theory of Suicide*. New York: Funk & Wagnalls.

Farberow, Norman L., and Maria D. Simon. 1969. "Suicides in Los Angeles and Vienna." *Public Health Reports* 84(5):389–403.

Farmer, Richard D. T. 1979. "Suicide by Different Methods." *Postgraduate Medical Journal* 55:775–79.

———. 1980. "The Relationship between Suicide and Parasuicide." In *The Suicide Syndrome*, edited by Richard Farmer and Steven Hirsch. London: Croom Helm.

Farmer, Richard D. T., and J. R. Rohde. 1980. "Effect of Availability and Acceptability of Lethal Instruments on Suicide Mortality." *Acta Psychiatrica Scandinavica* 62:436–46.

Federal Bureau of Investigation. 1981–85. *Crime in the United States*. Washington, D.C.: U.S. Government Printing Office.

Felson, Marcus, and Michael Gottfredson. 1984. "Social Indicators of Adolescent Activities Near Peers and Parents." *Journal of Marriage and the Family* 46:709–14.

Fox, Richard. 1975. "The Suicide Drop—Why?" *Royal Society of Health Journal* 95(1):9–20.

Freud, Sigmund. 1955. *An Outline of Psycho-analysis*. In *Standard Edition of the Complete Psychological Works of Sigmund Freud*, vol. 23, edited by J. Strachey. London: Hogarth. (Originally published 1940.)

Gabor, Thomas. 1978. "Crime Displacement: The Literature and Strategies for Its Investigation." *Crime and Justice* 6:100–106.

———. 1981. "The Crime Displacement Hypothesis: An Empirical Examination." *Crime and Delinquency* 26:390–404.

Gates, Don B. 1985. *Firearms and Violence*. San Francisco: Pacific Institute for Public Policy Research.

Gould, Leroy C. 1969. "The Changing Structure of Property Crime in an Affluent Society." *Social Forces* 48:50–59.

Halbwachs, Maurice. 1978. *The Causes of Suicide.* Translated by H. Goldblatt. London: Routledge & Kegan Paul. (Originally published 1930.)

Hamermesh, Daniel S., and Neal M. Soss. 1974. "An Economic Theory of Suicide." *Journal of Political Economy* 82(1):83–98.

Hassall, Christine, and W. M. Trethowan. 1972. "Suicide in Birmingham." *British Medical Journal* (March 18), pp. 717–18.

Hay, Peter, and Robert A. Bornstein. 1984. "Failed Suicide by Emission Gas Poisoning." *American Journal of Psychiatry* 141:592–93.

Heal, Kevin, and Gloria Laycock. 1986. *Situational Crime Prevention: From Theory into Practice.* London: H.M. Stationery Office.

Henry, Andrew F., and James F. Short. 1954. *Suicide and Homicide.* Glencoe, Ill.: Free Press.

Home Office. 1981–85. *Criminal Statistics: England and Wales.* London: H.M. Stationery Office.

Hope, Tim. 1985a. *Implementing Crime Prevention Measures.* Home Office Research Study no. 86. London: H.M. Stationery Office.

———. 1985b. "Preventing Alcohol-related Disorder in the City Centre: A Case Study." Paper presented at the annual meeting of the American Society of Criminology, San Diego, California, November 13–17.

Kreitman, Norman. 1976. "The Coal Gas Story: United Kingdom Suicide Rates, 1960–71." *British Journal of Preventive and Social Medicine* 30:86–93.

Kreitman, Norman, A. E. Philips, S. Greer, and C. R. Bagley. 1969. "Parasuicide." *British Journal of Psychiatry* 115:746–47.

Kreitman, Norman, and S. Platt. 1984. "Suicide, Unemployment, and Domestic Gas Detoxification in Britain." *Journal of Epidemiology and Community Health* 38:1–6.

Landers, Dennis. 1981. "Unsuccessful Suicide by Carbon Monoxide." *Western Journal of Medicine* 135:360–63.

Langan, Patrick A., and Christopher A. Innes. 1985. *The Risk of Violent Crime.* Washington, D.C.: U.S. Department of Justice, Bureau of Justice Statistics.

Lester, David. 1984. *Gun Control: Issues and Answers.* Springfield, Ill.: Thomas.

———. 1986. "Preventing Suicide: Past Failures and Future Hopes." Paper presented to the Conference on Suicide, King's College, London, Ontario, May 27–30.

Lester, David, and Mary E. Murrell. 1980. "The Influence of Gun Control Laws on Suicidal Behavior." *American Journal of Psychiatry* 137(1):121–22.

———. 1982. "The Preventive Effect of Strict Gun Control Laws on Suicide and Homicide." *Suicide and Life Threatening Behavior* 12:131–40.

Lorenz, Konrad. 1966. *On Aggression.* New York: Harcourt, Brace, Jovanovich.

Low, A. A., R. D. T. Farmer, D. R. Jones, and J. R. Rohde. 1981. "Suicide in England and Wales: An Analysis of 100 Years, 1876–1975." *Psychological Medicine* 11:359–68.

Maguire, Mike. 1980. "Burglary as Opportunity." *Home Office Research Unit Research Bulletin*, no. 10, pp. 6–9.

Malleson, Andrew. 1973. "Suicide Prevention: A Myth or a Mandate?" *British Journal of Psychiatry* 122:238–39, 123:612–13.

Marks, Alan. 1977. "Sex Differences and Their Effect upon Cultural Evaluations of Methods of Self-Destruction." *Omega* 8(1):65–70.

Mayhew, Patricia M., Ronald V. G. Clarke, Andrew Sturman, and J. Michael Hough. 1976. *Crime as Opportunity*. Home Office Research Study no. 34. London: H.M. Stationery Office.

Menninger, Karl A. 1938. *Man against Himself*. New York: Harcourt, Brace, & World.

Merton, Robert K. 1938. "Social Structure and Anomie." *American Sociological Review* 3:672–82.

Miller, H., D. Coombs, J. Leeper, and S. Barton. 1984. "An Analysis of the Effects of Suicide Prevention Facilities on Suicide Rates in the United States." *American Journal of Public Health* 74:340–43.

Morris, Norval, and Gordon Hawkins. 1970. *The Honest Politician's Guide to Crime Control*. Chicago: University of Chicago Press.

Morton, Frank. 1970. *Report of the Enquiry into the Safety of Natural Gas as a Fuel*. Ministry of Technology. London: H.M. Stationery Office.

Noomen, Peter. 1975. "Suicide in the Netherlands." In *Suicide in Different Cultures*, edited by Norman L. Farberow. Baltimore: University Park Press.

Office of Population Censuses and Surveys. 1959–85. *Mortality Statistics, England and Wales: Causes*. Series DH2. London: H.M. Stationery Office.

———. 1985. *Mortality Statistics, 1980–84: Serial Trends*. Series DH1, no. 15. London: H.M. Stationery Office.

Orr, L. D. 1984. "The Effectiveness of Automobile Safety Regulation." *American Journal of Public Health* 74:1384–89.

Patel, N. S. 1973. "Pathology of Suicide." *Medicine, Science and Law* 13:103–9.

Phillips, D. P. 1974. "The Influence of Suggestion on Suicide." *American Sociological Review* 39:340–54.

———. 1979. "Suicide, Motor Vehicle Fatalities and the Mass Media." *American Journal of Sociology* 84:1150–74.

Ramsay, Malcolm. 1986. "Preventing Disorder." In *Situational Crime Prevention: From Theory into Practice*, edited by Kevin Heal and Gloria Laycock. London: H.M. Stationery Office.

Rao, A. Venkoba. 1975. "Suicide in India." In *Suicide in Different Cultures*, edited by Norman L. Farberow. Baltimore: University Park Press.

Registrar General. 1900–40. *Report of the Registrar General for England and Wales*. London: H.M. Stationery Office.

———. 1959–73. *The Registrar General's Statistical Review of England and Wales*. Pt. 1, *Medical*. London: H.M. Stationery Office.

Reppetto, Thomas A. 1976. "Crime Prevention and the Displacement Phenomenon." *Crime and Delinquency* 22:166–77.

Rin, Hsien. 1975. "Suicide in Taiwan." In *Suicide in Different Cultures*, edited by Norman L. Farberow. Baltimore: University Park Press.

Sainsbury, Peter. 1983. "The Validity and Reliability of Trends in Suicide Statistics." *Quarterly Statistics of the World Health Organization* 36(3/4):339–45.

————. 1986. "The Epidemiology of Suicide." In *Suicide*, edited by Alec Roy. Baltimore: Williams & Wilkins.

Sainsbury, Peter, J. Jenkins, and A. Levey. 1980. "The Social Correlates of Suicide in Europe." In *The Suicide Syndrome*, edited by Richard Farmer and Steven Hirsch. London: Croom Helm.

Schneidman, Edwin. 1985. *Definition of Suicide*. New York: Wiley-Interscience.

Seiden, Richard H. 1967. "Suicide Capital? A Study of the San Francisco Suicide Rate." *Bulletin of Suicidology* 2:1–10.

————. 1977. "Suicide Prevention: A Public Health/Public Policy Approach." *Omega* 8(3):267–76.

Seiden, Richard H., and Mary Spence. 1983–84. "A Tale of Two Bridges: Comparative Suicide Incidence on the Golden Gate and San Francisco–Oakland Bay Bridges." *Omega* 14(3):201–9.

Stengel, Erwin. 1964. *Suicide and Attempted Suicide*. Harmondsworth: Penguin.

U.S. Department of Commerce. 1901–85. *Statistical Abstract of the United States*. Washington, D.C.: U.S. Government Printing Office.

Weissman, M. M. 1974. "The Epidemiology of Suicide Attempts, 1960–1971." *Archives of General Psychiatry* 30:737–46.

Wells, Nicholas. 1981. *Suicide and Deliberate Self-Harm*. London: Office of Health Economics.

Whitlock, F. A. 1975. "Suicide in Brisbane, 1956 to 1973: The Drug-Death Epidemic." *Medical Journal of Australia* 14:737–43.

Wilkinson, Paul. 1977. *Terrorism and the Liberal State*. London: Macmillan.

Williams, Trevor I. 1981. *A History of the British Gas Industry*. New York: Oxford University Press.

Wilson, James Q. 1975. *Thinking about Crime*. New York: Basic.

World Health Organization. 1967. *International Classification of Diseases*. Geneva: World Health Organization.

————. 1982. *Changing Patterns in Suicide Behavior*. European Reports and Studies no. 74. Copenhagen: World Health Organization.

Albert J. Reiss, Jr.

Co-offending and Criminal Careers

ABSTRACT

Understanding co-offending is central to understanding the etiology of crime and the effects of intervention strategies. The ratio of individual to co-offenders varies among crimes. Solo offending criminal careers are less common than those of exclusively co-offending but the typical criminal career is a mix of offenses committed alone and with others. Co-offending is more characteristic of juvenile than of adult criminality. Distinctions must be made between gangs, groups, and networks. Most delinquent groups are unstable. Desistance from co-offending results from transience, from the maturing of group members, and from the effects of interventions. Accomplice relationships are short lived, and active co-offenders thus tend to have many accomplices. Individuals who are both high-rate offenders and active recruiters to delinquent groups and to specific crimes may play an especially important role in co-offending and offer a potentially important target for intervention efforts. An increased understanding of co-offending, recruitment, and desistance and the implications of these for crime control policies can be gained from prospective longitudinal cohort studies that will include the experience of co-offenders of cohort members.

Offenders' criminal histories ordinarily are characterized by a mix of different types of offenses and by a mix of offenses committed alone and with accomplices. Accomplice offending, called "co-offending" in

Albert J. Reiss, Jr., is William Graham Sumner Professor of Sociology, Yale University, and lecturer in law, Yale University Law School. For their comments on this essay and earlier drafts, he owes a special debt to Larry Baron, Alfred Blumstein, Shari Diamond, David Farrington, Malcolm Klein, Richard Lempert, Lloyd Ohlin, James Parker, Elizabeth Piper, Brent Shea, James F. Short, Jr., Nigel Walker, Marvin Wolfgang, Stuart Wright, and Frank Zimring. He also owes special debts to Jerzy Sarnecki and Denise Galarraga. An earlier version of this essay appeared in Blumstein et al. (1986).

this essay, is more characteristic of juvenile than of adult criminal careers. This essay reviews the current state of knowledge about co-offending by juveniles and adults to illuminate how and when co-offending is relevant to strategies of intervention in criminal careers.

Relatively little research has been done on co-offending. Aggregate systems of criminal justice statistics and individual case records typically do not compile detailed information on co-offenders. Yet, the available evidence suggests that understanding major questions of social policy concerning crime may depend on knowledge of the differences between offenders who act alone and offenders who act with others and on knowledge about the effects of group processes on offending.

Selective incapacitation strategies aim to reduce the crime rate by removing from society those "career criminals" who have high individual rates of offending. In theory, the number of crimes and the number of victims should be reduced by the amount of crime incapacitated offenders would have committed were they not incarcerated. Within limits, that seems reasonable, provided the crimes are committed by a single offender. But whether incapacitating an offender prevents those crimes will also depend on the behavior of co-offenders and their affiliations. Crimes may not be reduced at all unless an offender's accomplices are deterred from offending by the offender's incapacitation. The accomplices may continue to commit the offenses alone, with one another, by recruiting new accomplices from within their group, or by recruiting new members to their network either as new participants in offending or by offending at increased rates. Network organization and group affiliations facilitate the search for accomplices, and it is possible that incapacitation may increase the crime rate if it leads to a marginal increase either in the number of offenders or in their individual rates of offending (Reiss 1980, pp. 15–16). It is important, consequently, to know to what extent patterns of recruitment into offending and changes in individual rates of offending may limit the capability of an incapacitation policy to reduce the crime rate.

A substantial proportion of all offending, including offending in serious crimes, occurs at young ages; the age of onset of offending is quite young (Farrington 1987). A serious juvenile career record appears predictive of high-rate offending in serious crimes as an adult (Chaiken and Chaiken 1982, p. 87). However, while many young people participate in crime, many stop fairly early (Wolfgang, Figlio, and Sellin 1972, p. 88), often without any official intervention to deter them from offending. Yet, at an early age, a sizable number of youthful offenders have high individual rates of offending (Wolfgang, Figlio, and Sellin 1972, p. 104). This raises the question of whether high-rate offenders can be identified at an early age so that they can be selected for special treatment in a juvenile or criminal justice system.

A related question is whether group affiliation is critical in onset, persistence, and desistance from offending; the role that groups play in juvenile criminal careers needs to be determined. If we could identify high-rate offenders who recruited a large number of persons into committing delinquent acts or who had a substantial effect on the individual crime rates of a large number of offenders, then these offender-recruiters might be targeted for special treatment.

Many crime control strategies aim to prevent offending either by incapacitating the offender or by encouraging desistance from crime in the free society. The latter refers to what are usually called individual-change strategies. Yet, other strategies are possible, such as altering group and other social structures or intervening in collective activity. If groups are important to onset, persistence, and desistance, direct intervention in group relationships or alteration of group structure to reduce the propensity for offending would be plausible crime control strategies. Or, recognizing that networks facilitate the search for accomplices, intervention in those networks to increase the costs of search behavior would be a plausible approach. The discussion that follows of the role of co-offending in criminal careers addresses the implications for intervention strategies.

Section I briefly reviews research on the scale of co-offending and considers the differences between the proportion of *offenses* committed by individuals and co-offenders and the proportion of *offenders* who commit offenses individually or with others. While a majority of criminal offenses are committed by individuals, a substantial number of offenders commit crimes with co-offenders.

Section II discusses research findings on various interactions between offending and involvement with accomplices or groups, including the effects of group size, age of onset, individual offending rates, duration of accomplice relationships, and the stability of delinquent and criminal groups.

Section III is concerned with characteristics of co-offenders, including variation in the extent of co-offending by sex, race, age, type of offense, relationships between victims and offenders, territorial concentration, and sibling relationships.

Section IV considers recruitment into delinquent and criminal networks and into participation as accomplices in specific crimes. There is substantial evidence that criminal groups and networks are unstable and that most accomplice relationships are short lived. Focusing on recruitment, in both senses, reveals the disproportionate importance of individuals who are both high-rate offenders and active recruiters.

Section V sets out several models for understanding why co-offending declines as offenders age and, correlatively, why sole offending increases.

Section VI considers desistance from crime generally and co-offending specifically, and Section VII considers the likely effects of various intervention strategies on participation in co-offending.

I. The Nature of Offending Behavior

There is no commonly accepted definition of "group" in research on delinquent and criminal behavior. Offending groups are often treated as synonymous with gangs, the gang being a territorially organized, age-graded peer group engaged in a wide range of activities and having a well-defined leadership (Miller 1975, p. 9). Most persons who engage in delinquency are not members of such highly structured groups (Klein and Crawford 1967; Morash 1983, p. 329). In most aggregates of twenty or more peers, people are only loosely associated with one another, leadership is unclear, and membership turnover is fairly high. Yablonsky (1959) refers to these peer aggregates as "near groups."

Before examining the basic dimensions of co-offending and their relation to criminal careers, a few issues that affect concepts and measures of co-offending should be considered. These are the relation of offending to crimes; defining and measuring lone, as opposed to group, offending; and the effects of criminal justice processing on group offending.

A. Criminal Incidents, Victims, and Offenders

Any criminal incident involves one or more crimes or offenses, one or more offenders, and, consenting and public-order crimes excepted, one or more victims. A number of relations are likely among a population of criminal incidents and their offenses, victims, and offenders. For example, the ratio of victims to incidents depends on the rate of multiple victimizations and the rate of victimization of the same person in different incidents. The number of offenders relative to the number of incidents depends on the number of offenders in an incident and their individual rates of offending. It is ordinarily assumed, moreover,

TABLE 1

Relations of Burglary Incidents and Offender Composition

Offender Composition	Number	Percent
Burglary incidents:		
With one offender	155	50.6
With two or more offenders	151	49.4
Total	306	100.0
Burglary offenders:		
One offender in incident	155	33.2
Two or more offenders in incident	312	66.8
Total	467	100.0

SOURCE.—Peoria Crime Reduction Council (1979).

that the number of offenders is well below the aggregate number of offenses and charges and that the differences are due primarily to variation in individual rates of offending and in the number of offenders in criminal incidents.

These relations can be illustrated using data on residential burglary and robbery collected by the Peoria (Illinois) Crime Reduction Council (1979) on all juveniles taken into custody for residential burglary from 1971 to 1978. During this period, 467 juveniles accounted for 306 separate burglaries. The relations of these burglary incidents to the number of offenders involved in them is shown in table 1.

Single offenders accounted for half of all residential burglaries. However, among offenders involved in burglaries, the half of the residential burglaries with a single offender involved only one-third of all offenders. The great majority of multiple-offender burglaries involved only two offenders.

How the number of offenders in crime incidents is related to the size of an offender population is seen even more dramatically for robbery offenses. Just over half of all robberies in the United States in 1982 involved a single offender (Bureau of Justice Statistics 1984, table 62). Nonetheless, as seen from the distribution in table 2, only one-fourth of all robbery offenders in those events offended alone, and there were about equal proportions of groups of two, three, and four or more offenders.

Note that, for about half of all robberies, the *same* robbery is part of the criminal history of more than one offender. Although there are on the average two offenders per robbery, in about one-fourth of all rob-

TABLE 2

Relations of Robbery Incidents and Number of Offenders

	Total Number	Percent Distribution by Number of Offenders			
		One	Two	Three	Four or More
Robbery incidents	1,149,000	51.5	24.2	14.3	10.0
Robbery offenders	2,215,272	26.7	25.1	22.3	25.9

SOURCE.—Bureau of Justice Statistics (1984, tables 52, 62).

beries, the same incident enters the criminal history of three or more offenders. If one knows the number of co-offenders in each offense in a criminal history, one can weight offenses accordingly and estimate more precisely the crimes prevented by incapacitating that offender. The larger the size of any participant's offending group, the less, on the average, that individual's absence should diminish the number of offenses.

B. Lone and Co-offenders in Criminal Careers

There is a firmly held view that most offenders are group offenders and that the career lone offender is uncommon (see, e.g., Shaw and McKay 1931). The statistical basis for this conclusion is ordinarily the number of offenders in criminal incidents rather than an analysis of the criminal histories or criminal careers for the offenders involved in those events.

The size distribution for a population of incidents is often used to estimate the participation rate of lone offenders. What is reported is a distribution of incidents by number of offenders, and the proportion of single-offender events is taken as an estimate of the prevalence of lone offenders. Such estimates are misleading because incidents rather than persons are counted. Corrections can be made by weighting the events by the number of offenders reported for them and using an appropriate population as the base for the rate.

Percentage distributions of the size of offending groups by the type of crime (the upper halves of tables 1 and 2) reflect the aggregate risk of being victimized by a group of a given size or by a single individual. By contrast, percentage distributions of the number of offenders involved in those incidents (the lower halves of tables 1 and 2) are offender-based statistics and state the probability that a randomly selected offender will commit that crime alone or with a given number of associates. The latter statistics are more appropriate in relating incidents to criminal careers or to offenders to be processed. When the interest lies in the rate of lone or co-offending crimes, statements should be made about a population of criminal incidents, but when the interest lies in lone- or co-offender participation rates, statements must be made about a population of offenders.

When all the incidents in a criminal history are considered, a large proportion of offenders exhibit neither exclusively lone nor exclusively co-offending. Most offender histories are characterized by a mix of offending alone and with accomplices. Although information on the number of accomplices in each incident in an offender's criminal history is generally lacking, some idea of the mix of lone and accomplice offending can be gained by examining the criminal histories of the juvenile offenders in the Peoria Crime Reduction Council study (1979). The 467 Peoria juveniles apprehended for at least one burglary during a 7.5-year period were involved in 2,820 offenses for which 3,426 charges were filed. Considering only co-offending among the 467 juveniles, seventy-nine (16.9 percent) always committed their offenses without accomplices from the study population, and ninety-one (19.5 percent) only acted with accomplices from the study population. The large majority (63.6 percent) sometimes acted alone and sometimes with others from the study population.[1]

Unfortunately, good estimates of the variation among criminal histories in the mix of lone and group offenses, of variation in the number of accomplices, and of the consistency and variation of co-offending in an individual's history are not available. With that information, individual-offender rates could be weighted by their partial contributions to crime events, especially when estimating the expected crimes saved by incapacitation. Such a weighted individual rate might be generally appropriate as a criterion for selective incapacitation (see Reiss 1980, p. 13).

C. Effects of Criminal Justice Processing on Estimates of Co-offending

Self-report studies of male delinquent behavior disclose a higher rate of lone offending than do official records of apprehension for the same

---

[1] Since the co-offending data in the criminal histories were tabulated only for offenders included in the study population, these are probably overestimates for lone offending.

offenders (Erickson 1971; Hindelang 1971, 1976b). The question arises, therefore, whether differential apprehension hazard is associated with violating the law with others (Erickson 1971, p. 121). For if violating with others increases the likelihood of being apprehended, the prevalence of lone offending will be underrepresented in official records.

Several attempts have been made to test whether there is a group-apprehension hazard by comparing self-reported and officially reported offenses in an offender's history. Erickson (1971, p. 125) concluded that, although there is a greater risk of apprehension for offenses that are officially known rather than self-reported, the selection bias is considerably less for the most serious offenses. Subsequent research by Hindelang casts doubt on the group-hazard hypothesis. While persons who offend only in groups have a higher risk of apprehension per crime than do those who always offend alone, those with a mix of lone and accomplice offending have comparable apprehension risks in both types of incidents.

Hindelang's work shows that "those engaging in illegal behaviour in groups are likely to engage in this behaviour more frequently than those engaging in the illegal behaviour alone" (1976b, pp. 121, 122). Indeed, the largest proportion of solitary offenders was found for delinquents with the lowest individual rates of offending and the smallest proportion of solitary offenders among those with the highest individual rates. This supports Erickson's conclusion that, among offending youths, solitary offenders are more likely to engage less frequently in crimes and to commit less serious crimes than group offenders.

Unfortunately, data are unavailable to determine whether adult solitary offenders are also disproportionately involved in the less serious offenses or have lower individual rates of offending. Because major crimes against persons involve higher rates of solitary offending, it is possible that adult solitary offending, in contrast to that of juveniles, is disproportionately concentrated on the more serious offenses.

II. Basic Features of Co-offending

Although a number of major longitudinal studies of criminal careers have followed samples of youths into their adult years (Glueck and Glueck 1930, 1937, 1940, 1943, 1946; Shannon 1978; Wolfgang 1978; Elliott et al. 1983), none has examined patterns of co-offending into adulthood. Thus, this discussion of co-offending must depend primarily on research on juvenile delinquency. Even that research, however, pays relatively little attention to individual rates of offending or the role of co-offending in careers; therefore, a single study or source of data must often be relied on.

A. Offenses and Number of Offenders

Breckinridge and Abbot (1917) were among the first to point out that most delinquent offenses are committed with at least one other person and that even most youths regarded as lone offenders occasionally engage in delinquency with a companion. Somewhat later, Shaw and Meyer (1929) and Shaw and McKay (1931) estimated from juvenile court samples that less than 20 percent of the offenders before the court committed offenses alone, that the modal number of offenders in a crime incident is small (two or three participants), and that most delinquency is not committed by well-organized groups. Shaw and McKay concluded, moreover, that, while such offending twosomes and threesomes commonly are combinations from a larger group, the whole group is rarely involved in the same delinquent or criminal act.

Large networks that link up to 200 youths ordinarily consist of fewer than thirty or forty active members organized into smaller cliques of five to ten members (Klein and Crawford 1967). In a cohort study of delinquency in a Swedish community, a youth gang was defined as a group of juveniles who were linked together because the police suspected them of committing crimes together (Sarnecki 1982, pp. 144–45).[2] There were well over 100 of these gangs in the study. Membership varied from two to thirty boys; the mean size was five boys. What was most evident, however, is that groups were constituted by co-offending relationships. These relationships consisted of links of co-offending to form chains of association. One such chain in this Swedish city involved 260 boys and a few girls and encompassed about 45 percent of the study population. Together they accounted for 86 percent of the crimes reported during the study period (Sarnecki 1982, pp. 144–45, 151).

Although accomplices in delinquency are drawn more often from smaller cliques than from the larger network, the number of accomplices in any delinquent act is much smaller than the number in the

[2] The study population was located in a southern Swedish industrial community of about 50,000 inhabitants. The records of the local police on all crimes whose suspects were under fifteen years old and from the police register (PBR) for all juveniles fifteen years and older were the main sources of information on offenses. Additional data sources included reports from police hearings, from police interviews with juveniles suspected of crimes, and from social service authorities (Sarnecki 1982, pp. 54–65; 1986, pp. 27–35).

clique (Short and Strodtbeck 1965; Klein and Crawford 1967). Considering only those offenses committed by two or more offenders, the modal number of offenders in a crime from age twelve onward is two participants. Four or more participants in a crime is relatively uncommon after age fourteen or fifteen. The majority of offenders have accomplices until their early twenties, after which the majority commit their offenses alone (Hood and Sparks 1970, pp. 87–88). There is some variation in lone and co-offending rates by country and considerable variation by type of offense (Sveri 1965).

The distribution of co-offenders for a criminal career has consequences for intervening in that career. A majority of most common crimes are committed by two or three offenders, and most offenders will have a substantial and continuing history of offenses in which their associates change from crime to crime. The larger the number of offenders in a crime, the more likely their co-offending is to be confined to a single incident unless they constitute a group specializing in specific targets of offending, as in terrorism or in some kinds of white-collar offending in which continuing use of organizational power is integral to committing offenses (Reiss and Biderman 1980).

B. Age of Onset

There is much controversy concerning whether the onset of delinquency is a consequence of induction by co-offenders. Glueck and Glueck (1934*a*, 1934*b*, 1937, 1943, 1950) contended that predelinquent and delinquent behavior begin at an early age in family and school socialization. They claimed that those with delinquent tendencies associate with one another rather than being led into their joint delinquent behavior by their associations. Their definition of delinquency is quite broad, including "delinquent tendencies" and behavior labeled as "antisocial" (1950, p. 42). Moreover, their conclusion is based not on information about the group composition of specific behavioral acts committed by offenders in their sample but on their observation that the onset of delinquency for their institutionalized delinquents occurred before age ten and before the time that peers play a significant role in a boy's life (1950, p. 41).

Eynon and Reckless, by contrast, found that the median age of youths when first contact with juvenile authorities occurred was thirteen for incarcerated juvenile offenders, and there were no significant differences in age of onset or in the presence or absence of companions at the first officially recorded delinquent act (1961, p. 169). The median age of onset for the first self-reported delinquent act ranged from eleven to fourteen years, depending on the type of offense. Self-reports on whether one had companions for each of seven offense types ranged from 56 percent of those who ran away from home to a not surprising 100 percent of those engaging in gang fights. Eynon and Reckless concluded that the "presence of companions is a major component of male delinquency, regardless of the age of delinquency onset." Companionship is present whether criminality begins early or late. But, as they note, what we still lack is information that tells us whether companionship experience relevant to the onset of delinquency causes delinquent behavior (1961, pp. 168, 170).

Most investigators seem to have missed the obvious point that companionship among children begins at a fairly early age. Although Thrasher (1927), in his classic study of what he called "youth gangs" in Chicago, was well aware that the kinds of groupings in which he was interested were found at quite young ages, he focused on territorial groupings. Subsequent work focused on "organized gangs" rather than on "companionship." These groups were largely territorially organized and were regarded as a phenomenon of adolescent and young adult ages. Recruitment and induction into these peer groups were seen as problematic, but no explicit attention was given to prior delinquent histories. This was partly because Thrasher devoted a great deal of attention to official records of delinquency, and a delinquent act rarely resulted in an official record prior to age twelve.

In any case, what is at issue is whether the onset of delinquency involves primarily lone offending or whether it is linked primarily to companionship or accomplice relationships. With answers to this key question, the problem of the role of peers in the onset and continuation of offending careers can be unraveled since there must be considerable desistance from offending, even at very early ages.

It is difficult to assess the role that companionship plays in the onset of delinquency because of the weak cross-sectional research designs of most etiological studies and because of the failure to specify a testable causal model. A longitudinal design that follows members of a birth cohort and all their accomplices who are not members of the cohort is necessary to test causal hypotheses about onset. Unfortunately, cohort studies to date have not examined the role of co-offending in criminal careers. Olson's (1977) multiple regression analysis of the personal interview data for a subset of the Racine birth cohort study (Shannon 1978) found that first police contact at a very young age was associated only with being male and having friends in trouble with the police. Yet those two variables accounted for at most one-fourth of the variance, indicating that the personal interview variables did not include the most important determinants of age at first police contact (Petersilia 1980, p. 349).

C. Group Affiliation and Individual Rates of Offending

Individuals vary considerably in their rates of offending (Farrington 1987). Most young offenders also have co-offenders and associate in other activities with still other offenders. An interesting question is how an individual's rate of offending is related to the offending rate of affiliated groups. Morash concludes that the delinquency rate of one's peers is a strong predictor of an individual's rate of delinquency. Boys who belonged to peer groups with a below-average rate of delinquency had below-average rates of delinquency, and boys with peers who had high individual rates of delinquency had an above-average individual rate of delinquency (Morash 1983, pp. 319, 321).

Juveniles with high offending rates typically commit those offenses with a large number of accomplices. Sarnecki found that the thirty-five most delinquent juveniles in the Swedish community he studied were linked to one another by membership in the largest gang and two smaller gangs. These were among the most criminally active gangs in the community. The thirty-five juveniles were involved with 224 accomplices in crime. Almost three in ten of the 799 other delinquents in the community committed at least one crime with one of these thirty-five high-rate offenders (Sarnecki 1982, pp. 171, 209). The accomplices of these thirty-five were usually selected from the criminally more active part of the total offending population (Sarnecki 1982, pp. 144–45).

High-rate juvenile offenders affiliate with one another in peer groupings. The thirty-five most active members were but 6 percent of the delinquents in Sarnecki's study population. They belonged to the three largest membership gangs, in which the mean number of suspected crimes per gang member was 22.3 during a three-year period—a rate that was three times that of the delinquent population as a whole. The members of the largest gang made up only 13 percent of the population of offenders, yet they accounted for 42 percent of all suspected crime (Sarnecki, p. 174).

D. Duration of Accomplice Relationships

Most pairings in committing delinquencies are of short duration. Sarnecki (1982, p. 140) found that only 13 percent of the 1,162 juvenile delinquency pairings in an offense in the Swedish community persisted beyond six months. Only 4 percent of the pairs were still committing crimes together after 1.5 years, but one of the 1,162 offending pairs was committing offenses together after 3.5 years, roughly half the six years that the study tracked offenders. The short life of any pairing in delinquency is partly a product of the shortness of most delinquent careers. Almost six in ten youths in the Swedish cohort were known to the police during only one six-month period of the six-year study (Sarnecki 1982, p. 141). Among those persisting in delinquency, the modal pattern was to change associates in committing offenses.

Sarnecki (1982, pp. 142–43) also found that the most criminally active usually commit their crimes in pairs and that they preserve particular pairings longer than do those who are less active. The most active and seriously delinquent juvenile suspects were forty-five times more likely to commit crimes with the same associates than were less active juveniles from the study population.

Quite clearly, accomplices in offending change quite frequently in juvenile careers. The larger the number of offenses committed by an offender, the larger the number of different accomplices linked to that offender's career. One's co-offenders as a juvenile are likely to be drawn from cliques or constellations of cliques with which one is affiliated. Ordinarily, these cliques are part of a network. Adults are perhaps more likely than juveniles to be linked in loose networks, ones in which they are linked by weak rather than strong ties (Granovetter 1973).

E. Stability of Group Affiliation

An important issue is how shifts among cliques of peers and co-offenders occur and how affiliation with cliques and larger networks is stabilized as well as disconnected and terminated. These issues are not dealt with systematically in the research on crime and delinquency.[3]

[3] Similarly, little is known about the stability of group affiliations among a population of nonoffenders. The stability of pair and group affiliations seems to vary by age and to be more stable during the preadolescent than the adolescent years. Still, it seems that all youths frequently change companions for conforming acts, such as walking to school, dating, going to the movies, and shopping. Much more needs to be known about pair and group affiliations for nondelinquents or all youths to assess the relative stability of delinquent affiliations. It is possible that delinquent pairings show greater stability than nondelinquent pairings. Choosing different companions for different activities, moreover, may simply be a characteristic of both youthful and adult behavior.

Thus, empirical studies on delinquent gangs and street-corner groups are used here to explore these issues.

It was quite evident in the Swedish community studied by Sarnecki that most gangs existed for only short periods of time. Only one gang persisted for the entire six-year period, and towards the end of that period, it split into two separate groups. Yet a third was spun off in the final six months of the study. The original gang was still the largest of the three at the close of the study period (Sarnecki 1982, p. 153). Although gangs can divide by schism, merge with other gangs, or join a network of gangs, their durability has consequences for individual careers. Career termination may result simply from the short duration of peer groups and the loose links that bind members, especially for those who rely primarily on group affiliation for accomplices and support in offending.

Suttles's study of street-corner groups in Chicago allows us to explore the stability of affiliations with offending groups. He identified thirty-two named street-corner groups in the Addams area of Chicago. With one exception, they were made up exclusively of males and averaged from twelve to fifteen members in size. Some had as few as eight members, and one had twenty-nine. Each of the groups had some members who lived outside the Addams area, ranging from 4 to 17 percent; 12 percent of the members of all the groups lived outside of the area. Outsiders were youths who either formerly lived in the area or were related by kinship to one of the group members (Suttles 1968, pp. 157–67).

Although Suttles does not provide detailed information on the duration of the thirty-two groups, he reports that one lasted but one year and that some lasted two or three years (1968, pp. 161, 166). All were subject to considerable turnover in membership, partly because of residential mobility.[4] Of those known to have quit membership in groups, 41 percent moved to another area of Chicago (p. 167).

One additional fact is worth noting. A substantial proportion of all boys in an area never affiliate with these larger groups (Short and Strodtbeck 1965, pp. 56–57; Suttles 1968, p. 173). Suttles reports that most of the unaffiliated are boys who regularly "band together" in small cliques (p. 169). Few boys, then, are isolates. The role of affiliation

---

[4] Klein and Crawford (1967) similarly reported high turnover in the black Los Angeles gangs they studied. They reported that "many members affiliate with the group for brief periods of from a few days to a few months, while others move out of the neighborhood or are incarcerated for periods sometimes exceeding a year" (p. 66).

with territorial delinquent groups in accounting for differences in individual rates of offending is unclear, however. Suttles (p. 220) reports that arrest rates were about equal for the affiliated and unaffiliated boys. Yet others, especially Short and Strodtbeck, report much higher individual rates of offending for gang-affiliated boys.

The stability of territorially based groups is threatened by three major contingencies: transiency, incarceration of members, and shifts to conventional careers.

1. *Transiency.* Slum neighborhoods, especially, are characterized by high residential transiency of families. That transiency has three major consequences for territorial youth organizations. Transiency makes the membership of any group volatile. To survive substantial annual turnover in membership, the group must obtain new members. From the perspective of the individual member, transiency means transitory affiliations with some group members and adapting to the exodus of former members and an influx of new members. Recruitment and replacement are age graded, and there is some preference for older rather than younger boys (Suttles 1968, p. 163). Even associations between gang boys appear age graded. Klein and Crawford (1967, p. 74) report that younger gang members are seldom seen in the company of older gang members.

Another consequence of transiency is that it spreads the network and influence of the group beyond the confines of its territory. Chicago appears similar to Sarnecki's Swedish community in that some youths who move into new areas affiliate with other territorial groups (Keiser 1969; Short and Moland 1976, p. 168). Transiency thus both expands the choice of accomplices and links territorially based groups. Just how widely such individual contacts spread across territorially based groups is unclear, but some of the most active and serious offenders are transient and use this larger network to search for accomplices.

Transiency also has important consequences for the continuity of territorially based groups over time. To survive, the group must continually invest in replacing members. The more formally organized a group and the more provision it makes for replacement of members, the more likely it is to survive, as studies of Chicago's black conflict gangs demonstrate. The Vice Lords, which incorporated as a not-for-profit organization, gained as many as 8,000 members in twenty-six divisions (Sherman 1970), while the informally organized Nobles barely survived (Short and Moland 1976, p. 168). The higher the residential transiency of an area, the more likely its youths are to be organized into a loose confederation and the fewer and less stringent are the criteria for entry and continuing affiliation with its territorial groups. Moreover, the combination of transiency and the aging of members, with replacement confined to a narrow range of age-mates, suggests that recruitment is limited to newly entering residents or, in a few cases, to mergers among gangs (Sherman 1970; Short and Moland 1976, p. 168). The combination of these contingencies suggests that, unless youth groups are formally structured to deal with turnover, they should have fairly high dissolution rates.

2. *Incarceration.* The second important source of instability in gang membership is the rate of incarceration of gang members. The more seriously delinquent the members of a gang, the more likely they are to be incarcerated for substantial periods of time. Short and Moland (1976, p. 168) report that nearly all the Vice Lords had been in correctional institutions at one time or another, and Short and Strodtbeck (1965) draw attention to the disruptions caused by incarcerating gang leaders. Unfortunately, they do not provide estimates of the rate of incarceration for any time interval.

3. *Conventional Careers.* A third important source of turnover in street-corner group membership is the shift to more conventional career affiliations by some members. At least half Suttles's (1968, p. 167) Addams-area group dropouts left because they married, went into the service, joined a job training program, or worked regularly in a job. Relatively few were lost to jail.

The general impression is that delinquents are organized into loose federations rather than highly organized groups. The federation is characterized by loose ties among individuals and cliques or clusters. Members are linked by a variety of activities in addition to delinquent offending. Individuals are not tightly bound either to large groups or to particular pairings within groups. Accomplices change quite frequently. According to Olofsson (1971), when compared to youths in the general population, Swedish male juvenile delinquents are less selective of companions, and their choices are less stable. It perhaps is reasonable to conclude that, while there are some highly structured territorial gangs that persist for periods of time (Miller 1958, 1975; Cloward and Ohlin 1960; Spergel 1964; Klein and Crawford 1967), associates in most delinquency offenses are drawn from much less structured networks in which nuclei of offenders are linked as nodes. Territorial gangs (Thrasher 1927; Whyte 1943) are perhaps more akin to nodes in networks than they are to independent groups in organized conflict relations (Bordua 1961, 1962; Yablonsky 1962). Over time, networks are durable while particular groups and pairings are transitory, and any individual's affiliations are of short duration.

An individual's offending history of some duration should be characterized by a large number of accomplice pairings, but, ordinarily, the same associates will be involved for only a short period of time. Moreover, the higher an individual's rate of offending and the more serious the crimes committed, the more likely that accomplices will be selected from a network.

Accepting the importance, even dominance, of networks in delinquent behavior should draw attention to the role of networks in offending and to the role that pairings, as contrasted with individual offending, play in the commission of crime.

III. Patterns in Group Offending

There is considerable variation in the extent to which offenders commit crimes alone and with others when this is examined in terms of the characteristics of the offense, the offender, and the victim. Unfortunately, the bulk of research on the role of groups in offending is done only with young offender populations. There are relatively few studies of the group behavior of youths in transition to adult status or of adult offenders at different ages. This makes it necessary to rely on single investigations or on case studies to infer patterns of group offending for adult offenders.

A. Sex

Somewhat over one in ten lone offenders in crimes of personal violence in the United States are female offenders (Bureau of Justice Statistics 1984, table 40). The proportion of female lone offenders varies by type of violent crime: it is negligible for the crime of rape and greatest for the crime of assault. Female offenders in violent crimes select females as their victims far more often than males select males. When females select male victims in violent crimes, they are most likely to assault men and least likely to rob them (Hindelang 1976a, p. 178).

Youths are more likely than adults to limit their choices to persons of the same sex. Not surprisingly, then, the associates of young persons in delinquency are almost always of the same sex. Shapland (1978, p. 262) reports that no boy in her sample of eleven- and twelve-year-olds, when interviewed at age thirteen or fourteen, admitted committing an offense with girls. The pattern is somewhat different when older offenders are included. Among violent, multiple-offender victimizations reported to the National Crime Survey (NCS) in 1982, 19 percent involved women as offenders, either with other women only (7 percent) or with men or both men and women (12 percent) (Bureau of Justice Statistics 1984, p. 49).

Only limited data are available to estimate the incidence of lone offending for both personal and property crimes by sex. The Federal Republic of Germany reports the size of arrested groups for a large number of offenses; the data show that the aggregate male rate of solo offending is somewhat below that of females but that the rate varies by offense. The West German police statistics for 1982 disclose that 68 percent of all males suspected of offenses were solo offenders, compared with 76 percent of all females. That difference is not large, but women are disproportionately found in offenses that have high proportions of lone offenders, such as assault, shoplifting, prostitution, and petty theft without contact. Moreover, given the low incidence of offending among women and the general absence of organized women's delinquent groups or gangs, it seems reasonable to conclude that women more commonly than men engage in offenses that make them more likely to offend alone. Some confirmation of this is also found in the fact that multiple-offender incidents in which all offenders are female are fewer in absolute numbers and proportionately (7 percent) than are those involving women as lone offenders (13 percent) (cf. Bureau of Justice Statistics 1984, tables 40, 45).

Women are less likely to be associated exclusively with other women than they are with men in committing violent crimes. Only 36 percent of the violent criminal victimizations involving one or more female offenders reported to the NCS in 1982 were made up entirely of female offenders; 64 percent involved association with men in the offense (Bureau of Justice Statistics 1984, table 45). Correlatively, only 12 percent of the violent, multiple-offender incidents involving male offenders also involved female associates.

Women are least likely to offend only with women in the more serious violent crimes of robbery and aggravated assault. Among crimes of violence toward persons, substantial involvement of women offenders with women victims is confined largely to simple assault.

B. Race

Blacks are somewhat less likely than whites to be solo offenders. Although data are lacking for a population of adult offenders, the NCS data for 1982 disclose that 72 percent of all violent criminal victimizations by whites, compared with 60 percent of those by blacks, were single-offender incidents (Bureau of Justice Statistics 1984, calculated from tables 44, 49).

Mixed-race offending is infrequent in multiple-offender victimizations. Less than 6 percent of all 1982 crimes of violence reported to the NCS involved a mix of black, white, or other races of offenders (Bureau of Justice Statistics 1984, table 49). There was little variation by type of violent crime.

Comparing mixed-sex with mixed-race offending, multiple-offender groups appear about twice as likely to include persons of the opposite sex (12 percent) as another race (6 percent) (Bureau of Justice Statistics 1984, tables 44, 49). Thus, accomplices from a different race and sex are uncommon, and most accomplices are of the same race and sex.

C. Age

Co-offenders are, in the aggregate, younger than solo offenders (Bureau of Justice Statistics 1984, tables 41, 46). In the NCS, offenses in which the offender's age was perceived by victims to be under twenty-one years were found more often among multiple- than single-offender victimizations (Hindelang 1976a, p. 172; Bureau of Justice Statistics 1984, tables 41, 46).

A study of apprehended burglars in the Thames Valley, England, found that somewhat over three-fourths of the adult burglars, compared with half the juvenile burglars, acted alone in the offense for which they were arrested. Considering only those offenses in which there were accomplices, adult burglars were more likely than juvenile burglars to act in pairs (Macguire and Bennett 1982, p. 184).

Information is lacking on the size of offending groups by age for a population of U.S. offenders. Hood and Sparks (1970, pp. 87–89), however, report data on size of offending group by age for apprehended offenders in London boroughs and for offenders convicted of theft in Norway. They concluded that, as offenders grow older, they are more likely to be apprehended or convicted for an offense committed alone. Not until they reach their mid-twenties, however, are lone offenders a majority of those apprehended or convicted. The age curve of solo offending is relatively flat until age sixteen, when the proportion of lone offenders begins to rise rather sharply. This shift is primarily accounted for by a rapid decline in apprehensions involving three, four, or more participants, especially the last. The proportion of apprehensions or convictions involving two offenders fluctuates far less over time than it does for lone offenders or for three or more offenders. The proportion with two or more offenders peaks at ages sixteen to eighteen, but there is no substantial decline with age. Lone offending exceeds pair offending by the late teens. Older offenders thus ordinarily commit offenses alone or with a single co-offender. Still, at least one in ten offenders in their mid-twenties is apprehended or convicted for offending with three or more offenders.

D. Type of Offense

Certain offenses are identified as committed typically by individuals or by co-offenders. With the exception of robberies and some assaults, the modal number of offenders reported by victims of major crimes against persons is a single offender; a pair of offenders is the next most common (Reiss 1980, table 1). But, with the exception of homicides and rapes without theft, the majority of offenders in crimes against persons commit their offenses with accomplices (Reiss 1980, table 2). The mean number of offenders per major common crime is between two and three for robbery and assaults and about 1.5 for all other offenses against the person and property (Reiss 1980, table 2).

Self-report studies show considerable variation by types of crime in the proportion of young persons committing offenses alone or with others. Much depends on how the self-report specifies the offense, especially as to the conditions of its occurrence. Shapland (1978, table 2) found, not surprisingly, that all the thirteen- and fourteen-year-olds she studied took money from home as a single offender. At the other extreme, more than nine of ten boys said they vandalized public property with others.

Most boys, nonetheless, report acting alone and with others for a variety of offenses. Shapland (1978, p. 262) calculated that the mean percentage involvement in group offending was 59.68 percent (standard deviation 15.6) for all boys aged thirteen to fourteen, whereas that for solitary offending was 30.02 percent (standard deviation 16.4). From this we can conclude that, although the typical offender history includes both lone and group offending in the same and different kinds of offenses, the ratio of co-offenders to solitary offenses in a youthful offender's career is, on the average, two to one.

Detailed information on the distribution of solo and co-offending for specific offenses is unavailable for the adult offender population of the

United States. Although the rate of solo offending appears to be higher for a population of offenders in the Federal Republic of Germany (Kaiser 1982, p. 103) and the German Democratic Republic (Kraeupl 1969, p. 63) than in the rest of Europe or in North America, police statistics for adult offenders in West Germany disclose marked variation in solo offending by type of offense. Among the major offenses in which at least eight of every ten offenders committed the offense alone were murder; sexual offenses, such as exhibitionism and sexual murder; drug abuse involving heroin and cocaine; and the white-collar offenses of embezzlement, forgery, and fraud. By contrast, most of the common crimes had much lower solo offending fractions. At least eight in every ten suspects in common thefts, robberies, breakings and enterings, and breaches of the peace had at least one co-offender (Federal Republic of Germany 1982).

The significance of group affiliation for young offenders is reinforced when variation in number of offenders is examined by age and type of offense. Even for homicide, which in the aggregate is a solo-offender crime and an infrequent offense among young offenders, Zimring (1984, p. 91) found that, the younger the homicide offender, the more likely he was to have killed with others and to have done so when engaging in a collateral felony, such as robbery-murder. In brief, young homicide offenders are far less likely than older ones to commit murder and felonious homicide alone.

E. Victims and Offenders

Prior relationships between victims and offenders are more characteristic of some crimes than others. Domestic assaults, for instance, are characterized by cohabitation of victim and offender, whereas assaults involving theft ordinarily occur between strangers. There is a modest relation between the size of an offending group and the relationship between offenders and their victims (Bureau of Justice Statistics 1984, tables 52 and 62). The modal offender in crimes of violence against strangers is a co-offender, whereas single offenders predominate when there is a prior relationship between victim and offender(s). Even the modal offender in robberies of nonstrangers is a lone offender, whereas it is a co-offender in robberies of strangers. The larger the number of offenders in robberies and assaults of strangers, the more likely victims are to be injured; however, a larger proportion of lone offenders inflict serious injury when the victim is a nonstranger rather than a stranger.

F. Territorial Concentration

Perhaps the single most noteworthy aspect about common crime is the territorial concentration of offenses, offenders, and, to a substantial degree, victims. A substantial majority of both personal and household crimes occur close to the residences of the offenders and their victims (Reiss 1967; Smith 1972; Pyle et al. 1974).

Juvenile offenders commonly belong to territorially based groups and typically select their co-offenders from those groups or the territory where they reside (Shaw and McKay 1931; Suttles 1968; West 1974, 1977, 1978; Sarnecki 1982). Shaw's (1938) tracing of the accomplices in the criminal careers of the five Martin brothers illustrates this territorial concentration of career offenders. In the course of their careers, these five brothers were implicated in theft with at least 103 other delinquents and criminals. The other offenders resided, for the most part, within seven-tenths of a mile of the Martin residence. Of the 103 co-offenders, twenty-eight were adjudicated in delinquent and criminal proceedings, and all but three of the twenty-eight served adult as well as juvenile institutional sentences (Shaw 1938, pp. 115–16). The geographic concentration of the Martin brothers' accomplice network was characteristic of both their juvenile and their young adult years, although some geographic diversification occurred through accomplices met during periods of incarceration.

Recent work on the neighborhood determinants of criminal victimization sheds additional light on the territorial concentration of offenders and on patterns of group offending. Smith (1986) reports that, the larger the proportion of single-parent households with children between the ages of twelve and twenty in a neighborhood, the higher the neighborhood's perceived risk and actual rate of victimization by crime. Sampson (1985, p. 25) finds that, the greater the proportion of female-headed households and the higher the density of settlement in a neighborhood, the greater the rate of victimization by crime. Sampson (1983, p. 172) also finds that juvenile offenders in neighborhoods with both high-density settlement and a large proportion of female-headed households commit a larger proportion of their offenses with others than do juveniles in areas with low density and a small proportion of female-headed households. Sampson's findings hold independent of the racial composition of the neighborhoods.

Additionally, Bottoms and Wiles (1986) report that delinquency rates in public housing projects in English industrial communities are correlated with the degree of concentration of single-parent households with youths of an age to offend. They conclude that high delinquency rates in public housing projects are partly a function of managers' concentrating single-parent households in selected public housing projects.

These studies lend support to the hypothesis that it is the territorial concentration of young males who lack firm controls of parental authority that leads them into a peer-control system that supports co-offending and simplifies the search for accomplices.

G. Siblings

Brothers in Crime, the classic study by Clifford Shaw (1938), traces the criminal careers of the five Martin brothers over a period of fifteen years. At the end of that period, the brothers ranged in age from twenty-five to thirty-five. Four of the five had by then terminated their criminal careers. Shaw describes the crime and criminal justice consequences of their careers in the following way: "The extent of their participation in delinquent and criminal activities is clearly indicated by the fact that they have served a total of approximately fifty-five years in correctional and penal institutions. They have been picked up and arrested by the police at least 86 times, brought into court seventy times, confined in institutions for forty-two separate periods and placed under supervision of probation and parole officers approximately forty-five times" (1938, p. 4).

These are but the official statistics of their five criminal careers. Autobiographical reports accounted for more than 300 burglaries, the theft of forty-five automobiles, and a host of other crimes involving theft, receiving stolen property, and armed robbery (Shaw 1938, p. 5).

The autobiographical accounts of these five brothers offer evidence of older brothers' recruiting their younger brothers into offending, thereby focusing on the role that siblings play in co-offending and how common siblings are as initial and continuing co-offenders. Whether one offends with siblings can be expected to depend on such characteristics as family size and sibling composition by sex and birth order. There is no reliable research on how much the co-offending of siblings accounts for group offending.

We can gain some notion of the role of siblings in criminal events from the Peoria study of residential burglary (Peoria Crime Reduction Council 1979). Of the 151 burglaries involving two or more offenders for which a juvenile was apprehended, roughly 24 percent involved two or more siblings (and sometimes nonsibling offenders as well). Of these, about two-thirds involved nonsiblings, and one-third involved only siblings.

What is apparent from these Peoria data is that more than one in ten adjudicated burglary events involved at least two members from the same family. Thus, among a population of offenders in residential burglary, a small proportion of families accounts for a disproportionate number of the adjudication decisions.

Little is known about the transmission of antisocial and criminal behavior within families and across generations of kin (see Loeber and Stouthamer-Loeber 1986). It has been recognized for some time that male delinquents come from larger families than do male nondelinquents of the same age and socioeconomic status (Ferguson 1952; West and Farrington 1973; Blakely, Stephenson, and Nichol 1974). Jones, Offord, and Abrams (1980) found that, in their comparisons of male probationers and controls, this difference in the size of sibling groups was due entirely to an excess of brothers. Probationers and controls did not differ in number of sisters (Jones, Offord, and Abrams 1980, p. 140).

Of special interest was the finding that the antisocial scores of the brothers of the delinquent male probationers were significantly higher than those of the brothers of their matched controls (p. 141). By contrast, among female probationers, both brothers and sisters were more antisocial than the siblings of their control counterparts (p. 144).

Even more striking was the discovery that the average antisocial score of the probationers' brothers increased with the number of brothers in the family when the number of sisters was held constant; it decreased with the number of sisters, holding the number of brothers constant (p. 142). Jones and his colleagues interpret these results to mean that sisters suppress antisocial behavior in their brothers, whereas brothers respond to one another in ways that stimulate their potential for antisocial behavior; that is, it is due less to learning antisocial behavior from siblings than to their mutual participation. Evidence on this point appears to be lacking.

IV. Role of Groups in Recruitment

Not much is known about how and why accomplices are selected. This section examines the structure of peer and adult networks that facilitate the search for co-offenders and discusses what is known about the search for and active recruitment of associates in offending.

A. Structure of Delinquent Peer Networks

There is some disagreement about how youth groups and their peer networks are structured. Most young males do not appear to belong to bounded groups that have a constant membership with strong social bonds from which they select their accomplices, if indeed selection is the appropriate model for describing how persons come to offend together. This exposition links youths in a web of affiliation or network of contacts and exchanges. Typically, sociometric techniques are used to define constellations that have a much smaller core membership that gathers together with some frequency (Yablonsky 1962; Short and Strodtbeck 1965; Gannon 1966; Klein and Crawford 1967; Sarnecki 1982). The core of active members within the larger constellation ordinarily is no more than one-fifth the total aggregate of affiliated youths, and it ranges in size from twenty to forty or so members (Hood and Sparks 1970, pp. 89–90). That core of firm or active members, in turn, often subdivides into clusters or cliques of five to ten members (Klein and Crawford 1967). These aggregations are best described as a loose web of affiliations because most persons have most of their contacts with others in their clique and little, if any, contact with others in the network.

Klein and Crawford studied the extent to which thirty-two youths in one gang had contacts with one another during a six-month period. The observed number of interactions of any member with all others during the six months ranged from one to 202. Of the 486 possible pair relationships among the thirty-two members, two-thirds involved no contact, and for three-fourths contact was limited to no or only one contact. Most of the contacts occurred within two cliques—one of nine members and the other of five, with the nine-member clique having a much greater frequency of contact than the five-member one (1967, p. 72).

Klein and Crawford divided the gang members into four clusters according to their individual rates of delinquency. Those labeled A and B in table 3 had relatively higher rates than those labeled C and D. Those in the A and B clusters also had continued gang relationships for longer than those in clusters C and D. Higher-delinquency group members were more likely to be members of the two major cliques and to have more of their delinquency contacts within the clique, as table 3 makes readily apparent.

We may conclude from these delinquency and group-affiliation data that delinquent contacts do not occur randomly. Indeed, a substantial

TABLE 3

Percentage Comparison of the Types of Contacts for Gang Boys in
Four Clusters with Different Rates of Delinquency

	Higher Delinquency Clusters (%)		Lower Delinquency Clusters (%)	
Type of Contact	A	B	C	D
Members in cliques	42	43	16	15
Mutual contacts among members of their cluster	81	72	20	32
Contacts that occurred only once	54	35	73	77
Member contacts made within clique	82	73	47	40

SOURCE.—Adapted from Klein and Crawford (1967, table 2); Hood and Sparks (1970, table 3.1).

amount of delinquency occurs within relatively small clusters that form within a larger network of affiliations. A minority of the contacts, nevertheless, are within the larger network, although they occur much less frequently.

B. Structure of Adult Networks

Surprisingly little is known about how adults make contacts and decide to offend together. Apart from highly organized criminal activity, most adult co-offending does not appear to arise from participation in groups of which they are members. Although some adults may form co-offending relationships that are stable over time, the typical co-offending relationship appears to be transitory, and there is a continual search for new co-offenders. Among the career thieves studied for the President's Commission on Law Enforcement and Administration of Justice, the search for opportunities and co-offenders was self-styled as "hustling." Hustling led to "connecting" with other individuals who were similarly "scouting" for opportunities to commit offenses and looking for buyers for their stolen goods (Gould et al. 1965, pp. 25–26). The particular set of accomplices often varies from crime to crime, and offenders must work with people according to the requirements of particular crimes. This is especially the case for what Sparks, Greer, and Manning (1982) describe as "crime as work" in "crimes for gain." Gould and his coworkers concluded, "While a few professional criminals work for extended periods of time with the same accomplices, most work from day to day, or week to week, with whomever they can put together for a particular job. Each job requires different personnel, different plans, different resources, and even a different working schedule" (1965, pp. 51–52).

Searches for accomplices and for means to dispose of illegal gain are facilitated by using networks as well as particular organizations. There are gathering places, organizational settings, and kinds of encounters that facilitate locating accomplices. Additionally, offenders are symbiotically linked to these settings by common residence in a community that is host to these organizations; the accomplice-offenders themselves constitute a loose web of affiliations and a resource for referrals in searches. The local pool halls, bars, and all-night restaurants (Gould et al. 1965, p. 25; Polsky 1969), the fences (Klockars 1974), the chop shops (shops that dismantle motor vehicles), and the legitimate businesses that deal in some stolen goods, such as parts shops, auto dealers, second-hand stores, and pawn shops (Gould et al. 1965, pp. 26–27, 37–39) are all places to search for accomplices and to dispose of illegal goods for gain. For some, the syndicate facilitates the search.

What seems to characterize the network among adult offenders is that adult offenders patronize the same places, make the same kinds of transactions, and often reside in the same area. The casual encounter can conclude the search as much as "putting out the word." Indeed, excepting recruitment for the more sophisticated crimes, which require a variety of highly specialized skills, the daily round suffices to select accomplices.

C. Dual Processes of Recruitment in Groups

Dual processes of recruitment go on in many delinquent and criminal groups. One process recruits members to a group, either to a loose affiliation with an informal group or, in the limiting case, to a structured position in an organized criminal syndicate. The recruit may be a "raw recruit" who is being initiated into delinquent or criminal activity, or, more commonly, the recruit has a history of offending.

A second kind of recruitment process involves group members recruiting accomplices in crimes. Although a member is more likely to recruit an accomplice from among fellow group members than from outside, offenders cross group boundaries to select accomplices.

1. *Recruitment into Offending Groups.*   Almost all groups that endure for any period of time experience turnover in membership. Even size of membership ordinarily does not remain constant over time (Suttles

1968, p. 161). Sarnecki (1982, p. 148) concludes that juveniles come into and leave gangs quickly; the boundaries of gangs are quite permeable. Normally, membership is shorter than six months, especially for the less delinquent. Members also appear to leave easily, generally without resistance or resentment by the group. This suggests that there is a kind of sifting and sorting going on in peer groups of delinquents. Yet, it is not necessarily high-rate offenders who remain. A number of studies (e.g., Sarnecki 1982, p. 148) report that a substantial number of high-rate offenders may leave after committing only a few crimes with accomplices drawn from the group. High-rate offenders often have contacts among a number of such groups, recruiting many of their accomplices from outside their own group. Thus, the stable core members of a group during the period it persists are generally neither the highest- nor the lowest-rate offenders.

2. *Recruitment of Accomplices.* Selection of accomplices is facilitated by the fact that some groups are linked with others to form networks. Those with older members, for example, are linked to ones with younger members, and those of the same ethnic origin are linked with one another. This loose linkage facilitates selection of accomplices from different groups. The most active offenders, moreover, belong to several groups, and so they themselves serve as links among their groups. They are the most likely to select accomplices from outside a group in which they may be regarded as a core member. What is not known from any of the studies, however, is whether the highly active members within these groups frequently are selected by others as accomplices. It would appear that they usually are not.

It is no simple matter to disentangle the effect of recruitment on offending rates from the selective recruitment of accomplices on the basis of prior record since longitudinal studies have not addressed recruitment of accomplices. There is no certain answer to the question of how previously unacquainted offenders find one another and become accomplices. The answer is less obvious than it may seem. Empey (1970), in a postscript to the account of an ex-offender, notes that ex-offenders continue to face blandishments from old friends to return to the old ways since friendship networks are one vehicle for entering into complicity to commit an offense. But he also reports (in a personal communication) that, when he moved delinquents from one school setting to another to provide them with the anonymity to change to a conventional life-style, within a few weeks they had formed associations with all the "local hoods in the new school." This suggests that active delinquents are continually signaling their interest in locating others with whom they may engage in offending. Such signaling is readily picked up by others who are similarly searching.

We need to understand how people search for accomplices in offending and how successful those searches are, especially among strangers. West (1974) concluded that local networks that uniquely identify offenders and their skills facilitate recruitment of accomplices in theft. Initial contacts are made when relevant information is passed about a named individual. But just how strangers search out one another to commit an offense is unclear. They may begin, as detectives do, by asking individuals they know to help them find a particular kind of accomplice. However, much searching probably is done by frequenting places where cues direct one to potential accomplices.

From his study of juvenile thieves who were serious offenders, West (1974, 1977, 1978) reports that it would be an exaggeration to say that most thieves learned how to practice thieving as a member of a group into which they were recruited. Rather, on the basis of his interviews and observations of high-rate juvenile thieves, he reports that theft is both endemic to and a highly visible occupation in many lower-class or working-class communities. Theft is a readily available activity for almost everyone in the community. Recruitment to high-rate offending in theft takes place, however, in loosely structured peer settings. West reports:

> Groups coalesce and disperse, individuals drift in and out of them, alone or in pairs. Almost all of the neighborhood youths have committed some petty varieties of theft during childhood. They are usually caught and labeled as secondary deviants. A great many teens know of the existence of theft through at least one peer who is thieving as an occupation. The symbiotic relationship between some older and younger clusters facilitates contact between peer groups and the potential recruits are able to meet the already initiated. . . . most teens do not need to befriend somebody to find a "partner in crime": they already have one. [1978, Pp. 177–78]

West goes on to describe how serious thieving is learned. Some learn by observing older, experienced thieves; for some there is anticipatory apprenticeship by modeling after an older thief and learning his skills. Some may even be self-taught, as in the case of one who had taken a locksmith course by mail and was in demand as an accomplice because he could pick locks. Especially important is the cultivation of contacts and relationships that provide information: "He needs colleagues, in most cases, who will 'cut him in' on jobs, angles, or 'hot tips,' warn him when 'the heat is on,' and lend him money when he gets down on his luck. He needs reliable fences and customers, who are aware of constrictions on his work and know how to 'play his game' or interact with him to minimize risks and maximize gain" (West 1978, p. 179).

Many jobs are carried out in partnerships, and some require an elementary division of labor (Shover 1973). All rely on supporting contacts and networks.

West's description can be restated in the following form. Minor delicts and theft are part of class culture and its organization in American society. Many youths engage in such behavior while growing up. Theft is common among preadolescent and adolescent peer groups. Minor delinquencies, such as truancy, theft, and vandalism, are committed at early ages. What is critical is how some get channeled into becoming high-rate or specialized offenders, such as in occupational theft. Loosely structured groups in networks are critical, perhaps, in leading to high-rate offending careers. To develop an occupational specialization in theft, one needs older offenders who serve as models and who inculcate necessary skills. Once the skills are acquired, however, whether an offense is committed with accomplices depends on whether a division of labor is required to commit the crime or whether one seeks to reduce risks by taking accomplices. Shoplifting can be done alone, for example, but risk may be reduced if an accomplice distracts clerks or watches for security personnel. Accomplices may, however, lower skill levels and increase the risk of apprehension.

From this perspective, the role of groups in recruiting members and inducing persons to offend with them is overstated. For, as W. G. West, Suttles, and others contend, the culture, group organization, and networks that constitute daily life in many neighborhoods create the necessary ecological environment for the development of offending careers.

All too little is known about how individual offending careers intersect and how such intersections are determined by individual and collective patterns of group affiliation and recruitment. Studies are needed that examine the intersection of careers for a cohort of offenders to determine the extent to which the members of a group contribute to one another's offending. But, since demographic processes and individual choice lead to selection of accomplices from outside the cohort, the study population must include all co-offenders of the cohort. Some indication of how substantial the external set of accomplices can be is found in Sarnecki's (1982) Swedish cohort study. The original cohort consisted of all persons born between 1957 and 1968 who were resident in the community and who the police concluded had committed at least one crime in the community between January 1, 1975, and December 31, 1977. There were 575 such individuals. But two additional study populations were added as the cohort's offending histories were followed. The first comprised those individuals who were born before 1957 but who police concluded had committed a crime during the study period with someone in the 1957–68 cohort or who had committed a crime with a juvenile who, in turn, had committed a crime with someone in the original cohort. The second group included persons who police concluded had committed a crime with someone in the 1957–68 cohort during the follow-up period from January 1, 1978, to December 31, 1980. These two additional populations included 259 individuals, so the total population studied was 834 individuals (Sarnecki 1982, pp. 50–51).

High-rate offenders may be youths who are highly susceptible to overtures from any offender to join in committing a delinquent act. Their high rate of offending with many different offenders could thus result from their being "joiners" rather than recruiters. Both the Peoria (Peoria Crime Reduction Council 1979) and the Swedish studies provide some evidence that it is primarily a recruiter effect. High-offenders who frequently change co-offenders may actually be composed of subpopulations of "joiners" or "recruits" and "recruiters."

Tracing the web of these relationships, Sarnecki became aware that the high-rate offenders were linked to other offending groups and individuals outside the city as members of groups extended their territorial range in the search for accomplices. By age eighteen to twenty, the cohort members still active in crime became part of new gangs that represented larger and larger areas and were increasingly composed of more high-rate offenders. The most active juveniles with high rates of offending thus became affiliated with groups whose members encompassed an entire city and, eventually, several cities (Sarnecki 1982, p. 241). Sarnecki even suggests that the web of affiliations over the careers of the most active members of this small group of gangs in one city links into a network that encompassed all the major gangs in Sweden. These remarks emphasize again the importance of looking at offending networks and the roles that individuals play in them. Some of the most effective intervention may lie in selecting individuals in terms of their place in offending networks.

Each offender potentially recruits others to offend together in a criminal incident since each may search for an accomplice. Yet, some offenders may be more open to recruitment and others to be recruiters. Evidence examined below strongly suggests that some offenders actively recruit co-offenders. Given their high individual rates of offending, recruiters seem more likely to recruit persons whose individual rate of offending is below theirs. These recruitments may well account for a considerable portion of a recruit's offending.

Evidence that there are recruiters comes from the Peoria juvenile residential burglary study. Recall that there were 306 residential burglaries, 151 of which involved at least two co-offenders (Peoria Crime Reduction Council 1979). Of these, seventy-four—or 49 percent—involved at least one offender who was previously apprehended and at least one who was never previously apprehended. This result is consistent with the view that an experienced offender selects a less experienced one. These juvenile "recruiters"—the recidivists apprehended with a first-time arrested—could logically be targets for special treatment.

Substantial evidence that there are recruiters is also found in Sarnecki's Swedish study. The thirty-five delinquents with the highest individual rates of offending had a total of 224 accomplices in crime, or one-third of all juveniles in the study population (Sarnecki 1982, p. 209). These high-rate offenders generally did not offend with the same accomplices in very many offenses, which strongly suggests they actively recruited other offenders. Moreover, Sarnecki found that, when high-rate offenders joined less criminally active groups, they recruited members to offending and appeared to introduce new members to a criminal career (p. 236). Finally, the most criminally active committed offenses with co-offenders from a larger territorial area (p. 171), which suggests that they were recruiting from a larger network.[5]

There is evidence, then, that individuals with high rates of offending often commit offenses with accomplices, most of whom have lower offending rates. Most of these high-rate offenders keep the same accomplice for only a short period of time. Thus, high-rate offenders commit

[5] Sarnecki was well aware that limiting the study to juveniles with police contacts and relying on official reports of delinquency limited the size of the network and its population and may have biased results in other ways (Sarnecki 1982, p. 235).

offenses with a substantial number of different accomplices and so must continually search for new accomplices. Still, they are not precluded from also committing some sizable proportion of offenses alone, and that often seems to be the case, increasingly so, perhaps, as they get older.[6]

D. Recruiter Effects on Offending

The review of patterns of lone and co-offending and their relation to individual rates of offending leads to a number of conclusions that have policy implications.

First, a relatively small number of very high rate youthful offenders can be identified retrospectively at a fairly young age (see, e.g., Blumstein, Farrington, and Moitra 1985). Their prevalence in a population of offenders will vary by age and place of residence. If these high-rate offenders could be identified and isolated prospectively, a substantial number of juvenile crimes, both those they commit alone and those attributable to recruiting others, could be averted. Moreover, to the degree that their incarceration deters or reduces the offending rate of a sizable proportion of their accomplices, considerable additional reductions in crime might be expected since it seems likely that these high-rate offenders seek accomplices who might otherwise not be as active in offending.

Second, although just under two-thirds of all crimes against persons and their property are estimated to have but a single offender (Reiss 1980, table 1), an estimated two-thirds of all offenders commit their crimes as members of groups (Reiss 1980, table 2). Roughly a third of all offenders offend in groups of four or more persons. Where group offending is involved, one would have to incapacitate a substantial proportion of the offending population since there is on the whole very little overlap in accomplices from one offense to the next, especially among older youthful and young adult high-rate offenders.

Third, the most efficient gains in reducing the crime rate might be made by incapacitating high-rate offenders who commit most of their offenses alone. But their number may be trivial even in the population of high-rate offenders. Indeed, since high-rate youthful offenders involve a substantial number of accomplices, and since the size of the

---

[6] Research is needed on the group composition of offenses in offending histories by age of offenders and accomplices.

offending group decreases with the age of offenders, it may be more efficient to incapacitate young high-rate offenders who are also recruiters.

Fourth, links among accomplices in offending provide a means to identify such high-rate individual offenders for intervention strategies. The use of network information may substantially increase the capacity to select high-rate offenders who account for the offending of others. Such identification requires that records be kept that uniquely identify all persons engaging in offenses. The Swedish police information system provides opportunities to trace such offenders, as does that of the police in Japan. Typically, U.S. juvenile courts uniquely identify offenders by name, family, personal characteristics, and address. They commonly identify co-offenders by name only, making little systematic effort to link co-offender records to each offending career. Similarly, although an adult police arrest record typically lists co-offenders arrested, no effort is made to select those individuals who may be systematic recruiters of accomplices.

Studies of offending and recruitment suggest that early intervention in the careers of high-rate offenders is possible by selecting those youths who fit the recruiter pattern characterized by a high individual rate of offending with a large number of different accomplices.

V. Models of Co-offending

One can postulate three kinds of criminal careers characterized by distinct types of offenders and patterns of offending. The first type of offender always offends alone. The second always offends with others. The third, by far the most common career, is characterized by both solo and co-offending.

The solo offender is relatively rare. For some, such as murderers, careers are very short, usually being limited to a single offense. Others begin their careers as solo offenders who commit a particular offense and never any other. This is characteristic of many sex offenders and is especially so for certain kinds of sex offending, such as voyeurism and pedophilia. Just how common a long career of solo offending is cannot be determined from existing investigations. Apart from sex offending, confidence forms of fraud, family assaults, and certain white-collar offending (e.g., embezzlement), most solo offending careers are probably of short duration.

There is also little known about careers characterized exclusively by group offending. Political criminals, such as terrorists, may be exclusively group offenders. A substantial proportion of very young delinquents who have short careers offend only with others. Indeed, desistance rates are probably greatest at young ages, often following a first apprehension (Wolfgang, Figlio, and Sellin 1972, pp. 87–89).

Generally, however, most criminal careers that endure are characterized by a diverse mix of individual and accomplice offending. It has long been known that most adult criminal careers in common crime begin with a juvenile delinquency career. Further, it is commonly assumed that most careers begin with at least a predominance of co-offending and that the rate of solo offending increases with age. This conclusion is based on the evidence previously summarized in this essay. First, solo offending is relatively uncommon at young ages and does not become the modal form of offending until the late teens or early twenties. Second, the mean number of co-offenders in crimes declines with age; incidents with three offenders become relatively uncommon after age twenty and with four or more become infrequent at an earlier age, perhaps by age seventeen. Third, solo offending begins to rise sharply at ages fifteen to sixteen, shortly before the peak age of juvenile offending, and becomes the dominant form of offending at about age twenty.

Yet, information from longitudinal studies of criminal careers is lacking that would determine whether aggregate statistics support the contention that offenders move from predominantly co-offending to predominantly solo offending in the course of a criminal career. Before alternative explanations for these aggregate changes are offered, several other findings merit attention because they are consistent with some alternative explanations. First, the peak participation rate in offending occurs around age seventeen or eighteen; the absolute size of the offender population declines rapidly thereafter. Second, there is a desistance from offending at every age but especially so in the early teens. Third, there are many careers of one or two offenses, and these predominate at the very young ages. Fourth, the participation rate declines markedly in the early twenties, suggesting either substantial desistance, declining average individual rates of offending, or both. Fifth, the proportionate increase in solo offending is largely at the expense of a decrease in offending by three or more offenders; the proportion of offenses committed by pairs remains fairly constant from late juvenile years through at least the mid-twenties. Sixth, juvenile offending networks are relatively unstable and few are linked to adult networks.

A number of models of co-offending in criminal careers can be postulated that are consistent with most, if not all, of the observations.

A *stochastic model* might provide a reasonable fit. One would expect that, as the size of the offending population decreases, especially in local areas, there would be fewer offenses with three or more co-offenders and more pair and solo offending. The rather steep rise in solo offending in the mid-teens, however, casts some doubt on how well such a model would fit if appropriate data were available to test it.

A *dynamic population model* assumes that offenders have considerable residential mobility, especially as they reach the point of establishing independence from their families. Residential and occupational mobility weaken group ties. Co-offending that is based on prior acquaintance with others should decline as age increases. Those offenders who remain active must either commit offenses alone or search for similar unaffiliated co-offenders. Since groups larger than two persons generally are unnecessary, the search can be truncated when one co-offender is found.

A *functional model* assumes that co-offending is necessary to commit at least some crimes. Whenever a division of labor is required to commit a particular offense, co-offending is necessary. The necessity for specialized skills, such as picking a lock, and for collaboration, such as driving an escape vehicle, are examples. Co-offending also may reduce the risk of apprehension, as when an accomplice diverts attention from the crime scene. Not uncommonly, moreover, offenders seem to require social support to plan and commit an offense. Social support appears to be more characteristic of juvenile than of adult offending since juvenile offending seems more closely linked to daily routines and activities. Most juvenile groups provide social support for characteristically juvenile crimes, such as vandalism or shoplifting.

This functional model is consistent with the selective attrition of low-offending persons, the decrease in the size of offending groups with the age of offenders, and the increase in solo offending by adults in offenses that usually do not require a division of labor. Yet, the functional model does not seem to account very well for the mix of solo and co-offending crime incidents characteristic of many criminal careers.

A *selective attrition of group offenders* or a *solo survivor model* tries to account for the sharp decline in co-offending with age, especially of large groups, and, correlatively, the marked increase in solo offending. The more general explanatory problem is whether the sharp rise in solo offending results from a greater survival of solo offenders and the selective attrition of co-offenders in a population of offenders or from a gradual shift of persisters from accomplice to solo offending. Several explanations seem worth exploring.

First, certain kinds of high-rate career offenders may shift towards solo offending because they require a substantial cash flow. This is characteristic, for example, of drug addicts who must commit a number of crimes each day to support their addiction, especially at the peak of dependence. The necessity to acquire cash quickly can lead to solo offending. The addict may consume search time in locating a buy rather than in locating co-offenders or be unwilling to take the time to commit enough crimes to split the income with a co-offender before making a buy. One expects drug dependence to create a substantial rise in solo offending for property crimes that provide cash, especially robbery. Nonaddict offenders, moreover, may shun offending with addicts because an addict in need of a fix may take risks that create a higher risk of apprehension.

Second, the mix of offenses in an offending career usually changes substantially over time. Very young offenders commit such accomplice offenses as vandalism and gang fighting. Later careers are characterized largely by offenses that can be committed alone—burglaries, thefts, armed robberies, and assaults.

Third, group offenders may be more likely to desist because their networks and group affiliations change substantially with age. There is considerable evidence that juvenile groups are unstable and do not persist for long and that many youth groups do not persist into the young adult years. Indeed, it seems reasonable to assume that the network structure of local communities is age graded so that, as offenders age, they move into adult networks, which are less likely to provide informal support for offending.[7] Attrition can be expected in any transitional process. We need to learn more about how such network transitions are made and how they affect offending behavior. It is likely that adult networks on the whole facilitate individual rather than group search behavior. Moreover, it is likely that the adult networks that facilitate individual searches for co-offenders are less cohesive and clique oriented than are those of juveniles. They also are more covert.

Research on criminal careers is needed to determine which of these explanations accounts for the aggregate shift towards solo offending. If it turns out that juveniles who shift early to high-rate, solo offending

[7] Excluding formally organized group behavior in which participation increases with age, it can be speculated that the propensity to do almost any activity alone or in pairs increases with age. But just what causes these changes is not well understood; maturation is a description, not an explanation, of what is taking place with age.

are most likely to have high-rate careers as adults, they are candidates for early intervention. What may be of special concern for timing incapacitative forms of intervention is identifying such individuals and detecting when the shift to predominantly solo offending occurs.

VI. Group Offending and Desistance

Earlier it was conjectured that the shift towards solo offending with age might occur because accomplice offenders desist at an early age. More generally, the question arises of whether, because of group processes, affiliation with groups affects offenders' desistance probabilities. This section reviews several empirical studies of desistance that take into account group characteristics and speculates on how group processes may enter into selective attrition from offending.

A. Empirical Studies of Desistance from Group Offending

There clearly is desistance from offending at every age. The reasons for desisting may well vary with career survival time. Some criminal histories are of very short duration, especially for those who enter at a very young age; others offend over a long period and desist or reduce their rate of offending substantially only at an advanced age (Blumstein, Farrington, and Moitra 1985). How these points in an offender's history determine the rate and form of desistance is explored below. Since most offenders begin offending by age sixteen, and since desistance rates appear to be greatest soon after entry, one expects greater aggregate desistance before age twenty than after.

Knight and West (1975) report on temporary and continuing delinquents in a long-term survey of a cohort of 411 boys in a working-class London neighborhood (see also West 1969). They selected eighty-three boys who constituted the most delinquent fifth of their cohort on the basis of prior convictions or admissions of delinquency. The eighty-three delinquents were divided into two groups. One group of thirty-three was labeled "temporary" delinquents because each had no official record of delinquency since turning age seventeen and denied committing any offenses at age eighteen to nineteen. The second group of forty-eight was labeled "continuing" delinquents because each had one or more major offenses.[8] Temporary delinquents were conviction free for a period of at least three years; continuing delinquents had a continuing record of convictions or acknowledged offenses.

---

[8] Two youths are not included in the analysis because they were not interviewed at ages eighteen to nineteen. One was killed in an accident at age seventeen, and the other was a fugitive from justice and could not be traced (Knight and West 1975, p. 43).

The largest single difference between the youths in these two groups was their involvement with adolescent peers in offending. Both official records and self-reports disclose that the continuing delinquents were more likely to commit their offenses alone. None of the official records for the temporary delinquents stated a boy was convicted alone, compared with 14 percent of the convictions for the continuing delinquents, a difference that was significant even when the larger number of convictions for continuing delinquents was taken into account. Although it is clear that the large majority of convictions for continuing offenders involved co-offending offenses, temporary delinquents had been involved only in co-offending (Knight and West 1975, p. 45).

Some explanation for this difference may be found in offenders' reported involvement in adolescent peer groups. Knight and West, like Scott (1956), found that involvement with peer groups declines with age and can be short lived. Temporary delinquents reported greater abandonment of their adolescent male peer groups than did continuing delinquents. Although all but one of the temporary delinquents had reported going about in an adolescent peer group of four or more boys between the ages of fifteen and seventeen, somewhat less than half of them said they were doing so at age seventeen and a half. The involvement of roughly 80 percent of the continuing delinquents in groups of this size remained unchanged during these years (Knight and West 1975, pp. 45–46). In disengaging from peer groups, the temporary delinquents did not become social isolates. Rather, they generally began to go about with only one or two companions in contrast to their earlier participation with four or more.

It is apparent once again that youths with more serious offenses that occur at a higher rate and who continue in delinquency include some who exhibit solo offending while continuing to associate with the members of network groups with which they are affiliated. In some sense the network may serve as a reference group and perhaps also as a resource for recruiting accomplices for offending since persisting offenders maintain a mix of individual and co-offending.

Suttles's (1968) work suggests that dropping out from the larger participatory group is a function of both mobility to other neighborhoods and a shift to more conventional roles, such as work, marriage, and military service, that bring new forms of association. In addition to the 41 percent of the Addams-area youths who quit their neighborhood group because they moved to another area of Chicago, 26 percent left Chicago for jobs or military service. Another 30 percent either married or went to work in Chicago. Only one left to serve a prison term, and only one left because he decided he did not want to belong to the group. The effect leaving has on offending behavior is unclear in Suttles's study, but the development of conventional bonds and the severing of old ties by moving out of the neighborhood or entering military service could account for a sizable proportion of desistance in the late teens and early twenties. The importance of environmental as well as status transitions on desistance rates is buttressed by a major study of adults paroled directly to the U.S. Army in World War II. Mattick (1960, pp. 49–50) found that the one-year parole violation rate was 5.2 percent for parolees in the army, compared with 22.6 percent for civilian parolees. Moreover, only 10.5 percent of the army parolees had committed an offense within eight years of discharge from prison, compared with an expected recidivism rate of 66.6 percent (1960, p. 54).

West (1978) found that just over half of forty high-rate juvenile thieves had retired from active criminality by age twenty. Comparing these "reformed" criminals with those who were still "active," West found that 86 percent of the reformed criminals, compared with only 11 percent of those still active, had formed conventional bonds with a woman, a job, or schooling (West 1978, p. 186). Of course, it is difficult from these behavioral data to determine whether the forming of the bond led to the desistance or whether the bond was formed as a means of escaping from a pattern of offending in a social network. Moreover, it is unknown whether those who were still active and had not formed such bonds had tried but failed to do so. The causal ordering of variables accounting for desistance is not easily resolved either theoretically or empirically.

Knight and West (1975) concluded that the delinquency of temporary delinquents is dominated by group solidarity rather more than by individual motivation to offend. As group offenders mature, many shift towards conventional work and family roles and to going about with one or two of "the boys" to sports events and bars or pubs. The "true" transient group delinquent in this sense is more likely to be a temporary delinquent whose affiliation is broken by transiency or by maturation into more conventional roles.

B. Group Processes in Selective Attrition from Criminal Careers

This section attempts to account for the selective attrition of accomplice offenders. In doing so, explanations are posited of how group and network processes account for desistance. Three explanatory models of desistance are presented—specific deterrence, status transitions, and disruption of group affiliations.

1. *Specific Deterrence.* This model assumes that punishing an offender not only leads the offender to desist but has consequences for the offending of friends and acquaintances as well. It assumes, moreover, that an individual is inducted into offending by others, often as a member of a family or peer group, and continues to offend with one or more accomplices until apprehended. The sanction of being caught (particularly if reinforced by parental or other sanctions) leads that individual to desist from offending. The experience of being sanctioned has a specific deterrent effect on the offender. Apprehending and punishing a member of a clique may increase the likelihood that other members, especially accomplices who are not punished, will also desist. The perception of the risk of being caught is increased by apprehension followed by punishment. This is a special kind of specific deterrence whereby the punishment of some specific and significant other leads to desistance. It is critical that one knows the person who is being punished and, consequently, has a more direct basis for vicariously experiencing the punishment and calculating one's risk.

This model probably accounts for much of the desistance at young ages and early in an offending career. The desistance rate is greatest following the first apprehension (Wolfgang, Figlio, and Sellin 1972, p. 87).

2. *Status Transitions.* Adolescence in American society is characterized by the substitution of peer for parental relationships and control, especially for males. As boys grow up, peer groups lose some of their influence and control over those affiliated with them. This loss of influence is closely tied to status transitions, particularly those connected with the transition to adult status. But from early adolescence on, individuals make transitions to more conforming affiliations. Such transitions decrease the influence of nonconforming peers.

This model can account for the desistance of individuals with low rates of offending. Such offenders usually offend with accomplices. They are recruited by others to participate in offenses others initiate, and they rarely, if ever, initiate offending. They are at most peripheral members in a clique and offend as occasional recruits. With marginal affiliations with offenders, they desist after one or a few such experiences because they find conforming activities more rewarding and less risky or because they are not selected as accomplices. These low-rate offenders normally desist in the early adolescent years.

This second model is especially germane, however, for persons who participate in delinquency as part of diversified peer activity. This is generally characteristic of the behavior of young males in peer activities, such as athletics, or as participants in street-corner society. Here one is gradually drawn into the cultural life-style of one's social class, including delinquency if that is part of that life-style. With aging, members turn to courtship, marriage, and having children as well as to regular employment to fulfill family responsibilities. They may withdraw from their peer group to assume these adult roles. Women and family may play a role in weaning the male delinquent from his peer group. Desistance, in this model, is a function of movement to adult status. This pattern probably explains the desistance of many lower-class ethnic males in the United States in their young adult years.

The desistance of group offenders may result not only directly from the declining influence of peers on a member's behavior but also from the indirect effect this has on group cohesiveness and the selection of co-offenders. With declining cohesiveness, groups become vulnerable to dissolution. There appears to be some discontinuity between the individual's maturation and group adaptation to the changing requirements of its members. Since such transitions do not occur at the same rate for all members, the group experiences selective attrition that gradually weakens it. Most groups cannot recruit replacements because the pool of those eligible also declines with transition to adult status. Failing to recruit enough members to maintain its status quo, the group disintegrates.

Much desistance of accomplice offenders and co-offending may be tied to the fate of the particular groups to which they belonged. Individuals who depend primarily on co-offending with accomplices affiliated with a particular group or network are particularly vulnerable to its demise. Inasmuch as the demise of delinquent peer groups is most commonly associated with the transition of their members from juvenile to adult status, group demise should account for at least some of the desistance of group offenders in their late teens. Desistance in this second model does not depend on apprehension and punishment. The model is consistent with explanations of selective attrition of accomplice offenders.

3. *Disruption of Group Affiliation.*   Individuals are particularly vulnerable to the disruption or dissolution of group ties. Where such ties are primarily responsible for or play a major role in reinforcing one's delinquent or criminal behavior, breaking them may lead to desistance.

This is especially likely to occur when the individual is unable to replace those bonds with others that permit continuation of the behavior. The three major ways that group bonds and affiliations that reinforce offending are dissolved are through residential mobility of an offender, affiliation with a total institution, and the dissolution of the reinforcing group itself.

Residential mobility breaks ties and makes problematic any reincorporation into a new group in the area to which one moves. Those who are unlikely to offend without group support drop out if they cannot affiliate with a new offending group or find accomplices. Residential mobility is often combined with other forms of social mobility, such as getting advanced schooling or a job or joining a military organization.

Total institutions also may affect desistance from careers. Two types of total institutions can have important consequences for desistance from criminal careers: prisons and the military. Incarceration affects one's position in a group, and, if that group still exists on release, one may have difficulty reentering. By disrupting patterns of search for co-offenders, incarceration may also shift offenders from predominantly accomplice to predominantly solo offending. Apart from disrupting co-offending patterns, incarceration may also have specific deterrent effects, especially for young group offenders. If so, incapacitation at young ages may be a viable strategy to bring about desistance from offending.[9]

Another major source of desistance through entry into a conventional total institution is the military. Some criminal careers obviously go on in the military, but many appear to be broken. Mattick (1960) found that 87 percent of the Illinois inmates paroled to the army were given honorable discharges and that their recidivism rates were far below those of civilian parolees. Research is necessary to examine the effect of military, merchant marine, and other forms of service on interrupting and terminating contemporary criminal careers since Mattick's (1958, 1960) research was on parole to the World War II army. Service in conventional total institutions is a potential alternative source of intervention in criminal careers.

This third model suggests that breaking group ties and relationships

---

[9] Imprisonment also introduces one to new offenders and networks. Just how influential such ties are on one's offending after leaving prison is not known. Such ties may not be as important as is commonly assumed because inmates with close ties are usually not released at the same time, and such ties and prison attitudes become less influential as release nears (Wheeler 1961).

may be a critical factor in desistance from offending. The breaking of bonds is facilitated by forming new relationships or movement to new environments. Such ties are most likely to be broken in the late teens or early adult years. Offenders who continue to offend after these years may be those who usually commit offenses alone or who select different accomplices, often strangers, for each offense. The adult career offender, then, is characterized by transient relationships with other offenders. Relationships with co-offenders are instrumentally contrived rather than being by-products of group affiliation.

VII. Intervention Issues and Co-offending

Co-offending is most characteristic of what we think of as juvenile delinquency and characterizes juvenile careers. Characteristically, the juvenile court deals with co-offenders rather than with a solo offender when considering a particular offense for which the juvenile is apprehended. Moreover, the juvenile career is more likely to be characterized by a predominance of accomplice offending when compared with adult careers. Additionally, the juvenile court is better able than is a criminal court to consider co-offenders in dispositions because it is less bound by many of the procedural safeguards attending criminal proceedings and by the obligation to try facts without knowledge of the prior record and current status of the offender and co-offenders. The juvenile court has greater latitude to investigate and dispose of matters involving joint offending and joint careers. When siblings are involved in juvenile offending, there is greater opportunity for family intervention. Given this greater latitude in investigating, examining, and disposing of juvenile cases and the fact that most adult criminal careers are initiated in the juvenile years, serious consideration must be given to identification of and intervention in those juvenile careers most likely to lead to adult careers. A number of issues relating to such interventions are examined below.

A. Probability of Being Caught in Co-offending

Earlier, attention was drawn to whether co-offending is more likely to lead to apprehension than is solo offending and whether risks of apprehension increase with the number of offenders in a criminal incident. Also, a current offender's probability of being apprehended as either a juvenile or an adult may well be a function of his prior record.

It seems reasonable to conclude that risk of apprehension is a function both of the individual's rate of offending and the rates of co-offenders. At least for juveniles, high-rate offenders with accomplices are more likely to engage in crimes than are those who commit the same acts alone (Hindelang 1976*b*, p. 122). There may also be interaction effects between an individual's rate of offending, the group mix of an individual's offenses, and the offending rates of co-offenders.

Inasmuch as one of the major ways of estimating an individual's rate of offending is from official records of apprehensions, it is important to know whether the probability of apprehension is substantially greater for accomplice offenders than for lone offenders who have the same individual rate of offending. This may well vary with age so that the risk of apprehension is a function of whether an individual offends alone or with others at both older and younger ages. It is also important to know whether apprehension is more likely to occur for a co-offending than for a solo offense, even for those careers characterized by a substantial proportion of solo offenses. Using official records of apprehension will substantially underestimate the individual rate of offending for those who engage predominantly in solo offenses and may overestimate the rate for accomplice offenders if the two are not distinguished.

Just how much the individual rate of offending, in comparison with the co-offender status of an offense, increases the risk of apprehension is most problematic for offenses against the person. A predominantly solo pattern of offending may disproportionately consist of nonstranger crimes against the person since that arrest rate is a function of victim identification at the time of the complaint. The rates of apprehension for solo offenses against persons who are strangers and against property may be substantially lower than those for others at risk. This suggests that it is important to separate solo from co-offending rates by type of offense in assessing apprehension risks.

B. Early Identification of Career Criminals

One of the barriers to early identification of adult career criminals has been that the high apprehension rate of juveniles creates a large population of offenders. Moreover, it is commonly presumed that at young ages it is difficult to distinguish high-rate from low-rate offenders. The Wolfgang, Figlio, and Sellin (1972) retrospective cohort study supports this conclusion by reporting probabilities of committing a next offense that are derived from the number of prior offenses and by reporting transition probabilities that are based on number and prior offense type. These probabilities were based on the entire juvenile career without respect to annualized individual rates of offending or to the time between offenses. This may be important information that may help to identify high-rate juvenile offenders at a fairly early age.

There is, of course, the possibility that many early high-rate offenders desist from a criminal career well before adulthood. There is no strong evidence that this is the case, however, and there is evidence that high-rate adult offenders can be identified by their juvenile offending rates (Chaiken and Chaiken 1982; Blumstein, Farrington, and Moitra 1985).

It has been suggested here that there is an important subset of juvenile offenders that should be identified for special adjudication. These are the high-rate offenders who have high rates of recruiting co-offenders. They would appear to be easily identified by both their high individual rates of offending and the number of offenses they commit with a large number of different co-offenders. It should be possible to distinguish between those high-rate co-offenders whose rate is primarily dependent on affiliation with a small number of co-offenders and those who are continually involved with new accomplices. Moreover, there is some evidence that these recruiters affect the participation rate of their co-offenders as well as the co-offenders' rates of offending. If that is the case, they are especially opportune targets for early intervention. In any event, the evidence presented suggests that the recruiter population for juvenile offenders is a small enough subset to warrant considering early intervention in their careers, perhaps even with strategies of incapacitation, since their incapacitation may have a marked effect not only on the aggregate crime rate but on participation and desistance rates of co-offenders as well. Investigation into these early intervention possibilities and their effects would add appreciably to our understanding of early criminal careers and the possibilities for intervening in them.

C. Sanctioning Co-offenders

Our adult system of justice is to a substantial degree based on preserving the individual integrity of co-offenders as they are processed in the criminal justice system. This means that not only must their individual history of offending generally be disregarded when trying a current set of charges but also individuals involved in the same offense can be treated differently on the basis of their role in the charged offenses. Differences in individual offenders' offending or personal histories can be taken into account at sentencing. The particular doctrine of sentencing will determine what will or may be taken into account, but there is a general presumption that the disposition for one offender need not be contingent on that of another. As noted above, the juvenile court has not been bound as tightly by these considerations and hence may have considerably more latitude to consider alternative strategies for sanctioning accomplices in an offense. Unfortunately, very little evidence about the effects of differences in sanctioning co-offenders is available to guide such choices.

One of the important issues in juvenile sanctioning is the extent to which early sanctioning may be a specific and a general deterrent to offending. It has been suggested here that punishment of an individual's co-offenders may increase the sense of risk. Also worth considering are whether early sanctioning of all co-offenders increases the desistance rate and whether differential sanctioning for offenders in the same offense has different specific deterrent and desistance effects for co-offenders. Where offenders are linked in the same networks, overlap in offending careers should be expected. Each of these careers can be treated independently to determine the extent to which sanctioning interventions affect each career.

D. Intervention Strategies and Co-offending

Intervention strategies disrupt the lives of individuals and affect their criminal careers. Although many interventions are individual-change strategies, some aim to change the external conditions believed to cause the behavior of individuals. Klein and Crawford (1967, pp. 65–66) concluded that "elimination of external sources of cohesiveness of gangs, in most cases, would be followed by dissolution of a relatively large proportion of gang membership." They reached this position by observing that the internal sources of gang cohesion are weak and that the gang is maintained by strong external pressures (p. 66). From this perspective, juvenile gangs are rather fragile entities. They lack the stability of internally generated group goals, have high turnover in membership, generate few unique group norms, and lack a lasting identity with a group name (Klein and Crawford 1967, p. 66). There is also considerable evidence that these internally unstable gangs are kept together by external pressures, such as conflict with other groups (Klein and Crawford 1967, pp. 65–66) or political activity (Jacobs 1976; Short and Moland 1976).

Disrupting the internal structure of such gangs to diminish their members' delinquency is not likely to be successful. Klein and Crawford (1967) concluded that interventions by group workers with black delinquent gangs in Los Angeles tended to increase the social cohesiveness of the gangs, thereby resulting in increased individual rates of offending. Similarly, Short and Strodtbeck (1965) concluded that disrupting the gang leadership in the black gangs they studied failed to disrupt the gang and may actually have contributed to increased rates of minor delinquent acts.

Although the group workers' intervention strategies that aimed at disrupting group structure and processes may not have achieved their intended result, other strategies of intervention aimed at disrupting networks may, nonetheless, be consequential for individual careers. Klein and Crawford (1967) suggested that strategies that weaken group cohesion may have that effect.

Incapacitation of offenders similarly does not necessarily disrupt gang structure. Jacobs (1976, 1977, 1983) described the U.S. prison of the 1960s and 1970s in our most urbanized states as organized around an inmate system that was an extension of the gang organization and the conflict relations from which the prison population was drawn. He suggested, moreover, that the prison society tended to increase the cohesion of those gangs and their importance to their members because they performed a wide variety of functions for them. The gangs also recruited members within the prison, especially as the inmate system became politicized (Jacobs 1976, 1977, pp. 145–49). On release, a substantial number of the recruits and many of the former members of the supergangs (which include juvenile and adult divisions in the community and in juvenile and adult correctional institutions) retained ties with at least some former gang members. The prison of this period appeared to extend the network of adult co-offenders through inmate recruitment into the gangs while incarcerated, and it sustained at least some of them on release.

E. Group Recruitment and Replacement Processes

When more than one individual is involved in offending, incapacitation of one of the offenders will not necessarily affect the crime rate. Much depends on what happens to the individual rate of offending of co-offenders. The current practice is to discount the "crimes saved" through incapacitation of an offender by weighting the individual's contribution to the incident, using the mean size of offending groups for that offense. If the mean size of offenders is two, for example, an individual's crime saved is calculated as half. Yet, there is no empirical evidence to conclude that individuals reduce their crime rate, on the average, in this way. There is some reason to believe they might not. One would expect that the incapacitation of recruiters, for example, would have a far greater effect on the crime rate than would the incapacitation of followers or many of their co-offenders, even granted equal rates of offending.

What is needed is a comparison of overlapping criminal careers to determine whether incapacitation in the career of any offender has any effect on the individual rate of offending of his co-offenders subsequent to incapacitation. Because the more organized gangs of career criminals may be more adept at recruiting replacements for incarcerated members, incarceration may save only those crimes that are solo offenses. If so, one should not only aim to incapacitate individuals with high solo offending rates but expect little effect from incapacitating individuals who have high co-offending rates as accomplices. If this were to be verified empirically, one would also expect to gain less from incapacitating juveniles than adults since their solo offending rates are, on the average, lower.

One might also expect to gain more by disrupting processes of recruitment and replacement of co-offenders in juvenile than in adult populations since juvenile networks that facilitate offending are seemingly based more on solidaristic and personal relationships than on rational choice and impersonal contact. For most juveniles, the selection of co-offenders is far more restricted than it is for adults, as they are limited to one neighborhood and its environs. We need to know more about how adults recruit their co-offenders and the extent to which their co-offenders are dispersed rather than concentrated in space and time. We clearly need both ethnographic and network studies of adult offending populations to explore these issues of co-offending and their effects.

Research on co-offending is disproportionately concentrated on juveniles and has focused almost exclusively on documenting how pervasive it is and on speculating on its role in the etiology of delinquency. The etiological questions therefore remain murky, and the consequences of groups for criminal career development remain unexplored. We need, therefore, to devote far more attention to detailed studies of offending careers and to pay special attention to co-offending in those careers, treating each individual's career in terms of its intersections with others. Not only do such investigations provide sociometric information so that techniques such as block modeling (White, Boorman, and Breiger 1976) can isolate particular networks, but also they permit us to examine how criminal justice interventions have consequences for the offending of all individuals in the same network.

Examination of the consequences of solo and co-offending is but part of a larger need to order over time the life events of offenders with their offending histories. Further study of co-offending requires far more information on how juvenile and adult careers are linked. Information linking criminal careers must be obtained from prospective longitudinal cohort studies that approximate more closely the design of the Swedish community study undertaken by Sarnecki (1982). That design is based on a social-network approach and expands the study population to include all co-offenders who are not initially part of the cohort. It is well to bear in mind that in a dynamic society there is considerable movement into and out of communities and that individuals are drawn into different networks over time. The artificial divorce of the cohort from a changing environment and its reduction to a population of individuals unrelated in time and space restrict considerably what can be learned about individual careers.

REFERENCES

Blakely, R., P. S. Stephenson, and H. Nichol. 1974. "Social Factors in a Random Sample of Juvenile Delinquents and Controls." *International Journal of Social Psychiatry* 20:203–17.

Blumstein, A., J. Cohen, J. A. Roth, and C. A. Visher, eds. 1986. *Criminal Careers and "Career Criminals."* Vol. 2. Washington, D.C.: National Academy Press.

Blumstein, A., D. Farrington, and S. Moitra. 1985. "Delinquency Careers: Innocents, Desisters, and Persisters." In *Crime and Justice: An Annual Review of Research*, vol. 6, edited by M. Tonry and N. Morris. Chicago: University of Chicago Press.

Bordua, D. J. 1961. "Delinquent Subcultures: Sociological Interpretations of Gang Delinquency." *Annals of the American Academy of Political and Social Science* 338:120–36.

———. 1962. "Some Comments on Theories of Group Delinquency." *Sociological Inquiry* 32:245–46.

Bottoms, A., and P. Wiles. 1986. "Housing Tenure and Changing Crime Careers in Britain." In *Communities and Crime*, edited by A. J. Reiss, Jr., and M. Tonry. Vol. 8 of *Crime and Justice: A Review of Research*, edited by M. Tonry and N. Morris. Chicago: University of Chicago Press.

Breckinridge, S. P., and E. Abbot. 1917. *The Delinquent Child and the Home.* New York: Russell Sage.

Bureau of Justice Statistics. 1984. *Criminal Victimization in the United States, 1982.* National Crime Survey Report no. NCJ-92820. Washington, D.C.: U.S. Government Printing Office.

Chaiken, J., and M. Chaiken. 1982. *Varieties of Criminal Behavior.* Santa Monica, Calif.: Rand.

Cloward, R. A., and L. E. Ohlin. 1960. *Delinquency and Opportunity.* Glencoe, Ill.: Free Press.

Elliott, D. S., S. S. Ageton, D. Huizinga, B. Knowles, and R. J. Canter. 1983. *The Prevalence and Incidence of Delinquent Behavior: 1976–1980.* Boulder, Colo.: Behavioral Research Institute.

Empey, L. T. 1970. "Postscript." In *The Time Game*, edited by A. Manocchio and J. Dunn. Beverly Hills, Calif.: Sage.

Erickson, M. 1971. "The Group Context of Delinquent Behavior." *Social Problems* 19:114–29.

Eynon, T. G., and W. C. Reckless. 1961. "Companionship at Delinquency Onset." *British Journal of Criminology* 2:162–70.

Farrington, David P. 1987. "Predicting Individual Crime Rates." In *Prediction and Classification: Criminal Justice Decision Making*, edited by D. M. Gottfredson and M. Tonry. Vol. 9 of *Crime and Justice: A Review of Research*, edited by M. Tonry and N. Morris. Chicago: University of Chicago Press.

Federal Republic of Germany. 1982. *Police Statistics, 1982.* Bonn: Bundesamt.

Ferguson, T. 1952. *The Young Delinquent in His Social Setting.* London: Oxford University Press.

Gannon, T. M. 1966. "Emergence of the Defensive Gang." *Federal Probation* 30:44–48.

Glueck, S., and E. T. Glueck. 1930. *Five Hundred Criminal Careers.* New York: Knopf.

———. 1934a. *Five Hundred Delinquent Women.* New York: Knopf.

———. 1934b. *One Thousand Juvenile Delinquents.* Cambridge, Mass.: Harvard University Press.

———. 1937. *Later Criminal Careers.* New York: Commonwealth Fund.

———. 1940. *Juvenile Delinquents Grown Up.* New York: Commonwealth Fund.

———. 1943. *Criminal Careers in Retrospect.* New York: Commonwealth Fund.

———. 1946. *After Conduct of Discharged Offenders.* London: Macmillan.

———. 1950. *Unraveling Juvenile Delinquency.* New York: Commonwealth Fund.

Gould, L., E. Bittner, S. Chaneles, S. Messinger, K. Novak, and F. Powledge. 1965. *Crime as a Profession: A Report on Professional Criminals in Four American Cities.* President's Commission on Law Enforcement and Administration of Justice. Washington, D.C.: U.S. Government Printing Office.

Granovetter, M. S. 1973. "The Strength of Weak Ties." *American Journal of Sociology* 78:1360–80.

Hindelang, M. J. 1971. "The Social versus Solitary Nature of Delinquent Involvements." *British Journal of Criminology* 11:167–75.

————. 1976a. *Criminal Victimization in Eight American Cities: A Descriptive Analysis of Common Theft and Assault.* Cambridge, Mass.: Ballinger.

————. 1976b. "With a Little Help from Their Friends: Group Participation in Reported Delinquency." *British Journal of Criminology* 16:109–25.

Hood, R., and R. Sparks. 1970. *Key Issues in Criminology.* London: World University Library.

Jacobs, J. B. 1976. "Stratification and Conflict among Prison Inmates." *Journal of Criminal Law and Criminology* 66:476–82.

————. 1977. *Stateville: The Penitentiary in Mass Society.* Chicago: University of Chicago Press.

————. 1983. *New Perspectives on Prisons and Imprisonment.* Ithaca, N.Y.: Cornell University Press.

Jones, M., D. Offord, and N. Abrams. 1980. "Brothers, Sisters, and Antisocial Behavior." *British Journal of Psychiatry* 136:139–45.

Kaiser, G. 1982. *Jugendkriminalität: Rechtsbruche, Rechtsbrecher, und Opfersituationen im Jugendalter.* 3d. ed. Basel: Weinheim.

Keiser, L. 1969. *The Vice Lords: Warriors of the Streets.* New York: Holt, Rinehart & Winston.

Klein, M., and L. Y. Crawford. 1967. "Groups, Gangs and Cohesiveness." *Journal of Research in Crime and Delinquency* 4:142–65.

Klockars, C. B. 1974. *The Professional Fence.* New York: Free Press.

Knight, B. J., and D. J. West. 1975. "Temporary and Continuing Delinquency." *British Journal of Criminology* 15:43–50.

Kraeupl, G. 1969. "Der Einfluss Sozial Fehlentwickelter Jugendlicher auf die Entstehung, Entwicklung, Struktur und Funktion Krimineller Gruppen 14–25 Jähriger." *Staat und Recht* 18:63–75.

Loeber, R., and M. Stouthamer-Loeber. 1986. "Family Factors as Correlates and Predictors of Juvenile Conduct Problems and Delinquency." In *Crime and Justice: An Annual Review of Research*, vol. 7, edited by M. Tonry and N. Morris. Chicago: University of Chicago Press.

Macguire, M., and T. Bennett. 1982. *Burglary in a Dwelling.* London: Heinemann.

Mattick, Hans W. 1958. "Parole to the Army." M.A. thesis, University of Chicago, Department of Sociology.

————. 1960. "Parolees in the Army during World War II." *Federal Probation* 14:49–55.

Miller, W. B. 1958. "Lower Class Culture as a Generating Milieu of Gang Delinquency." *Journal of Social Issues* 14:5–19.

————. 1975. *Violence by Youth Gangs and Youth Groups as a Crime Problem in Major American Cities.* Washington, D.C.: U.S. Government Printing Office.

Morash, M. 1983. "Gangs, Groups, and Delinquency." *British Journal of Criminology* 23:309–31.

Olofsson, B. 1971. *Vad Var Det Vi Sa! Om Kriminellt Och Konformt Beteende Bland Skolpojkar.* Stockholm: Utbildningsforlaget.

Olson, M. R. 1977. "A Longitudinal Analysis of Official Criminal Careers." Ph.D. dissertation, Department of Sociology, University of Iowa. Ann Arbor, Mich.: University Microfilms.

Peoria Crime Reduction Council. 1979. *Criminal Activity of Juvenile Residential Burglars.* Peoria, Ill.: City of Peoria.

Petersilia, J. 1980. "Criminal Career Research: A Review of Recent Evidence." In *Crime and Justice: An Annual Review of Research,* vol. 2, edited by N. Morris and M. Tonry. Chicago: University of Chicago Press.

Polsky, N. 1969. *Hustlers, Beats and Others.* Garden City, N.Y.: Doubleday.

Pyle, G. E., E. Hanten, P. Williams, A. Pearson, J. Doyle, and K. Kwofie. 1974. *The Spatial Dynamics of Crime.* Chicago: University of Chicago, Department of Geography.

Reiss, A. J., Jr. 1967. *Studies in Crime and Law Enforcement in Major Metropolitan Areas.* Vol. 1, *Measurement of the Nature and Amount of Crime: Field Surveys III.* President's Commission of Law Enforcement and Administration of Justice. Washington, D.C.: U.S. Government Printing Office.

———. 1980. "Understanding Changes in Crime Rates." In *Indicators of Crime and Criminal Justice: Quantitative Studies,* edited by S. E. Fienberg and A. J. Reiss, Jr. Washington, D.C.: Bureau of Justice Statistics.

Reiss, A. J., Jr., and A. D. Biderman. 1980. *Data Sources on White-Collar Law-breaking.* Washington, D.C.: U.S. Department of Justice.

Sampson, R. J. 1983. "The Neighborhood Context of Criminal Victimization." Ph.D. dissertation, State University of New York at Albany.

———. 1985. "Neighborhood and Crime: The Structural Determinants of Personal Victimization." *Journal of Research in Crime and Delinquency* 22:7–40.

Sarnecki, J. 1982. *Brottslighet och Kamratrelationer: Studie av ungbrottsligheten i en svensk kommun.* Report 1982.5. Stockholm: Brottsforebyggnderadet (National Council for Crime Prevention). Portions translated in 1984 by Denise Galarraga as *Criminality and Friend Relations: A Study of Juvenile Criminality in a Swedish Community.* Washington, D.C.: National Institute of Justice, Criminal Justice Reference Service.

———. 1986. *Delinquent Networks.* Report No. 1986:1. Stockholm: National Council for Crime Prevention.

Scott, P. D. 1956. "Gangs and Delinquent Groups in London." *British Journal of Delinquency* 7:5–26.

Shannon, L. W. 1978. "A Longitudinal Study of Delinquency and Crime." In *Quantitative Studies in Criminology,* edited by C. Wellford. Beverly Hills, Calif.: Sage.

Shapland, J. 1978. "Self-reported Delinquency in Boys Aged 11 to 14." *British Journal of Criminology* 18:255–66.

Shaw, C. R. 1938. *Brothers in Crime.* Chicago: University of Chicago Press.

Shaw, C. R., and H. D. McKay. 1931. "Male Juvenile Delinquency as Group Behavior." In *Report on the Causes of Crime.* No. 13. Washington, D.C.: National Commission on Law Observance and the Administration of Justice.

Shaw, C. R., and E. D. Meyer. 1929. "The Juvenile Delinquent." In *The Illinois Crime Survey.* Peoria, Ill.: Illinois Association for Criminal Justice.

Sherman, L. W. 1970. "Youth Workers, Police, and the Gangs: Chicago, 1956–1970." M.A. thesis, University of Chicago, Department of Sociology.

Short, J. F., Jr., and J. Moland, Jr. 1976. "Politics and Youth Gangs: A Follow-Up Study." *Sociological Quarterly* 17:162–79.

Short, J. F., Jr., and F. L. Strodtbeck. 1965. *Group Processes and Delinquency*. Chicago: University of Chicago Press.

Shover, N. 1973. "The Social Organization of Burglary." *Social Problems* 20:499–514.

Smith, D. 1986. "The Neighborhood Context of Police Behavior." In *Communities and Crime*, edited by A. J. Reiss, Jr., and M. Tonry. Vol. 8 of *Crime and Justice: A Review of Research*, edited by M. Tonry and N. Morris. Chicago: University of Chicago Press.

Smith, M. W. 1972. "An Economic Analysis of the Intracity Dispersion of Criminal Activity." Ph.D. dissertation, North Carolina State University, Department of Economics.

Sparks, R. F., A. Greer, and S. A. Manning. 1982. *Crime as Work: Theoretical Studies*. Final Report to the National Institute of Justice of the U.S. Department of Justice under grant 80-IJ-CX-0060. Newark, N.J.: Rutgers University.

Spergel, I. 1964. *Racketville, Slumtown and Haulburg*. Chicago: University of Chicago Press.

Suttles, G. D. 1968. *The Social Order of the Slum*. Chicago: University of Chicago Press.

Sveri, K. 1965. "Group Activity." *Scandinavian Studies in Criminology* 1:173–85.

Thrasher, F. 1927. *The Gang*. Chicago: University of Chicago Press.

West, D. J. 1969. *Present Conduct and Future Delinquency*. London: Heinemann.

West, D. J., and D. P. Farrington. 1973. *Who Becomes Delinquent?* London: Heinemann.

West, W. G. 1974. *Serious Thieves: Lower Class Adolescent Males in a Short-Term Deviant Occupation*. Ph.D. dissertation, University of Toronto.

———. 1977. "Serious Thieves: Lower Class Adolescent Males in a Short-Term Deviant Occupation." In *Crime and Delinquency in Canada*, edited by E. Vaz and A. Lodhi. Toronto: Prentice-Hall.

———. 1978. "The Short Term Careers of Serious Thieves." *Canadian Journal of Criminology* 20:169–90.

Wheeler, S. 1961. "Socialization in Correctional Communities." *American Sociological Review* 26:699–712.

White, H., S. A. Boorman, and R. L. Breiger. 1976. "Social Structure from Multiple Networks. I. Blockmodels of Roles and Positions." *American Journal of Sociology* 81:730–80.

Whyte, W. F. 1943. *Street Corner Society*. Chicago: University of Chicago Press.

Wolfgang, M. 1978. "Overview of Research into Violent Behavior." Testimony to the Subcommittee on Domestic and International Scientific Planning, Analysis, and Cooperation of the House Committee on Science and Technology, 95th Cong., 2d Sess.

Wolfgang, M., R. M. Figlio, and T. Sellin. 1972. *Delinquency in a Birth Cohort*. Chicago: University of Chicago Press.

Yablonsky, L. 1959. "The Delinquent Gang as a Near-Group." *Social Problems* 7:108–17.

———. 1962. *The Violent Gang*. New York: Macmillan.

Zimring, F. E. 1984. "Youth Homicide in New York: A Preliminary Analysis." *Journal of Legal Studies* 13:81–99.

James B. Jacobs

The Law and Criminology of Drunk Driving

ABSTRACT

Reliable information on patterns and frequency of drunk driving is difficult to obtain. The evidence suggests that driving under the influence is widespread—particularly among males. Today, a set of interrelated criminal laws, procedures, and administrative laws makes it easier to arrest, convict, and punish drunk drivers. Criminal investigation and law enforcement in drunk-driving cases have become simpler as impediments to apprehension, investigation, arrest, and conviction have been systematically removed. The effectiveness of the campaign against drunk driving has been difficult to assess because of the poor quality of data, the lack of carefully planned evaluations, and the difficulty in disentangling the effects of simultaneous intervention programs. Some drunk-driving campaigns seem to have short-term deterrent effects. Driver's license suspensions and revocations may play an incapacitative role. Alcohol treatment programs, however, do not appear to reduce recidivism among drunk drivers. Public education must be directed toward changing popular attitudes and behaviors associated with alcohol consumption.

Drunk driving is the intersection of two American institutions: drinking and driving. Americans devote enormous energy to the pursuit of leisure, and alcoholic beverages (beer, wine, spirits) are an integral component of leisure activities and celebrations. From cocktail parties to sporting events, from dining out to wakes and christenings, from fraternity bashes to clambakes, alcohol both facilitates and symbolizes celebration, conviviality, camaraderie, or intimacy. For many drinkers,

James B. Jacobs, professor of law, New York University School of Law, is grateful to professors Richard Bonnie and Franklin Zimring for their reviews of an earlier draft and to David Wasserman for assistance in preparing the manuscript. This work was supported by the Filomen V'Agostino and Max E. Greenberg Research Fund of the New York University School of Law.

alcohol serves important psychological functions—reduction of tension, guilt, anxiety, and frustration, and enhancement of fantasy, sensuality, aggressiveness, and self-esteem. The beer, spirits, and wine industries advertise aggressively and creatively, linking alcohol consumption to positive cultural symbols and psychological needs (Jacobson, Atkins, and Hacker 1983).

Per-capita alcohol consumption has risen steadily over the last several decades (Malin et al. 1982). On the average, each person over fourteen years old consumes the annual equivalent of 591 twelve-ounce cans of beer, 115 bottles (fifths) of table wine, or thirty-five fifths of eighty-proof whiskey, gin, or vodka. Since a third of the population are abstainers, the drinking population consumes much more than the per-capita average. The heaviest drinking tenth of the population consumes half of the alcoholic beverages sold (U.S. Department of Health and Human Services 1983).

Alcohol is associated with many personal and social problems and with much human misery. In addition to drunk driving, a great deal of criminality, suicide, and family violence is related to alcohol abuse. At some point in their lives, perhaps 10–15 percent of American men consume eight or more drinks per day (Vaillant 1983). Alcoholics and problem drinkers account for a disproportionate share of drunkenness and severe alcohol-related problems. In the aggregate, however, moderate drinkers account for an even greater absolute number of drunk days and destructive and dangerous alcohol-related events. According to Moore and Gerstein, "problems associated with drinking are distributed rather broadly through the population of drinkers" (1981, p. 47).

The American love affair with the automobile is well known (see Meyer and Gomez-Ibanez 1981; Lewis and Goldstein 1983). The car is a symbol of social status and personal life-style; for many people, it fulfills deep psychological needs for power, aggression, fantasy, and control. There are more cars and miles of roadway per person in the United States than in any other nation in the world. Americans show less interest in public transportation than do other peoples and drive greater distances between home, work, and play. American roadways are dotted with restaurants, bars, and taverns. It is hardly surprising, then, to find drinking and driving combined, often destructively.

Although its role cannot be precisely determined, drunk driving is estimated to cause between 30 and 50 percent of all traffic fatalities (U.S. Department of Transportation 1985) and a smaller but still substantial fraction of other crashes (see Reed 1981).

Drunk driving dates from the advent of the automobile (King and Tipperman 1975). For the last decade, there have been more than a million drunk-driving arrests every year in the United States, making drunk driving (commonly called "driving while intoxicated" [DWI] or "driving under the influence" [DUI]) our most commonly prosecuted criminal offense.

While the magnitude of the problem has long been recognized, it has only recently been accorded high priority. This has resulted in large part from the efforts of anti-drunk-driving groups, which are a major lobbying force at local, state, and federal levels. Anti-drunk-driving messages appear frequently in television public service announcements, in magazines, and on billboards. Insurance companies, automobile manufacturers, and the liquor industry support public education campaigns. The crusade against drunk driving is featured in leading news magazines and has been the subject of numerous television documentaries and dramatizations.

Politicians have taken note of the intensified citizen interest in doing something about drunk driving. Congress has proclaimed an anti-drunk-driving week each December and has enacted two laws making availability of federal highway funds to states contingent on, among other things, passage of "per-se laws" that make it illegal to operate a motor vehicle with a blood-alcohol content (BAC) greater than .10 and increase the minimum drinking age to twenty-one.[1] States have enacted hundreds of new anti-drunk-driving laws that mostly seek to reduce drunk driving through stricter enforcement and tougher sanctions, including mandatory jail terms, severe fines, and more expeditious and longer license suspensions and revocations (U.S. Department of Transportation 1985). Some states have abolished or restricted plea bargaining for drunk-driving cases. Local police departments have given increased priority to drunk-driving arrests. Many have implemented nighttime roadblocks (Jacobs and Strossen 1985). The courts have upheld most of these measures and have added their own initiatives, including punitive civil damages against drunk drivers (e.g., Taylor v. Superior Court, 24 Cal. 3d 890, 598 P.2d 854, 157 Cal. Reporter 693 [1979]), and have expanded liability for commercial alcohol dispensers (e.g., Lopez v. Maez, 98 N.M. 625, 651 P.2d 1269 [1982]) and even social hosts (e.g., Kelly v. Gwinnell, 96 N.J. 538, 426 A.2d 1219 [1984]).

[1] 23 U.S.C. § 408; 23 U.S.C. § 158.

Research on the incidence, causes, and control of drunk driving has received far less attention than has research on its lethal effects. While a corps of mostly governmental researchers has been investigating these questions since the late sixties, their work, much of it unpublished, is little known to criminologists and to legal scholars. The issues of jurisprudence raised by recent legislative initiatives against drunk driving have received even less scrutiny. The purpose of this essay is to bring the work of the drunk-driving specialists to the criminological community and to raise issues about the definitions and grading of drunk-driving offenses that have been neglected in the rush to stricter enforcement.[2]

Section I examines what is known about patterns of offending and offenders. Section II analyzes the legal definition and grading of drunk driving and examines several ways in which these offenses strain criminal jurisprudence.[3] Section III reviews the enforcement process, noting how the campaign against drunk driving has eroded traditional restraints on police practices. Section IV examines initiatives and research on a wide variety of control strategies and ends on a note of qualified optimism.

I. Patterns of Offending

This section summarizes research findings on the patterns and frequency of drunk driving and on the characteristics, criminal records, and personal psychologies of drunk drivers.

[2] Drunk driving can be studied from a variety of perspectives. Over the last fifteen years, the federal government's National Institute of Alcohol Abuse and Alcoholism (NIAAA) has helped to generate an enormous body of research on drinking practices, alcohol abuse and alcoholism, and treatment modalities (see U.S. Department of Health and Human Services 1983). Research on drunk driving, particularly in relation to serious and fatal accidents, dates back at least to the 1930s (e.g., Holcomb 1938). Pioneering work was carried out in the 1950s (see *Proceedings of the Second International Conference on Alcohol and Road Traffic* 1955) and early 1960s (e.g., Haddon, Suchman, and Klein 1964; Borkenstein et al. 1974). Research on the psychology, sociology, and epidemiology of drunk driving has steadily accumulated (see U.S. Department of Transportation 1979, 1985). This research is regularly reported in publications such as the *Journal of Safety Research, Accident Analysis and Prevention,* the *Journal of Studies on Alcohol,* and *Abstracts and Reviews in Alcohol and Driving*. Research on the measurement of alcohol levels and the accuracy of breath-testing devices is also reported in the *Journal of Forensic Science*. An enormous body of unpublished research is accessible through the National Highway Traffic Safety Administration (NHTSA) and the National Technical Information Service.
[3] Nevertheless, there are dozens of law review articles, notes, and comments that, in addition to their analyses of constitutional, statutory, and jurisprudential issues, often bring together important data and information. The 1983 "Alcohol and the Law Symposium" in the *North Dakota Law Review* contains an excellent legal bibliography on drunk driving. For case law and statutory developments, see the bimonthly *Drinking/Driving Law Letter*.

A. Frequency of Offending

A crime is committed each time an individual drives a motor vehicle while having a BAC exceeding legal limits. There are no available estimates of the total amount of drunk driving. The vast majority of individual offenses do not come to light, and the "dark figure" is unknown. While drunk driving is not a victimless crime, it usually does not produce victims, unless one considers those motorists, cyclists, and pedestrians whom drunk drivers put at risk. Most of these "victims" are unaware of having been placed at risk.

A number of sample surveys have sought to determine the amount of drunk driving (see, e.g., Gallup 1977). Oddly, it is sometimes difficult for an individual to know whether he has committed a DWI offense. Many people who drive while intoxicated do not remember the event (e.g., as they would a burglary) either because they were too drunk or because it was so uneventful. Others may admit to having driven when they felt they had too much to drink even though, had they been tested, they would not have exceeded the legal BAC limit. Moreover, even if we knew how many people had ever driven while intoxicated, we would not know the frequency of their intoxicated driving and therefore could not estimate the total amount of offending.[4]

At the request of the insurance industry's All-Industry Research Advisory Council (1985), the Roper Organization recently surveyed 1,491 randomly chosen adults over the age of eighteen. Thirty-seven percent of the respondents answered affirmatively to the question, In the past year have you driven after drinking alcohol? Affirmative responses were positively correlated with being male, having a higher education or a greater income, living in the North Central region, and being eighteen to thirty-four years old. Unfortunately, these findings shed very little light on the incidence of drunk driving. The survey question does not ask about drunk driving but only about drinking and driving. It does not specify time or quantity, thus leaving in a quandary the respondent who recalls having driven home hours after having had a single glass of wine at lunch. It does not ask about frequency of

---

[4] In response to Gallup's (1977) question, "Have you ever driven when you thought you had too much to drink to drive safely?", 37 percent of respondents answered affirmatively. The question seems to require the respondent to search his entire past for a drinking and driving episode and, if one is recalled, to remember what he thought at the time. Even if it is accurately recalled and reported, what have we learned? The respondent's judgment at the time may have been poor. After consuming a dozen beers, he may not have appreciated any risk, or, after consuming two beers, he may have been unwarrantedly concerned.

drinking and driving, foreclosing any inferences about rates of offending.

Roadside surveys are another way to estimate the amount of drunk driving (see Palmer and Tix 1985). Random samples of drivers are stopped and asked to submit voluntarily to a Breathalyzer to determine BAC. In theory, roadside surveys could produce very accurate data on the percentages of drinking drivers of different ages, sexes, income levels, and so forth at different times of the day and night. Unfortunately, because such surveys are expensive to mount and difficult to implement, their theoretical potential has not been realized. They have often failed to achieve two critical objectives: obtaining BAC tests from a representative sample of drivers and obtaining a sufficiently high rate of voluntary cooperation. Ideally, a random sample should include all types of drivers, from all types of communities, at all times of the day and night. The frequency of drunk driving surely varies from place to place, depending on religion, ethnicity, drinking practices, the age mix of the population, the percentage of the population living in urban areas, and other demographic characteristics. Results will be distorted, for instance, if the roadways tested have disproportionate numbers of particularly heavy drinkers, such as college students or blue-collar workers, or if times of the day are chosen when a disproportionate number of drunk drivers are on the road. For reasons of expense and logistics, no feasible study could achieve an ideal sampling. Instead of attempting to estimate the frequency of drunk driving over a twenty-four hour period, many roadside surveys have sought to determine the incidence of drunk driving during the highest risk periods (weekends, late-night hours) or to determine the role of alcohol in fatal accidents by stopping drivers at sites where and at times when fatal drunk-driving crashes have previously occurred (see Palmer and Tix 1985).

For the results of roadside surveys to be credible, it is also necessary to obtain near-universal cooperation from drivers who are stopped. It is quite likely that drunk drivers will disproportionately refuse to cooperate. Thus, roadside surveys underestimate the amount of drunk driving, although by how much is not clear. The results can be of little value if large numbers of drivers refuse to submit to the voluntary BAC testing. By promising drivers anonymity and immunity from prosecution (see Valverius 1982), rates of cooperation in excess of 90 percent have occasionally been achieved.

The small number of roadside surveys reported in the literature are a valuable source of information. The most famous is the "Grand Rapids

Study" of Robert Borkenstein et al. (1974), in which drivers were tested at all times of the day and night at sites where and at times when accidents had occurred during the previous three years. The results showed that only .75 percent of all drivers who were tested had a BAC above .10 percent; another 2.47 percent had a BAC between .05 and .09 percent. Only 10 percent of all drivers tested positively for *any* trace of alcohol.

The only nationwide roadside survey was carried out in 1973 by the University of Michigan's Highway Research Institute (see Wolfe 1974). It sought to test only late-night weekend drivers—those most likely to be driving while intoxicated. The researchers found that 3.2 percent of all drivers tested between 10:00 P.M. and midnight had a BAC at or above .10, and 6.3 percent had a BAC between .05 and .09. The period between 2:00 A.M. and 3:00 A.M. showed 11.1 percent of the drivers with a BAC above .10 and 13.5 percent with a BAC from .05 to .09 (Wolfe 1974). Nineteen of the communities designated to participate in the federally funded Alcohol Safety Action Projects conducted night-time random roadside breath-test surveys. Five and two-tenths percent of the drivers had a BAC over .10 (Voas 1981).

A recently completed roadside survey in Minnesota (Palmer and Tix 1985) found that of 838 drivers on the road between 8:00 P.M. and 3:00 A.M., 82.3 percent tested negative for alcohol, 9.3 percent tested positive (but not illegal) between .01 and .04, 6.0 percent tested between .05 and .09 (a recognized but lesser DWI offense in some states), and only 2.4 percent tested above the legal limit of .10. These results almost certainly underestimate the presence of alcohol because almost 25 percent of the drivers who were stopped refused to cooperate.

The disparities in the results of these surveys illustrate the effects of time, place, and differential cooperation. If one tried to generalize from these surveys, perhaps 5–10 percent of late-night weekend drivers and less than 1 percent of daytime drivers may be driving under the influence of prohibited levels of alcohol. There must also be a large number of additional drivers who are under the influence of licit and illicit drugs and whose offending cannot be brought to light by the BAC testing procedures.

B. Who Is the Drunk Driver?

In 1984, according to the FBI's *Uniform Crime Reports* (1985), there were 1.8 million drunk-driving arrests, which made up more arrests than those for any other offense for which national crime statistics are compiled. While these arrest data are certainly significant, they cannot be taken as representative of the offending population. Who gets arrested depends on the enforcement priorities of thousands of state and local police departments around the country. Furthermore, certain subgroups are disproportionately vulnerable to arrest. For example, the police are more alert to the offenses of young men than to those of women or of older men (although young drivers who qualify as juvenile offenders may be "adjusted" rather than arrested). Young men are not only disproportionately likely to come to the attention of the criminal justice system, but also they are the most likely arrestees to "hassle" police officers, and they are the worst drivers (Zylman 1973).

The *Uniform Crime Reports* (UCRs) show that drunk driving, like street crime, is an overwhelmingly male activity (FBI 1985). Almost 90 percent of arrestees are male; whites constituted 89.8 percent of those arrested in 1984. This is the highest percentage of whites among persons arrested for any crime reported in the UCRs. The race-specific rates of arrests for DWI may result partly from the lower level of car ownership among minorities, the lower level of driving in urban areas in which most racial minorities live, and the lower priority the urban police traditionally give to drunk driving.

There is a good deal of confusion and a growing literature about the age distribution of drunk drivers. Teenagers are not much overrepresented among drunk-driving arrestees despite their high vulnerability to police attention, their inferior driving skills, their lesser drinking experience, and their propensity for nighttime weekend driving. Sixteen- to twenty-year-olds account for a smaller percentage of arrestees for DWI than for any other UCR offense. In its 1973 roadside BAC testing study, the University of Michigan's Highway Safety Research Institute found that between 10:00 P.M. and 3:00 A.M., 88.4 percent of the sixteen- to seventeen-year-olds and 81.5 percent of the eighteen- to twenty-year-olds had BAC scores at the lowest level, .01, or less. Only 8.2 percent of the sixteen- to seventeen-year-olds and 11.2 percent of the eighteen- to twenty-year-olds had BACs over .05 (Wolfe 1974, p. 48). Their scores were slightly lower than those of the next older-aged cohort. Nevertheless, teenagers are overrepresented among traffic fatalities and are more dangerous drivers with or without alcohol (Zylman 1973).

C. Recidivism and Other Prior Criminal Records

The UCR data do not tell us how many individuals account for the total DWI arrests. According to the National Highway Traffic Safety

Administration's *Review of the State of Knowledge* (1978), 93 percent of arrestees have no previous arrests. Like all first-offender statistics, this one must be handled with care. The likelihood of being arrested for drunk driving is extremely low,[5] and DWI defendants often plead guilty to lesser traffic offenses, which may not show up in criminal histories. Since most studies use motor vehicle records to test for recidivism, previous drunk-driving arrests and convictions often are not revealed. Certainly, it cannot be assumed that a first-time arrestee is a first-time offender.

While a large majority of persons arrested for DWI have no previous drunk-driving convictions, those drunk drivers who cause serious injuries and deaths are more likely to have previous drunk-driving and other serious traffic convictions. Goldstein and Susmilch (1982) found that 31 percent of drunk drivers in Madison, Wisconsin, who caused serious injuries had accumulated a significant number of convictions for traffic violations. If all facts were known, DWI offenders could be sorted along a continuum according to their rates of offending. Unfortunately, we do not know the rates of offending for high- and low-rate offenders, nor whether chronic, intermittent, or infrequent drunk drivers are the most dangerous.

The popular image of the drunk driver (as opposed to the killer drunk) is of a white middle-class law-abiding fellow whose drunk driving is aberrational and inadvertent. This image is not completely accurate. Data from Massachusetts, for example, show that 32.6 percent (of males) in a statewide sample of 1,300 DUI defendants had been previously arraigned for criminal offenses other than drunk driving, 8.8 percent had been previously arraigned only for drunk driving, 23.1 percent had been previously arraigned for both drunk driving and other criminal offenses, and 38.7 percent had never before been arraigned (Massachusetts Department of Public Health 1984). If this pattern holds in other jurisdictions, our image of the drunk driver needs refocusing. To a greater extent than previously thought, this may be a group that engages in a large amount of antisocial behavior.

D. The Social Psychology and Psychopathology of Drunk Drivers

Unlike most other offenses, drunk driving risks significant injury to the offender and often to his friends and family members. How do drunk drivers deny or rationalize their risk-taking behavior? There is

---

[5] Borkenstein (1975) estimated the chances of being arrested for drunk driving at one in 2,000.

no research that bears directly on this subject, but it is not difficult to generate hypotheses. Several studies have shown that the typical drunk driver is on his way to or from a tavern or restaurant. Yoder and Moore (1973) found that 52 percent of all DWI arrestees in their study had been drinking in a bar or pool hall prior to arrest. Palmer and Tix (1985) found that drivers whose trips began at a bar or restaurant had an average BAC nearly four times greater than those whose trip began at the next most frequent location, a friend's or relative's house. Taverns play a major role in male social life and, unlike in British pubs, the focus is almost exclusively on drinking, and the hours are much longer. Gusfield, Kotarba, and Rasmussen's (1984) ethnography of bar culture found that bar regulars seek to maintain face as competent drinking drivers and rarely challenge one another's competency, even when an objective observer would conclude that a particular drinker was far too intoxicated to drive safely.

Any explanation of why people drive after drinking should begin by taking note of the enormously different offense rates of men and women. Women drive less than men, but this difference alone cannot account for their vastly different arrest rates. From an early age, women also drink less than men; four times as many eighteen- to twenty-year-old men as women (20 percent vs. 5 percent) can be classified as heavy drinkers (U.S. Department of Health and Human Services 1983). Alcohol consumption has a different social meaning for men than it does for women. Some male social groups accord prestige to hard drinking; a "real man" can consume large quantities of alcohol and "hold his liquor." For men, heavy drinking takes place in groups, while for women it often occurs alone. Cars and driving have a great deal more symbolic significance to men than to women.

Researchers have used a variety of screening instruments to determine whether drunk drivers are primarily alcohol abusers and alcoholics. Ehrlich and Selzer (1967), Waller (1967), Selzer (1969, 1971), and Yoder and Moore (1973) all concluded that more than 50 percent of the DWI arrestees in their respective samples were alcohol abusers or alcoholics. In Yoder and Moore's study, 26 percent of the first offenders and 48 percent of the repeaters answered yes when asked if they had ever thought they might have a drinking problem. Because of the plasticity of the categories, there is room to quarrel with the assumptions and judgments that underlie the accuracy of labeling people "alcoholics" and "alcohol abusers," but there seems little doubt that a high percentage of people arrested for drunk driving are heavy drinkers.

Indeed, it takes heavy drinking to reach the BAC .10 level and very heavy drinking to reach the much higher levels of many arrestees.[6]

Whether most drunk-driving arrestees (and, by inference, drunk drivers) can accurately be characterized as alcoholics or the near equivalent, alcoholics are heavily involved in traffic accidents and traffic violations (Selzer et al. 1967). In fatal accidents, the majority of drivers who had been drinking had very high BAC levels, often exceeding .20. Such high levels indicate alcoholism or serious alcohol abuse.[7]

Among alcohol abuse researchers, there has long been a debate between those who view alcohol abuse as symptomatic of severe psychological problems and those who see psychological problems as symptomatic of alcohol abuse. The same debate reverberates through drunk-driving and traffic accident research. For example, in Yoder and Moore's (1973) sample of DWI arrestees, "a problem or event" was given as a reason for drinking by 17 percent (see also Selzer, Rogers, and Kern 1968). A few researchers have investigated the possibility that some fraction of those involved in serious traffic accidents are consciously or unconsciously bent on suicide or that they are extremely depressed, paranoically aggressive, or otherwise psychologically disturbed (Selzer et al. 1967; Tabachnik 1973). For such individuals it would be quite wrong to say that alcoholism or alcohol abuse "caused" their wanton driving.

The hypothesis linking suicide and alcohol-related traffic death bears continuing study. Sixty percent of all alcohol-related traffic fatalities are single-car fatalities. Many are the result of high-speed crashes on clear roads on clear nights. It is hard to avoid the suspicion that some of these are conscious or unconscious suicides (see Tabachnik 1973). Alcohol is present in about one-third of U.S. suicides (Gerstein 1981), and it has been estimated that alcoholics commit suicide from six to fifteen times more frequently than the general population (U.S. Department of Health and Human Services 1983). Drunk driving might be an especially appealing form of suicide to persons anxious not to have their deaths revealed as suicides.

---

[6] The New York State Department of Transportation's "Drink/Drive Calculatory" indicates that a 180-pound person who drinks five drinks in an hour will reach a BAC level of almost .09; in two hours his BAC would be just under .08. People will vary according to what they have eaten and other personal characteristics.

[7] There are dissenters to this view. For example, Vingilis (1983) concluded that alcoholics and drivers who drink are not the same population, that the majority of drivers who drink are not alcoholics, and that within an alcoholic population there are alcoholics with certain characteristics who seem to be the high-rate drivers.

These are only hypotheses. There is no single explanation for drunk driving or for any single type of drunk driver. Researchers would do well to produce typologies of drunk drivers, perhaps grouping offenders according to the frequency of offenses (e.g., high, medium, low, one-time) and the most salient explanation (e.g., alcoholism, psychological problems, peer pressure, misjudgment). Until such research is produced, control strategies must be formulated in a vacuum.

II. Jurisprudence of Driving While Intoxicated

The legal history of drunk driving is marked by "a protracted struggle to define scientifically a standard for intoxication and to provide some objective evidentiary basis on which to determine guilt or innocence" (King and Tipperman 1975, p. 547). It is also marked by an extraordinary effort to ease the path of enforcement and foreclose opportunities for avoiding arrest or conviction. The result is a comprehensive web of substantive and procedural criminal and administrative laws that, over time, has made it easier to arrest drunk drivers, and thereafter to convict and punish them. Jurisprudential and constitutional values that figure prominently in the evolution of criminal law and criminal procedure generally seem to be ignored or slighted when it comes to drunk driving.

A. Why Is Drunk Driving a Crime?

There can be no serious quarrel with research that shows that almost everybody drives worse when under the influence of alcohol, but why should there be a special offense for driving with this impairment? How does drunk driving differ from any other form of poor or irresponsible driving? What makes driving under the influence of alcohol more dangerous, more culpable, or more appropriate for special formulation as a crime than driving while sleepy, angry, distracted, depressed, or sick? If erratic driving attributable to those causes can be punished by general-purpose traffic laws—reckless driving, speeding, following too closely, crossing the center line—why not similarly punish erratic driving caused by intoxication?

A drunk-driving conviction does not require reckless driving or violation of any other traffic law. A person operating a motor vehicle under the influence of alcohol is treated as something akin to a ticking bomb. The definition of drunk driving as a criminal offense means that there is no need to wait for the explosion before taking preemptive action. Of course, the same logic and strategy could theoretically be deployed to control sleepy, distracted, or depressed driving. But these forms of potential danger would be even less detectable and less amenable to legislative proscription and court adjudication than driving while intoxicated.

It is plausible to argue that intoxicated driving is more culpable than distracted or sleepy driving. The risks associated with driving under the influence are better known, or at least easier to visualize, than the risks of other forms of faulty driving. There may be a sense in which sleepy or distracted driving is generally excusable, while drunk driving is not. Driving under the influence means that the defendant consumed alcoholic beverages to the point of drunkenness, which itself is widely considered to be inappropriate behavior, while distractedness and sleepiness certainly are not.

Of course, there are more mundane explanations for the existence of a special crime of driving while intoxicated. Intoxicated driving is simpler to identify and prove than, for example, distracted driving. Once apprehended and confronted by a police officer, the distracted driver will no longer be distracted, but, despite his best efforts, the intoxicated driver may be unable to pass for sober. Then, too, intoxication can be measured by chemical or mechanical testing, whereas distractedness cannot be. The capacity to test for alcohol levels makes possible much of the law defining drunk driving and its enforcement.[8]

B. Defining Drunk Driving

That there should be a crime of drunk driving or of driving under the influence does not tell us how such a crime should be formulated or defined. What should be criminalized? Driving while "drunk"? Driving while "intoxicated"? Driving while "under the influence of alcohol"? Driving within a certain period of time after some specified amount of drinking? "Dangerous" driving after drinking?

In most American jurisdictions, there are two formulations of drunk driving, often located in the same DWI statute: the traditional crime, prohibiting "driving under the influence" or "driving while intox-

---

[8] Robert Force (1979) has proposed the abolition of drunk driving as an offense and the creation of a new set of traffic offenses "aggravated by alcohol." His proposal would essentially abandon the strategy of treating driving under the influence as an inchoate crime and would give more attention to the defendant's dangerous driving. Still, if the "aggravation" factor sharply escalated the punishment (which is likely), the practical effect of his proposal might be very small. Under current law, most drunk-driving arrests are made after the driver has been stopped for speeding, reckless driving, or some other traffic violation.

icated," and a newer per se offense of driving with a BAC greater than some specified level, usually .10. Both formulations present analytical or conceptual problems. The first formulation suffers from serious vagueness problems and delegates extraordinary power to the police to determine whether an offense has occurred. The second suffers from overinclusiveness and also raises questions of adequate notice.

1. *Driving under the Influence.*   What does it mean to be under the influence of alcohol or intoxicated? Any alcohol ingestion produces some physiological and psychological effects, even if they are so slight that neither the drinker nor the observer could discern them. At what point is a person under the influence? Neither prevailing cultural norms nor law mean to prohibit all driving and drinking; presumably, driving following light and moderate consumption is acceptable, if not desirable. What is unacceptable is driving following excessive, irresponsible, or abusive drinking. But these are adjectives requiring subjective judgment. Given that people differ in size, age, maturity, and experience with alcohol, and given that drinking contexts differ widely, how can this legal prohibition be formulated as a neutral, objective standard capable of routine, predictable, uniform enforcement?

Intoxication does not have a scientific definition. It is a social judgment, like "pretty" or "good," that has different meanings for different individuals and subgroups. This is not to deny a high degree of consensus about extreme forms of intoxication; we can all agree about the condition of someone who conforms to one of the stereotypes of the drunk. In the real world, however, most drinkers, even heavy drinkers, do not conform to such caricatures.

There is a serious, unavoidable, linguistic imprecision in the legal definition of driving under the influence or driving while intoxicated. Unfortunately, courts typically glide over the problem with a "we know it when we see it" reaction. *People v. Cruz*, an important New York Court of Appeals case, is a good example. It rejected a challenge to the DWI law as "void for vagueness." The court found a "definite and ascertainable meaning" of "intoxication" in the alcohol-induced loss of "the mental or physical abilities needed to, for instance, form a specific intent, understand the nature and effect of a contract, or testify truthfully and accurately."

One might be forgiven for failing to grasp the relation between the minimum standard for understanding a contract or testifying at trial, even if readily ascertainable, and the minimum standard for operating a motor vehicle. In *Cruz*, the court's application of the standard to driving was hardly more helpful. For purposes of the statute, it found an individual to be intoxicated "to the extent that he is incapable of employing the physical and mental abilities which he is expected to possess in order to operate a vehicle as a reasonable and prudent driver."[9] Admittedly, the average citizen has a great deal more experience with driving than with contracts or trial testimony. Nevertheless, there is bound to be uncertainty and confusion about what mental and physical abilities one is expected to possess in order to operate a vehicle in a socially acceptable manner.[10] Standards for issuing driver's licenses are modest, and recertification is not required. The operative assumption seems to be that the opportunity to drive should be universal or nearly so (see Reese 1971). Thus, the minimum standard is quite low. The law does not require all drivers to operate close to their personal best. It is therefore possible that an "impaired" driver might still be driving more skillfully and with better control than a good number of unimpaired drivers and, in any event, above the minimum objective standard. In a sense, the drunk-driving laws superimpose a relative standard of competency over an objective standard.

One of the vices of a vague law is the wide latitude that it gives to police, judges, and juries in interpreting the standard. This problem is exacerbated in the case of intoxication because of the range of alcohol habits, attitudes, and tolerances. Judges and juries are drawn from a society made up of people with vastly different drinking habits. At least 30 percent of the American adult population are alcohol abstainers, and another third claims to have no more than a few drinks per month. The heaviest drinking third consumes 95 percent of all alcohol; the heaviest drinking tenth accounts for 50 percent of total consumption (Moore and Gerstein 1981). People whose own drinking habits differ so widely must have very different ideas about what it means to be under

---

[9] People v. Cruz, 48 N.Y. 2d 419, 427 (1979). Due process requires that criminal statutes be reasonably definite as to the persons and conduct within their scope. In determining whether a criminal law is void for vagueness, a court must determine whether the law gives fair notice to those persons subject to it, and whether the law adequately guards against arbitrary and discriminatory enforcement (LaFave and Scott 1986).

[10] Holding people to an undefined standard of care is not an unknown feature of our jurisprudence. The tort law entreats us to act "reasonably," and negligence appears, albeit infrequently (and often in the driving context), in the criminal law. Telling the citizenry they must not drive while intoxicated is perhaps no more vague than telling them to act reasonably. Of course, this begs the question. Negligence could be criticized, and has been, as an improper standard for imposing criminal liability (Hart 1968), not only because it ensnares the hapless, but also because the standard is so subjective that different judges and juries are bound to apply different standards.

the influence, intoxicated, and impaired and will govern their own behavior by their subjective standards.

Furthermore, the facts by means of which the defendant's intoxication is assessed typically consist of the police officer's subjective labeling of the defendant's condition and behavior. In many jurisdictions, the police officer is entitled to testify as an expert on the subject of intoxication, basing his opinion on the defendant's glassy eyes, slurred speech, alcoholic breath, and inability to pass a police-administered field sobriety test (walking a line, touching the nose, and adding and subtracting. If it went to trial, a case prosecuted on the basis of such testimony might devolve into little more than a clash of opinion between the police officer and the defendant.[11] Occasionally, a court will balk at such exclusive reliance on subjective police judgment. The Wyoming Supreme Court (Crum v. City of Rock Springs, 652 P.2d 27 [Wyo. 1982]) found the prosecution's case to be legally insufficient when it consisted of nothing more than the testimony of the arresting officer that the defendant's face was flushed, his speech was slurred, he was having some trouble maintaining his balance, and he could not perform the field sobriety tests "too well."

This difficulty of proof has led over the past four decades to continuous efforts to define the offense more specifically and scientifically. As breath-testing methods became available in the early 1940s and implied consent laws were adopted in the 1950s and 1960s, it became possible to obtain scientific evidence of the driver's BAC level in a large proportion of cases. Statutes provided that certain BAC levels could be treated as presumptive evidence of driving under the influence. In New York, for example, a driver whose BAC score exceeded .15 was presumptively intoxicated; a driver whose BAC fell between .08 and .15 was presumptively impaired (the lesser offense). In cases where no BAC test was available, however, the states had to prosecute under the intoxicated or under-the-influence standards. The final step in the progression was to define the offense in terms of the driver's BAC.

2. *Per Se Laws.* According to a January 1985 National Highway

[11] The U.S. Supreme Court has warned against just such situations. In a concurring opinion striking down a New Orleans ordinance prohibiting the use of "obscene or opprobrious language" toward a police officer, Justice Lewis Powell explained: "this ordinance . . . confers on police a virtually unrestrained power to arrest and charge persons with a violation. Many arrests are made in 'one-on-one' situations where the only witnesses are the arresting officer and the person charged. All that is required for conviction is that the court accept the testimony of the officer . . ." (Lewis v. City of New Orleans, 415 U.S. 130 [1974]).

Traffic Safety Administration (NHTSA) survey (U.S. Department of Transportation 1985), all but eight states have adopted drunk-driving per se laws that make it an offense to operate a motor vehicle with a BAC greater than .10. This type of statute does not require proof that the defendant was intoxicated or impaired. It requires only a demonstration that the defendant operated a vehicle with a BAC above .10.

The amount of alcohol necessary to bring a drinker over the prohibited .10 level depends, among other things, on weight, body type, the amount of food in the stomach, and the speed of alcohol consumption (see, generally, American Medical Association Committee on Medicolegal Problems 1970). For example, a 180-pound man must consume approximately six to eight drinks in two hours to reach this level. The BAC level dissipates at a rate of about one drink per hour; there is no way to accelerate this process.

If, in effect, traditional driving-under-the-influence statutes make it a crime to be in a dangerous condition, the per se laws criminalize the probability of being in a condition that increases the probability of crashing. While this type of prophylactic is not unique (e.g., laws prohibit carrying guns in public even though countless individuals could carry guns safely), it involves a kind of conclusive presumption that is not common and is not favored in the criminal law (Underwood 1977).

The .10 BAC level does not mark a scientific divide between impaired and unimpaired driving. It is the result of increasing political pressure to attack the drunk-driving problem. A decade ago, many states set BAC .15 as the level at which a presumption of intoxication became operative, but the pressure of lobbyists, the saliency of the issue, and the recent passage of a federal law tying highway funds to state adoption of BAC .10 as the standard of criminal liability is leading inexorably to a national BAC .10 standard. According to a study by the American Medical Association Committee on Medicolegal Problems (1970), at BAC .10 approximately half of all people will show signs of intoxication. It is quite possible that lobbying efforts will push the prohibited BAC level still lower.

There seems to be no scientific justification for reducing the prohibited BAC level lower than .05. The classic study of accident and control drivers' BAC levels by Borkenstein et al. (1974) in Grand Rapids in the early 1960s showed that the chance of an accident increased sharply at levels above .05. Drivers with BAC levels below .04 had no greater probability of an accident than drivers with zero BAC. While it might be that even lower BAC levels are dangerous for certain categories of drivers, especially young people, this has yet to be shown scientifically.

The .05–.10 range is less clear. In England, for example, the prohibited level is .08. The higher the standard, the less overinclusiveness; the lower the standard, the less underinclusiveness. In effect, we are dealing with political judgments. The realities of social control support the BAC .10 level. If the DWI laws are seen to criminalize only serious, irresponsible, and aberrational driving after drinking, they may be able to draw on broad-based citizen sentiment. If, however, the prohibited BAC level is lowered too far, the behavior of more people, and more moderate drinkers, and more unimpaired drivers will be subject to criminal sanction. Drunk-driving laws that criminalize routine, socially accepted behavior run the risk of alienating large segments of the public. Moreover, the challenge of delivering swift and serious punishment to far greater numbers of defendants would be insurmountable.

3. *BAC Testing.* What is unique about the per se laws is that they make the results of a mechanical test (see Nichols 1983) almost entirely dispositive of the defendant's guilt or innocence. While the BAC test is highly accurate, it is hardly infallible.[12]

---

[12] There is a substantial scientific and legal literature on BAC testing (see Nichols 1983). The most common form of BAC testing is a breath test, which is conducted (usually at the station) by requesting the arrested driver to blow deeply into one of several types of machines. Since the late 1940s, the most popular has been the Breathalyzer (see Borkenstein 1960), but today there are several competitors (e.g., the Intoximeter). The Washington Court of Appeals (State v. Baker, 56 Wash. 2d 846, 355 P.2d 806 [Ct. App. 1960]) has described the operation of the Breathalyzer as follows: "The breathalyzer is a machine designed to measure the amount of alcohol in the alveolar breath and is based on the principle that the ratio between the amount of alcohol in the blood and the amount in the alveolar breath from the lungs is a constant 2,100:1. In other words, the machine analyzes a sample of breath to determine the alcoholic content of the blood. . . . To operate the machine, the subject blows into the machine through a mouthpiece until he has emptied his lungs in one breath. The machine is so designed that it traps only the last 521/2 cubic centimeters of air that has been blown into it. This air is then forced, by weight of a piston, through a test ampoule containing a solution of sulphuric acid and potassium dichromate. This test solution has a yellow hue to it. As the test sample bubbles through the test solution, the sulphuric acid extracts the alcohol, if any, therefrom, and the potassium dichromate then changes the alcohol to acetic acid, thereby causing the solution to lose some of its original yellow color. The greater the alcoholic content of the breath sample, the greater will be the loss of color of the test solution. By causing a light to pass through the test ampoule and through a standard ampoule containing the same solution as the test ampoule (but through which no breath sample has passed), the amount of the change in color can be measured by photoelectric cells which are connected to a galvanometer. By balancing the galvanometer, a reading can be obtained from a gauge which has been calibrated in terms of the percentage of alcohol in the blood." There is little for the Breathalyzer operator to do other than start the machine, insert the ampoule, check that the machine is not defective by blowing into it himself, and read the defendant's score off the display.

Every machine has a small error factor, which varies at different alcohol levels. The air-to-blood ratio varies slightly from person to person (Jones 1978).[13] Some researchers claim that BAC can vary with air temperature, humidity, breathing pattern, and body temperature (Hlstala 1985). The machine test can be distorted if the subject has vomit or other foreign matter in his mouth at the time he blows into the machine. The chemicals could be defective or the machine improperly calibrated. Only recently, it was revealed that several Smith and Wesson Intoxilyzer models provided distorted BAC results when operated in the presence of radio frequency interference, thus registering false scores when operated in the presence of a police radio. Many convictions were reversed before these models were adapted to correct the problem (see, e.g., Kelly and Tarantino 1983; Durand v. City of Woonsocket, 82-4808 [Super. Ct. R.I. 1982]).

Since the accuracy of the BAC test is practically the only contestable issue in most drunk-driving cases, it is not surprising that there is considerable litigation over the accuracy of the machine or its operation in a particular case. In recent years, defense lawyers around the country have asserted the state's obligation to preserve the breath ampoule so that it can be submitted for independent testing if the defendant wishes. State courts ruled both ways on the question before the Supreme Court held that due process provides no such right (California v. Trombetta, 104 Sup. Ct. 2528 [1984]). Subsequently, some state supreme courts, on state constitutional grounds, have reaffirmed the state's obligation to save the used ampoules or to provide the defendant a second test to fortify confidence in the accuracy of the procedure.

4. *Due Process: The Notice Requirement.* While it may be more precise to define DWI in terms of BAC rather than intoxication, it also provides drinkers less notice of when they are in violation. Drinkers can monitor their own sensations, behavior, and speech for the tell-tale signs of intoxication, but they cannot be expected to carry around their own breath-testing devices. This would not be a problem if BAC level corresponded closely with the outward symptoms of intoxication, but it does not always do so. There are many heavy drinkers who have no mental or physical indication of intoxication at the point when their BAC level crosses .10. Some drinkers who reasonably believe that the effects have dissipated to a safe level may not feel drunk even though their BAC is illegally high.

---

[13] Recently the Nebraska Supreme Court rejected a BAC test because individual variation in individual breath/blood ratios could have elevated the defendant's BAC level from a lawful to an unlawful score (State v. Burling, 40 CrL 2400 [1987]).

The courts that have rejected "notice" challenges have done so on the ground that the approximation is close enough. A .10 BAC requires a "significant quantity" of alcohol, and "any person with common sense will know when consumption is *approaching* a meaningful amount." At that point he proceeds at his own risk (State v. Muehlenberg, 347 N.W.2d 914 [Wis. App. 1984]). Those concerned with problems of vagueness and notice in the criminal law will be no more satisfied with this formulation than with the DWI or DUI formulations. If individuals differ significantly on whether a person is "intoxicated" or "under the influence," they will hardly agree on when drinking "is approaching a meaningful amount."

A stronger and more realistic response to the notice argument would emphasize that drivers have constructive notice of their potential criminal liability. While drinkers cannot be expected to carry pocket breath-testing devices, they can be expected to consult readily available pocket conversion tables that indicate how many drinks it takes to bring them above the legal limit. Unfortunately, however, these tables are neither consistent nor reliable. Because there is variation in the amount of drinking necessary to bring a person in a given weight range over the proscribed BAC level, the figures are necessarily rough averages. The choice of averages is essentially political. There is strong motivation for the table constructors to underestimate the unlawful number of drinks. Indeed, to overestimate the number would provide a plausible reliance defense for a defendant who reached the prohibited level despite having relied (by definition, reasonably, and in the absence of contrary indication) on the table's guidance (Wisconsin v. Hinz, 121 Wis. 2d 282, 360 N.W.2d 56 [1984]).[14]

C. Mens Rea

Criminal liability is generally conditioned on the concurrence of a *mens rea* (guilty mind) and *actus reus* (guilty act). Strict liability offenses, or those defined without a mens rea, are not unheard of, but are few in number and light in penalty (compare Wasserstrom 1960 with Hart 1968). Traffic offenses might at first seem exceptional, because they typically affix responsibility and impose punishment whether the violator acted intentionally, knowingly, recklessly, or even, in some

---

[14] Ironically, widespread dissemination of the conversion tables might actually lead to more drinking. My experience is that most people underestimate the number of alcoholic drinks necessary to bring them over the legal limit. With more accurate information, they might be encouraged to consume more.

cases, negligently. Nonetheless, traffic offenses are not true crimes, but rather a species of less serious administrative infractions or quasi-crimes. They impose neither criminal stigma nor severe punishment, but are recognized as a necessary part of the regulatory framework governing vehicular travel.

Drunk driving has one foot in the traffic offense category and one foot in the category of real crime. It has been tempting for legislators and judges to treat drunk driving as a regulatory crime, one of many rules and conventions about proper motoring conduct. There has, however, been a countervailing tendency to separate DWI from the regulatory framework and brand its perpetrators as criminals.

In the 1980s, there has been a definite trend toward treating drunk-driving defendants with the opprobrium reserved for criminal defendants and punishing them accordingly. In most states, a first drunk-driving conviction is a misdemeanor, and a second conviction within a lengthy time period (e.g., in New York, five years; Pennsylvania, seven years) is a felony. First offenders face mandatory jail terms in many states and recidivists face prison time.

Remarkably, although drunk driving is the most commonly prosecuted offense in our criminal courts, there is little case law on the applicable mens rea. Some courts have simply ignored the subject. Others, like the Wyoming Supreme Court, have treated drunk driving as a strict liability offense, requiring only the actus reus to be proven: "The elements of the offense are that the accused was (1) driving or in actual physical control of the vehicle; and (2) under the influence of an intoxicating liquor to a degree that renders him incapable of safely driving a motor vehicle, and (3) within the City of Rock Springs at the time of the driving" (Crum v. City of Rock Springs, 652 P.2d 27, 28 [Wyo. 1982]).[15]

It might be thought that legislative and judicial inattention to the mens rea of drunk driving is not important since anyone who drinks alcoholic beverages and drives is at least acting recklessly. The effects of alcohol are well-known, and the possibility of having to drive a car is so foreseeable that any drinker can, arguably, be considered to meet the criminal law standard of recklessness vis-à-vis driving while intoxicated.

---

[15] The absence of mens rea requirements is particularly disturbing because, as discussed earlier, DWI is an inchoate offense. Courts traditionally pay close attention to the mens rea required for inchoate offenses; for example, attempt crimes almost always require the highest level of mens rea.

Despite its superficial appeal, this reasoning is laden with conclusive presumptions about whole categories of persons, activities, and behaviors—presumptions that are incompatible with a criminal jurisprudence that claims to focus on individual culpability. If recklessness is inherent to drunk driving, it should not be difficult for prosecutors to prove. Moreover, requiring proof of recklessness would leave open the possibility of acquittal when that level of culpability is absent. Perhaps the defendant did not know that the substance he drank was alcoholic; perhaps he had explicitly and reasonably (though mistakenly) assured himself that it was not. Perhaps the defendant was unaware that he had consumed too much alcohol because his glass was refilled without his knowing it, or because he inadvertently miscounted. Perhaps his friend deliberately served him double-strength, deceptively sweet drinks. Furthermore, even if the defendant was reckless (or perhaps just negligent in becoming intoxicated), this culpability should not, it might be argued, automatically be transferred to the defendant's driving.

As penalties for drunk driving become heavier, disregard of mens rea becomes an increasingly serious defect. Driving while intoxicated is steadily evolving as a harm defined by criminal law while its formulation and enforcement follow an administrative or regulatory model.

D. Grading Drunk-driving Offenses

There are two basic drunk-driving offenses: DWI and the per se offense, driving with a BAC greater than .10. Many courts have held that a defendant can be charged and convicted, but not sentenced, for both.

1. *DWI: Lesser and Greater Forms.*   Some states, like New York, have developed a lesser traffic offense called "driving while ability-impaired" (DWAI), which has a per se analogue—driving with BAC greater than .05 (New York) or .07 (Connecticut). Driving while ability-impaired was created to discourage prosecutors from offering DWI defendants pleas to non-alcohol-related offenses like reckless driving or speeding. In time, at least in New York, DWAI came to be chargeable in its own right. This is problematic because it makes it an offense to drive in a condition that is not clearly dangerous.

Drunk driving is not a monolithic form of behavior. Drunk drivers present a continuum of dangerousness. At one end are drunk drivers who show no sign of impairment. A little further along are those who overcautiously hug the shoulders of the road. At the far end of the continuum is the vehicular equivalent of the fighting drunk, which is the grossly intoxicated driver who tears through traffic at eighty miles an hour, seemingly indifferent to human life, including his own. Because drunk driving varies so greatly, one might well ask whether a single offense category lumps together offenders who should properly be distinguished. While distinctions between cases can be made at the sentencing stage, these may not be adequate to reflect the enormous range of dangerousness and culpability. This is especially true if there are mandatory sanctions or fixed sentences.

The Scandinavian countries distinguish between driving with a very high BAC level (e.g., greater than .15) and driving under lesser degrees of intoxication. Punishments are calibrated accordingly. The only American state following this pattern is New Hampshire, which makes driving with a BAC greater than .20 an aggravated form of DWI.

2. *Traffic Infractions, Misdemeanors, and Felonies.*   Most jurisdictions treat a first DWI offense as a misdemeanor, precluding a sentence to state prison. A second offense within a certain number of years (typically between five and ten) is graded as a felony and is punishable by a maximum of several years imprisonment (more than thirty New Yorkers are now serving felony prison time for DWI). Increased enforcement and restrictions on plea bargaining mean that more drunk drivers will be treated as felons. More recidivists will be sentenced to felony probation or state prison terms. This trend raises the general problem of whether recidivists should be treated more severely than first offenders, an issue usually raised in the context of sentencing. Some commentators see no persuasive philosophical justification for punishing a person more severely because he has been previously convicted of a crime (e.g., Singer 1979). Others argue that treating the recidivist more severely is really a decision not to extend the leniency shown to first offenders (Morris 1974). Still others argue that the repeat offender confirms the predictive judgment that he is dangerous and warrants enhanced punishment and incapacitation. Whatever the rationale, American sentencing practice generally permits a previous criminal record to serve as an aggravating factor for sentencing purposes, and many statutes provide greatly extended sentences for habitual offenders. There seems, therefore, no sound reason to object to legislation that makes recidivist drunk driving a more serious substantive offense carrying a more severe sentence.

3. *Drunk Driving Resulting in Injury.*   It could be argued that the drunk driver who causes serious injury or death is no more dangerous, but just more unlucky, than the drunk driver who injures no one. In

individual cases this may be true. Overall, however, this is almost certainly untrue. As a group, crash-causing drunk drivers are unlikely to be a random sample of all drunk drivers. The Grand Rapids study (Borkenstein et al. 1974) demonstrated that the probability of a serious accident varied directly with BAC level above .04. Drivers who caused serious injury or death are disproportionately likely to have been acting more dangerously than those who have not, although there will be counterexamples.

Many states have a felony offense of "causing injury by means of drunken driving," or some equivalent. In states without such specialized laws, injuries resulting from drunk driving can be prosecuted as aggravated assault. These statutes raise a general issue for criminal law: Is there a justification for taking resulting harms into consideration in defining the seriousness of offenses? That is, if two comparably situated people who have consumed the same amount of alcohol leave the same party at the same time to drive home, and one encounters no other moving vehicles while the other, because of slow reaction time, runs into another car, should the latter be punished for the resulting damage or injury? Both drivers were equally culpable and equally reckless. Only one, however, caused harm.

While this is an issue that excites jurisprudential controversy, the criminal law generally takes resulting harm into account in grading and punishing (Schulhofer 1974). Attempted crimes are usually punished less severely than completed crimes, assaults less seriously than homicides. The Model Penal Code (American Law Institute 1960) treats the crime of reckless endangerment less seriously than reckless homicide. This might be justified on the ground that a driver who injures someone is more dangerous than a driver who injures no one: on the average, people who injure others may be more careless or more foolhardy than people who cause no injuries. Even if this is not true and only chance accounts for the resulting harm caused by one of two equally dangerous and culpable offenders, it seems appropriate to impose on the wrongdoer the risk of those harms he foresaw or ought to have foreseen. Defendants are burdened with the risk of foreseeable harms throughout the criminal law.

4. *Drunk Driving Resulting in Death.*   Nearly 45,000 people died in traffic collisions in 1984. While there is good reason to discount as exaggerated the oft-repeated estimate that 50 percent of these deaths are alcohol-related (Zylman 1974; Reed 1981), let us accept it for the sake of discussion. Of drunk-driving victims, 60 percent are drunk drivers

themselves. This leaves 9,000 fatalities who are passengers in drunk drivers' cars or are innocent motorists, bicyclists, or pedestrians. How should the criminal law deal with these deaths? Should they be treated as vehicular homicides, manslaughters, or even murders?

In the 1950s, many states passed "vehicular homicide" or "causing death by means of a motor vehicle" statutes. The rationale was that juries would not convict killer motorists of manslaughter, let alone murder, because they would regard the stigma of such a conviction as outweighing the gravity of the wrongdoing. I know of no empirical evidence to support this familiar rationale. In any case, punishments for this junior species of homicide, usually probation or a short jail term, were typically less than those for manslaughter.

The anti-drunk-driving crusade of the 1980s has challenged the reluctance to prosecute drunk drivers for common law homicides. Images and profiles of the killer drunk emphasize the horrors of drunk driving. The suggestion that a killer drunk driver deserves a lesser penalty than other reckless killers is anathema to groups like Mothers Against Drunk Driving and Remove Intoxicated Drivers. Under their prodding, and in an atmosphere of intense anti-drunk-driving sentiment, more prosecutors are charging drunk drivers with manslaughter or murder ("*People v. Watson:* Drunk Driving Homicide" 1983).

The added burden of proof imposed by this charge escalation is not as great as might appear. The typical manslaughter statute is satisfied by showing that the defendant caused a death by gross negligence. There seems little doubt that driving while intoxicated, in the absence of some extraordinary excuse, would satisfy most current statutory definitions of gross negligence (e.g., a gross deviation from the standard of behavior expected of a reasonable person). The prosecution should be required to show, however, not just that the defendant was driving while intoxicated, but that he was grossly negligent with respect to the death that he caused. This would exempt defendants who drove carefully despite their intoxication, or whose careless driving was not the cause of an unavoidable fatality.

In some states, the desire to ease the path of prosecution in drunk-driving homicide cases has extended the idea of strict liability from the DWI context to the homicide context. A recent Florida statute (Fla. Rev. Stat. [§] 860.01[2]) provides that:

It is unlawful for any person, while in an intoxicated condition or under the influence of intoxicating liquor, model glue . . . or any [controlled substance] to such an extent as to deprive him of full possession of his normal faculties, to drive or operate over the highways, streets, or thoroughfares of Florida any automobile, truck, motorcycle, or other vehicle. . . . and if the death of any human being be caused by the operation of a motor vehicle by any person while intoxicated, such person shall be deemed guilty of manslaughter, and on conviction be punished as provided by existing law relating to manslaughter.

The prosecution must prove only that a death occurred, that the death resulted from the operation of the defendant's vehicle, and that the defendant was intoxicated. No mens rea and no relation between the driver's intoxication and the death need be proved. The Florida Supreme Court explained (in Baker v. State, 377 So.2d [1979]) that the legislature's intent to make this a strict liability offense was justified by the gravity of the drunk-driving problem.

Florida is not alone in emasculating its homicide law to more easily snare and punish killer drunks. A recent Colorado statute (Colo. Rev. Stat. § 18–3–10–6 (1)(b)(I)), provides: "If a person operates or drives a motor vehicle while under the influence of any drug or intoxicant and such conduct is the proximate cause of the death of another, he commits vehicular homicide. This is a strict liability offense."

What could this mean? Apparently, the prosecution does not have to prove gross or even simple negligence in getting drunk, getting behind the wheel, or driving. Once the prosecution proves that the defendant was intoxicated and proximately caused a fatal injury, manslaughter is established unless, as the Colorado Supreme court vaguely suggested, the defendant could show that he had not acted "voluntarily."

The homicide liability here is even stricter than that imposed by traditional felony-murder statutes. The Colorado statute does not require even a causal relation between the defendant's impaired condition and the victim's death. Thus, when a pedestrian kills himself by jumping in front of the defendant's vehicle, the defendant would be guilty of murder if his BAC tested above .10, even if he was driving with reasonable care and could not have avoided the collision.

5. *Murder Convictions.* The anti-drunk-driving groups have called for killer drunk drivers to be prosecuted as murderers, and some prosecutors have obliged. This development presents formidable conceptual difficulties (see "Murder Convictions for Homicides Committed in the Course of Driving while Intoxicated" 1977; "*People v. Watson:* Drunk

Driving Homicide" 1983). Historically, murder prosecutions have been reserved for the most serious forms of homicide. Under the common law, murder required a showing of malice; under the Model Penal Code it requires either an intent to kill or "recklessness manifesting extreme indifference to the value of human life" (i.e., extreme recklessness). Some courts that have upheld murder convictions emphasize the evils of drunk driving in the abstract rather than the defendant's reckless conduct. For example, in *People v. Watson* (637 P.2d 279 [Cal. Sup. Ct. 1981]), the California Supreme Court said: "One who willfully consumes alcoholic beverages to the point of intoxication knowing that he must thereafter operate a motor vehicle, thereby combining sharply impaired physical and mental faculties with a vehicle capable of great force and speed, reasonably may be held to exhibit a conscious disregard of safety of others."

This language is broad enough to support a murder conviction of any drunk driver who causes a fatality. While consistent with popular outrage, it rides roughshod over the jurisprudence of homicide.

A better analysis would focus on the specified behavior leading to the fatal collision. Did Watson act maliciously and wantonly? Did he consciously disregard the risk of a serious crash? In fact, Watson drove in excess of eighty miles per hour through village streets; he nearly collided with one vehicle, and drove away and crashed into a second vehicle, killing three people. His BAC level was .25. Under a traditional "reckless indifference" standard, Watson may well have been guilty of murder. Thus, the court did not need to base its judgment on a generalized analysis of drunk driving as reckless behavior manifesting gross indifference to human life. Watson's behavior may be a quintessential example of such indifference, but not simply because it involved drunk driving. The court's needlessly broad language paves the way for the murder convictions of all drunk drivers who cause death.

III. Enforcing the Drunk-driving Laws

Criminal procedure strengthens the web that substantive criminal law has spun around the drunk driver and displays similar impatience with traditional limits on state power. A lenient standard of reasonable suspicion gives the police wide latitude in stopping vehicles to investigate for intoxicated driving. Recently, a majority of state supreme courts that have considered the matter have given the police a green light to set up drunk-driving road blocks, at which they may stop all drivers, dispensing with probable cause altogether. After they are stopped, drivers are coerced ("encouraged") to cooperate with the breath-testing procedures on pain of license forfeiture. Once they are charged with drunk driving, a conviction will almost certainly follow. The whole process has become increasingly automatic, a prime example of the mass processing of criminal cases characteristic of our criminal justice system.

A. *Vehicle Stops and Investigations*

Arrests for drunk driving are typically made when a police officer stops a car for violating a traffic law (or comes on the scene of an accident) and determines in the course of the stop that there is probable cause to believe that the driver is intoxicated. The Supreme Court decided that cars cannot be stopped at random in hopes of turning up an unlicensed driver,[16] but that traditional probable cause is not required. If the police officer has an articulable suspicion that a traffic offense is being committed, he may make the stop. Thus, if the police officer observes a vehicle drifting in and out of its lane, or speeding, or failing to have proper operating lights, he may pull it over.

These legal standards provide police enormous latitude in choosing which vehicles to stop. Given the number and complexity of traffic laws, articulable suspicions are ubiquitous. Furthermore, some courts have held that a traffic violation may not even be necessary (see, for example, State v. Goetaski, 104 N.J. 458, 517 A.2d 443 [1986]).

A police officer striving to stay within the bounds of legality, but willing to press his authority to the limits, has enormous opportunity to make vehicle stops. Moreover, police officers who do not feel constrained to abide by legal standards can stop whatever vehicles they like, confident that they can always manufacture reasonable suspicion if necessary. Who could dispute a police officer's claim that a vehicle stop was justified by the vehicle's excessive speed or by its weaving or erratic

---

[16] The Supreme Court (Delaware v. Prouse, 440 U.S. 648 [1979]) said "except in those situations in which there is at least articulable and reasonable suspicion that a motorist is unlicensed or that an automobile is not registered, or that either the vehicle or an occupant is otherwise subject to seizure for violation of law, stopping an automobile and detaining the driver in order to check his driver's license and the registration of the automobile are unreasonable under the Fourth Amendment." The Maine Supreme Court's (State v. Griffin, 459 A.2d 1086 [1983]) slightly different formulation of the same standard is also instructive: "In order to initiate an investigation short of a formal arrest, a law enforcement officer must act on the basis of specific and articulable facts which taken together with rational inferences from those facts, reasonably warrant that intrusion; however, the basis for the investigatory stop need not amount to probable cause for an arrest and, in fact, the observed conduct giving rise to the officer's suspicion of criminal activity may be wholly lawful in itself."

maneuvers? A motorist who is stopped, checked for license and alcohol, and sent on his way with a warning to drive carefully is hardly likely to complain about mistreatment.

Once the vehicle is stopped, the officer has authority to order the driver out of the vehicle and to subject him or her to a frisk for weapons (Pennsylvania v. Mimms, 434 U.S. 106 [1977]). The officer may observe the driver's demeanor and take note of his general condition and speech. If the officer has a further articulable suspicion that the driver is intoxicated, he may ask the driver to submit to a field sobriety test or to blow into an Alco-sensor, a portable breath-testing device that provides a reasonably accurate reading of the driver's BAC level. Some states have passed preliminary breath-testing laws, which purport to give the police authority to require a preliminary breath test from *any driver* lawfully stopped for a traffic violation or accident (e.g., N.Y. Vehicle and Traffic Law § 1193[a]). As is shown in section C, most courts have not objected to this type of coerced cooperation. If, in the officer's subjective opinion, the driver fails the field sobriety test or scores above the prohibited limit on the Alco-sensor, the officer will have probable cause to arrest him for driving while intoxicated.

B. Roadblocks

In the early 1980s, the anti-drunk-driving movement and the Presidential Commission on Drunk Driving (1983) urged the establishment of sobriety checkpoints, which would stop all drivers on a given road and subject them to brief investigations for intoxication. If there was reason to suspect driver intoxication, the officer would press on with the investigation by ordering the driver to pull off the road for a field sobriety or Alco-sensor test. By 1984, these roadblocks were operational in at least twenty-one states (National Transportation Safety Board 1984).

Roadblocks raise serious questions of constitutional law and the proper role of the police ("Curbing the Drunk Driver under the Fourth Amendment" 1983; Jacobs and Strossen 1985). The Fourth Amendment protects the citizenry from unreasonable searches and seizures. Traditionally, a search without probable cause was per se unreasonable (see, generally, LaFave and Israel 1985). For example, the police could not stop and search everyone in a park for drugs, interrogate all motorists about terrorist activities, or search all homes in order to turn up evidence of crime. Such dragnets, hallmarks of authoritarian regimes, are inconsistent with fundamental American legal and cultural values.

In the last two decades, however, the Supreme Court and lower federal courts have recognized certain limited exceptions to the proscription against searches and seizures without probable cause and have upheld a few police practices according to a doctrine of "general reasonableness." The Supreme Court first recognized this exception in *Camara v. Municipal Court* (387 U.S. 523 [1967]), where the constitutionality of area-wide building inspections in Baltimore, Maryland, was in question. Even though there was no probable cause to suspect violations at any of the particular premises, the Court found that these inspections were reasonable because they were not personal, they had a long history of public acceptance and served a primarily administrative purpose, and there was no other effective way to guarantee that the code regulations were being followed.

In the next decade, the Court upheld probable cause-less (and warrantless) permanent roadblocks at or near the country's borders to detect illegal aliens (United States v. Martinez-Fuerte, 428 U.S. 543 [1976]). These roadblocks, which stopped all (or every *n*th) motorists along the road to allow a brief search for illegal aliens, were clearly not supported by probable cause. The Court's rationale for upholding them, a mix of precedent and balancing, was similar to that in *Camara*. In subsequent years, the Court also recognized a few other limited exceptions, particularly inspections of certain highly regulated industries (Donovan v. Dewey, 452 U.S. 594 [1978]). In *Delaware v. Prouse*, the Court refused to permit *random stops* to determine whether drivers had proper licenses and vehicle registrations. The Court's dictum, however, indicated that roadblocks used to achieve the same ends would be permissible: "This holding does not preclude the State of Delaware or other states from developing methods for spot checks that involve less intrusion or that do not involve the unconstrained exercise of [the police officer's] discretion. Questioning of all oncoming traffic at roadblock-type stops is one possible alternative" (440 U.S. 648, 663 [1979]).

This was all the encouragement that some states needed. The National Highway Traffic Safety Administration added further encouragement. It listed roadblocks as one of several drunk-driving countermeasures that would qualify a state for supplemental highway safety funds.[17] The President's Commission added its blessing. Soon roadblocks began to appear across the United States.

---

[17] Highway Safety Act of 1966 as amended, 28 U.S.C. § 408 (1982). The regulation specific to roadblocks is found at 23 C.F.R. § 1309.6 (1984).

These proliferating roadblocks were challenged under the Fourth Amendment and its state constitutional analogues. The majority of state courts approved the roadblocks (e.g., State v. Deskins, 234 Kan. 529, 673 P.2d 1174 [1983]; Little v. State, 300 Md. 485, 479 A.2d 903 [1984]; People v. Scott, 63 N.Y.2d 518, 473 N.E.2d 1 [1984]; State v. Martin, 496 A.2d [1985]; City of Las Cruces v. Betancourt, 41 CrL 2093 [N.M. Ct. App. 1987]), provided that they were implemented pursuant to departmental criteria and not according to the whim of individual line officers.[18] These courts purported to balance the necessity for and the intrusiveness of roadblocks against the interest in highway safety, as the Supreme Court had balanced analogous concerns in *Camara* and *Martinez-Fuerte*. Like the Supreme Court, most state courts concluded that the necessity outweighed the intrusion.

Courts reaching the opposite conclusion have emphasized roadblocks' incompatibility with traditional Fourth Amendment values and have questioned the claim that roadblocks are a more effective general deterrent to drunk driving than traditional police strategies (State v. Bartley, 125 Ill. App. 3d 575; 466 N.E.2d 346 [1984]; Nelson v. Lane County, 720 P.2d 1291 [Ore. App. 1986]; State v. Crom, 383 N.W. 2d 461 [Neb. Sup. Ct. 1986]).[19] Research on the deterrent effects of various drunk-driving strategies is discussed in Section IV. If the burden of proof is on those who would expand police powers, these courts are correct. There are at present no reliable data to support the claim that sobriety checkpoints have a significant marginal deterrent effect, or that whatever effect they do have could not be matched by committing equivalent resources to other enforcement strategies.

Like the administrative searches upheld in *Camara* and in *Martinez-Fuerte*, drunk-driving roadblocks are a striking departure from the traditional balance that has been struck between state power and individual autonomy. Motorists are detained and investigated without any

[18] Several courts have disapproved of specific sobriety checkpoints because of lack of adequate protections against arbitrary enforcement (e.g., State ex. rel. Ekstrom v. Justice Court, 136 Ariz. 1, 663 P.2d 992 [1983]; Jones v. State, 459 So.2d 1068, Fla. Dist. Ct. App. [1984]).

[19] As the Oklahoma Court of Criminal Appeals (State v. Smith, 674 P.2d 562, Okla. Crim. App. [1984]) declared in rejecting drunk-driving roadblocks: "The Court finds drunk [-driving roadblocks] . . . draw dangerously close to what may be referred to as a police state. Here, the state agencies have ignored the presumption of innocence, assuming that criminal conduct must be occurring on the roads and highways, and have taken an 'end justifies the means' approach. . . . [A] basic tenet of American jurisprudence is that the government cannot assume criminal conduct in effectuating a stop. . . . Were the authorities allowed to maintain such activities . . . the next logical step would be to allow similar stops for searching out other types of criminal law offenders."

reason to believe they have violated any laws. Sobriety checkpoints do not target for investigation individuals reasonably suspected of having committed a crime. Rather, on the chance of turning up criminal law violators, police officers investigate all motorists who pass through the checkpoints. That this police practice appears "logical," "necessary," and "appropriate" reflects the current saliency of drunk driving as a social problem and the tendency to think of drunk driving in the context of traffic offenses where fundamental rights and liberties do not seem to be threatened.

The departure from traditional restraints is actually far greater for sobriety checkpoints than for building or border checks. Unlike the procedures upheld in *Camara* and *Martinez-Fuerte*, drunk-driving roadblocks are not a form of administrative regulation, but a technique of criminal law enforcement; their purpose is apprehension, punishment, and deterrence. Not only is the threat to personal liberties greater than in administrative searches, but the justification is also far weaker: traditional enforcement techniques produce more arrests for drunk driving than for any other offense for which national data are collected, and crackdowns, which increase the resources available to the police, have invariably been able to produce more arrests. The roadblocks are, at best, a marginal supplement to the already massive anti-drunk-driving effort. Moreover, the acceptance of sobriety checkpoints on a wide scale might have profound implications for American policing, paving the way for other mass searches, sweeps, and dragnets.[20]

C. Right to Counsel

In some jurisdictions, a drunk driver is formally arrested before being asked to take a Breathalyzer test; elsewhere, the suspect must be given an opportunity to take the Breathalyzer before being placed under arrest. Whenever the formal arrest occurs, however, once a driver is placed in custody, he must be given Miranda warnings, which inform him that anything he says may be used against him in criminal

[20] Once accepted in the drunk-driving context, this dragnet technique could be extended to other pressing law enforcement problems, such as possession of narcotics or firearms and muggings, shoplifting, or bank robberies. There is a strong parallel between a drunk-driving roadblock investigation that is based on the statistical likelihood that a certain number of passing drivers will be under the influence of alcohol and, for example, a requirement that all pedestrians on a certain street submit to a frisk or magnetometer search that is based on the statistical likelihood that some of them will be carrying a gun or knife illegally.

proceedings (Berkemer v. McCarty, 104 Sup. Ct. 3138 [1984]). At the same time that he is told of his right to counsel, he is informed that he must submit to a Breathalyzer test for alcohol and that if he refuses to submit, he will automatically lose his license. In those states where a refusal will be admissible at the criminal trial, the suspect must be so informed.

Most courts have held that there is no right to consult an attorney before deciding whether to take the Breathalyzer test.[21] Miranda does not apply because the police request for a BAC sample is not interrogation for testimonial evidence (see section D). The Sixth Amendment right to counsel does not attach because the election of whether to take a BAC test is not a critical stage of the criminal proceeding (Davis v. Pope, 197 S.E.2d 861 [Ga. 1973]; Newman v. Hacker, 530 S.W.2d 376 [Ky. 1975]; Dunn v. Petit, 388 A.2d 809 [R.I. 1978]).[22] Nevertheless, laymen might be surprised to learn that the decision about whether to take the Breathalyzer test is not a critical stage of the criminal proceeding against the drunk driver, since the test results constitute practically the state's entire case or the defendant's entire defense.

A slightly different question arises if the defendant asks to speak with a lawyer before deciding whether to cooperate in the BAC test procedures. Even though there is no right to counsel at this stage, courts are clearly uneasy about permitting police officials to refuse such requests. Thus, the New York Court of Appeals (People v. Craft, 28 N.Y.2d 274, 279 [1971]) held that "there is a vast difference between a failure to advise or warn a defendant of his rights . . . and a flat refusal . . . to afford him 'access to counsel' after he has requested the assistance of a lawyer." The Court called denial of a direct request for counsel "so offensive as to taint the subsequent criminal trial." Yet, it saw no contradiction in holding that it is unnecessary to inform a defendant that he has a right to contact an attorney for consultation.

---

[21] Some statutes, however, give suspects the right to consult with counsel by phone, as long as contact can be made within the short time period before the BAC level begins to dissipate. Until 1981, Illinois' implied consent law permitted a suspect ninety minutes in which to consult with an attorney to decide whether to take the test (Ill. Rev. Stat. ch. 95 1/2 § 11–501.1(a) [1979], repealed and superseded by P.A. No. 82–311, § 11–501-11–501.2 [1981]).

The Minnesota Supreme Court held that a state law providing suspects the right to counsel gives DWI suspects facing a decision about whether to take the Breathalyzer test the right to contact an attorney within a reasonable amount of time (Prideaux v. State Dept. of Public Safety, 247 N.W.2d 385 [Minn. 1976]).

[22] Thus, for example, criminal defendants have a right to counsel at a *post*indictment line-up, but not at a *pre*indictment line-up (United States v. Wade, 388 U.S. 218 [1967]).

D. *Implied Consent Laws*

The laws that demand that drunk-driving arrestees provide a breath, urine, or blood sample on pain of license revocation are called "implied consent" laws.[23] New York State passed the first such law in 1953. Every state subsequently passed similar laws.[24] They are referred to as implied consent because they are predicated on the fiction that in applying for a license to drive, a person gives implied consent to cooperate in a BAC testing procedure if requested to do so by a police officer with probable cause to suspect DWI. Ironically, there is no real consent and, since the state conditions the license on cooperation with the enforcement procedures, nothing is implied. The state's authority to demand the test is specified in the vehicle and traffic law (see Lerblance 1978).

Some implied consent laws (e.g., New York's) give the defendant a choice of taking the chemical test or of refusing the test and accepting a license suspension. Others demand that the test be taken, state the penalties for refusal, but say nothing of a choice. This silence may mean that if the police have probable cause they have the authority to administer the test forcibly, usually by extracting blood. The Supreme Court upheld this practice (Schmerber v. California, 384 U.S. 757 [1966]). In reality, except in cases when the defendant is in a medical setting because of an accident, the police will rarely exercise this apparent option.

If the defendant refuses to submit to the BAC test, his license will be revoked, although he is entitled to an administrative hearing to determine certain limited issues (Bell v. Burson, 402 U.S. 105 [1977];

---

[23] The New York statute is typical (N.Y. Vehicle and Traffic Law § 1194): "Any person who operates a motor vehicle in this state shall be deemed to have given his consent to a chemical test of his breath, blood, urine, or saliva for the purposes of determining the alcoholic or drug content of his blood provided that such test is administered at the direction of a police officer: (1) having reasonable grounds to believe such person to have been driving in an intoxicated condition or, while his ability to operate such motor vehicle or motorcycle was impaired by the consumption of alcohol or the use of a drug as defined in this chapter. . . . If such person having been placed under arrest or after a breath test indicates the presence of alcohol in his system and thereafter having been requested to submit to such chemical test refuses to submit to such chemical test, the test shall not be given, but the commissioner shall revoke his license or permit to drive and any non-resident operating privilege. . . ."

[24] Nationwide adoption of implied consent laws was "encouraged" by NHTSA requirements that must be met in order for a state to qualify for highway safety funds. See Highway Safety Program Standard No. 8, Alcohol in Relation to Highway Safety, 23 C.F.R. § 204.4–8. An approved program must provide that: "Any person placed under arrest for operating a motor vehicle while intoxicated or under the influence of alcohol is deemed to have given his consent to a chemical test of his blood, breath, or urine for the purpose of determining the alcohol content of his blood."

Mackey v. Montrym, 443 U.S. 1 [1979]; Illinois v. Batchelder, 103 Sup. Ct. 3513 [1983]). Did the police officer have probable cause to demand the Breathalyzer test? Did the defendant truly refuse? The hearing need not be held prior to the license revocation.

The threat of automatic revocation leads the majority of drunk drivers to cooperate in the testing procedures, thereby assuring the evidence that the state needs to prosecute defendants under the per se laws. One suspects, however, that as criminal penalties for drunk driving increase, more defendants will refuse to incriminate themselves with a breath sample. Thus, states have begun to escalate the penalties for refusal. Some states permit the defendant's refusal to be placed in evidence at his criminal trial. Some states even make refusal a crime![25] Many states have recently passed administrative per se laws that make license suspension automatic and immediate as soon as the arrestee fails the Breathalyzer test (see National Transportation Safety Board 1984). The police may seize the defendant's driver's license at the station house. The defendant has a right to request a subsequent hearing on the issue of whether he actually refused the test.

The Supreme Court has rejected a variety of challenges to implied consent procedures. The Court has ruled that drivers are not entitled to a presuspension or prerevocation hearing (Dixon v. Love, 431 U.S. 105 [1977]; Mackey v. Montrym, 443 U.S. 1 [1979]). More important, perhaps, the Court has held that encouraging or coercing arrestees to take the breath test does not violate the Fifth Amendment right against compelled self-incrimination, because the amendment protects against being forced to provide incriminating *testimony*, not against being compelled to provide *physical evidence* like urine, saliva, blood, or breath (Schmerber v. California, 384 U.S. 757 [1966]).

The Court faced a somewhat subtler issue in 1983, when a drunk-driving defendant in South Dakota challenged the state law that permitted the prosecution to enter into evidence at the criminal trial the defendant's refusal to submit to a chemical test for BAC. The refusal, it was argued, constituted compelled testimony. The Supreme Court disagreed (South Dakota v. Neville, 459 U.S. 553 [1983]). It held that the Fifth Amendment was not violated because the evidence, whether it could be characterized as testimonial or not, was not compelled. The Court explained that South Dakota was not compelling people arrested

---

[25] See Alaska Stat. § 28.35.032(f) and State v. Jensen, 667 P.2d 188 (Alaska Ct. App. [1983]).

for drunk driving to refuse to take a BAC test and thereby provide evidence against themselves in a criminal trial; to the contrary, the state was trying to compel people arrested for drunk driving to take the test and provide physical (nontestimonial) evidence of BAC that could be used against them at a criminal trial. Thus, the results of the BAC have been held admissible because they are not testimonial, while the refusal to take the test, though arguably testimonial, has been held not to be compelled.

E. Postarrest Proceedings

Once a defendant has been charged with DWI, the chance of escaping conviction is small. In this respect, not surprisingly, drunk driving parallels the processing of crimes generally. The overwhelming majority of DWI defendants, like most criminal defendants, plead guilty. Joseph Little's (1973) careful empirical study of the administration of justice in drunk-driving cases found that 58.5 percent of apprehended DWI offenders were convicted as charged, and 89.2 percent were convicted of either the original or a lesser charge. In their study of drunk driving in Madison, Wisconsin, Goldstein and Susmilch (1982) found 88 percent of DWI defendants were convicted of that charge; there were no acquittals in an entire year's sample of cases. The FBI's Uniform Crime Reports consistently report a DWI conviction rate of over 90 percent.

It is a myth that juries regularly acquit drunk drivers. For one thing, under the Sixth Amendment, the right to a jury trial attaches only if there is a possible sentence of more than six months incarceration (Baldwin v. New York, 399 U.S. 66 [1970]).[26] In states where a first DWI offense does not carry a maximum jail sentence of that length, there is no federal right to a jury trial.[27] When a jury trial right is available to a DWI defendant, it is very rarely exercised. Jury trials are rare events in

[26] Some state constitutions are more liberal, guaranteeing a jury trial when the federal Constitution does not. See, e.g., Brenner v. Caster, 723 P.2d 558 (Wyo. 1986), in which a crime punishable by *any* jail term triggers the right to a jury trial.

[27] In June 1987, the 5th Circuit Court of Appeals ruled that a state DWI defendant is entitled to a jury trial even though the maximum punishment is less than six months because "Even though DWI is classified as a petty offense according to Louisiana's statutory scheme, and even though the penalty may reflect a considered legislative judgment, we are not persuaded that DWI should not be classified as a 'serious' offense triable to a jury. However, the offense is truly *malum in se*. Recent statistics indicate that nearly one of every two people in this country will be involved in an alcohol-related automobile collision. The loss of life, impairment of body and destruction of property present a devastating social problem in America today" (Landry v. Hoepfner, 41 CrL 2209 [1987]).

American criminal justice, accounting for less than 5 percent of criminal dispositions. The strongest disincentive for requesting a jury trial is the likelihood of a harsher sentence on conviction. There are also higher legal fees and the unpleasant experience of living for months with a pending criminal case.

The vast majority of drunk-driving prosecutions result in negotiated pleas of guilty. In jurisdictions where plea bargaining is based on charge bargaining, drunk-driving charges are typically reduced to lesser traffic offenses, unless there is a special lesser included alcohol-related offense. A recent NHTSA-sponsored study shows that even in states where there are mandatory rules against plea bargaining in drunk-driving cases, charges in a high percentage of cases are nevertheless reduced. In jurisdictions where plea negotiation is carried on by sentence bargaining, drunk drivers typically plead guilty to obtain a sentence more lenient than the statutory maximum.[28]

The convicted DWI defendant is likely to be fined, have his driver's license suspended or revoked, and perhaps be sentenced to a short jail term. The severity of the license suspension may be eased by a provisional or occupational license, which permits the defendant to drive to work. The severity of the jail sentence, if any, may be reduced by weekend scheduling and by giving two days credit for a stint that begins just before midnight Friday and ends Saturday night just after midnight. A fine may, in fact, also be discounted if it is not collectable, which is a serious problem in many courts. On the other hand, the financial cost of conviction may be augmented by program costs, lawyers' fees, and insurance surcharges.

F. Conclusion

Law enforcement and the administration of justice in DWI cases have become automatic. One by one, impediments to apprehension, investigation, arrest, and conviction of drunk drivers have been removed. While the police cannot stop vehicles randomly to check for drunk driving, they can stop them on suspicion of violating any traffic

---

[28] The National Highway Traffic Safety Administration's August 1979 summary of the Alcohol Safety Action Project initiative contains the following revealing statement about how criminal procedure is regarded by anti-drunk-driving advocates: "A major element in making the increased enforcement activity effective must be a rapid, low cost flow of the apprehended drivers through the courts. Unless there is a high proportion of 'satisfactory' outcomes of court prosecutions, an increased arrest rate cannot be maintained. This puts an emphasis on finding streamlined procedures that permit rapid processing of first offenders."

law or without suspicion at a properly established sobriety checkpoint. Once a driver is stopped, he can be subjected to a field sobriety test on the slightest suspicion of alcohol, or he can be required to submit to a preliminary breath test without any suspicion. If probable cause surfaces from these investigations, the driver can be arrested. His cooperation in providing a breath sample for use in later criminal prosecution will be "encouraged" by threat of license suspension for refusal. If he passes the Breathalyzer test, he will probably be released. If he fails the test, his license can be seized on the spot and he will be subject to DWI charges.

Contrary to popular belief, very few drunk-driving defendants contest their guilt. In part, this is because most of the sanctions can be applied against them administratively, whether or not they are convicted. Many states now limit plea bargaining in drunk-driving cases. Neither prosecutors nor defense lawyers have many options. The "going rate" is well-known and predictable. The occasional wealthy defendant may contest the charges, retaining expert witnesses to impeach the Breathalyzer and its administration, but the number of such cases is insignificant. In processing drunk-driving cases, the criminal justice system functions as a guilt-stamping machine.

IV. Effectiveness of Controls

Efforts to reduce drunk driving have been pursued with vigor and imagination over the last two decades. Pressed by citizens' lobbying efforts, state legislatures have passed hundreds of laws (see U.S. Department of Transportation 1985) increasing administrative and criminal sanctions, authorizing enforcement campaigns and roadblocks, implementing public education initiatives, funding rehabilitation programs, and establishing new anti-drunk-driving agencies.

Criminologists constantly warn policy makers of the limitations of criminal sanctions in eradicating deviant behavior and solving social problems. This message seems to be better understood for drunk driving than for other deviant behaviors. Although there have been continuous pressures to make criminal sanctions more pervasive and more severe, the criminal law has never been the exclusive social control strategy for drunk driving.

That the anti-drunk-driving effort is multifaceted does not assure its success. In any event, "success" is difficult to define. It may encompass reduction in alcohol-related traffic injuries and minimization of undesirable secondary effects, like unacceptable strains on the criminal justice system. "Success" may also require a long-term perspective; for example, some of today's public education efforts may not show results for a generation.

Success is difficult to determine because accurate data are not available on how much drunk driving is occurring and has occurred. Thus, it is difficult to determine whether a particular intervention policy has influenced the amount of drunk driving. Furthermore, the agencies responsible for anti-drunk-driving campaigns rarely plan for careful evaluation, and their vested interest in continuing their programs creates a bias in favor of demonstrating good results. Even the federal government's pioneering Alcohol Safety Action Project did not provide for comprehensive testing and evaluation (Zimring 1978).[29] To further complicate evaluation, there are so many interventions occurring simultaneously that it is practically impossible to attribute a success, assuming one could be verified, to any particular policy.

Fatal traffic accidents in the United States, after peaking in the early 1970s, began a steady decline. Unfortunately, no comparable statistics exist for traffic crashes resulting in nonfatal injuries.[30] The decline in fatalities may be the result of safer cars, better emergency medical care, the fifty-five mile an hour speed limit, aging of the population, less drunk driving, or other unknown factors, or any combination of these. It seems unlikely that the primary factor is the anti-drunk-driving movement. If it were, we would expect single-vehicle nighttime fatalities—those most likely to be alcohol-related—to be declining faster than other types of fatal traffic crashes, and this has not occurred (see Hedlund et al. 1983).

A. Deterrence

Most efforts to reduce drunk driving have been based on deterrent rationales. According to deterrence theory, a decrease in the aggregate amount of drunk driving will occur if the audience of potential drunk drivers perceives an increase in the expected cost, defined as a function

[29] Researchers for the U.S. Department of Transportation initially claimed, on the basis of reduced numbers of single-vehicle nighttime fatalities, that the Alcohol Safety Action Project initiatives had indeed reduced drunk driving (U.S. Department of Transportation 1974). A later and more comprehensive independent analysis of this evaluation demonstrated that these claims could not be substantiated (Zador 1976; but see Johnson, Levy, and Voas 1976; also see Zador 1977).

[30] In 1979, NHTSA established the National Accident Sampling System, a computerized file of police-reported accidents, in order to permit estimation of the total injury and property damage accidents in the United States (see National Center for Statistics and Analysis 1981).

of the expected probability of apprehension, conviction, and punishment and the magnitude of the punishment (Zimring and Hawkins 1973; Cook 1980).

There has been remarkably little credible evaluation research on anti-drunk-driving initiatives (see Cramton 1969; Ennis 1977; Cameron 1979; National Highway Traffic Safety Administration 1978, 1985; Reed 1981). The first major effort emerged out of the federal government's Alcohol Safety Action Projects of the early 1970s, which were ultimately implemented in thirty-five communities. Its goal was to determine whether a mix of intensive countermeasures (enforcement, rehabilitation, and public information) and a "systems approach" (coordinated efforts by police, courts, and treatment agencies) could reduce drunk driving. Arrests increased significantly in all jurisdictions, in some by more than 300 percent, and rehabilitation programs processed thousands of offenders. A significant positive effect on reducing drunk driving could not, however, be demonstrated (Zador 1976; Levy et al. 1978; Nichols et al. 1978; U.S. Department of Transportation 1979; Voas 1981).

Much of what we know about deterring the drunk driver is attributable to H. Laurence Ross, who has analyzed the effects of various anti-drunk-driving laws and enforcement initiatives in the United States (1974), Britain (1973), France (1981), and Scandinavia (1975). This research, and that of others, is compactly summarized in Ross's book, *Deterring the Drinking Driver: Legal Policy and Social Control* (1982; see also Ross 1984, 1985).

Ross has consistently followed a straightforward methodology to determine whether a new law or police crackdown produced a decline in drunk driving. Because there are no accurate data on the amount of drunk driving, he has used single-vehicle, nighttime fatalities as a surrogate dependent variable, reasoning that these are more likely than other automobile fatalities to be the consequence of drunk driving. (The same strategy was followed in the U.S. Department of Transportation's evaluation of the Alcohol Safety Action Projects and in most agency evaluations.) Ross employs interrupted time series analyses in order to avoid mistaking a momentary perturbation or a regression to the mean for a real effect. This methodology requires data on daytime and nighttime fatalities over reasonably long periods before and after the passage of a new law or implementation of an enforcement crackdown. Even if a real decline is identified (and found to be statistically significant), it cannot be attributed to the anti-drunk-driving intervention if all other categories of traffic fatalities decreased by the same amount during the same time. In that case, something else, like better emergency medical care, must be at work. Ross would confirm a marginal deterrent effect only if single-vehicle nighttime fatalities declined more than other kinds of vehicle fatalities.

On the basis of evaluations in Finland, Chicago, and an anonymous city in Australia, Ross was unable to confirm that the announcement of more severe penalties for drunk driving produced a deterrent effect. He concluded that tougher penalties, unaccompanied by increased certainty of apprehension, are unlikely to have much effect, and speculated that draconian penalties are unlikely to be carried out. He also was unable to confirm that tough Scandinavian laws had actually reduced drunk driving; it is possible that these laws reflect (rather than cause) Scandinavian attitudes of temperance. In any case, because these laws were implemented so many decades ago, it would be very hard to demonstrate that they have had an effect on the modern rate of drunk-driving in Scandinavia (but see Votey 1982).

Ross did conclude that the 1967 British Road Safety Act reduced drunk-driving fatalities in the short run. However, within two years, the effect was dissipated, and the number of drunk-driving deaths reverted to its earlier level. Ross found a similar short-term (several months long) deterrent effect for the French drunk-driving roadblock program of 1978, and indications of a similar pattern in Canada, the Netherlands, and several Alcohol Safety Action Project jurisdictions. Wherever Ross has identified a deterrent effect, it has dissipated and eventually disappeared. Thus, Ross somewhat pessimistically concludes, "deterrence-based policies are questionable in the long run. No such policies have been scientifically demonstrated to work over time under conditions achieved in any jurisdiction. This fact does not mean that such policies are hopeless but rather that success—if achievable— probably will involve something other than what has been done in the past. Moreover, the option of merely increasing penalties for drinking and driving has been strongly discredited by experience to date. The most hopeful opportunities for further deterrent accomplishments would seem to lie in increasing the actual probabilities of apprehension and conviction of drunk drivers" (1982, p. 111). While Ross's own empirical research and literature review is the most meticulous deterrence analysis yet done, his conclusions may be unduly pessimistic. His methodology may underestimate the effect of DWI countermeasures on drunk driving because it assumes that a drunk-driving decline will be reflected in reduced single-vehicle nighttime fatalities (see Heeren et al. 1985). But what if, as seems plausible, drivers involved in fatal accidents are a peculiar subset of all drunk drivers—severely alcoholic, highly dangerous, and highly troubled—who may be particularly resistant to deterrent measures? It is possible that run-of-the-mill drunk drivers (e.g., social drinkers) are being deterred and that alcohol-related *nonfatal* crashes would show a decline if appropriate data were available (see Andenaes 1984; Simpson 1985).

Ross's methodology may mask or mute the deterrent effect of drunk-driving countermeasures on single-vehicle nighttime fatalities because many of these crashes are *not* alcohol related and therefore could not be affected by anti-drunk-driving measures. If we assume that 40 percent of single-vehicle nighttime fatalities are not alcohol related, a policy initiative that reduced alcohol-related fatalities by 10 percent would reduce all single-vehicle nighttime fatalities by only 6 percent.

Ross's conclusions assume "current levels of threat." This assumption may no longer hold. Since his book was published, there has been a broadly based drive to step up enforcement and increase punishments. Many states have enacted mandatory jail terms (usually one or two days for first offenders, seven to fourteen days for second offenders), greatly increased fines ($500 to $1,000 for first offenders; up to $2,500 for repeat offenders), special "penalty assessments," and lengthy periods of license suspension and revocation. While it is always important to ask whether these increased penalties are actually being imposed (see U.S. Department of Transportation 1983; Ross and Foley 1984; Goldstein 1985), there is good evidence that the penal cost of drunk driving is increasing (National Institute of Justice 1984). A National Institute of Justice evaluation of mandatory jail sentences for first-time drunk drivers found that there was "a dramatic increase in incarceration rates for convicted drunk drivers in each of the four jurisdictions where mandatory confinement" had been implemented. The evaluation continued: "This finding is clear and consistent and includes drunk drivers convicted of their first offense. In Seattle, only 9 percent of convicted drunk drivers were sentenced to jail before mandatory confinement was introduced; afterwards, the incarceration rate was 97 percent. In Memphis the incarceration rate was 29 percent before mandatory sanctions and virtually 100 percent afterwards. In Cincinnati and Minneapolis, similar increases occurred. Only California, where judges have discretionary power to impose probation instead of confinement for drunk driving offenses, failed to show a consistent increase in incarceration rates" (1984, p. 7).

Despite the apparent inability of Alcohol Safety Action Project jurisdictions to achieve reductions in single-vehicle nighttime fatalities,
Ross believes that greater deterrent effects may be achieved by increasing the probability of apprehension than by increasing the expected
punishment. If he is right, there is reason to be encouraged by the more
than 50 percent increase in DWI arrests from 1975 to 1984 (see Federal
Bureau of Investigation 1985). The perception of the risk of apprehension may have risen enormously because of the publicity that has been
given to crackdowns and especially to sobriety checkpoints (roadblocks).

Ross also seems unduly pessimistic in discounting the short-term
successes he documents. Short-term successes should not be mini-
mized, especially when success is measured by fewer fatalities. Moreover, Ross's analysis suggests the possiblities of building on short-term
successes by planning a long-term anti-drunk-driving program on the
basis of periodic outbursts of highly publicized activity. In any case,
even short-term success shows that the promulgation and enforcement
of criminal law can affect drunk driving.

It is important to be realistic about the capacity of the criminal justice
system to sustain a long-term perception that the risks of drunk driving
have increased. There are many demands on police time and resources,
and drunk driving cannot be a top priority forever. Even the effects of
roadblocks may diminish over time as drivers learn where they are set
up and how they can be avoided, and that the chances of being
identified as a drunk driver at a roadblock are slight (Jacobs and Strossen 1985). Overcrowding necessarily limits the amount of jail time that
can be allocated to drunk drivers, unless the definition of "jail" can be
stretched to encompass the use of community institutions like schools
or armories as holding facilities (see National Institute of Justice 1984)
and quasi-incarcerative alternatives like house arrest (see Ball and Lilly
1986). While such makeshift arrangements could expand the system's
capacity to impose some type of confinement on drunk drivers, this
might have the unwelcome effect of signaling that drunk driving is less
serious than other offenses.

B. Incapacitation

In other contexts, disillusion with the deterrent effects of punishments has led many criminologists to focus their attention on incapacitating the high-risk offender; this usually means imprisonment
(see, e.g., Cohen 1983; Blumstein et al. 1986). For drunk-driving of-

fenders, incapacitation can be achieved in theory by suspending or revoking the offender's license, or by seizing his vehicle.

License suspension is a common punishment for drunk drivers (Waller 1985). In New York State, for example, there were almost 73,000 suspensions or revocations for drunk driving and for refusal to take the Breathalyzer test in 1984. Nevertheless, the incapacitation resulting from these sanctions is only partial. A California study revealed that two-thirds of suspended and revoked drivers operated their vehicles in violation of license restrictions (National Transportation Safety Board 1984). Willet (1973) came to a similar conclusion on the basis of a 1973 study in England. That suspended and revoked drivers continue to drive is hardly surprising, given the importance of driving for participation in economic and social life. Still, this finding is not inconsistent with the existence of an incapacitation effect. The minority of drivers who do not drive at all during their period of suspension are fully incapacitated. As a group, those who drive in violation of license restrictions almost certainly drive less often, less far, less dangerously, and less drunk. This too amounts to an important incapacitation effect.

License suspension and revocation is diluted by limited enforcement as well as by limited compliance. Most states offer defendants, especially first offenders, an occupational license that allows operation of a vehicle during certain hours and/or for certain purposes, such as commuting to work. Authorizing occupational licenses for run-of-the-mill first offenders makes it much more likely that a defendant will comply with a license sanction. This is important, because a draconian policy of license revocations would not be enforceable. Two million license revocations and suspensions a year could not be backed up with a credible threat of apprehension and significant punishment (see Goldstein and Susmilch 1982; Goldstein 1985). License suspensions, forfeitures, and restrictions must be backed by credible threats if they are to deliver their incapacitative effect successfully. Most jurisdictions "provide for" a jail sentence for driving in violation of restriction, but few offenders are actually sent to jail.

Vehicle forfeiture or impoundment offers a potentially powerful incapacitative effect, particularly as a supplement to a license sanction. Impounding the drunk driver's car for thirty, sixty, or ninety days would make it harder (although obviously not impossible) for him to commit another DWI offense. National Highway Traffic Safety Administration regulations list vehicle impoundment as one of the countermeasures that states can implement in order to qualify for highway incentive grants. Several states do prescribe this sanction for driving while under suspension or revocation for an alcohol-related offense or for (usually repeat) DWI itself. Curiously, the sanction has rarely been used. My impression, on the basis of interviews with motor vehicle personnel, is that impoundment is perceived to be too harsh a penalty, which is surely an irony in a country that considers incarceration a normal response to a vast range of undesirable behaviors. It is true that a DWI offender's family may suffer from the loss of the vehicle, but why is this a compelling objection? An offender's family suffers from all sanctions. Moreover, mobilizing the drunk driver's family and friends against his offending would be a powerful form of social control. While reluctance to impose impoundments may also stem from inhibition and unease over the use of new sanctions, police departments have substantial experience impounding vehicles that are abandoned, used in crimes, or illegally parked and, as a practical matter, should have little difficulty executing an impoundment strategy.

Another possibility for more effective incapacitation of drunk drivers is house arrest, perhaps using electronic monitoring devices (Ball and Lilly 1986). It might be appropriate to sentence most drunk drivers to home detention during weekend evenings and nights for a period of months. Keeping potential drunk drivers at home during these hours might have a significant collective incapacitation effect.

C. Rehabilitation

Since the late 1960s, the alcohol treatment community has been a major force in the politics of drunk driving. Alcohol abuse is one of the nation's major public health problems, and an extensive network of programs and treatment professionals now exists (U.S. Department of Health and Human Services 1983). The treatment community views drunk driving as an alcohol problem and an alcohol arrest as an opportunity to pull alcohol abusers into treatment. Many jurisdictions require an alcoholism assessment for every drunk-driving defendant.

Many Alcohol Safety Action Projects and other state and local programs used an arrest to divert drunk drivers into treatment. Defendants were screened by treatment personnel and, depending on diagnosis and eligibility, were assigned to a DWI school, an outpatient alcohol abuse program, or an inpatient facility. Successful completion of the diversion program sometimes meant release from the DWI charge, eligibility for plea bargaining, full or partial remittance of the fine, or eligibility for an occupational license. Some of these programs were open only to first offenders, which meant closing the door to those most in need of treatment.

It is not unrealistic to regard DWI treatment programs as a type of sanction. Attending a treatment program is likely to be inconvenient and burdensome. It is also likely to be psychologically painful if the offender is forced to confront an image of himself as sick or bad.

For reasons of expense, administration, and the need for the defendant's cooperation, the vast majority of DWI defendants in "treatment" have been channeled through DWI schools, most of which are based on the Phoenix prototype (Stewart and Malfetti 1970) whose curriculum consists of approximately sixteen hours of movies, classes, lectures, and group discussion. The classes, led by an alcoholism counselor, attempt to heighten participants' awareness of the dangers of drunk driving and the symptoms of alcohol abuse and alcoholism. The curriculum is clearly geared to social drinkers who, it is assumed, can be convinced to separate their drinking and driving more effectively. I know of no national figures on the number of Americans who have passed through DWI schools during the last one-and-a-half decades. However, New York State's program alone processed more than 185,000 people from 1975 to 1983, and it currently handles about 30,000 people per year. Some states have used home-study courses in lieu of the drinking/driving school and claim comparable results.

Like rehabilitation efforts generally, drunk-driver rehabilitation is now on the defensive. The 1983 President's Commission on Drunk Driving criticized diversion programs for delaying disposition of the criminal case and imposition of license restrictions, and concluded that their effectiveness could not be demonstrated. This criticism appears warranted. Studies comparing the recidivism rates of drunk drivers who have graduated from treatment programs with those of control groups have repeatedly failed to find better results for the treatment group (see Preusser, Ulmer, and Adams 1976; Nichols et al. 1978; Michelson 1979). A majority of defendants apparently will not recidivate (or at least will not be caught recidivating) whether or not they enroll in the safe-driving school. A stubborn minority continues to recidivate whether or not enrolled in DWI school.

Nevertheless, the DWI treatment programs have survived, though often not as diversion programs; instead, they are increasingly deployed as a condition of probation or as a condition for obtaining an occupational license. They have also achieved a good measure of fiscal independence by charging defendants a fee.

Even if rehabilitative success cannot be demonstrated, these schools may have symbolic value, marking societal concern about drinking and driving, and may possibly contribute over time to attitudinal change. Moreover, continued diagnostic, curricular, administrative, and evaluative efforts may discover more successful treatment strategies. In any event, attending the schools may be perceived as a sanction and thus assist in the furtherance of specific and general deterrent goals.

A minority of DWI offenders are channeled into long-term outpatient and inpatient alcohol abuse therapy. This is not the place for a lengthy review of alcoholism treatment in the United States today. While research and treatment experimentation continue, there have been no extraordinary breakthroughs. There still is no cure for alcoholism, and no particular treatment has been clearly demonstrated superior to the others. Vaillant (1983) modestly advises treaters not to expect too much, and to be resigned to inevitable disappointments when patients do not improve, or when they revert to abusive drinking after a period of remission (see also Polich, Armor, and Braiker 1980).

D. Public Education

In the long run, significant reductions in drunk driving will require changes in popular attitudes, behaviors, and lifestyles. By symbolizing societal disapproval, the promulgation, enforcement, and imposition of criminal sanctions has an important role. Public education efforts can publicize the sanctions that attach to drunk driving, create negative images of DWI offenders, and explain the logic of the law. However, it would be simplistic to believe that if people are told that drunk driving is dangerous, irresponsible, illegal, and punishable by serious labeling and sanctioning, they will forever desist from this behavior. Such messages have always been abundant, coming from parents, friends, teachers, and media. Beyond giving people information, it is necessary to change both what they desire and how they behave.

Changing attitudes and behavior through public education concerning drinking and driving may be harder than initiatives against smoking and in favor of seat belts, initiatives which themselves have not been altogether successful. The antismoking message is clear: "Smoking is dangerous to your health; don't smoke." Likewise, the seat belt message is unequivocal: "Always buckle up!" Contrast these with the ambiguous message that is beamed to potential drinking drivers: "Driving is okay; drinking is okay; driving after light (and perhaps moderate) drinking is okay; but driving after heavy drinking is dangerous, irresponsible, and unlawful." While the message makes perfect sense, one can readily see how it could fail to make a strong impression on men and women who like to drink, who do not consider their drinking excessive, and who believe themselves able to drink and drive competently. Cigarette smoking, by contrast, while important and addictive to millions of people, is not as central to American culture as alcohol. Unlike alcohol, cigarette smoking is not a part of our cultural rituals; we have no public occasions at which smoking is required or expected. In assessing the potential of mass education campaigns to change peoples' attitudes and feelings about drinking and driving, we must also bear in mind the staggering number of counter-messages beamed to the American public through advertisements and through television and movie depictions of hard-drinking heroes and heroines (see Jacobson, Atkins, and Hacker 1983).

There are a number of other reasons why changing drunk driving by means of public education is more difficult than changing smoking and seat belt behavior. Smoking and driving without seat belts are constantly repeated behaviors to which people are committed or habituated. Perhaps educational campaigns can weaken or eradicate these habits. Drunk driving is much less likely to be a commitment or strong habit (except perhaps for a small fraction of people). Many drunk-driving episodes are aberrational for the individuals involved. For most drunk drivers, the "facts" are not an issue.

There is a growing literature on the effect of mass education on behavior in general and drunk driving in particular (Haskins 1969, 1985; Blane and Hewitt 1977; Hochheimer 1981). Unfortunately, most of the anti-drunk-driving media campaigns have not built on the knowledge base that social psychologists and communications specialists have accumulated. Hochheimer (1981) persuasively argues that anti-drunk-driving campaigns must go beyond denouncing drunk driving; they must demonstrate how people can change their behavior to avoid driving drunk. This means that their drinking, their driving, or their driving after drinking will have to change. Perhaps people can be shown how to resist pressure to drink more or how to plan their social activities so that they can effectively separate their drinking from their driving. Mass media campaigns alone cannot achieve these goals. Education also needs to take place at the individual and group levels.

Another strategy for reducing drunk driving through mass education is to change the behavior of those people who are in a position to prevent the drunk driver from committing his offense. The slogan,

"Friends do not let friends drive drunk," is meant to appeal to third parties' affections and loyalties. Sports figures and other respected role models espouse such messages in order to convince people that it is socially acceptable to restrain, or refuse to drive with, someone who is drunk. To have an effect, however, campaigns must do more than tell people not to let their friends drive drunk. They must show people how to restrain their friends without fights and rancor.

Some states threaten third parties with civil and even criminal liability for permitting or assisting driving under the influence. There is a clear trend toward imposing dram shop liability on commercial alcohol dispensers whose patrons cause alcohol-related injuries (see Jacobs 1988; Beitman [various issues]). A few states have extended such liability to social hosts as well. A server or passenger who knowingly assists an act of drunk driving could be charged with aiding and abetting drunk driving and, if convicted, punished for DWI (see, e.g., State v. Morgan, 598 S.W.2d 796 [1979]). The threat of such accomplice liability, however remote, might make it easier for hosts and passengers to restrain prospective drunk drivers.

The anti-drunk-driving groups have not limited their educational efforts to the cultivation of negative stereotypes. They have brought speakers and movies to the schools and have developed educational materials for children of all grade levels. They have worked with high school groups, parents, and teachers to design ways for students to get home from parties and proms without driving drunk. They have tried to work with tavern owners by training bartenders to identify and control intoxicated patrons. Changing bar culture seems an especially rich area for policy initiatives and research.

E. Reducing the Costs of Drunk Driving

It will be difficult to get millions of people to change their patterns of drinking and locomotion, particularly those who suffer from pathological drinking and other problems. It may make sense to pursue control or loss-reduction strategies that do not depend on individual choice and decision making. For more than twenty years, students of drunk driving have speculated about the feasibility of automobiles that could not be operated by a drunk driver. While such a technological fix may now be possible,[31] it is unlikely that the automobile manufacturers

[31] The following report appeared in the *Drinking/Driving Law Letter*: "Guardian Interlock Systems of Denver, Colorado, claims to have developed an alcohol-sensitive automobile ignition system which would lock the starter system of a car if the driver's alcohol

will voluntarily produce such vehicles, or that Congress will require them to do so; some courts have ordered the installation of these devices as a condition of probation.

The technological fix that does have a chance of implementation is the construction of all vehicles with passive restraints, automatic seat belts or airbags. Although seat belts are extremely effective in preventing serious injuries in the event of collisions, until recently less than 15 percent of the American public seemed willing to wear them. The passage of mandatory seat belt usage laws in some states has increased this percentage, although it is not yet clear whether this is a short-term or a permanent effect. Air bags could save perhaps 10,000 lives per year (see Motor Vehicles Mfrs. Ass'n v. State Farm Mut. Auto Ins. Co., 183 Sup. Ct. 2856 [1983]), not just of drunk-driving victims but of all collision and crash victims. There is surely great irony in people's willingness to support extraordinary efforts to deter, identify, capture, and punish drunk drivers and their unwillingness voluntarily to adopt trivial measures to protect themselves. Likewise, there is irony in the government's willingness to invest in unproven enforcement and punishment policies, but not in proven safety strategies.

F. Regulating the Sale and Consumption of Alcohol

If one assumes, not unreasonably, that there is a positive relation between per capita consumption of alcoholic beverages and the frequency of drunk driving, one might consider strategies for reducing alcohol consumption—increasing taxes, restricting the number of establishments, reducing hours, and raising the minimum purchase age (Moore and Gerstein 1981). All such strategies "penalize" the entire drinking public in order to change the behavior of the minority of law violators (see Bonnie 1985). Nevertheless, some of these strategies might well be utilized as part of an overall effort at controlling drinking and driving.

One possibility is to increase taxes on alcoholic beverages. Moore and

---

level rendered him unsafe to drive. The device consists of a tube into which the driver must breathe, and an alcohol sensor that allegedly determines the alcohol level of the driver. Each time the car is started the driver exhales into the tube continuously for four seconds to stimulate the alcohol sensor. If the driver's alcohol level is in an acceptable range to drive, Guardian claims that a green light will appear on the device and the car will start. A yellow light is an indication to the driver that his alcohol level is nearing the legal limit and he should use caution in driving, but the car will continue to start. If the driver's alcohol level is above the legal limit, a red light is supposed to appear, the car's ignition system will lock, and the car will not start" (Nichols 1984, p. 8).

Gerstein (1981) conclude that there is a significant relation between the price of alcohol and the level of alcohol-related problems, including drinking and driving (hence, the title of their book, *Beyond the Shadow of Prohibition*). So far the anti-drunk-driving organizations have not pressed for increased liquor taxes, perhaps perceiving that this would be unpopular.

In many jurisdictions, taverns have long hours and are permitted to remain open late into the night. Not surprisingly, the proportion of drinking drivers and the number of single-vehicle fatalities are highest during these late night hours. Mandating earlier tavern closing times might reduce the amount of drinking and the amount of driving after drinking although the effects are obviously speculative (e.g., extent of enforcement, drinkers' adaptations).

Several researchers have found a relation between the per capita number of on-premises liquor outlets and various alcohol-related problems, particularly cirrhosis (Harford et al. 1979; McGuiness 1979; Colon 1981). It is conceivable that reducing the number of taverns would decrease drunk driving, although the opposite effect is also possible; drivers might seek out taverns at ever further distances, thereby increasing the number of miles they drive while drunk (Waller 1976). In any event, the political impediments to such a move seem insurmountable.

The only popular and politically feasible prohibition-type social control strategy is raising the minimum purchase age. A large body of research on the effect of the minimum purchase age on traffic fatalities shows that when the purchase age was lowered, more deaths occurred, and that when it was raised, fatalities declined (see Williams, Rich, and Zador 1975; Smart 1977; Douglas 1980; Weschler 1980; Wagenaar 1983; Williams et al. 1983; Smith et al. 1984; Cook and Tauchen 1984; Bonnie 1985). Of course, if the alcohol consumption of any age cohort could be reduced, its drunk-driving deaths also would decrease. A 1985 federal law (23 U.S.C. § 158) withholds certain highway funds from states that do not have a twenty-one-year-old minimum purchase law. The U.S. Supreme Court recently upheld the law against a challenge that it was beyond the power of Congress under the spending clause of the Constitution and a violation of the Twenty First Amendment, which repealed prohibition and left alcohol regulation substantially to the states (South Dakota v. Dole, 55 U.S.L.W. 4971 [1987]). Thus, the United States is moving rapidly toward a uniform standard prohibiting sale of alcohol to persons below age twenty-one.

G. Summary

It is simply not possible to say definitively whether drunk driving is declining in the United States. It is, however, possible to conclude that it is not increasing. There are many signs that societal attitudes are changing. Opinion polls show that large percentages of people regard drunk driving as dangerous and antisocial and are prepared to change their behavior and to make efforts to prevent their friends from driving drunk. A well-established anti-drunk-driving movement shows every sign of remaining active for the foreseeable future. There is continuous proliferation of anti-drunk-driving initiatives through the criminal justice, public health, transportation, and public education systems which, taken together, create a very strong societal anti-drunk-driving message. While it is not realistic to expect an unconditional victory over drunk drivers, it is realistic to expect that steady inroads can be made, especially in influencing the vast numbers of drivers who are not alcoholics or alcohol abusers.

REFERENCES

"Alcoholism and the Law Symposium Issue." 1983. *North Dakota Law Review* 59 (3).

All-Industry Research Advisory Council. 1985. "A Survey of Public Attitudes Toward the Civil Justice System, Reasons for Lawsuits, Drunk Driving, and Other Topics." All-Industry Research Advisory Council, mimeographed.

American Law Institute. 1960. *American Law Institute Model Penal Code and Commentaries*. Draft no. 10. Philadelphia: American Law Institute.

American Medical Association Committee on Medicolegal Problems. 1970. *Alcohol and the Impaired Driver: A Manual on the Medicolegal Aspects of Chemical Tests for Intoxication with Supplement on Breath/Alcohol Tests*. Chicago: National Safety Council.

Andenaes, Johannes. 1984. "Drinking and Driving Laws in Scandinavia." *Journal of Scandinavian Studies in the Law*. Pp. 13–23.

Ball, Richard A., and J. Robert Lilly. 1986. "The Potential Use of Home Incarceration for Drunken Drivers." *Crime and Delinquency* 32:224–47.

Beitman, Ronald S., ed. Various issues. *Dram Shop and Alcohol Reporter*. Falmouth, Mass.: Seak.

Blane, Howard T., and Linda E. Hewitt. 1977. "Mass Media, Public Education and Alcohol: A State-of-the-Art Review." Final Report. Washington, D.C.: National Institute on Alcohol Abuse and Alcoholism.

Blumstein, Alfred, Jacqueline Cohen, Jeffrey Roth, and Christy Visher, eds. 1986. *Criminal Careers and "Career Criminals."* 2 vols. Washington, D.C.: National Academy Press.

Bonnie, Richard J. 1985. "Regulating Conditions of Alcohol Availability: Possible Effects on Highway Safety." In *Proceedings of the North American Conference on Alcohol and Highway Safety,* edited by Thomas B. Turner, Robert K. Borkenstein, Ralph K. Jones, and Patricia B. Santona. Suppl. 10, *Journal of Studies on Alcohol.*

Borkenstein, Robert F. 1960. "The Evolution of Modern Instruments of Breath Alcohol Analysis." *Journal of Forensic Sciences* 5:395–444.

———. 1975. "Problems of Enforcement, Adjudication, and Sanctioning." In *Alcohol Drugs and Traffic Safety,* edited by S. Israelstam and S. Lambert. Toronto: Addiction Research Foundation of Ontario.

Borkenstein, Robert, R. F. Crowther, R. P. Shumate, W. P. Ziel, and R. Zylman. [1964] 1974. "The Role of the Drinking Driver in Traffic Accidents (The Grand Rapids Study)." In *Blutalkohol: Alcohol, Drugs, and Behavior,* Vol. 11, 2d ed. Suppl. 1. Hamburg: Steintor.

Cameron, Tracy. 1979. "The Impact of Drinking-Driving Countermeasures: A Review and Evaluation." *Contemporary Drug Problems* 8:495–566.

Cohen, Jacqueline. 1983. "Incapacitation as a Strategy for Crime Control: Possibilities and Pitfalls." In *Crime and Justice: An Annual Review of Research,* vol. 5, edited by Michael Tonry and Norval Morris. Chicago: University of Chicago Press.

Colon, I. 1981. "Alcohol Availability on Cirrhosis Mortality Rates by Gender and Race." *American Journal of Public Health* 71:1325–28.

Cook, Phillip. 1980. "Research in Criminal Deterrence: Laying the Groundwork for the Second Decade." In *Crime and Justice: An Annual Review of Research,* vol. 2, edited by Norval Morris and Michael Tonry. Chicago: University of Chicago Press.

Cook, Phillip, and G. Tauchen. 1984. "The Effect of Minimum Drinking Age Legislation on Youthful Auto Fatalities 1971–1977." *Journal of Legal Studies* 13:169–90.

Cramton, Roger. 1969. "Driver Behavior and Legal Sanctions: A Study of Deterrence." *Michigan Law Review* 67:421–54.

"Curbing the Drunk Driver under the Fourth Amendment: The Constitutionality of Roadblock Seizures." 1983. *Georgetown Law Journal* 71:1457–86.

Douglas, Richard L. 1980. "The Legal Drinking Age and Traffic Casualties: A Special Case of Changing Alcohol Availability in a Public Health Context." *Alcohol Health and Research World* 4(2):101–17.

Ehrlich, N. J., and M. L. Selzer. 1967. *A Screening Procedure to Detect Alcoholism in Traffic Offenders in the Prevention of Highway Injury,* edited by M. L. Selzer, P. W. Gikas, and F. F. Hueke. Ann Arbor, Mich.: University of Michigan, Highway Safety Research Institute.

Ennis, J. 1977. "General Deterrence and Police Enforcement: Effective Countermeasures against Drinking and Driving." *Journal of Safety Research* 9:15–25.

Federal Bureau of Investigation. 1985. *Uniform Crime Reports: Crime in the United States.* Washington, D.C.: U.S. Department of Justice.

Force, Robert. 1979. "The Inadequacy of Drinking Driving Laws: A Lawyer's View." In *Proceedings of the Seventh International Conference on Alcohol, Drugs, and Traffic Safety,* Melbourne, Australia, January 23–28, 1977. Canberra: Australian Government Publishing Service.

Gallup, George. 1977. "Four in Ten Drive after Boozing." Princeton, N.J.: Gallup Poll.

Gerstein, Dean. 1981. "Alcohol Use and Consequences." In *Alcohol and Public Policy: Beyond the Shadow of Prohibition,* edited by Mark Moore and Dean Gerstein. Washington, D.C.: National Academy Press.

Goldstein, Herman. 1985. *Early Impressions of the Impact of Increased Sanctions on the Arrest, Prosecution, Adjudication, and Sentencing of Drinking Drivers in Madison, Wisconsin.* Madison: University of Wisconsin School of Law.

Goldstein, Herman, and C. Susmilch. 1982. *The Drinking Driver in Madison: A Study of the Problem and the Community's Response.* Madison: University of Wisconsin School of Law, mimeographed.

Gusfield, Joseph, J. Kotarba, and P. Rasmussen. 1984. "The Social Control of Drunk Driving: An Ethnographic Study of Bar Settings." *Law and Policy* 6:45–66.

Haddon, William, Jr., Edward Suchman, and David Klein. 1964. *Accident Research: Methods and Approaches.* New York: Harper & Row.

Harford, Thomas C., Douglas A. Parker, Charles Paulter, and Michael Wolz. 1979. "Relationship between the Number of On-Premise Outlets and Alcoholism." *Journal of Studies on Alcohol* 110(11):1053–57.

Hart, H. L. A. 1968. *Punishment and Responsibility.* New York: Oxford University Press.

Haskins, J. B. 1969. "Effects of Safety Communication Campaigns: A Review of Research Evidence." *Journal of Safety Research* 1:58–66.

———. 1985. "The Role of Mass Media in Alcohol and Highway Safety Campaigns." In *Proceedings of the North American Conference on Alcohol and Highway Safety,* edited by Thomas B. Turner, Robert K. Borkenstein, Ralph K. Jones and Patricia B. Santona. Suppl. 10, *Journal of Studies on Alcohol.*

Hedlund, J., R. Arnold, E. Cerrilli, S. Partyka, P. Hoxie, and D. Skinner. 1983. "An Assessment of the 1982 Traffic Fatality Decrease." Staff Report. Washington, D.C.: National Highway Traffic Safety Administration.

Hereen, T., R. A. Smith, S. Morelock, and R. W. Hingson. 1985. "Surrogate Measures of Alcohol Involvement in Fatal Crashes: Are Conventional Indicators Adequate?" *Journal of Safety Research* 16(3):127–34.

Hlstala, Michael. 1985. "Physiological Errors Associated with Alcohol Breath Testing." *Champion* 9(6):16–19, 39.

Hochheimer, John. 1981. "Reducing Alcohol Abuse: A Critical Review of Educational Strategies." In *Alcohol and Public Policy: Beyond the Shadow of Prohibition,* edited by Mark H. Moore and Dean R. Gerstein. Washington, D.C.: National Academy Press.

Holcomb, R. L. 1938. "Alcohol in Relation to Traffic Accidents." *JAMA* 3:1076–85.

Jacobs, James B. 1988. "The Impact of Insurance and Civil Law Sanctions on Drunk Driving." In *The Social Control of Drunk Driving*, edited by Michael Lawrence and Franklin Zimring. Chicago: University of Chicago Press.

Jacobs, James B., and Nadine Strossen. 1985. "Mass Investigations without Individualized Suspicion: A Constitutional and Policy Critique of Drunk Driving Roadblocks." *U.C. Davis Law Review* 18:595–680.

Jacobson, Michael, Robert Atkins, and George Hacker. 1983. *The Booze Merchants: The Inebriating of America*. Washington, D.C.: Center for Science in the Public Interest.

Johnson, P., P. Levy, and R. Voas. 1976. "A Critique of the Paper 'Statistical Evaluation of the Effectiveness of Alcohol Safety Action Projects.' " *Accident Analysis and Prevention* 8:67–77.

Jones, A. W. 1978. "Variability of the Blood: Breath Alcohol Ratio in Viva." *Journal of Studies on Alcohol* 39(11):1931–39.

Kelly, Michael A., and John A. Tarantino. 1983. "Radio Frequency Interference and the Breathalyzer: A Case Analysis." *Rhode Island Bar Journal* 31:6–8.

King, J., and M. Tipperman. 1975. "Offense of Driving While Intoxicated: The Development of Statutes and Case Law in New York." *Hofstra Law Review* 3:541–604.

LaFave, Wayne R., and Jerome Israel. 1985. *Criminal Procedure*. St. Paul, Minn.: West.

LaFave, Wayne R., and Austin W. Scott, Jr. 1986. *Handbook on Criminal Law*. St. Paul, Minn.: West.

Lerblance, Penn. 1978. "Implied Consent to Intoxication Tests: A Flawed Concept." *St. John's Law Review* 53:39–64.

Levy, Paul, Robert Voas, Penelope Johnson, and Terry M. Klein. 1978. "An Evaluation of the Department of Transportation's Alcohol Safety Action Projects." *Journal of Safety Research* 10(4):162–76.

Lewis, David, and Lawrence Goldstein. 1983. *The Automobile and American Culture*. Ann Arbor: University of Michigan Press.

Little, Joseph. 1973. "An Empirical Description of Administration of Justice in Drunk Driving Cases." *Law and Society Review* 7:473–96.

Malin, H., J. Coakley, C. Koelber, N. Murrch, and W. Holland. 1982. "An Epidemiological Perspective on Alcohol Use and Abuse in the United States." In *Alcohol and Health*. Alcohol Consumption and Related Problems, monograph no. 1. Washington, D.C.: U.S. Department of Health and Human Services.

Massachusetts Department of Public Health. 1984. "An Evaluation of Drunk Driving in Massachusetts under Chapter 373, Acts of 1982." Boston: Massachusetts Department of Public Health, Office of the Commissioner of Probation and the Division of Alcoholism, mimeographed.

McGuiness, T. 1979. *An Econometric Analysis of Total Demand for Alcoholic Beverages in the U.K., 1956–1975*. Edinburgh: Scottish Health Education Unit.

Meyer, J., and J. Gomez-Ibanez. 1981. *Autos, Transit, and Cities: A Twentieth Century Fund Report*. New York: Twentieth Century Fund.

Michelson, Larry. 1979. "The Effectiveness of an Alcohol Safety School in Reducing Recidivism of Drinking Drivers." *Journal of Studies on Alcohol* 40(11):1060–64.

Moore, Mark H., and Dean R. Gerstein. 1981. *Alcohol and Public Policy: Beyond the Shadow of Prohibition.* Washington, D.C.: National Academy Press.

Morris, Norval. 1974. *The Future of Imprisonment.* Chicago: University of Chicago Press.

"Murder Convictions for Homicides Committed in the Course of Driving while Intoxicated." 1977. *Cumberland Law Review* 8:477–94.

National Center for Statistics and Analysis. 1981. *Report on Traffic Accidents and Injuries—1981.* Washington, D.C.: National Highway Traffic Safety Administration.

National Highway Traffic Safety Administration. 1978. *Review of the State of Knowledge.* Washington, D.C.: National Highway Traffic Safety Administration.

———. 1979. *Review of the State of Knowledge.* Washington, D.C.: National Highway Traffic Safety Administration.

———. 1985. *Review of the State of Knowledge.* Washington, D.C.: National Highway Traffic Safety Administration.

National Institute of Justice. 1984. "Jailing Drunk Drivers: Impact on the Criminal Justice System." Washington, D.C.: National Institute of Justice, mimeographed.

National Transportation Safety Board. 1984. *Safety Study, Deterrence of Drunk Driving: The Role of Sobriety Checkpoints and Administrative License Revocation.* Washington, D.C.: National Transportation Safety Board.

Nichols, Donald H. 1983. "Toward a Co-ordinated Judicial View of the Accuracy of Breath Testing Devices." *North Dakota Law Review* 59:329–48.

Nichols, Donald H., ed. 1984. "New Device Prevents Intoxicated Driving." *Drinking/Driving Law Letter* 4(17):8 (August 23).

Nichols, James, Elaine Weinstein, Vernon Ellingstad, and David L. Struckman-Johnson. 1978. "The Specific Deterrent Effects of ASAP Education and Rehabilitation Programs." *Journal of Safety Research* 10(4):177–87.

Palmer, John W., and Paul E. Tix. 1985. Minnesota Alcohol Roadside Survey. Minneapolis: St. Cloud University, Department of Health Education, typescript.

"*People v. Watson:* Drunk Driving Homicide—Murder or Enhanced Manslaughter?" 1983. *California Law Review* 71:1298–1323.

Polich, J. Michael, David J. Armor, and Harriet B. Braiker. 1980. *The Course of Alcoholism: Four Years after Treatment.* Santa Monica, Calif.: Rand.

Presidential Commission on Drunk Driving. 1983. *Final Report.* Washington, D.C.: U. S. Government Printing Office.

Preusser, David, Robert Ulmer, and James Adams. 1976. "Driver Record Evaluation of a Drinking Driver Rehabilitation Program." *Journal of Safety Research* 8(3):98–105.

Proceedings of the Second International Conference on Alcohol and Road Traffic. 1955. Toronto: Garden City.

Reed, David R. 1981. "Reducing the Costs of Drinking and Driving." In *Alcohol and Public Policy: Beyond the Shadow of Prohibition,* edited by Mark H. Moore and Dean R. Gerstein. Washington, D.C.: National Academy Press.

Reese, John. 1971. *Power, Politics, People: A Study of Driver Licensing Administration.* Washington, D.C.: National Research Council.

Ross, H. Laurence. 1982. *Deterring the Drinking Driver: Legal Policy and Social Control*. Lexington, Mass.: Lexington.

———. 1984. "Social Control through Deterrence: Drinking-and-Driving Laws." *Annual Review of Sociology* 10:21–35.

———. 1985. "Deterring Drunk Driving: An Analysis of Current Efforts." *Journal of Alcohol Studies*. Suppl. 10:122–28.

Ross, H. Laurence, and James P. Foley. 1987. "Judicial Disobedience of the Mandate to Imprison Drunk Drivers." *Law and Society Review* 21:315–24.

Schulhofer, Stephen. 1974. "Harm and Punishment: A Critique of Emphasis on the Results of Conduct in the Criminal Law." *University of Pennsylvania Law Review* 122:1497–1607.

Selzer, Melvin. 1969. "Alcoholism, Mental Illness, and Stress in 96 Drivers Causing Fatal Accidents." *Behavioral Science* 14:1–10.

———. 1971. "The Michigan Alcoholism Screening Test: The Quest for a New Diagnostic Instrument." *American Journal of Psychiatry* 127:1653–58.

Selzer, Melvin, L., Charles Payne, Franklin Westervelt, and James Quinn. 1967. "Automobile Accidents as an Expression of Psychopathology in an Alcoholic Population." *Quarterly Journal of Studies on Alcohol* 28:505–16.

Selzer, Melvin L., J. E. Rogers, and S. Kern. 1968. "Fatal Accidents: The Role of Psychopathology, Social Stress, and Acute Disturbance." *American Journal of Psychiatry* 124:1028–36.

Simpson, Herbert M. 1985. "Human Related Risk Factors in Traffic Crashes: Research Needs and Opportunities." In *Proceedings of the North American Conference on Alcohol and Highway Safety*, edited by Thomas B. Turner, Robert K. Borkenstein, Ralph K. Jones, and Patricia B. Santona. Suppl. 10, *Journal of Studies on Alcohol*.

Singer, Richard G. 1979. *Just Deserts: Sentencing Based upon Equality and Desert*. Cambridge, Mass.: Ballinger.

Smart, Reginald G. 1977. "Changes in Alcoholic Beverage Sales after Reduction in the Legal Drinking Age." *American Journal of Drug Alcohol Abuse* 4(1):101–8.

Smith, R. A., R. W. Hingson, S. Morelock, T. Heeren, M. Mucatel, T. Mangione, and N. Scotch. 1984. "Legislation Raising the Legal Drinking Age in Massachusetts from 18 to 20: Effect on 16 and 17 year olds." *Journal of Studies on Alcohol* 45:534–39.

Stewart, Ernest I., and James L. Malfetti. 1970. *Rehabilitation of the Drunken Driver*. New York: Teachers College Press.

Tabachnik, Norman. 1973. *Accident or Suicide: Destruction by Automobile*. Springfield, Ill.: Thomas.

Turner, Thomas B., Robert K. Borkenstein, Ralph K. Jones, and Patricia B. Santona, eds. 1985. *Proceedings of the North American Conference on Alcohol and Highway Safety*. Suppl. 10, *Journal of Studies on Alcohol*.

U.S. Department of Health and Human Services. 1983. Fifth Special Report to Congress on Alcohol and Health from the Secretary of Health and Human Services. Washington, D.C.: National Institute on Alcohol Abuse and Alcoholism.

U.S. Department of Transportation. 1974. *Alcohol Safety Action Projects: Evalu-*

228   James B. Jacobs

ation of Operations—1972. Washington, D.C.: National Highway Traffic Safety Administration.

———. 1978. *Alcohol and Highway Safety: A Review of the State of Knowledge 1978*. Washington, D.C.: National Highway Traffic Safety Administration.

———. 1979. *Alcohol Safety Action Projects Evaluation of Operations: Data, Tables of Results and Formulations*. Washington, D.C.: National Highway Traffic Safety Administration.

———. 1983. *DWI Sanctions: The Law and the Practice*. Washington, D.C.: National Highway Traffic Safety Administration.

———. 1985. *Digest of State Alcohol-Highway Safety Related Legislation*. 3d ed. Washington, D.C.: National Highway Safety Administration.

Underwood, Barbara. 1977. "The Thumb on the Scales of Justice: Burdens of Persuasion in Criminal Cases." *Yale Law Journal* 86:1299–1348.

Vaillant, George. 1983. *The Natural History of Alcoholism*. Cambridge, Mass.: Harvard University Press.

Valverius, M., ed. 1982. *Roadside Surveys: Proceedings of the 8th International Conference on Alcohol, Drugs and Traffic Safety*. Stockholm: Swedish Council of Information on Alcohol and other Drugs.

Vingilis, E. 1983. "Driving Drinkers and Alcoholics: Are They from the Same Population?" In *Research Advances in Alcohol and Drug Problems*, vol. 7, edited by R. G. Smart, F. B. Glaser, Y. Isreal, H. Kalant, R. E. Potham, and W. Schmidt. New York: Plenum.

Voas, Robert. 1981. "Results and Implications of the ASAPS." In *Alcohol, Drugs, and Traffic Safety*, vol. 3, edited by L. Goldberg. Stockholm: Almqvist & Wiksell.

Votey, Harold L., Jr. 1982. "Scandinavian Drinking-Driving Control: Myth or Intuition?" *Journal of Legal Studies*. 11:93–116.

Wagenaar, Alexander C. 1983. *Alcohol, Young Drivers, and Traffic Accidents*. Lexington, Mass.: Lexington.

Waller, Julian. 1967. "Identification of Problem Drinking among Drunken Drivers." *JAMA* 200:114–20.

———. 1976. "Alcohol Ingestion, Alcoholism and Traffic Accidents." In *The Legal Issues in Alcoholism and Alcohol Usage*. Boston: Boston University, Law-Medicine Institute.

Waller, Patricia. 1985. "Licensing and Other Controls of the Drinking Driver." In *Proceedings of the North American Conference on Alcohol and Highway Safety*, edited by Thomas B. Turner, Robert K. Borkenstein, Ralph K. Jones, and Patricia B. Santona. Suppl. 10, *Journal of Studies on Alcohol*.

Wasserstrom, Richard. 1960. "Strict Liability in the Criminal Law." *Stanford Law Review* 12:731–45.

Weschler, H., ed. 1980. *Minimum-Drinking-Age Laws*. Lexington, Mass.: Heath.

Willett, T. C. 1973. *Drivers after Sentence*. London: Heinemann.

Williams, Allen F., R. F. Rich, and P. L. Zador. 1975. "The Legal Minimum Age and Fatal Motor Vehicle Crashes." *Journal of Legal Studies* 4:219–39.

Williams, Alan F., Paul L. Zador, Sandra S. Harris, and Ronald S. Karpf. 1983. "The Effect of Raising the Legal Minimum Drinking Age on Involvement in Fatal Crashes." *Journal of Legal Studies* 12:169–79.

Wolfe, A. C. 1974. "Characteristics of Late-Night Weekend Drivers: Results of the U.S. National Roadside Breath-Testing Survey and Several Local Surveys." In *Alcohol, Drugs, and Traffic Safety: Proceedings of the Sixth International Conference on Alcohol, Drugs, and Traffic Safety*, edited by S. Israelstam and S. Lambert. Toronto: Addiction Research Foundation of Ontario.

Yoder, Richard, and Robert Moore. 1973. "Characteristics of Convicted Drunken Drivers." *Quarterly Journal of Studies on Alcohol* 34:927–36.

Zador, P. 1976. "Statistical Evaluation of the Effectiveness of Alcohol Safety Action Projects." *Accident Analysis and Prevention* 8:51–66.

———. 1977. "A Rejoinder to a Critique of the Paper 'Statistical Evaluation of the Effectiveness of Alcohol Safety Action Projects.' " *Accident Analysis and Prevention* 9:15–19.

Zimring, Franklin. 1978. "Policy Experiments in General Deterrence: 1970–1975." In *Deterrence and Incapacitation: Estimating the Effects of Criminal Sanctions on Crime Rates*, edited by Alfred Blumstein, Jacqueline Cohen, and Daniel Nagin. Washington, D.C.: National Research Council, National Academy of Sciences.

Zimring, Franklin, and Gordon Hawkins. 1973. *Deterrence: The Legal Threat in Crime Control*. Chicago: University of Chicago Press.

Zylman, Richard. 1973. "Youth, Alcohol and Collision Involvement." *Journal of Safety Research* 5(2):51–72.

———. 1974. "A Critical Evaluation of the Literature on 'Alcohol Involvement in Highway Deaths.'" *Accident Analysis and Prevention* 6:163–204.

Alfred Blumstein

Prison Populations: A System Out of Control?

ABSTRACT

The dramatic rise in prison populations characteristic of the last fifteen years results from no single cause. The politicization of imprisonment policy, which began in the 1970s, and the changing age composition of the American population due to the postwar baby boom are important factors. One of the most troublesome aspects of prison populations is the overrepresentation of blacks. This cannot be explained solely or predominantly by racial discrimination in the criminal justice system: the bulk of the differential presence of blacks in prison appears to result from their differential involvement in those kinds of crime for which prison sentences are often imposed. Three basic approaches exist for relieving prison crowding. First, offenders can be diverted from prison by sentencing them to nonincarcerative punishments (a "front-door" approach). Second, prison sentences can be shortened, by a variety of mechanisms (a "back-door" approach). Third, prison capacity can be increased by constructing more facilities. States that are formulating strategies to alleviate prison crowding should consider a mixture of these approaches.

Federal and state prison populations in the United States have grown steadily since 1972. This is in stark contrast to the first three quarters of this century when the U.S. incarceration rate remained strikingly stable. That stability, at least in part, reflected the availability of various "safety valves" that could adjust prison populations when they outpaced the available capacity. The most important of these was parole release, augmented by correctional administrators' discretion over good time, furloughs, assignment to community centers, and home release.

Alfred Blumstein is dean and J. Erik Jonsson Professor of the School of Urban and Public Affairs, Carnegie-Mellon University.

Parole release, however, has been under intense assault for fifteen years, and has been eliminated in a number of states; and no corresponding institutional arrangement has emerged to replace it.

At the end of December 1986, there were 546,659 prisoners in state and federal prisons (U.S. Bureau of Justice Statistics 1987a). In mid-1986, local jails housed an additional 274,444 prisoners (U.S. Bureau of Justice Statistics 1987b), and that number also has been increasing. Thus, on any particular day, there are over 820,000 people in jail or prison in the United States. This is more than one-third of 1 percent of the U.S. population; one of every 300 people living in America on any day is in jail or prison.

While this ratio may not seem particularly large, it takes account of every child and elderly widow, two groups that are very unlikely to appear in prison. Females, for example, make up about 51 percent of the population but only 4 percent of the prisoners. Similarly, people over thirty make up about half of the U.S. population, but only about 28 percent of prisoners. The demographic group at highest risk of imprisonment, black males in their twenties, has an incarceration rate about twenty-five times that of the general national average; about 8 percent, or one of every twelve, is in prison or jail on any given day— an astonishing and profoundly disturbing level of incarceration for any such identifiable group. If the focus were restricted even more narrowly to residents of inner cities and included not only those who are in prison on any day but those who have recently been there or might soon be, the proportions would be even larger.

Only fifteen years earlier, imprisonment rates were strikingly different. In 1970, there were 196,429 prisoners in state and federal prisons, and the incarceration rate was ninety-six per 100,000 population (U.S. Bureau of Justice Statistics 1982). This was somewhat below the average rate of 110 per 100,000 population that had prevailed (with a standard deviation of only eight per 100,000) since the 1920s (Blumstein and Cohen 1973). By the end of 1986, the prison population had nearly trebled, and the incarceration rate had more than doubled to 227 per 100,000 population.

This sharp growth is conveyed by figure 1, which depicts the U.S. prison population and incarceration rates since 1925. The rate was fairly steady until about 1972, with only minor fluctuations, except for a dip during World War II. It then began a steady climb that has continued through 1986, and gives every indication of continuing to climb. In both absolute numbers and percentage terms, this fifteen-

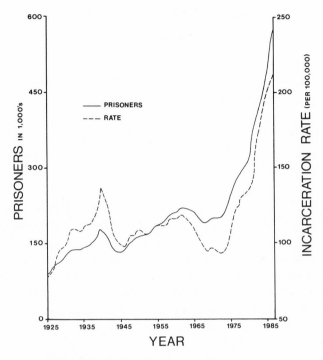

FIG. 1.—Growth in relationship between sentenced prisoners and incarceration rate. Source: U.S. Bureau of Justice Statistics 1987*a*.

year period represents the most rapid growth of prison populations in the United States since the first prisons were established early in the nineteenth century.

Some perspective on the U.S. incarceration rate may be derived from comparisons with other nations. The United States has an incarceration rate that is appreciably higher than most countries whose cultures and values we share, and with which we typically compare ourselves.

Table 1 presents recent data on incarceration rates in a number of countries. Rates per 100,000 vary markedly, from a low of sixteen prisoners per 100,000 population in Sweden to a high in the United States of 194. Comparisons such as these are often invoked as the basis for claims that the American criminal justice system is more punitive than are those of other countries. It is not clear, however, that use of incarceration rates per capita is the right measure of comparative "punitiveness." A better measure would relate incarceration to crime, rather than to population.

TABLE 1

Incarceration Rates for Eight Countries

Country	Population (Millions)	Prisoners	Prisoners per 100,000 Population	Rank
Australia	15.1	9,698	64	6
Hong Kong	5.2	5,339	102	3
Singapore	2.4	2,775	114	2
New Zealand	3.1	2,635	84	5
England/Wales	55.9	49,471	89	4
Finland	4.8	1,094	23	7
Sweden	8.3	1,344	16	8
United States	226.5	438,830	194	1

Nations that differ in their crime rates might be expected to differ in their incarceration rates. If two nations' incarceration rates were proportionate to their crime rates, the countries could be considered comparable in punitiveness. Comparisons between countries that consider only incarceration rates are incomplete if they fail to take account of differences in crime rates.

Crime rates in the United States are higher than those in many countries. Thus, when prison use is compared relative to numbers of reported crimes, rather than relative to population, the international comparisons could look very different. Whether incarceration is thought of as a mechanism for imposing retribution for offenders' crimes, or as a mechanism for utilitarian crime prevention through incapacitation, deterrence, or rehabilitation, or as all of these, one would expect higher rates of crime in any given country to be associated with increased use of incarceration, with no implied increase in punitiveness.

Table 2 illustrates this approach to comparing national punitiveness. If country A's incarceration and crime rates are respectively half of the incarceration and crime rates of country B, the two countries could be regarded as comparable in their punitiveness (assuming the patterns of crime were also comparable).

Relative to population, country C appears much more punitive than A or B, and country B appears more punitive than A. Looked at in relation to crime rates, however, country C is less punitive than either of the others, and countries A and B, despite their drastically different incarceration rates, are comparably punitive. Of course, the ratios of

TABLE 2

Hypothetical Crime* and Incarceration Rates

Country	Incarceration Rate	Crime Rate	Ratio of Incarceration Rate to Crime Rate
A	100	50	2.0
B	200	100	2.0
C	300	200	1.5

* Assuming that the distributions of offense types are comparable in each country and that crime reporting and recording practices are comparable.

incarceration rates to crime rates are not the only plausible way to compare punitiveness, but this adds an important dimension that comparison of incarceration rates alone fails to address.

Comparisons between countries in terms of gross crime rates can also be misleading, however, because patterns of crimes may vary substantially between countries. Other things equal, countries where crimes of violence are a larger fraction of all crimes might reasonably be expected to be more punitive in the punishments imposed on convicted offenders. In most countries—probably in all countries—murder and robbery are regarded as two of the most serious "prison-eligible" crimes. One way to compare different countries' patterns of punishment is to compare the relation in each country between incarceration rates and numbers of robbery or homicide. Table 3 offers comparative data on numbers of prisoners in relation to numbers of reported murders and robberies in the eight countries identified in table 1.

Comparison of numbers of prisoners per serious crime is one coarse measure of the degree to which imprisonment is focused on those most serious offenses. If this punitiveness ratio is high (i.e., relatively many prisoners per murder or robbery), then it may be that imprisonment is being used predominantly for less serious offenses, or that sentences for these less serious offenses are very long. If the ratio is very low, then that would suggest that robbery and homicide probably represent a significant fraction of the prison population, and that sentences for them are not excessive—indicative of low punitiveness.

Table 3 shows that Australia's ratios of imprisonment to reported robberies and homicides are close to those of the United States, while those in Hong Kong, Singapore, New Zealand, and England and Wales are significantly greater than in the United States. The ratios for

TABLE 3

Prisoners Related to Serious Crimes in Eight Countries

Country	Prisoners per Murder	Rank	Prisoners per Robbery	Rank
Australia	23.4	5	1.01	4
Hong Kong	55.6	3	.45	7
Singapore	56.2	2	2.0	3
New Zealand	34.6	4	8.1	1
England/Wales	66.8	1	2.2	2
Finland	4.2	7	.56	6
Sweden	3.3	8	.42	8
United States	22.7	6	.88	5

Sweden and Finland are substantially lower than those for the United States, but the difference is much less than the differences between the two Scandinavian countries and the United States in simple imprisonment rates (see table 1).

Tables 1 and 3 taken together show that conventional claims that the United States is one of the most punitive countries in the world (usually, it is said, in company with South Africa and the Soviet Union) are grossly oversimplified because they are based only on comparison of incarceration rates. When crime rates are taken into account, the United States appears to be less punitive than most of the countries represented in the tables.

Nonetheless, the observation that the United States is not egregiously punitive should not detract from the fact that prison populations in the United States are higher than ever before and appear to be increasing. This essay examines a number of major empirical and policy issues associated with current levels of prison crowding and patterns of prison use. Section I examines the respective roles of politicization of criminal justice policy-making and demographic change in causing or exacerbating current levels of prison crowding. Section I also examines the evidence concerning the substantial overrepresentation of blacks in the American prison population. Section II examines major ways to address the crowding problem—develop more "safety valves," incorporate prison capacity constraints in decision making about incarceration, and build more prisons. Section III discusses the contours of a mixed strategy containing features of each.

I. Factors Contributing to Prison Population Growth

Incarceration rates in the United States were relatively stable from the mid-1920s until the early 1970s, and then started the climb that has seen them almost triple since then. A variety of factors have contributed to that dramatic growth. One is the decline in faith in the effectiveness of rehabilitative correctional programs. A second is the movement to reduce reliance on parole release as a "safety valve" within the criminal justice system. Parole release has been abolished in some states; in others, parole guidelines and more punitive release policies have been used to assure that offenders serve more time in prison. There has been a growing public demand for toughness in dealing with offenders, including calls for mandatory sentencing legislation and increased pressures on judges to send more people to prison and for longer terms. A final factor, and one that is outside the control of the criminal justice system, is the changing age composition of the U.S. population that has increasingly brought the large numbers of persons in the "baby-boom" generation into those ages when they are most likely to be imprisoned.

A. *Politicization of Imprisonment Policy*

There was a widespread consensus on punishment policy when parole release was introduced and widely adopted in the United States in the early years of the twentieth century (Rothman 1981). That consensus was noteworthy both for its duration and for the extent of agreement it embodied.

Punishment systems looked much the same throughout the United States. In pursuit of "individualized punishment," judges had broad discretion to decide who went to prison. Judges usually set maximum sentences, and often set minimum sentences, but everywhere it was the parole board that determined when prisoners were released. In most jurisdictions, at most times, parole release decision making was ad hoc and discretionary and, in theory, premised on rehabilitative considerations. Only in the 1970s did some jurisdictions begin to structure release decisions by means of guidelines.

The consensus accepted offender rehabilitation as the primary objective of imprisonment. Associated with rehabilitation was the indeterminate sentence. This could range from wholly indeterminate sentences (one day to life) in Washington and California to the more common minimum-maximum, often constrained by a requirement that the minimum sentence be no greater than one-third or one-half the maximum. The decision to release a prisoner was made within those constraints by a parole board, which had to assess each offender's prospects for returning to the community with his crime-committing tendencies eliminated or greatly reduced.

This discretion gave parole boards the flexibility to react to fluctuations in prison populations. Those fluctuations could result from shifts in political mood and its effect on sentencing toughness, from demographic changes, or from variations in unemployment and its contributions both to crime (perhaps through need or deprivation) and to judges' sentencing decisions (through consideration of the economic self-sufficiency of a convicted offender as a factor in letting him back on the street). When prisons became too congested, the parole board might be willing to take more risk in deciding who should be released to make more room for incoming prisoners. These marginal shifts were certainly reasonable, especially in light of the great difficulty of making a good prediction of recidivism (Blumstein et al. 1986; Gottfredson 1987).

During the 1970s, however, the powers of parole boards were eliminated or reduced in part because the rehabilitative rationales for parole board discretion lost their credibility. The evaluations summarized and publicized by Martinson (1974), reported in more detail by Lipton, Martinson, and Wilks (1975), and confirmed by Sechrest, White, and Brown (1979), conveyed the impression that rehabilitation did not "work." This impression became conventional wisdom and stimulated a movement to divorce release decisions from rehabilitative considerations, especially as it became clear that most of the information that parole boards considered in making release decisions was available to judges at the time of sentencing.

With this denigration of parole boards as setters of time served, a scramble developed among legislatures, judges, and sentencing commissions over the exercise of that authority. In many states, there was a move toward greater determinacy in the establishment of sentences. In some states, this resulted in elimination of parole release, with determinate sentences replacing the indeterminate sentence. The elimination of parole release removed the parole board's capacity to adjust release decisions to respond to conditions of crowding in the prisons. If every prisoner arrives for a predetermined period, there is little flexibility to release some early to make room for new arrivals.

The shift toward determinate sentencing in many states resulted from a convergence of the interests of liberals and conservatives. To liberals, the diverse—and seemingly arbitrary—decisions by the parole boards represented a source of unwarranted disparity, with too much potential for bias and discrimination because of the lack of standards. Conservatives were offended by what they viewed as excessive leniency by the parole boards. Each group believed that the determinate sentence could redress these concerns. (See Messinger and Johnson 1978 for a blow-by-blow account of the politics of California's Uniform Determinate Sentencing Law.)

To liberals, the determinate sentence eliminated the potential for arbitrariness in parole release decisions and lessened the likelihood of decision making that discriminated against members of minority groups. Of course, different offenders—even those who committed the same crime—might well differ in their conviction offense. Any particular offense can be treated in many ways. A prosecutor might classify a burglary as a larceny or as possession of stolen goods. Similarly, there are degrees of homicide that reflect variations in premeditation, circumstances, and intent, and many degrees of assault depending on the amount of harm inflicted and the nature of the intent to inflict harm. Thus any legal category of an offense can cover a wide range of criminal culpability, and the dominant exercise of that discretion rests with the prosecutor in his initial charge of the defendant (Blumstein et al. 1983).

Different offenders might also differ in their prior record, or in other factors that the prosecutor might or might not choose to invoke in making decisions about charges, plea negotiations, or sentence recommendations, all of which influence the choice of a presumably "determinate" sentence. Thus there was still considerable room left for discretion in the classification of convicted offenders, and much of that discretion is lodged in the office of the prosecutor.

The determinate sentence removes much of the judge's sentencing discretion, and with the elimination of later review by the parole board, there is little opportunity for major revision of the sentencing decisions that are shaped or influenced by the prosecutors' discretionary choices. This gives prosecutors leverage in bargaining with a defendant to encourage a plea of guilty and the opportunity to achieve more severe sentences. Furthermore, those classification decisions are made shortly after conviction, and changes in the offender's behavior or personality while in prison cannot readily be taken into account.

The conservative concern about leniency focused on the disparity between the sentence that the judge imposed and the time actually served. In an indeterminate sentencing environment, the sentence imposed is inherently ambiguous. The public's view of the sentence is dominated by what it learns from the press, which almost always reports only the maximum sentence. The *New York Times*, for example, recently noted of Bess Myerson, a prominent New York political figure accused of corrupt practices, "if convicted, Ms. Myerson could face up to 30 years in prison and fines up to $513,000" (October 11, 1987, Sec. E, p. 11). This accumulation of theoretical maximum sentences for all charges filed is not uncommon in the newspapers, and it gives the general public a misimpression of the severity of criminal sentences. That the theoretical maximum penalties are misleading is shown by the actual sentence of another New York City official accused (and convicted) of public corruption; and mentioned in the same news story: "Anthony Ameruso, the former Transportation Commissioner, was sentenced to sixteen weekends on Rikers Island for lying under oath to a panel investigating corruption but he will keep an annual city pension of nearly $50,000."

In a totally indeterminate system, the maximum sentence has very little meaning. Even when judges set minimum and maximum sentences, there is usually a presumption in favor of parole release at the earliest possible time, which is often less than half of the maximum term. In the absence of serious prison misconduct, release on parole at first eligibility is the norm for all but the shortest sentences. In such jurisdictions, the minimum sentence is most properly thought of as the imposed sentence, and the difference between the time served and the maximum sentence is much more a matter of political rhetoric than a distortion of the judge's true intent. Of course, the pronouncement of minimum and maximum terms is an arrangement that enables a judge to act tough to satisfy public demands for severe punishment, while expressing through the minimum sentence what he views to be the appropriate sentence to be served.

Attention to this disparity between actual time served and nominal maximum sentences increased the tension resulting from the growing public pressure for more severe sanctions and judges' attempts to retain less severe sentences reflecting the deserts they viewed as "just." If a judge felt it appropriate to imprison an offender for, say, two years, then he would have to adjust his sentence accordingly. If the judge imposed a sentence of one year minimum and two years maximum, then there was a high—and growing—probability that the offender would be on the street in one year, or perhaps even less with various good-time rules. The judge had to raise the maximum sentence to perhaps five years in order to assure two years of imprisonment. When this adjustment by the judges led to excessive prison populations, a corrections commissioner might be induced to find ways to permit earlier release, which in turn would encourage judges to impose even higher nominal sentences.

There emerged a growing disparity between sentences imposed and times served that led to greater public cynicism about the sentencing process. Parole boards were blamed for this seeming hypocrisy and for the "leniency" that was becoming increasingly unacceptable in a political environment that punished severely politicians accused of being "soft on crime."

Whether because the parole board's release power was eliminated, or because parole boards adapted to a changed political environment by delaying release dates, the parole boards' ability to accommodate prison populations to available capacity diminished. The move to determinate sentences—especially when they were set by the legislature—led to increased pressure for raising those sentences (e.g., Zimring 1977; Messinger and Johnson 1978). Consequently, prison populations grew and the parole boards' safety-valve function in many states was disabled.

Some states adopted legislation to reintroduce such a safety-valve function. In its determinate sentencing law, for example, Illinois provided for good time of as much as 50 percent of the determinate sentence. The Illinois Department of Corrections later used a forced-release program to try to keep up with the growing flow of prisoners (Austin 1986). The courts put a stop to that.

In North Carolina, the legislature has repeatedly liberalized rules permitting "good time" (good conduct) and "gain time" (prison labor credits) with the result that the percentage of the declared determinate sentence actually served has steadily declined for a decade (Clarke 1987). However, judicial and public resistance to this has led to repeated efforts to revise the sentencing and good time systems.

Michigan established an Emergency Powers Act, which brought numerous agencies into the process: a corrections commission declared the prisons to be overcrowded; the governor was then mandated to reduce minimum sentences by up to ninety days to increase the pool of prisoners eligible for parole; and, finally, the parole board could act to release the good risks among those newly eligible. That came to an end when Governor Blanchard refused to invoke the sentence-reduction authority. In Illinois and Michigan, the fundamental function of providing a safety valve was reintroduced, but with only limited success for a limited time.

There is a widespread perception that sentencing practices have become tougher; that shift is generally attributed to the general politicization of sentencing that has reduced parole discretion. It has been difficult to find definitive evidence to document that perception, however. The growth in prison populations shows that more people are being sent to prison, or that those who are sent are staying a longer time. It is still not yet well established, however, how much of that shift is attributable to limits on judges' discretion, how much is attributable to shifts in the severity of the offenses being committed, and how much is attributable to changes in the convicted composition of the population.

B. Changing Age Composition

The move toward tougher sentences and diminished use of parole could not have come at a more inopportune time from a demographic perspective. It occurred just as the leading edge of the population wave known as the "postwar baby boom" was moving into the peak ages for imprisonment. Even under traditional indeterminate sentencing systems, the prisons would have been pressed to deal with increased numbers. Without the flexibility to accommodate the surge, the management problems posed by demographic change were severely exacerbated.

The structure of the baby-boom generation is shown in figure 2, which illustrates the age composition of the U.S. population in 1985 in terms of the number of people of each age. The same figure can also be read backwards to indicate the sizes of various birth cohorts in the U.S. population. For example, the group that was twenty years old in 1985 was born in 1965, and that cohort included 4.1 million people in 1985. The group that was forty in 1985 was born in 1945, just before the start of the "baby boom." Thus, the horizontal axis can be labeled both with the ages of the groups in 1985 and with the years in which each of those cohorts was born. (The size of each such age group is not identical to the number of persons born in the United States in their year of birth, however; they differ because of mortality from the original U.S. birth cohort and in-migration of those born outside the Unites States.)

The figure shows that the baby boom began in 1947, with an increase of about 30 percent in the size of that cohort compared with the 1946 cohort. After the end of World War II in 1945, about one year was

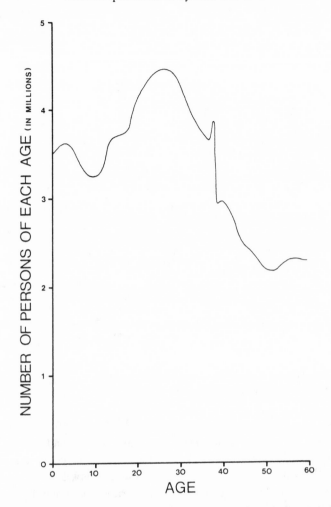

FIG. 2.—Age composition of the United States on July 1, 1985 (smoothed data except for ages thirty-eight and thirty-nine). Source: U.S. Bureau of the Census 1986.

consumed in separation from service and in family formation. The large pent-up increment in births that occurred in 1947 was followed by a steady growth in the sizes of successive cohorts until around 1960. A generally steady decline ensued until the beginning of the "echo boom," the generation of children born to baby-boom children, following the trough in 1976.

This age-composition information must be considered in light of what we know about the age sensitivity of crime and imprisonment. Crime commission is primarily an activity of the young, and this is

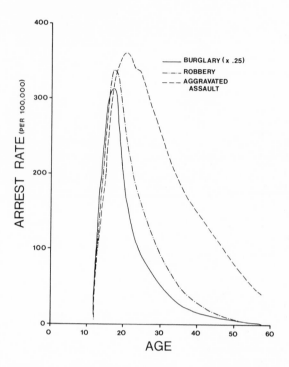

FIG. 3.—Age-specific arrest rates for burglary, robbery, and aggravated assault. Source: Federal Bureau of Investigation 1984.

reflected in the age-specific arrest rates shown in figure 3 (see also Farrington 1986). The data reported in figure 3 are broadly indicative of involvement in crime, albeit with some error, since young offenders may well be more likely to be caught, but perhaps less likely to be recorded as arrested when they commit a crime than are older offenders. Hindelang, Hirschi, and Weis (1979) compared victims' reports of offender characteristics with the characteristics of arrestees, and found general consistency; this suggests that the gross indications of figure 3 are probably correct. The basic conclusion here is that involvement in most kinds of crime peaks at ages sixteen to eighteen, depending on the type of crime, and then declines rapidly thereafter. For example, property crimes peak at age sixteen and fall to half the peak rate by age twenty-one. Robbery peaks at about seventeen or eighteen and reaches half its peak by age twenty-three. The fall-off in the assaultive crimes is slowest, with the peak occurring in the period eighteen through twenty-one, and the rate does not fall to half the peak until age thirty-five.

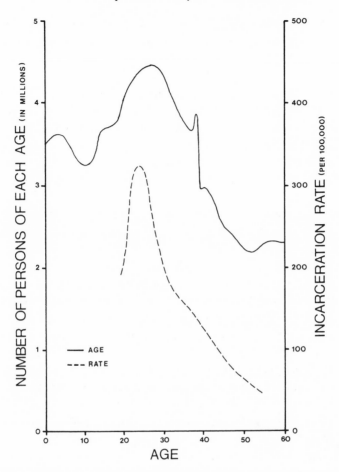

FIG. 4.—Age-specific incarceration rate compared to 1985 U.S. age composition

We can also compare the age distribution of the U.S. population (from figure 2) with the age-specific incarceration rates of prisoners (in figure 4) (derived from U.S. Bureau of Justice Statistics Survey of Prisoners in 1979—Reference Profile 1979, table 2, for prisoners, and U.S. Bureau of the Census, 1986, table 2, for the population). Figure 4 shows an age sensitivity of the incarceration rate that is similar to that of figure 3, though somewhat less pronounced. There is also an important shift in the peak age. In contrast to the offending-rate peak at about age sixteen to eighteen, the age-specific incarceration rate peaks at about age twenty-three. This delay is easily explained. Juveniles under eighteen are rarely sent to prison, and most first-time offenders—in

many places, for most offenses, even second- or third-time offenders—
are not sent to prison. Thus, even though figure 3 suggests that most
offenders desist from crime by age twenty-three, it is the relatively few
who continue to be active who create the highest rate of incarceration.

The largest single age group in 1985 was the twenty-four-year-old
cohort, those born in 1961. We thus see in figure 4 the coincidence of
this population peak with the peak of the incarceration rate. This coincidence would undoubtedly have contributed to growth in prison populations on the basis of demographic considerations alone.

An issue of continuing interest is whether the aging of the large
baby-boom age cohorts might soon contribute to a decline in the prison
population. One way to examine this is provided in figure 5, in which
the population composition of 1995 is simulated simply by shifting the
1985 population (of figure 4) to be ten years older, but leaving fixed the
age-specific incarceration rate. The bulk of the baby-boomers will be
well past the age of primary prison vulnerability, and the changing age
composition should therefore soon contribute to a reduction in prison
population. Of course, that influence may well be countered by other
influences, such as growth in crime rates or continuing pressure on
judges for tougher sentences, and only the net effects will be evident.

Thus, in summary, we see that in 1975—when the first wave of the
baby boom, the 1947 cohort, was twenty-eight—the early waves of the
baby boom were moving into the peak imprisonment ages, and undoubtedly contributed to the initial growth of prison populations. In
1985, the incarceration rate peak and the age composition peak were
coincident, suggesting a peaking of the demographic influence on the
prison population. By 1994, the baby-boom generation should be well
past the peak incarceration rate ages, and the changing age composition
should work to diminish prison populations.

C. The Racial Disproportionality in Prison

There is a large difference in incarceration rates between blacks and
whites in the United States. The age-specific incarceration rate for
blacks is shown in figure 6, which shows an age pattern that is generally
similar to that for whites, with the peak age-specific incarceration rate
at about the same age, twenty-three. The incarceration rate for blacks,
however, is about seven times that for whites, and so blacks constitute
almost half of the United States' prison populations.

This disproportionality has been viewed as a manifestation of the
"racism" of the criminal justice system (see, e.g., Dunbaugh 1979).

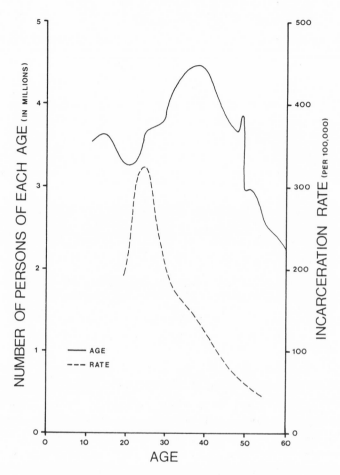

FIG. 5.—Simulated relationship between incarceration rate and age composition of the U.S. population in 1995.

Extensive research efforts from a wide variety of perspectives have been directed at establishing the existence and magnitude of racial discrimination within the criminal justice system.

The dominant research strategy involves collecting a sample of sentenced cases, then identifying variables that could reasonably contribute to the sentence outcome, adding the offender's race as one more variable, and then testing to see whether the coefficient associated with the race variable (black or white) is statistically significantly different from zero (see reviews of this research in Blumstein et al. [1983] and Hagan and Bumiller [1983]). That approach, however, has a number of

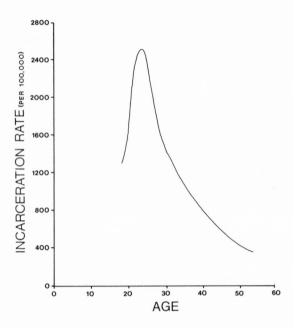

FIG. 6.—Incarceration rate by age for black males. Source: U.S. Bureau of Justice Statistics 1979, and U.S. Bureau of the Census 1986.

important weaknesses. First, not all variables that might possibly affect sentencing can be included in an analysis. The influence of excluded variables that do have a racial correlation may be mistakenly attributed to included variables that are thought to have a racial link.

Second, a spurious race correlation could result from nonlinearities in the functional relationships; if the presumed linear model (a simple weighted sum of the relevant influential variables) is inappropriate, then the stray influence could be attributed to any of the included variables, including race.

Third, if there is any race effect, and if the sample size is large enough, then the residual statistical error would be small and the coefficient, however small, will be viewed as "statistically significant" (although the word "discernible" more appropriately conveys the sense, because it avoids the misinterpretation of "significant" as "large").

Fourth, there could also be bias due to selection effects. If, for example, a prosecutor was systematically favoring whites by dropping less serious cases only for them, then the whites convicted for a particular offense would have committed more serious crimes than would the nonwhites; judges who were perfectly race-blind in their sentencing would impose harsher sentences on white offenders than on nonwhite offenders. This apparently harsher treatment of whites (as it might be seen by people who did not understand the prosecutor's screening policies) would camouflage a systematic bias against nonwhites. This is merely one of the ways by which discrimination that did exist could be masked.

Another is the phenomenon known as "victim discounting," when offenders whose victims are blacks receive lesser sentences than do those whose victims were white. This has been highlighted for capital punishment cases in particular (Baldus, Pulanski, and Woodworth 1983). Since the great majority of black offenders offend against black victims, this discrimination against black victims would appear as an average benefit to black offenders when compared with whites. Also, since most black offending occurs in urban areas, and urban courts typically impose less severe sentences than do suburban or rural courts (perhaps because the volume of offending in urban areas is so high that judges are inured to less serious kinds of offending), the relative leniency in the urban courts would also tend, on average, to benefit black offenders in any analysis that aggregated urban and rural areas, as is the case for most state cross-sectional analyses.

Thus, such statistical studies using regression analyses can contribute in only a limited way to understanding the nature and extent of racial discrimination in the criminal justice system. Findings of "significant" coefficients could be spurious or could indeed represent evidence of racial discrimination. While discrimination is patently abhorrent and to be eliminated wherever possible, it would not be surprising to find some. Given the gross disproportionality of racial representation in prisons, the important question is not whether racial discrimination exists at all (it almost certainly does to some degree in places), but to what extent it contributes to this enormous difference. In contrast, for example, the disproportionality of representation between the sexes is even larger, twenty-four to one. That difference is readily attributed predominantly to differential involvement in crime by males rather than to sex discrimination against males.

Blumstein (1982) tried to address this issue by comparing the racial distributions of prisoners and arrestees, but controlling for the type of crime involved. The results (which were based on data in 1978 and 1979, but were found to be insensitive to year-to-year variations) show that there is generally a close approximation between the two distributions. For example, 51.6 percent of arrestees for murder are black, whereas 52.3 percent of prisoners in prison for murder are black. Among arrestees for robbery, 57.1 percent are black, and 61.2 percent

TABLE 4

Fraction of Prison Racial Disproportionality Not Accounted for by Differential Involvement in Arrest

Crime Type	Fraction (%)
Homicide	2.8
Aggravated assault	5.2
Robbery	15.6
Aggregate (all crimes)	20.5
Forcible rape	26.3
Burglary	33.1
Larceny/auto theft	45.6
Drugs	48.9

SOURCE.—Blumstein (1982, p. 1274).

of prisoners sentenced for robbery are black. Murder and robbery together account for 40 percent of American prison populations, and the correspondence between the race distribution of prisoners and the race distribution of arrestees is reasonably close. Taking account of all crime types, Blumstein's estimate is that 80 percent of the racial disproportionality in prison populations is explainable by differences between the races in their involvement in arrest. The explanation is primarily that robbery and murder account for a large fraction of the prison population, and the race ratio at arrest so closely matches that in prison.

As attention shifts to the relatively less serious types of crime, the disparities between arrestees and prisoners become greater. Table 4 indicates for each type of crime the percent of the disproportionality in prison that is *not* accounted for by differential involvement in arrest. The table also includes the aggregate for the total prison population, with each type of crime weighted by its representation in prison. As the focus shifts toward the less serious offenses, the latitude for racial discrimination becomes greater. The offense itself becomes less determinative of whether a prison sentence is imposed and other factors, such as the extent of prior record, employment, seriousness of the offense within the class—and also possibly race—become more salient.

If the race distributions at arrest were identical to race distributions of imprisonment for each type of crime, the black proportion in prison in 1979 would shift from 49.1 percent to 47.1 percent. While that shift would have been very meaningful to the 10,000 individuals involved, relative to the total prison population and its aggregate disproportionality, the shift would not have a major impact; the shift would be most pronounced in the lesser types of crime, and prisoners convicted of those make up a relatively small fraction of the prison population.

In the aggregate, then, it appears that the races differ in their involvement in arrest, and that this difference accounts for 80 percent of the disproportionality in prisons. Some of the remaining 20 percent could be attributable to factors other than the type of crime at arrest (such as differences in prior record or in probation or in employment status) that are at least arguably appropriate for consideration within the sentencing decision. These effects could also be moderated by practices that are not necessarily nondiscriminatory but that do favor black defendants (such as victim discounting or relative leniency in urban courts).

This evidence suggests that there is not a major shift in the racial disproportionality of representation between arrest and imprisonment, at least when types of crime are weighted by their relative representation in prison populations. One challenge that might be raised to this analysis is that arrests may reflect police discrimination against non-whites and, as a result, comparisons of racial proportions at arrest and in prisons are inherently misleading. That critique, however, is undermined to a significant degree by the similarity found by Hindelang (1978) between the racial distributions reported by victims of robbery and assault and the corresponding racial distributions of people arrested for these crimes. These results, which were consistently found in a number of jurisdictions, serve to counter the hypothesis that the major racial disproportionalities in arrests are largely attributable to police discrimination. Again, one need not conclude that there is no such discrimination, but rather that the discrimination that is there—and which should, of course, be eliminated to the degree possible—does not account for the gross racial differences in arrests.

A more fundamental political critique of racial disproportionality in prison concedes the comparable disproportionality in arrests and in offending, but argues that the United States discriminates against non-whites by treating harshly those offenses that nonwhites disproportionately commit and treating leniently those offenses, such as environmental or business regulatory offenses, that whites disproportionately commit. This critique simply does not hold up. The two offenses that are most represented in prison are murder and robbery. They represent large proportions of prisoners, partly because those crimes are more easily solved, and partly because there is a widespread feeling of repugnance toward them. This engenders a motivation for imprisonment for reasons both of retribution and incapacitation. This view is shared across a wide range of times, settings, and cultures. It may well be that the less frequently solved, white-collar offenses could be punished more severely, but it is not likely that that would reduce the number or length of sentences for crimes like murder and robbery, nor would it contribute many more prisoners to prison.

Another facet of racial disproportionality in prison is portrayed in table 5, which shows the American states (omitting those smaller states that have so few black prisoners that no incarceration rate is estimated) and their incarceration rates (prisoners per 100,000 resident population of each of the races) for white and black males (U.S. Bureau of Justice Statistics 1984). The last column of table 5 lists the ratio of the black and white incarceration rates (which average 6.5 for all the prisons in the United States) as an indicator of the racial disproportionality of each state's prison population. The states with a high ratio are those that are most disproportionate in their imprisonment of their black residents, and the states with the lowest ratios have the closest approximation between black and white incarceration rates.

Table 5 lists the states in order of this ratio of black-to-white incarceration rates. The lowest ratios are displayed by the southern states, and the highest ratios by the states that are conventionally regarded as liberal and least likely to engage in gross racial discrimination. The table thus prompts speculation about the factors contributing to this seemingly anomalous pattern of racial disproportionality. Perhaps, for example, the blacks in the "liberal" states are more concentrated in urban areas where involvement in crime, and therefore the probability of incarceration, is greater. Or perhaps blacks in these states are more likely to be recent arrivals and thus less subject to the conventional forms of social control, while blacks in the South are more likely to have been residents longer, and because of their roots in local communities, to be more comfortable and socialized to the local legal and behavioral norms.

Some of the differences might also reflect a generally greater level of punitiveness toward offenders in the South. This difference is reflected in the higher rate of incarceration in the South, which is the highest region in the nation (U.S. Bureau of Justice Statistics 1984). Since the differential racial involvement in crime is greatest for murder and robbery, and less for the less serious crimes, the more punitive a state is (as reflected in a high incarceration rate in relation to its serious crime rate, for example), the greater is the proportion of its prison population that will be accounted for by the less serious offenses. Since whites commit

TABLE 5

Ratio of Black-to-White Incarceration by State

State	Incarceration Rates		Black/White Ratio
	White Males	Black Males	
South Carolina	340	1,144	3.36
Georgia	292	1,183	4.05
Nevada	545	2,285	4.19
North Carolina	320	1,355	4.23
Mississippi	196	857	4.37
Tennessee	221	994	4.50
Alabama	245	1,150	4.69
West Virginia	159	753	4.74
Kentucky	174	842	4.84
Oklahoma	318	1,617	5.08
Texas	353	1,828	5.18
Arkansas	198	1,097	5.54
Florida	351	2,007	5.72
Missouri	202	1,170	5.79
Virginia	197	1,148	5.83
Louisiana	206	1,304	6.33
Indiana	227	1,473	6.49
Colorado	179	1,169	6.53
Arizona	368	2,438	6.62
New York	192	1,300	6.77
Delaware	348	2,540	7.30
Ohio	185	1,544	8.35
Washington	230	2,032	8.83
Maryland	190	1,695	8.92
Kansas	174	1,632	9.38
Michigan	147	1,441	9.80
Illinois	101	1,067	10.56
Connecticut	226	2,460	10.88
New Jersey	101	1,132	11.21
Massachusetts	114	1,416	12.42
Pennsylvania	89	1,160	13.03
District of Columbia	130	1,835	14.12
Wisconsin	120	1,948	16.23
Minnesota	70	1,522	21.74

SOURCE.—U.S. Bureau of Justice Statistics (1984, p. 23).

a higher proportion of these lesser offenses, this would tend to lower the black-white ratio of incarceration rates.

The evidence is still insufficient to explain the ordering among the states shown in table 5. Regardless of the cause, however, the ranking of the states in terms of their black-to-white incarceration rate ratios challenges the more common expectation that the disproportionality derives from discrimination, and so should be greatest in the South.

The basic conclusion I draw is that the bulk of the differential presence of blacks in prison is attributable to differential involvement in crime rather than to racial discrimination. If this is substantially true, that also cuts off one potential avenue for relief from the prison crowding crisis. If disproportionality were attributable to racial discrimination, then that would warrant—and major support could probably be amassed for—political and legal efforts to end that repugnant practice, and thereby to reduce prison populations significantly. If discrimination is not the explanation, however, that approach will not substantially relieve the crowding problem.

The conclusion that racial imbalance in prison is not largely explained by discrimination makes the crowding problem look even bleaker, because of the changing racial composition of the U.S. population. At ages twenty to twenty-four, the ratio of white to black males in the general population is 6.35. For the ages of ten to fifteen—those not yet eligible for prison, but contributing to the next generation of prisoners—the ratio is 17 percent lower, 5.27 (U.S. Bureau of the Census 1986). This suggests that in the absence of some significant shifts in the factors contributing to the differences between the races in their involvement in crime, the proportion of black prisoners is likely to increase, and thereby exacerbate the continuing problems of prison crowding and of racial disproportionality in prison. The differential involvement in crime may diminish if the United States moves more vigorously toward eliminating the inequalities in its society, but trends in recent years do not make one optimistic that this will happen very quickly.

II. Approaches to Relieving Prison Crowding

There are three basic ways of dealing with the present crowding conditions in prison. The first involves diverting people to sentences other than prison (a "front-door" approach). Probation is the most common such means, and is now offered to the large majority of convicted first-time offenders.

The second involves shortening the lengths of prison sentences served (a "back-door" approach). This is what parole boards have been doing for many years, and the opposition to such practices has contributed to the current crowding problem.

Third, more prisons can be built to provide additional capacity. This requires considerable costs, however, and also introduces some concern that the additional capacity will continue to be used in the future even if crime rates decline. Provision of additional capacity inevitably involves a delay, often up to four to seven years from initial planning before that capacity becomes operational. Given the difficulty of forecasting prison populations into the future, that capacity may not become available until after it is no longer needed.

A. Approaches to Population Reduction

The "front-door" approach involves finding alternatives to prison for those whom a judge might want to send there. This is not intended for the most serious offenders, for those who commit heinous crimes, or for those who represent a serious continuing risk in the community. It is, however, a possibility for the marginal offenders who might otherwise be candidates for probation but who may already have had one or more prior sentences to probation, and who warrant something more severe. The problem is to develop a rich array of nonprison punishments so that the judge, the victim, and the community are satisfied that the level of punishment is adequate and that there is some hope that the punishment will reduce the probability that the offender will persist in crime. The alternatives most often considered are some combination of intensive probation, restitution, community service, or residence in a group home with tighter surveillance but with the right to go to work during the day.

These programs handle a mixture of offenders—some who would otherwise have gone to prison if the programs were not available, and others for whom prison would not have been likely and who would have been put on probation. Most evaluations have found that the programs handle mostly individuals who would have been on probation ("widening the net of social control") rather than those who would have gone to prison (Austin and Krisberg 1982). Analyses of some programs, however, are uncovering possibilities for moving in the other direction (Winterfield 1982).

While front-door strategies operate to divert offenders from entering prison, back-door strategies—such as adjustments in parole release, good-time policies, and emergency-release laws—are concerned with increasing the release rate by shortening the time served by those who do go to prison. In the presence of constraints on total prison capacity, one can choose between sending more people to prison for shorter times, or fewer people can be imprisoned for longer times. Considerations of both deterrence and incapacitation argue for the former.

Research has consistently supported the position that sentence "severity" (i.e., the time served) has less of a deterrent effect than sentence "certainty" (the probability of going to prison) (Blumstein, Cohen, and Nagin 1978). Thus, it makes sense to increase certainty, even if it must be done at the expense of severity.

From the standpoint of incapacitation, the longer the time served, the more likely it is that the individual would have terminated his criminal activity even if he were not in prison. In this sense, additional prison time after the end of the criminal career is "wasted." Studies of the duration of criminal careers suggest that 10 to 20 percent of offenders "retire" from crime each year (Blumstein and Cohen 1985). Furthermore, findings in rehabilitation research that most correctional programs do not reduce recidivism rates suggest that this dropout rate is not significantly affected by the imposition of prison sentences or by the length of imprisonment. In any given year one might expect about 10 percent of the individuals in prison to have terminated their criminal activity even if they were on the outside. The interest of incapacitation is best served by incarcerating individuals during the period when they are most likely to be criminally active, which turns out to be the period closest to the time of conviction (Blumstein et al. 1986). Thus, from both incapacitation and deterrence perspectives, more shorter sentences are to be preferred to fewer longer ones.

These considerations do not negate the value of long sentences for retributive reasons, but it should be recognized that long retributive sentences in the face of a capacity constraint may reduce efficiency in crime prevention and reduction.

B. Population-Sensitive Flow-Control Strategies

Sentencing policies can be linked more directly to prison population. It is possible to devise strategies that explicitly tie a measure of crowding (e.g., the excess of prison population over available capacity) to sentencing practices (see Knapp 1987).

I here consider three somewhat different approaches to a population-sensitive incarceration strategy: (1) a planned policy that uses sentencing guidelines and links those guidelines to prison capacity; (2) a policy that employs a population-responsive "safety valve" to release prisoners when overcrowding becomes excessive; and (3) a strategy that allocates prison spaces to each court and its judges or prosecutors, who must take their limited allocation into account in making their own decisions.

The best example of a planned population-sensitive incarceration policy is the sentencing guidelines matrix developed by the Minnesota Sentencing Guidelines Commission (Knapp 1987). The commission's work followed from an explicit legislative mandate to give "substantial consideration" to prison capacity in developing sentencing guidelines, and used prison capacity as a constraint on the sentencing standards that emerged. Thus, if the commission were to increase the presumptive sentence for robbery, the forecasted increase in prison population would have to be offset by decreasing presumptive sentences for other categories of offenders or by shifting some categories of offenders from presumptive prison sentences to presumptive nonprison sentences. Such a procedure requires some kind of simulation or estimation model that enables the policy group to calculate for each possible sentencing schedule the prison capacity it would consume. This in turn requires information on the expected number of convicted offenders in each category (based, in Minnesota's case, on an offense severity score and on the length of the offender's prior conviction record) in order to estimate the prison capacity that the schedule would consume.

The existence of a prison-capacity constraint imposes a useful discipline on the policy debate. In most settings where sanction policies are debated, advocates of tougher sentences gain political benefits without having to consider the costs of their actions. The methods developed by the Minnesota Sentencing Guidelines Commission deserve much credit for the fact that in 1981, when the U.S. prison population as a whole increased 12.1 percent from 1980, Minnesota had one of the lowest rates of increase, only 1.1 percent. There remains the important question, however, of whether the willingness of the Minnesota criminal justice system—and especially its judges—to accept the discipline of sentencing guidelines is likely to be repeated in other jurisdictions where the commitment to rational government is less strong.

The Minnesota system is rather elaborate; a greater number of jurisdictions might be more comfortable with the "safety valve" policy adopted by the Michigan legislature in 1981 that was discussed above. A corrections commission was charged with monitoring the population of the state's prisons in relation to their capacity, and with reporting to the governor when the incarcerated population exceeded the prison's capacity for longer than thirty days. Upon receipt of such a report, the governor was then enabled to reduce the minimum sentences of every prisoner by up to ninety days, thereby increasing the population eligible for parole. This did not represent an automatic release of all these prisoners because they still had to appear before the parole board, which can still retain the most dangerous offenders until their maximum sentences expire.

This strategy diffuses the political cost of accommodating prison population to capacity. The legislature enacts the law; the independent corrections commission declares the condition of overcrowding; the governor orders the reduction of minimum sentences; and the parole board orders the actual release. This approach provides all participants with a politically palatable means of acting responsibly to avoid the consequences of prison crowding.

Finally, a more radical approach has been proposed by John Manson, the late commissioner of corrections of Connecticut. A "ration" of prison cells would be allocated to the individual courts within the state, or possibly even to the prosecutors (Blumstein and Kadane 1983). If a court used up its allocation and wanted to send an additional convicted offender to prison, the court would be required to identify which cell from among its allocation should be vacated. The judge would then release a current occupant in order to obtain the needed space for the new one. This approach would force the judge (or the prosecutor before him) to acknowledge the costs of prison crowding, and to take those costs into account in making sentencing decisions. Such a policy seems highly unlikely to be implemented, but it certainly forces thinking about the allocation issues, and directs attention to the Michigan or Minnesota approaches.

All of the approaches to population-sensitive flow control require an explicit formulation of the excessively flexible concept of "prison capacity." As long as double- or triple-celling is a possibility, capacity remains a poorly defined notion and imposes only a weak constraint on policy-making or decision makers. When capacity does become a more meaningful limit, explicit policy statements can be formulated to define it. This can be done by a commission, including representatives of the legislature, the judiciary, the correctional administration, and prosecutors.

C. Provision of Additional Capacity: Effect on Prison Admissions

Additional prison capacity would permit keeping the same number of prisoners (or more), but under more acceptable conditions. Providing the additional capacity costs money, however; construction costs typically range between $50,000 and $75,000 per cell. Additional money is needed each year—about $10,000–$15,000 per prisoner—to maintain, guard, and manage the prisoners. These high costs were undoubtedly influential in the rejection several years ago by New York State voters of a bond issue to provide additional prison space.

Additional capacity does not, however, become available instantly. Many bureaucratic processes are involved: deciding to provide the additional capacity; agreeing on a site, and especially gaining acceptance by the prison's neighbors; authorization and appropriation of funds by the legislature; architectural design; and finally construction. Although a series of National Institute of Justice–sponsored publications demonstrates that additional prison space can sometimes be added quickly and inexpensively (DeWitt 1986a, 1986b), prison construction normally takes four to seven years or more. Thus, a commitment to provide additional capacity to solve today's crowding problem may not provide the capacity for several years. By that time, the crowding problem may have diminished on its own. By 1992, for example, the earliest date by which new prisons begun in 1988 might become available, the population in the prison-prone ages will have decreased significantly, and the age component of the crowding problem will begin to be alleviated.

One issue that has been of continuing concern regarding prison populations—and especially in an era when prison crowding creates a need for additional prison capacity—is the mutual influence between population and capacity. One view is that prison populations follow their own Parkinson's Law—the population will expand to fill the available capacity. Thus, if more capacity is provided, the threshold of which offenders warrant imprisonment will simply drop and the capacity will be filled. The other view holds that any jurisdiction has some reasonably well-defined criteria (that may well differ across jurisdictions) that define a prison "tariff," and that the capacity should be large enough to accommodate that tariff.

Anecdotal evidence is available on both sides. Many judges maintain that they have their own view of sentences, and that the availability of slack capacity does not encourage them to be harsher and crowded conditions do not inhibit their imposition of imprisonment. They see prison management as someone else's problem. Other judges admit that crowded prisons do influence their imposition of prison sentences, perhaps raising the threshold of offense or offender characteristics that warrant imprisonment.

This issue has been raised most vigorously by those who argue for a moratorium on prison construction or argue against construction of additional capacity, on the Parkinsonian grounds that any additional capacity will be filled, irrespective of crime rates. The proponents of this position can point to a number of cases where additional capacity was provided and quickly became filled. Of course, there are counterarguments. One is that those who have responsibility for establishing the capacity simply anticipated future populations. It is also the case that many state prison systems had excess capacity in the 1960s, a time when prison populations were decreasing.

The interaction between prison population and prison capacity became a major theme of a $1 million study of American prisons and jails by Abt Associates (Mullen, Carlson, and Smith 1980). Abt researchers formulated two competing statistical models, one having prison population as the dependent variable and the other having prison capacity as the dependent variable. The independent variables were the various measures of previous years' capacity and prison populations and no other exogenous factors. In both models, most of the coefficients were found to be negligibly small, but in one—the model with prison population as a dependent variable—they found a coefficient of 1.02 associated with changes in capacity two years earlier. The other coefficients were much smaller and all less than 0.1. This surprising result seemed to confirm the Parkinsonian argument and to demonstrate that it was indeed the available capacity that influenced prison populations two years later almost precisely on a one-to-one basis. That finding became the subject of considerable public attention, was the theme of an article in the *New York Times*, and was explicitly incorporated as an element of a National Institute of Corrections policy (Mullen and Smith 1980).

The data that gave rise to the conclusion were reanalyzed by Blumstein, Cohen, and Gooding (1983), and the coefficient of 1.02 was found to have resulted from a mistake in entering the missing value statements in the Statistical Package for the Social Sciences (SPSS) analysis program. When the mistake was corrected, the coefficient dropped from 1.02 to .254. Even that coefficient was shown to be largely the product of two anomalous data points out of 1,000 that were used; omitting those two data points dropped the resulting coefficient below 0.1, no different from the others, which were also not statistically significantly different from zero, and the finding disappeared.

It is not surprising that so complex an issue as the relationship of prison population to prison capacity could not be adequately expressed by so simple a model. Considerations such as state revenues, budget surpluses or deficits, court interventions in the corrections system, crime rates, unemployment, and many other factors can affect prison construction, prison population, or both. A simultaneous statistical model is needed that reflects the mutual influence of population growth on the construction of capacity, and the influence of capacity limitations in encouraging or inhibiting the growth of prison populations. Such simultaneous models recognize that either can influence the other (just as, in economics, changes in supply can influence demand and vice versa). Analysis of such situations, however, requires isolation of the factors that influence each independently, and particularly those factors that influence one without affecting the other. For example, unemployment rates are likely to influence commitment rates to prison but not likely to influence the capacity provided, whereas a state budget surplus may influence decisions to provide additional capacity but are not likely to have a direct influence on prison populations. The existence of judicial interventions in prison management because of crowding is likely to influence both judges' commitment decisions and political decisions to provide additional capacity.

During the 1960s, for example, when incarceration rates were less than half what they were in 1984, there was considerable surplus capacity, but prison populations continued to decline. Thus, the inevitability of the use of available capacity was certainly not the case during that period.

Showing the incorrectness of the Abt "proof" of the influence of capacity on population does not demonstrate the contrary, that is, that population is unaffected by capacity. It is still possible for such influences to occur, but no scientific or statistical evidence yet supports that causal hypothesis.

III. A Reasonable Mixed Strategy

As a state formulates its strategy for dealing with its prison crowding, it must consider approaches that will work in the short run to alleviate the immediate congestion—a problem faced by virtually all states—and it must develop a long-run strategy. As a first step it is important for a state to develop a projection of its demography, including anticipated in- and out-migration. That projection should extend to at least the year 2000, when the baby-boom generation will have exited the high-imprisonment age brackets. For states whose demography is not dominated by migration, such a projection should be reasonably accurate, since all individuals of interest to an adult prison system in the year 2000 were born by 1982.

The demographic projection should be augmented by an analysis of trends in demographic-specific crime rates (particularly in the crimes of murder, robbery, and burglary, which account for a majority of the prison population) and of trends in the punitive responses of the state's criminal justice system. If there has been a strong trend toward greater incarceration resembling that reflected in table 1, then the factors causing the trend should be isolated, and the state must face the hard assessment of whether those trends will continue or will reverse. Demographic projections, in combination with judgments about future punitiveness, should provide a reasonable basis for estimating the size of the prison population for the remainder of the century.

Construction cannot solve the short-term congestion problem. The introduction of a "safety valve" on the Michigan model, however, appears to be entirely appropriate; it could be made politically acceptable, and it could be readily implemented. In the absence of such a safety valve, or of the legislative leadership necessary to create one, means such as good-time release that will permit reduction of the time served by prisoners should be considered as a back-door strategy.

For the intermediate term, many states will find it desirable to provide temporary extra capacity for the next decade. This could be done by converting vacated state mental hospitals or other such state-owned residential facilities that are no longer used for the human services for which they were originally constructed.

In addition, states should establish a linkage between their sentencing policies and their prison capacities. They can do this first by establishing legislative, judicial, or executive commissions charged with establishing a formal prisoner capacity for each of the state's prisons. Once the aggregate prison capacity has been calculated, a sentencing commission can be established. The role of the sentencing commission is to examine current sentencing patterns and to reconsider sentencing practice in terms of appropriate norms. The commission should then establish a schedule of sentencing guidelines consistent with those norms in a relative sense and scaled to the available (or anticipated) capacity in an absolute sense. The commission should also continually assess the relation between prison capacity and sentencing policy and practice, and should be in a position to adjust sentences downward or to recommend the construction of additional facilities as population exceeds capacity.

Meanwhile, research should continue on improving the selection process in sentencing and on the overall prison planning process. Research on selective incapacitation should be pursued carefully through a sequence of prospective studies that test the usefulness of various kinds of predictors of high-frequency predatory offenders.

Research is also needed to enable a state or its sentencing commission to better estimate the impact of policies on prison populations. Such methods of prediction have proved particularly important in Minnesota in developing its sentencing guidelines and in Pennsylvania, where they helped shape a sentencing policy compatible with a reasonable level of new construction. There is a need for further development and dissemination of methodologies that are applicable to any state that wants to pursue its policies in a similar responsible way.

The prison congestion problem will remain serious throughout the 1980s, and well into the 1990s at least. The problem can be addressed responsibly in a variety of ways without imposing inhumane conditions on prisoners or suffering the disastrous risks of doing nothing. Effective action, however, requires a level of political leadership that has rarely been mobilized to address prison problems. Those who manage and live in the prisons, and who alone suffer from the effects of overcrowding, control none of the levers that can provide solutions.

There is consequently an urgent need for coordination across the criminal justice system—just the sort that the old Law Enforcement Assistance Administration (LEAA) was created to provide. Such coordination was difficult for LEAA to achieve, in large part because *its* problems were predominantly those of growing crime rates, and there is only very weak knowledge of the effects of policy changes on crime rates. It is ironic that following the demise of the LEAA in 1980, prison crowding emerged as the dominant problem. This was the kind of problem that criminal justice planning can effectively support. Unfortunately, however, the money and the organizational structures disappeared with the end of the LEAA program, and so most states cannot now pursue this critical opportunity for cross-system planning.

REFERENCES

Austin, James. 1986. "Using Early Release to Relieve Prison Crowding: A Dilemma in Public Policy." *Crime & Delinquency* 32:404–501.

Austin, James, and Barry Krisberg. 1982. "The Unmet Promise of Alternatives." *Crime & Delinquency* 28:374–409.

Baldus, David, Charles Pulanski, and George Woodworth. 1983. "Comparative Review of Death Sentences: An Empirical Study of the Georgia Experience." *Journal of Criminal Law and Criminology* 74:661–753.

Blumstein, Alfred. 1982. "On the Racial Disproportionality of United States'
Prison Populations." *Journal of Criminal Law and Criminology* 73:1259–81.

Blumstein, Alfred, and Jacqueline Cohen. 1973. "A Theory of the Stability of
Punishment." *Journal of Criminal Law and Criminology* 64:198–207.

———. 1985. "Estimating the Duration of Adult Criminal Careers." Paper
presented at the 1985 meeting of the International Statistical Institute, Am-
sterdam, August.

Blumstein, Alfred, Jacqueline Cohen, and William Gooding. 1983. "The Influence of Capacity on Prison Population: A Critical Review of Some Recent
Evidence." *Crime & Delinquency* 29:1–51.

Blumstein, Alfred, Jacqueline Cohen, Susan Martin, and Michael Tonry, eds.
1983. *Research on Sentencing: The Search for Reform.* 2 vols. Washington, D.C.:
National Academy Press.

Blumstein, Alfred, Jacqueline Cohen, and David Nagin, eds. 1978. *Deterrence
and Incapacitation: Estimating the Effects of Criminal Sanctions on Crime Rates.*
Panel on Research on Deterrent and Incapacitative Effects, Committee on
Research on Law Enforcement and Criminal Justice, Assembly of Behav-
ioral and Social Sciences, National Research Council. Washington, D.C.:
National Academy of Sciences.

Blumstein, Alfred, Jacqueline Cohen, Jeffrey Roth, and Christy Visher, eds.
1986. *Criminal Careers and "Career Criminals."* 2 vols. Washington, D.C.:
National Academy Press.

Blumstein, Alfred, and Joseph B. Kadane. 1983. "An Approach to the Allocation of Scarce Imprisonment Resources." *Crime & Delinquency* 29:546–60.

Clarke, Stevens. 1987. *Felony Sentencing in North Carolina 1976–1986: Effects of
Presumptive Sentencing Legislation.* Chapel Hill: Institute of Government, University of North Carolina.

DeWitt, Charles. 1986a. *New Construction Methods for Correctional Facilities.* Construction Bulletin, March. Washington, D.C.: U.S. Department of Justice,
National Institute of Justice.

———. 1986b. *California Tests New Construction Concepts.* Construction Bulletin,
June. Washington, D.C.: U.S. Department of Justice, National Institute of
Justice.

Dunbaugh, Frank M. 1979. "Racially Disproportionate Rates of Incarceration
in the United States." *Prison Law Monitor* 1(9):March.

Farrington, David P. 1986. "Age and Crime." In *Crime and Justice: An Annual
Review of Research,* vol. 7, edited by Michael Tonry and Norval Morris.
Chicago: University of Chicago Press.

Federal Bureau of Investigation. 1984. *Age-Specific Arrest Rates.* Uniform Crime
Reporting Program. Washington, D.C.: U.S. Government Printing Office.

Gottfredson, Steven. 1987. "Prediction: An Overview of Selected Methodological Issues." In *Prediction and Classification: Criminal Justice Decision Making,*
edited by Don M. Gottfredson and Michael Tonry. Vol. 9 of *Crime and*

Justice: A Review of Research, edited by Michael Tonry and Norval Morris. Chicago: University of Chicago Press.

Hagan, John, and Karen Bumiller. 1983. "Making Sense of Sentencing: A Review and Critique of Sentencing Research." In *Research on Sentencing: The Search for Reform*, vol. 2, edited by Alfred Blumstein, Jacqueline Cohen, Susan Martin, and Michael Tonry. Washington, D.C.: National Academy Press.

Hindelang, Michael. 1978. "Race and Involvement in Common Law Personal Crimes." *American Sociological Review* 43:93–109.

Hindelang, Michael J., Travis Hirschi, and Joseph Weis. 1979. "Correlates of Delinquency: The Illusion of Discrepancy between Self-Report and Official Measures." *American Sociological Review* 44:995–1014.

Knapp, Kay. 1987. "The Sentencing Commission's Empirical Research." Chapter 7 in *The Sentencing Commission and Its Guidelines*, by Andrew von Hirsch, Kay Knapp, and Michael Tonry. Boston: Northeastern University Press.

Lipton, Dugan, Robert Martinson, and Judith Wilks. 1975. *The Effectiveness of Correctional Treatment: A Survey of Treatment Evaluation Studies*. New York: Praeger.

Martinson, Robert M. 1974. "What Works? Questions and Answers about Prison Reform." *Public Interest* 35:22–54.

Messinger, Sheldon, and Phillip Johnson. 1978. "California's Determinate Sentence Laws." In *Determinate Sentencing: Reform or Regression*, edited by the National Institute of Justice. Washington, D.C.: U.S. Government Printing Office.

Mullen, Joan, Kenneth Carlson, and Bradford Smith. 1980. *American Prisons and Jails*. Vol. 1, *Summary Findings and Policy Implications of a National Survey*. Washington, D.C.: U.S. Government Printing Office.

Mullen, Joan, and Bradford Smith. 1980. *American Prisons and Jails.*. Vol. 3, *Conditions and Costs of Confinement*. Washington, D.C.: U.S. Government Printing Office.

Rothman, David J. 1981. "Perspectives on the History of Sentencing." Paper presented at the National Research Council Conference on Sentencing Research, Woods Hole, Mass., July.

Sechrest, Lee, Susan O. White, and Elizabeth D. Brown, eds. 1979. *The Rehabilitation of Criminal Offenders: Problems and Prospects*. Washington, D.C.: National Academy of Sciences.

U.S. Bureau of the Census. 1982. "Estimates of the Resident Population of the United States, by Age, Race, and Sex: July 1, 1970 to July 1, 1981." *Current Population Reports: Population Estimates and Projections*, Series P-25, no. 917. Washington, D.C.: U.S. Government Printing Office.

———. 1986. "Estimates of the Population of the United States by Age, Sex, and Race: 1980 to 1985." *Current Population Reports: Population Estimates and Projections*, Series P-25, no. 985. Washington, D.C.: U.S. Government Printing Office.

U.S. Bureau of Justice Statistics. 1979. *Profile of State Prison Inmates: Sociodemo-*

graphic Findings from the 1974 Survey of Inmates of State Correctional Facilities. National Criminal Justice and Statistics Service, Special Report No. SD-NPSL-SR-5. Washington, D.C.: U.S. Government Printing Office.

———. 1982. *Prisoners 1925–81.* National Prisoner Statistics Bulletin No. NCJ-85861. Washington, D.C.: U.S. Government Printing Office.

———. 1984. *Prisoners in State and Federal Institutions on December 31, 1982.* National Prisoner Statistics Bulletin No. NCJ-93311. Washington, D.C.: U.S. Government Printing Office.

———. 1987*a. Prisoners in 1986.* Bureau of Justice Statistics Bulletin No. NCJ-104864. Washington, D.C.: U.S. Government Printing Office.

———. 1987*b. Jail Inmates 1986.* Bureau of Justice Statistics Bulletin No. NCJ-107123. Washington, D.C.: U.S. Government Printing Office.

Winterfield, Laura. 1982. "Community Corrections: A Realized Alternative to Corrections." Working Paper. Pittsburgh: Urban Systems Institute, Carnegie-Mellon University.

Zimring, Franklin E. 1977. "Making the Punishment Fit the Crime: A Consumer's Guide to Sentencing Reform." *Hastings Center Report* 6(6):13–21.

Michael Tonry

Structuring Sentencing

ABSTRACT

Since the modern sentencing reform movement began in the
mid-seventies, much has been learned about the effects of efforts to
structure sentencing discretion. Many new programs failed to achieve
their objectives; some innovations seem inherently flawed. Mandatory
sentencing laws seem always to create injustice in individual cases and to
produce efforts by judges and lawyers to avoid their application.
Voluntary sentencing guidelines have consistently been shown to have
little effect on sentences. By contrast, prosecutorial plea bargaining bans
and rules and parole guidelines have regularized decision making and
produced more consistent decisions. Both presumptive sentencing
guidelines and statutory determinate sentencing laws can reduce
sentencing disparities and change sentencing patterns in ways sought by
policymakers, without substantial increases in work loads, case processing
times, or trial rates, and without significant decreases in guilty plea rates.
The major policy initiatives as yet not addressed or evaluated are the
development of guidelines for nonprison sentences, development of
judicial controls on plea bargaining, and development of ways to sustain
momentum and maintain desired levels of compliance after structured
sentencing systems have been implemented.

Between 1935 and 1975, every American state, the District of Colum-
bia, and the federal system had an indeterminate sentencing system.
Between 1975 and 1988, major changes in sentencing institutions, prac-

Michael Tonry is managing editor of *Crime and Justice—A Review of Research*. Numer-
ous friends helped improve successive drafts of this essay. These include David Boerner,
Stevens Clarke, John Kramer, Sheldon Messinger, Norval Morris, Lloyd Ohlin, Dale
Parent, Roxanne Park, Sandra Shane-DuBow, Andrew von Hirsch, Richard Will, and
Franklin E. Zimring. An earlier version of portions of this essay appeared in Tonry
(1987).

tices, and laws were considered or adopted in nearly every jurisdiction. The changes receiving the greatest amount of national attention were associated with the effectuation of the Federal Sentencing Reform Act of 1984. These include the creation of the U.S. Sentencing Commission, the sentencing guidelines developed by the commission that took effect on November 1, 1987, the elimination of parole release for federal offenders sentenced under the new guidelines, and the establishment of a system of appellate sentence review.

By 1988, there was no longer "an American system of sentencing," as there had been during most earlier parts of the twentieth century, when indeterminate sentencing systems looked much the same everywhere: judges decided who went to prison and parole boards decided when the imprisoned were released, in both cases on ad hoc individualized bases justified by the need to individualize punishments and by the relevance of rehabilitative considerations.

Instead, by 1988, there was great diversity. Many jurisdictions remained indeterminate and in profile looked in 1988 much as they had in 1935. Those jurisdictions making major changes between 1975 and 1988 shared a premise—that the traditional system was undesirable in some respect—but not a conclusion as to what to establish in its place. No single approach predominated.

Some jurisdictions abolished parole release, parole supervision, or both. Some adopted parole guidelines. Some enacted statutory determinate sentencing laws. Some adopted presumptive sentencing guidelines. Some adopted "voluntary" sentencing guidelines at the state or local levels, for some or all offenses. Most enacted mandatory sentencing laws. A few tried to invigorate appellate sentence review. Underlying most of these initiatives is the notion that officials' discretionary decisions should be structured by rules and be made accountable to higher authorities.

This essay summarizes the evaluative literature that has accumulated on the consequences of efforts to structure sentencing. The focus is on sentencing narrowly defined as decisions made or ratified by judges concerning the sanctions meted out to convicted offenders. In an important sense, however, parole boards' release decisions are difficult to distinguish from judges' time-setting decisions, and many prosecutorial decisions are tantamount to sentencing decisions when they create meaningful constraints on the exercise of judicial discretion (examples include decisions to charge offenses subject to mandatory minimum sentences or to charge bargain under a presumptive sentencing guidelines system). Research on parole guidelines and efforts to structure prosecutorial discretion are mentioned briefly, but the primary focus is on structured judicial decision making.[1]

There is substantial evidence that efforts to structure sentencing discretion can achieve increased consistency (and reduced disparity) in sentencing decisions, and can achieve substantial changes in sentencing outcomes, without major disruption to court processes. Some of the most robust findings defy conventional wisdom:

1. Determinate sentencing laws, whether expressed in statutes or sentencing guidelines, often do not increase sentencing severity.

2. Radical changes in sentencing practice, including plea bargaining bans and shifts from indeterminate to determinate sentencing systems, often do not decrease guilty plea rates, increase trial rates or average case processing time, or in general impose substantial additional demands on court personnel and resources.

3. Determinate sentencing laws, presumptive sentencing guidelines, and plea bargaining bans often do not meet with widespread circumvention or manipulation at the hands of the officials whose discretions they constrain.

4. Appellate sentence review need not generate a caseload that overwhelms the appellate courts.

That the horribles paraded by opponents of change need not occur does not, of course, mean that all efforts to structure sentencing have succeeded. "Voluntary" sentencing guidelines have not been shown by evaluations to have much effect (though anecdotal evidence tells a somewhat different story in some jurisdictions). Many statutory determinate sentencing laws set standards that are so general or so unrealistically severe that they appear to be widely disregarded. Similarly, that presumptive sentencing guidelines systems can by and large achieve their goals does not mean that they will: more sentencing commissions have failed in their efforts to develop and implement presumptive sentencing guidelines than have succeeded.

This essay presents and discusses the research on which the foregoing assertions are based. The focus is on the impact of changes on sentencing decisions, case processing, and the behavior of lawyers and judges. Section I comments generally on the nature and limits of the existing impact evaluation literature. Sections II, III, and IV discuss

---

[1] The research on plea bargaining bans and guidelines and parole guidelines is summarized in Cohen and Tonry (1983) and Tonry (1987).

voluntary sentencing guidelines, presumptive sentencing guidelines, and determinate sentencing laws. Section IV also briefly considers mandatory sentencing laws. Section V integrates conclusions reached in the preceding sections, discusses the current generation of policy problems (notably the handling of plea bargaining in systems of structured discretion and the problem of maintaining momentum after the initial reform enthusiasm abates), and considers likely next steps in policy development.

I. An Introduction to the Research

Several prefatory matters warrant mention before the impact evaluation literature is discussed. First, it is sometimes hard to know how to weigh the effectiveness of legal or procedural innovations. Is the goal to achieve what the innovation's draftsmen said they wanted to accomplish, to achieve the results indicated by a literal analysis of the plain meaning of the law or rule, to make a slight change in direction toward outcomes more consistent with the values or principles underlying the change, or something else? Second, a number of methodological and interpretive problems confront efforts to generalize from the sentencing literature; some characterize the literature en masse and others affect individual studies. Third, there is the problem of separating cause from effect. Doctor Johnson accused doctors, particularly, of confusing subsequence for consequence, and that confusion is a special problem for analyses of the effects of legal changes.

A. What Kind of "Impacts"?

Whether an innovation can be said to succeed must depend on the criteria chosen for success. For many statutes, success can be measured straightforwardly. If a new law requires use of seat belts in cars, measuring compliance is relatively easy. With sentencing laws, it is sometimes more difficult. For some sentencing innovations, such as mandatory sentencing, the real goal of legislation may be achieved merely by its passage. Legislators may wish to be seen to be "tough on crime" and may support laws that many of them realize are unlikely to be enforced.

Setting aside that special category, by what measure should a sentencing innovation be assessed? Here are several possibilities.

Has the innovation achieved the declared goals of its proponents— reduced sentencing disparity, increased sentencing severity, whatever?

Has the new law been complied with literally? If, for example, it requires three-year prison sentences for persons convicted of robbery, have those sentences actually been imposed?

Has the innovation achieved those goals that are conceptually implied in the legislation, whether reduction of discrimination in sentencing outcomes, reduction in the extent of sentencing disparities, increased severity, more use of alternative sentencing resources?

Has the innovation affected the volume, distribution, or nature of crime by increasing the deterrent or incapacitative efficacy of sanctioning?

Has the innovation affected the processing of cases and the behavior of judges, prosecutors, defense lawyers, probation officers, and policemen?

This essay summarizes the evidence concerning the effects of structured sentencing initiatives on sentencing patterns, sentencing severity, disparity, case processing (including guilty plea and trial rates and case processing time), and court procedures, including plea bargaining practices, but does not address crime control effects or achievement of proponents' goals.

The effects of sentencing changes on crime rates are not discussed for three reasons. First, a number of major assessments of these impacts have been completed by others and are readily available (see, e.g., Beha 1977; Loftin and McDowall 1981, 1984; Carlson 1982). Second, the technical issues implicated by efforts to assess deterrent and incapacitative effects require a different degree of technical sophistication than this essay aims for (e.g., Blumstein, Cohen, and Nagin 1978). Third, not much can usefully be said about crime control impacts because most of the sentencing impact evaluations do not investigate them.

There are several reasons why I do not discuss whether innovations achieved their proponents' goals. First, there may be no authoritative source from which the proponents' goals can be ascertained. Second, the "authoritative" sources may be disingenuous, ambiguous, or contradictory; legislators often try to "make a record" to support an interpretation of a law in a way they prefer but that they failed to persuade their legislative colleagues to adopt. Third, different proponents may have had different goals. In many jurisdictions, liberals supported law changes because they hoped to make sentencing more fair and less severe, and conservatives supported the same changes because they hoped to make sentencing more consistent (less room for leniency) and more severe (see, e.g., Messinger and Johnson 1978; Casper, Brereton, and Neal 1983). Whichever result occurs, one set of proponents will be frustrated.

B. Limitations of the Literature

Although a complete bibliography on modern sentencing reform would be lengthy, the credible bases for developing generalizations about the consequences of innovations are few in number and subject to important methodological limitations.

1. *Sparseness.* The impact evaluation literature on sentencing is tiny, especially in light of the enormous volume of reform activity of the last decade. Although many agencies of government routinely collect statistics for management purposes, these are seldom collected with the needs of impact evaluations in mind and are seldom more than suggestive. Special purpose impact evaluations are required if generalizations concerning impact are to be offered with some confidence. Of the many sentencing innovations undertaken since 1975, only the enactment of California's determinate sentencing law in 1976 precipitated the funding and conduct of a significant number of impact evaluations (see Section IV below). Much more commonly, when major changes were initiated, no formal independent evaluation was undertaken, or if one was, it was of limited duration and scope. For example, no major independent evaluation has reported on the operation of presumptive sentencing guidelines in Washington and Pennsylvania, two of the three states where they have been promulgated by sentencing commissions. The major evaluation of Minnesota's sentencing guidelines, probably the single best known sentencing reform initiative in the United States and, outside North America, of the United States, was completed by the commission's research staff (Knapp 1984a; more recently, an outside evaluation was completed; see Miethe and Moore 1987).

Evaluations of other sentencing innovations have also been few in number. Mandatory sentencing laws, for example, though in effect in forty-nine states, have been seriously evaluated in only five jurisdictions—New York (Joint Committee on New York Drug Law Evaluation 1978), Massachusetts (Beha 1977; Rossman et al. 1979; Pierce and Bowers 1981), Michigan (Heumann and Loftin 1979; Loftin, Heumann, and McDowall 1983), Florida (Loftin and McDowall 1984), and Pennsylvania (Pennsylvania Commission on Crime and Delinquency 1986). Determinate sentencing laws that abolished parole and established sentencing standards have given rise to major evaluations only in California and North Carolina (Clarke et al. 1983; Clarke 1984, 1987), even though at least nine states have adopted such systems.

For purposes of this essay, the scantness is no great problem. What is important is the potential of sentencing reforms to achieve particular results and, when it can be demonstrated that those results are obtainable sometimes, under some circumstances, that may be all that is needed.

2. *Research Designs.* Many of the sentencing reform impact evaluations are simple before-after studies, often with relatively short time periods under consideration, and this necessarily limits the confidence with which their findings can be declaimed. When the "before" period extends, say, six months or a year from the date of implementation, and the "after" period extends six months or a year after, it is difficult to know what to make of apparent differences in behavior or sentencing outcomes during the two periods.

These kinds of before-after studies may fail to recognize long-term trends. Sentencing may have been changing gradually but systematically over an extended term, and a before-after comparison may miss the trend altogether and characterize the contrasts between the two periods as the result of a legal change. A before-after study may mislead because behavior during either period, or both, may not be representative of normal behavior. Decision makers may, for example, consciously decide to act according to the new system before it formally takes effect, thereby making the before-after contrast look less substantial than it was. Conversely, there may be a gradual phase-in period during which decision makers learn about, come to understand, and adapt to a new system. Or there may be a period of resistance that wanes as time passes. In any of these cases, behavior during the first six months or year after a change takes effect may be very different from behavior thereafter.

3. *Sample Selection.* The samples of cases examined in studies of felony sentencing often come from cases that have already entered the felony courts. If a changed sentencing system affects pre-indictment or pre-arraignment charging or bargaining patterns, the mix of cases entering the felony courts after implementation of the new system may be significantly different from those entering before. The solution to this problem is, in theory, simple (Sparks 1983). Begin data analysis and sample selection with arrests or complaints and follow cases through the system to sentencing. This theoretically easy answer is seldom practicable. Research budgets and schedules often preclude com-

prehensive long-term data collection and analysis. Waiting for arrests to penetrate entire systems may require delays that cannot be accommodated. And, even if these constraints are not insuperable, the lack of integration of official records systems can create logistical barriers that are often more than researchers can manage. Sample selection affects some evaluations more than others, but it is not a trivial problem: a considerable number of impact evaluations indicate that changes in felony sentencing produced changes in pre-arraignment charging and bargaining practices.

4. *Maturation.*   Evaluations that compare sentencing patterns during brief periods before and after a change encounter another problem. Just as there is evidence that periods immediately before a change may not be representative of practices before the innovation was seriously contemplated, because behavior changes in anticipation of the new regime, so behavior immediately after implementation of the change may be unrepresentative of what happens twelve or twenty-four months later. Practitioners must learn how to use the new systems. They must deal with grandfathered cases that arose in the old system but are being resolved under the new one, and for a time must sometimes simultaneously handle parallel sets of grandfathered cases under the old rules and new cases under the new rules. Practitioners must form a view as to whether the new system is to be taken seriously and, if it is, whether it is to be generally complied with or systematically circumvented. All of these processes happen during the early months of implementation, and it is likely that a new equilibrium will have been established twelve or twenty-four months after implementation. Whether the experience during months one to six or one to twelve is an adequate proxy for the experience during months twenty-four to thirty will vary from place to place, but certainly in many cases the two will differ substantially.

5. *What to Make of Research Limitations?*   Notwithstanding its limitations, the current research literature is more reliable than what preceded it, and future research will be better still. Until the 1970s, there were few impact evaluations available, and most were little more than impressionistic descriptions offered by advocates of programs. For several states, evaluations now cover both multiyear periods before and after the change (for North Carolina, see Clarke 1987; for Minnesota, see Knapp 1984 and Miethe and Moore 1987; for California, see Cohen and Tonry 1983). The problems with the literature limit the confidence with which any specific conclusion of most individual studies can be urged. Certainly they create a need to verify tentative conclusions from

multiple sources. This essay does not devote substantial attention to details of research design and resulting limitations. That has been done by others elsewhere (Blumstein et al. 1983).

C. Legal Change from a Distance

One causal conundrum for assessments of the effects of sentencing reforms is to determine whether behavior after implementation should be seen as a consequence of the change or, along with the change, as the consequence of underlying changes in political attitudes, ideology, social values, and culture. California illustrates the problem. Some of the impact evaluations of California's determinate sentencing law seemed to show that the proportion of convicted offenders receiving prison sentences increased after the new law took effect (e.g., Lipson and Peterson 1980). This research, however, involved simple before-after studies looking at short time periods. When one research team looked at sentencing over a longer period, including several periods before the new law took effect, and several afterwards, it became apparent that there was a long-term trend toward increased imposition of prison sentences, and it significantly predated the statutory change (Casper, Brereton, and Neal 1982). That may suggest that the trend and the law change were both symptomatic of underlying social forces in California, and that the sentencing patterns after implementation would have happened in any event. That does not mean that they would have happened in exactly the same way or affected the same people, but that in broad outline sentencing might have continued to become more severe in California even if the determinate sentencing law had not been enacted.

The same underlying dynamic may apply in jurisdictions across the country. Clarke (1986, 1987), for example, describes a gradual seven-year drop in North Carolina in the proportion of maximum prison sentences served before parole release from 51 percent in 1973–74 to 38 percent in 1980–81, the last year before the determinate sentencing law took effect. The average proportion of prison sentences served after the law took effect was lower still at 34 percent (because of the effect of "good" and "gain" time laws), and Clarke (1986, p. 13) notes that, because of the earlier trend, "the percentage served might have continued to drop anyway."[2] Pre-existing trends of this type, reflecting

---

[2] Clarke's analysis dealt with prison terms of forty-eight months or less. The pattern for longer sentences may be different (1987, pp. 14–15).

deeper social forces, undermine the sense of efforts to identify the impacts of change. This sort of analysis should not be pushed too far or it ends in nihilism, determinism, or both, but its cautions cannot be ignored when considering the effects of legal changes.

With the ground now cleared of caveats and explanations, it is time to turn to the impacts of sentencing reforms.

II. Voluntary Sentencing Guidelines

Voluntary sentencing guidelines were among the earliest of the sentencing innovations of the seventies. The earliest versions were based on "implicit sentencing policies" revealed by empirical research on past sentencing practices and were seen as a method for reducing sentencing disparities (Wilkins et al. 1978; Kress 1980). Although there was a boom in voluntary guidelines activity in the late seventies and early eighties, it has since subsided.

The guidelines are "voluntary" because judges are not required to comply with them. Nothing happens if a judge ignores the guidelines altogether or imposes a sentence not specified in the applicable guidelines. The guidelines lack statutory force or mandate and generally are not adopted as court rules. As a result, a defendant has no legal right to be sentenced according to the guidelines and has no legal right to appeal a sentence that is contrary to the guidelines.

The earliest voluntary guidelines projects were efforts to apply methods and experience derived from development of parole guidelines. Consequently, before discussing the major research on voluntary sentencing guidelines, some comments on parole guidelines may be in order.

For most of this century, both parole and sentencing were premised on the desirability of individualized decision making in which a judge or parole board would consider the circumstances of each individual case and then, acting within wide limits of discretion, would make the most appropriate decision. In the early 1970s, however, the U.S. Parole Commission elected to set standards for its release decisions, based on empirical research into the Parole Board's "implicit policies," and thereby to structure its own discretion by means of parole guidelines (Gottfredson, Wilkins, and Hoffman 1978).

The parole guidelines offered a way to make decision makers accountable by setting presumptions for their decisions and then requiring them to explain why decisions were made contrary to the applicable presumption. They made policy explicit and thereby helped to lessen both the probability and the appearance that decision making was capricious or idiosyncratic. Both the prevailing criticism of individualized decision making and the potential benefits of guidelines appeared to some to be as applicable to sentencing as to parole and, in 1974, the National Institute of Justice initiated a multiyear project to study the feasibility of empirically based guidelines for sentencing. In the first instance, support was provided to the researchers who had been instrumental in development of the parole guidelines to test the feasibility of sentencing guidelines. The feasibility study was undertaken in state courts in Vermont and in Denver, Colorado (Wilkins et al. 1978).

There are, however, a number of important differences between parole and sentencing, and these have confounded efforts to transfer parole guidelines approaches to sentencing. One difference is that parole boards have one critical decision to make—how long should a prisoner be held in prison before release? Judges, by contrast, have two critical decisions to make—should a convicted defendant be imprisoned and, if so, for how long? After deciding to impose a prison sentence, trial judges in many jurisdictions have to make decisions concerning both minimum and maximum sentences.

A second difference is that, within constraints created by minimum or maximum sentences imposed by the judge or by statute, the parole board can set a release date to its liking. Judges, however, are part of a "work group" consisting primarily of the prosecutor, the defense lawyer, and the judge, but influenced by probation officers and police. As a consequence, judges in some ways are not as independent as parole boards. The judges' independence is often limited by plea bargains, prevailing notions of "going rates," and the need to maintain relatively smooth functioning of the courts in cooperation with other key actors.

A third difference is that parole boards are able to monitor the decisions made by examiners and to establish management controls and appeal procedures to assure that guidelines are applied properly. The organized judiciary lacks similar controls over individual trial judges and, certainly in the 1970s, there was no reason to expect appellate sentence review to serve as an effective monitoring mechanism (see, e.g., Zeisel and Diamond 1977).

The combination of these differences between parole and sentencing had two major ramifications. First, the research effort to identify "implicit policies" was much more complex for sentencing than for parole. Second, in those early days, the prospects that the Denver judiciary would agree to establish sentencing guidelines as presumptive decision-making standards were so slight as not to be considered; this meant that the resulting guidelines had to be "voluntary." There was some hope on the part of the guidelines' developers that the guidelines would have a logical or moral force that might incline judges to comply with them. The notion was that judges would welcome information on "going rates" and, for "ordinary" cases, might be inclined to set sentences in accordance with those going rates (Wilkins et al. 1978). At the very least, guidelines should help identify aberrantly lenient or severe sentences, and thereby lessen their frequency.

After the initial feasibility study was completed in Denver (Vermont fell by the wayside), the federal government funded guidelines projects in criminal courts in Denver, Newark, New Jersey, Chicago, and Phoenix. The aim was to build on the feasibility study and develop and implement voluntary sentencing guidelines (see Kress [1980] for accounts of those four implementation projects). Parallel projects were undertaken, but under local direction in Philadelphia and at the state level in New Jersey (Sparks and Stecher 1979; Rich et al. 1982).

At about the same time, the National Institute of Justice initiated the Multijurisdictional Sentencing Guidelines Program. Unlike the earlier guidelines, which generally dealt with sentencing in a single city or county, these projects were intended to test the feasibility of voluntary sentencing guidelines on a statewide basis. In each of the two participating states, Maryland and Florida, research on sentencing practices was undertaken in a number of demographically and culturally diverse counties with the aim of developing a single set of guidelines for use in all of the counties (Carrow et al. 1985a). The rationale was that if such diverse counties could share a single set of guidelines, there was no reason why guidelines should not be a viable sentencing reform mechanism on a statewide basis.

Between 1975 and 1980, voluntary sentencing guidelines were the single most energetically pursued sentencing innovation. By 1980, one count showed that voluntary guidelines had been developed or were under way in a majority of states (Criminal Courts Technical Assistance Project 1980). A more recent survey described sentencing guidelines activities in thirty-five states by 1983 (Carrow et al. 1985b, figs. A-1, A-2).

Whether voluntary sentencing guidelines will be retained in many jurisdictions remains to be seen. The auguries are not good. Most of the original guidelines systems have been abandoned or supplanted. The second generation of federally supported guidelines, in Denver, Chicago, Phoenix, and Newark, were displaced by statutory determinate or presumptive sentencing laws. The initial set of statewide sentencing guidelines in New Jersey also was displaced by a presumptive sentencing law. The statewide experimental guidelines in Florida and Maryland survived, however, and have been institutionalized; the Florida voluntary guidelines were revised by a sentencing commission and were converted into presumptive guidelines in 1983. Guideline systems have recently been adopted, after long development periods, in Massachusetts, Michigan, Utah, Rhode Island, and Wisconsin (Shane-DuBow, Brown, and Olsen 1985).

Notwithstanding the volume of voluntary guidelines activity in the United States, not much has been written about the impact of the guidelines. One early evaluation of statewide guidelines in Massachusetts (and to a lesser degree in other states) found that the guidelines were poorly conceived, poorly developed, and not effectively implemented (Sparks et al. 1982). The National Center for State Courts conducted an assessment of the development and impact of voluntary guidelines in Denver, Chicago, Newark, and Phoenix (Rich et al. 1982). Cohen and Helland (1982) completed a modest assessment of the impact of guidelines in Newark. Abt Associates (Carrow et al. 1985a) conducted an evaluation of the multijurisdictional voluntary sentencing guidelines in Florida and Maryland. In broad outline, all four evaluations concluded that the guidelines had few significant impacts on sentencing outcomes or sentencing processes in the courts studied.

One of the ironies of evaluation research is that results are often available too late to influence policy-making. The evaluation of the first guidelines projects (Rich et al. 1982) was not available even in a draft version until 1981, after the development of the "multijurisdictional" guidelines projects was far advanced. Had the evaluation been available earlier, it might have contributed importantly to the shaping of those projects. The evaluation is discussed at some length in the report of the National Academy of Sciences Panel on Sentencing Research (Blumstein et al. 1983), and so only the broadest conclusions are summarized here.

Rich and his colleagues identified major methodological and analytical defects in the development of the Denver guidelines. The evaluation concluded that the Denver guidelines had no important influence on judicial decisions whether to incarcerate, and that compliance rates for lengths of prison terms were disappointingly low. Moreover, the report concluded that it was highly unlikely that sentencing guidelines affected the overall severity of sentences in either Denver or Philadelphia. The evaluators also found that the guidelines failed to reduce sentencing disparity. The overall conclusion: "The various measures employed . . . converge on a single conclusion: sentencing guidelines have had no detectable, objectively manifested impact on the exercise of judicial sentencing discretion" (Rich et al. 1982, p. xxiv).

The effects in Florida and Maryland were not much greater. Concerning Florida, Carrow and her colleagues (1985a, pp. 275–76) concluded:

Sentences were *less* uniform . . . during the test year than during the year before. Thus, guidelines clearly did not reduce unwarranted sentence disparity. . . . There were substantial differences in sentence severity across the sites. . . . The Florida guidelines did not begin to mitigate differences in local sentencing practice.

In Maryland, the findings were mixed. The researchers found evidence that sentencing disparities were significantly reduced in Baltimore during the first year of guidelines use, but "no changes in sentencing variation were detected in the other three Maryland test sites" (Carrow et al. 1985a, p. 14).

Using a combination of quantitative analyses, interviews, and participant observation, the evaluators investigated the effects of the guidelines on sentencing disparity and compliance rates, whether written reasons were provided for departures, and patterns of adaptive responses. Interviews revealed that many judges in the urban county in Florida rarely referred to the guidelines, especially in plea bargained cases, and that while most Maryland judges claimed to use the guidelines, they often did so after having first decided what sentence to impose. Evaluators found that the guideline scoring sheets were often not completed. In Florida, score sheets were filed for only 57 percent of the eligible burglary cases; the score sheet filing rate in Maryland was 70 percent.

Nominal compliance with the guidelines was not high. Although a majority of cases were sentenced within the guidelines, 78 percent in Florida and 68 percent in Maryland, the guidelines ranges were so wide

TABLE 1

Maryland Sentencing Matrix Offenses against Persons Offender
Score

Offense Score	0	1	2	3	4	5	6+
1	P	P	3M-2Y	3M-2Y	3M-2Y	3M-2Y	2Y-5Y
2	P-1Y	3M-2Y	3M-2Y	3M-2Y	3M-2Y	1Y-4Y	3Y-8Y
3	P-2Y	1Y-5Y	3Y-8Y	3Y-8Y	3Y-8Y	3Y-8Y	5Y-10Y
4	P-3Y	3Y-8Y	3Y-8Y	4Y-10Y	4Y-10Y	4Y-10Y	5Y-10Y
5	P-4Y	3Y-9Y	4Y-9Y	4Y-10Y	4Y-10Y	6Y-12Y	8Y-14Y
6	3Y-6Y	3Y-10Y	4Y-10Y	5Y-10Y	5Y-10Y	8Y-15Y	10Y-20Y
7	3Y-7Y	4Y-10Y	5Y-10Y	5Y-10Y	5Y-10Y	9Y-15Y	12Y-20Y
8	4Y-8Y	5Y-10Y	6Y-12Y	6Y-12Y	6Y-12Y	10Y-15Y	12Y-25Y
9	4Y-10Y	6Y-12Y	8Y-15Y	8Y-15Y	8Y-16Y	15Y-30Y	25Y-L
10	8Y-15Y	8Y-15Y	8Y-16Y	8Y-16Y	10Y-25Y	15Y-30Y	25Y-L
11	9Y-16Y	9Y-16Y	9Y-16Y	15Y-30Y	17Y-30Y	17Y-30Y	25Y-L
12	12Y-20Y	12Y-20Y	15Y-30Y	18Y-35Y	18Y-35Y	25Y-L	25Y-L
13	14Y-22Y	14Y-22Y	18Y-35Y	20Y-40Y	20Y-40Y	25Y-L	30Y-L

SOURCE.—Carrow et al. 1985*b*, p. E-12.
NOTE.—P = probation, M = months, Y = years, L = life.

that this could happen as easily by coincidence as by purpose.[3] In
Florida, the upper limit of most guideline ranges is at least twice the
lower limit. Thus, typical burglary ranges are 3½–7 years, 5½–12
years, and 7–17 years (*Florida Rules of Criminal Procedure*, Rules 3.701
and 3.988). Table 1 shows the revised Maryland grid for *minimum*
sentences for violent offenses (Maryland retains parole release and the
parole board determines the actual length of prison terms). Compared
with any of the presumptive sentencing guidelines grids shown later in
this essay, these ranges are enormous. Finally, judges departing from
guidelines in Florida complied with the requirement that they provide
written reasons in 80 percent of such cases; only 50 percent of extra-
guidelines sentences in Maryland were accompanied by explanations
(Carrow 1984).

The question naturally arises as to why the Maryland and Florida
guidelines seem to have achieved so little. Although Carrow and her

---

[3] Revised Florida guidelines were promulgated effective October 1, 1983, pursuant to
legislation creating a sentencing commission and giving the guidelines presumptive force.
As discussed in Section III, compliance with presumptive guidelines in Florida has not
been much more impressive than compliance with voluntary guidelines in Florida.

colleagues identify a variety of political and public relations strategies that might help a guidelines project achieve acceptance, the central problem seems simply to have been that compliance with the guidelines was voluntary:

> it seems that purely voluntary systems are unlikely to achieve the kinds of compliance needed to make guidelines a meaningful approach to sentencing reform. Strong requirements for compliance with the basic conditions of guidelines are necessary, whether that be through court rule or legislative mandate. In addition . . . without some capacity to review the validity of reasons for extra-guidelines sentences . . . , guidelines ultimately offer relatively little as a means of structuring judicial discretion. [Carrow et al. 1985a, p. 172]

Of course, the evaluations described here should not, by themselves, be taken as conclusive evidence that voluntary sentencing guidelines cannot reduce sentencing disparities or serve as a means for structuring sentencing and increasing judicial accountability. After all, the Maryland guidelines did appear to reduce sentencing disparities in Baltimore. Stuart Simms, the prosecuting attorney in Baltimore, reports in personal communication that the Baltimore guidelines have significantly affected plea bargaining because both judges and defense lawyers treat the minimum guideline sentence as the starting point from which to sentence bargain downward. If this can be confirmed by empirical analyses, it would demonstrate a greater impact of voluntary guidelines than has heretofore been shown. Research in Philadelphia on voluntary bail guidelines has shown some successes in reducing bail disparities (Goldkamp and Gottfredson 1985). Unfortunately, the lack of published independent evaluations of statewide voluntary guidelines, like those in Wisconsin and Michigan, limit the bases for generalizations. The evaluations of the Denver, Florida, and Maryland experiences are, however, reason to be skeptical about the long-term promise of voluntary sentencing guidelines.

In retrospect, the notion of voluntary guidelines was a good one, well worth investigating; it simply did not work out as its proponents hoped. Voluntary sentencing guidelines served as a crucial intermediate step in the development of presumptive sentencing guidelines which offer the key features that voluntary guidelines lacked—a statutory mandate and appellate sentence review.

III. The Sentencing Commission and Presumptive
   Sentencing Guidelines

The strength of the sentencing commission approach is its combination of the sentencing commission, presumptive sentencing guidelines, and appellate sentence review (Frankel 1972; von Hirsch, Knapp, and Tonry 1987). Appellate sentence review has been available in various jurisdictions from time to time throughout this century, and probably earlier. However, it seldom amounted to much in the United States, primarily because there was no substantive sentencing law (see Zeisel and Diamond 1977). Most criminal statutes simply authorized maximum lawful sentences. If the maximum for robbery was fifteen years, there were no governing standards to guide a judge in deciding whether probation, five years, ten years, or fifteen years was the appropriate sentence to impose. By contrast, in most legal matters, when an appeal is taken from a trial judge's decision, the appellate court can look to the applicable statutes and the case law for guidance in deciding whether the trial judge's decision was correct.

In most jurisdictions that have appellate sentence appeal, the scrutiny given to appealed sentences has been slight, and doctrines of extreme deference to the trial judge have developed. It is hard to see what else could have happened. The long maximum sentences in indeterminate sentencing systems were intended to permit judges to individualize sentences. For an appellate judge to have reversed a sentence, in the absence of established standards for evaluating the appropriateness of sentences, would have seemed, and been, ad hoc and arbitrary.

The sentencing commission approach changed that. The judge is directed to impose a sentence consistent with the guidelines unless there is a good reason to do otherwise. This is also what makes appellate sentence review feasible. There is no significant difference, in principle, between considering whether a trial judge rightly decided a question of property law and considering whether a trial judge rightly decided to impose a sentence at odds with the applicable guidelines. In both instances, the appellate judges must consider the standard rule and any cases that apply or interpret it, and then decide whether the reasons given for the disputed decision are persuasive. Before the research on the effects of presumptive guidelines on sentencing outcomes and court processes is discussed, the next section introduces the major presumptive guidelines systems in Minnesota, Pennsylvania, and Washington.

TABLE 2

Minnesota Sentencing Guidelines Grid (Presumptive Sentence Length in Months)

Security Levels: Conviction Offenses	Criminal History Score						
	0	1	2	3	4	5	6 or More
I: Unauthorized use of motor vehicle; possession of marijuana	12*†	12*†	12*†	13†	15†	17†	19 (18–20)
II: Theft-related crimes ($250–$2,500); aggravated forgery ($250–$2,500)	12*†	12*†	13†	15†	17†	19†	21 (20–22)
III: Theft crimes ($250–$2,500)	12*†	13†	15†	17†	19 (18–20)	22 (21–23)	25 (24–26)
IV: Nonresidential burglary; theft crimes (over $2,500)	12*†	15†	18†	21†	25 (24–26)	32 (30–34)	41 (37–45)
V: Residential burglary; simple robbery	18†	23†	27†	30 (29–31)	38 (36–40)	46 (43–49)	54 (50–58)
VI: Criminal sexual conduct, second degree	21†	26†	30†	34 (33–35)	44 (42–46)	54 (50–58)	65 (60–70)

VII: Aggravated robbery	24 (23–25)	32 (30–34)	41 (38–44)	49 (45–53)	65 (60–70)	81 (75–87)	97 (90–104)
VIII: Criminal sexual conduct, first degree; assault, first degree	43 (41–45)	54 (50–58)	65 (60–70)	76 (71–81)	95 (89–101)	113 (106–120)	132 (124–140)
IX: Murder, third degree; murder, second degree (felony murder)	105 (102–108)	119 (116–122)	127 (124–130)	149 (143–155)	176 (168–184)	205 (195–215)	230 (218–242)
X: Murder, second degree (with intent)	120 (116–124)	140 (133–147)	162 (153–171)	203 (192–214)	243 (231–255)	284 (270–298)	324 (309–339)

Source.—Knapp (1985, p. 107).

Note.—Numbers in parentheses denote the range within which a judge may sentence without the sentence being deemed a departure. Offenders with nonimprisonment felony sentences are subject to jail time according to law. First-degree murder is excluded from the guidelines by law and continues to have a mandatory life sentence.

* One year and one day.

† At the discretion of the judge, up to a year and/or other nonjail sanctions can be imposed as conditions of probation. Numbers not followed by a † denote presumptive commitment to state imprisonment.

A. Overview of Guidelines Systems

Major systems of presumptive sentencing guidelines are now in operation in Minnesota, Washington, and Pennsylvania. The federal guidelines took effect in November 1987. The Florida voluntary guidelines were converted to presumptive guidelines in 1983. Commissions are at work in Louisiana, Oregon, and Tennessee. Several states have tried but failed to establish presumptive guidelines.

1. *Minnesota.* Minnesota became in 1978 the first jurisdiction to establish a sentencing commission. The Minnesota Commission made a number of bold policy decisions (Knapp 1984). First, it decided to be "prescriptive" and explicitly to establish its own sentencing priorities; the voluntary sentencing guidelines systems being developed elsewhere purported to be "descriptive," to be attempting to replicate existing sentencing patterns. Second, the commission decided to de-emphasize imprisonment as a punishment for property offenders and to emphasize imprisonment for violent offenders; this was a major sentencing policy decision because research on past Minnesota sentencing patterns showed that repeat property offenders tended to go to prison, and that first-time violent offenders tended not to. Third, in order to attack sentencing disparities, the commission established very narrow sentencing ranges (e.g., thirty to thirty-four months, or fifty to fifty-eight months) and authorized departures from guideline ranges only when "substantial and compelling" reasons were present. Fourth, the commission adopted "Just Deserts" as the governing premise of its imprisonment policies. Fifth, the commission interpreted an ambiguous statutory injunction that it take correctional resources into "substantial consideration" as a mandate that its guidelines not increase the prison population beyond existing capacity constraints. This meant that the commission had to make deliberate trade-offs in imprisonment policies. If the commission decided to increase the lengths of prison terms for one group of offenders, it had also either to decrease prison terms for another group or to shift the "in/out" line and divert some group of prisoners from prison altogether. Sixth, the commission forbade consideration at sentencing of many personal factors—such as education, employment, marital status, living arrangements—that might directly or indirectly discriminate against minorities, women, or low-income groups. A recent book by Dale Parent (1988), the commission's first director, provides a full account of the commission's work.

Minnesota's guidelines, which are set out as table 2, initially proved more successful than even the commission anticipated. Rates of compliance with the guidelines were high. Relatively more violent offenders and relatively fewer property offenders went to prison than before the guidelines took effect. Disparities in prison sentences diminished. Prison populations remained under control.

Later there was backsliding; as time passed, sentencing patterns came more closely to resemble those that existed before the guidelines. The differences between sentencing in Minnesota before and after the guidelines took effect remained, however, substantial. One recent opinion survey showed that "a clear majority (66 percent) of judges and public defenders viewed the guidelines as an improvement over the indeterminate system" (Miethe and Moore 1987, p. xiv). The Minnesota guidelines system has been a remarkable success with important long-term consequences.

2. *Pennsylvania.* The Pennsylvania Commission on Sentencing was established in 1978 and began its work in April 1979. The commission proposed guidelines to the legislature in January 1981. They were rejected in March 1981, and the commission was directed to revise and resubmit the guidelines, to make the sentencing standards more severe in a variety of specified ways, and to increase judicial discretion under the guidelines. In numerous ways the commission complied, and the resulting guidelines were submitted to the legislature in January 1982 and took effect on July 22, 1982. (Martin [1984] describes the guideline development process in Pennsylvania.)

The current Pennsylvania guidelines grid is set out as table 3. Parole release has been retained, and the guidelines prescribe ranges only for minimum sentences; the judge retains full discretion over the maximum sentence and, of course, the parole board is not bound to release prisoners when the minimum sentence has been served.

For every offense, including misdemeanors, the guidelines specify three "ranges"—a normal range, an aggravated range, and a mitigated range. The judge may impose a sentence from within any of the three ranges and may do so for any reason, so long as he states it. The guidelines set no general criteria for imposition of aggravated or mitigated sentences, or for "departures" from the guidelines, and no special findings of fact need be made. There are, in addition, no rules governing when consecutive sentences may be imposed.

Pennsylvania annually publishes statistical analyses of the guidelines' impact. Overall "compliance rates" are very high, but it is unclear what this means; the guidelines are broad (e.g., nine to thirty-six months), and substantial disparities can occur even within the guidelines because

TABLE 3

Pennsylvania Sentencing Range Chart, Effective June 6, 1986

Offense Gravity Score	Prior Record Score	Standard Range*	Aggravated Range*	Mitigated Range*
10 (third-degree murder)†	0	48–120	Statutory limit‡	36–48
	1	54–120	Statutory limit‡	40–54
	2	60–120	Statutory limit‡	45–60
	3	72–120	Statutory limit‡	54–72
	4	84–120	Statutory limit‡	63–84
	5	96–120	Statutory limit‡	72–96
	6	102–120	Statutory limit‡	76–102
9 (e.g., rape; robbery inflicting serious bodily injury)†	0	36–60	60–75	27–36
	1	42–66	66–82	31–42
	2	48–72	72–90	36–48
	3	54–78	78–97	40–54
	4	66–84	84–105	49–66
	5	72–90	90–112	54–72
	6	78–102	102–120	58–78
8 (e.g., kidnapping; arson [Felony I]; voluntary manslaughter)†	0	24–48	48–60	18–24
	1	30–54	54–68	22–30
	2	36–60	60–75	27–36
	3	42–66	66–82	32–42
	4	54–72	72–90	40–54
	5	60–78	78–98	45–60
	6	66–90	90–112	50–66

288

7 (e.g., aggravated assault causing serious bodily injury; robbery threatening serious bodily injury)†			
0	8–12	12–18	4–8
1	12–29	29–36	9–12
2	17–34	34–42	12–17
3	22–39	39–49	16–22
4	33–49	49–61	25–33
5	38–54	54–68	28–38
6	43–64	64–80	32–43
6 (e.g., robbery inflicting bodily injury; theft by extortion [Felony III])†			
0	4–12	12–18	2–4
1	6–12	12–18	3–6
2	8–12	12–18	4–8
3	12–29	29–36	9–12
4	23–34	34–42	17–23
5	28–44	44–55	21–28
6	33–49	49–61	25–33
5 (e.g., criminal mischief [Felony III]; theft by unlawful taking [Felony III]; theft by receiving stolen property [Felony III]; bribery)†			
0	0–12	12–18	Nonconfinement
1	3–12	12–18	1½–3
2	5–12	12–18	2½–5
3	8–12	12–18	4–8
4	18–27	27–34	14–18
5	21–30	30–38	16–21
6	24–36	36–45	18–24
4 (e.g., theft by receiving stolen property less than $2,000; by force or threat of force; or in breach of fiduciary obligation)†			
0	0–12	12–18	Nonconfinement
1	0–12	12–18	Nonconfinement
2	0–12	12–18	Nonconfinement
3	5–12	12–18	2½–5
4	8–12	12–18	4–8
5	18–27	27–34	14–18
6	21–30	30–38	16–21

Continued on next page

TABLE 3 (Continued)

Offense Gravity Score	Prior Record Score	Standard Range*	Aggravated Range*	Mitigated Range*
3 (most misdemeanor I's)†	0	0–12	12–18	Nonconfinement
	1	0–12	12–18	Nonconfinement
	2	0–12	12–18	Nonconfinement
	3	0–12	12–18	Nonconfinement
	4	3–12	12–18	1½–3
	5	5–12	12–18	2½–5
	6	8–12	12–18	4–8
2 (most misdemeanor II's)†	0	0–12	Statutory limit‡	Nonconfinement
	1	0–12	Statutory limit‡	Nonconfinement
	2	0–12	Statutory limit‡	Nonconfinement
	3	0–12	Statutory limit‡	Nonconfinement
	4	0–12	Statutory limit‡	Nonconfinement
	5	2–12	Statutory limit‡	1–2
	6	5–12	Statutory limit‡	2½–5
1 (most misdemeanor III's)†	0	0–6	Statutory limit‡	Nonconfinement
	1	0–6	Statutory limit‡	Nonconfinement
	2	0–6	Statutory limit‡	Nonconfinement
	3	0–6	Statutory limit‡	Nonconfinement
	4	0–6	Statutory limit‡	Nonconfinement
	5	0–6	Statutory limit‡	Nonconfinement
	6	0–6	Statutory limit‡	Nonconfinement

SOURCE.—Pennsylvania Commission on Sentencing (1986, pp. 7–8).

* Weapon enhancement: At least twelve months and up to twenty-four months confinement must be added to the above lengths when a deadly weapon was possessed in the crime.

† These offenses are listed here for illustrative purposes only.

‡ Statutory limit is defined as the longest minimum sentence permitted by law.

judges can use the aggravated and mitigated ranges at will and because no efforts have been made to account for the role of plea bargaining.

Because the Pennsylvania guidelines concern only minimum sentences, there is no structural reason for appellate judges to take appellate sentence review seriously—the parole board makes release decisions and, if it chooses, can disregard idiosyncratic maximum sentences. Thus the parole board remains the primary mechanism for review of maximum sentences. Only the appellate courts, however, can review minimum sentences, and there is reason to be skeptical that they will do so in a meaningful way. More important, because the guideline ranges are broad, and because there are no rules governing when judges may depart from them, Pennsylvania appellate courts may have difficulty knowing the substantive criteria by which a sentence appeal can or should be evaluated. An unpublished 1985 paper by a member of the commission's research staff analyzes the sentence appeal case law and concludes that, at that time, the appellate courts in Pennsylvania had dealt primarily with procedural issues and had not dealt with the substantive bases of sentences (McCloskey 1985).[4]

3. *Washington.*   The Washington State Sentencing Commission, like the Minnesota Commission, took a comprehensive and principled approach to policy problems. When the proposed guidelines were submitted to the Washington legislature, they passed amidst relatively little controversy and have been in effect since July 1, 1984. A recent book by Boerner (1985) describes Washington's guideline system.

The Washington guidelines, which are set out as table 4, resemble Minnesota's. Sentencing ranges are much narrower than those in Pennsylvania but are somewhat broader than those in Minnesota. The guidelines set out illustrative aggravating and mitigating circumstances and permit departures only, as in Minnesota, in the presence of "substantial and compelling" circumstances. Parole release has been abolished. As in Minnesota, the commission decided to shift sentencing policy toward more incarceration of violent offenders and less incarceration of property offenders. Unlike the Minnesota guidelines, which provide guidance primarily concerning felony sentences to state prison, the Washington guidelines set presumptions for all felony sentences.

The early evaluations of Washington's guidelines suggest considerable successes: the shift toward imprisonment of violent offenders and

---

[4] The annotations to the commission's *Sentencing Guidelines Implementation Manual* (Pennsylvania Commission on Sentencing 1986b) indicate, however, that the appellate courts are beginning to address substantive sentencing issues.

TABLE 4
Washington Sentencing Guidelines Grid

Seriousness Level	Offender Score									
	0	1	2	3	4	5	6	7	8	9 or More
XIV	Life Sentence without Parole/Death Penalty									
XIII	23y4m 240–320	24y4m 250–333	25y4m 261–347	26y4m 271–361	27y4m 281–374	28y4m 291–388	30y4m 312–416	32y10m 338–450	36y 370–493	40y 411–548
XII	12y 123–164	13y 134–178	14y 144–192	15y 154–205	16y 165–219	17y 175–233	19y 195–260	21y 216–288	25y 257–342	29y 298–397
XI	6y 62–82	6y9m 69–92	7y6m 77–102	8y3m 85–113	9y 93–123	9y9m 100–133	12y6m 129–171	13y6m 139–185	15y6m 159–212	17y6m 180–240
X	5y 51–68	5y6m 57–75	6y 62–82	6y6m 67–89	7y 72–96	7y6m 77–102	9y6m 98–130	10y6m 108–144	12y6m 129–171	14y6m 149–198
IX	3y 31–41	3y6m 36–48	4y 41–54	4y6m 46–61	5y 51–68	5y6m 57–75	7y6m 77–102	8y6m 87–116	10y6m 108–144	12y6m 129–171
VIII	2y 21–27	2y6m 26–34	3y 31–41	3y6m 36–48	4y 41–54	4y6m 46–61	6y6m 67–89	7y6m 77–102	8y6m 87–116	10y6m 108–144

	0	1	2	3	4	5	6	7	8	9 or more
VII	18m 15–20	2y 21–27	2y6m 26–34	3y 31–41	3y6m 36–48	4y 41–54	5y6m 57–75	6y6m 67–89	7y6m 77–102	8y6m 87–116
VI	13m 12+–14	18m 15–20	2y 21–27	2y6m 26–34	3y 31–41	3y6m 36–48	4y6m 46–61	5y6m 57–75	6y6m 67–89	7y6m 77–102
V	9m 6–12	13m 12+–14	15m 13–17	18m 15–20	2y2m 22–29	3y2m 33–43	4y 41–54	5y 51–68	6y 62–82	7y 72–96
IV	6m 3–9	9m 6–12	13m 12+–14	15m 13–17	18m 15–20	2y2m 22–29	3y2m 33–43	4y2m 43–57	5y2m 53–70	6y2m 63–84
III	2m 1–3	5m 3–8	8m 4–12	11m 9–12	14m 12+–16	20m 17–22	2y2m 22–29	3y2m 33–43	4y2m 43–57	5y 51–68
II	0–90 Days	4m 2–6	6m 3–9	8m 4–12	13m 12+–14	16m 14–18	20m 17–22	2y2m 22–29	3y2m 33–43	4y2m 43–57
I	0–60 Days	0–90 Days	3m 2–5	4m 2–6	5m 3–8	8m 4–12	13m 12+–14	16m 14–18	20m 17–22	2y2m 22–29

SOURCE.—Washington State Sentencing Guidelines Commission 1985, p. 7.

NOTE.—Numbers represent presumptive sentence ranges in months. 12+ equals one year and one day. For a few crimes, the presumptive sentences in the high offender score columns exceed the statutory maximums. In these cases, the statutory maximum applies. Additional time added to the presumptive sentence if the offender was armed with a deadly weapon: 24 months (Rape 1, Robbery 1, Kidnapping 1), 18 months (Burglary 1), 12 months (Assault 2, Escape 1, Kidnapping 2, Commercial Burglary 2).

away from imprisonment of property offenders is happening. Compliance with the guidelines has been high. Trial rates have not increased.

4. *Other Sentencing Commissions.* Sentencing commissions have been established in a number of other states and in the federal system, but at the time of writing the only other major presumptive guidelines system that has been in effect for a significant period of time is Florida's.

Notwithstanding the limited impact of Florida's voluntary guidelines, the Florida legislature in 1982 created a sentencing guidelines commission; presumptive sentencing guidelines took effect on October 1, 1983. The scant empirical evidence on the presumptive guidelines' effects is not encouraging (see the following subsection). Legislation to abolish the sentencing guidelines was introduced in 1987 but did not pass (Holton 1987). The Florida Commission itself proposed that the Florida Supreme Court adopt rule changes that would greatly have weakened the guidelines. The court rejected most of the proposals (*Florida Rules of Criminal Procedure re Sentencing Guidelines* [rules 3.701 and 3.988], Florida Supreme Court, Case No. 69,411, April 2, 1987).

The work of the U.S. Sentencing Commission has been mired in controversy. It published three different sets of draft guidelines (U.S. Sentencing Commission 1986, 1987*a*, 1987*b*), and each draft was widely criticized; despite numerous calls for delay, the federal guidelines took effect on November 1, 1987.

The New York State Committee on Sentencing Guidelines was appointed in 1983 and submitted proposed guidelines to the legislature in 1985 (New York State Commission on Sentencing Guidelines 1985). The proposed guidelines were rejected and the commission ceased operation. A sentencing commission in Connecticut, after developing a "descriptive" sentencing grid, "went on record stating that it was strongly *opposed* to the adoption of the sentencing guidelines system" (Shane-DuBow, Brown, and Olson 1985, p. 48) and urged enactment of a statutory determinate sentencing system. A sentencing commission was appointed in Maine in 1983; many of its members decided they did not favor sentencing guidelines, and the commission's report to the legislature (Phillips 1984) called primarily for appointment of a new commission. Legislation to reestablish the commission was passed in 1986, but the commission was not reconstituted. Finally, a sentencing guidelines commission was established in South Carolina in 1982, and proposed guidelines were submitted to the legislature in 1985. They were rejected.

Despite this checkered history, new efforts are under way. The Canadian Sentencing Commission, a study group, has recently recommended establishment of a permanent Canadian national sentencing commission charged to develop presumptive sentencing guidelines (Canadian Sentencing Commission 1987). Sentencing commissions are at work in Tennessee, Oregon, and Louisiana and are under serious consideration in a number of other states.

B. The Impacts of Commission Guidelines

This subsection summarizes the findings of the evaluations of the impact of sentencing commission–promulgated guidelines in Minnesota, Pennsylvania, Florida, and Washington. The Minnesota guidelines have been in effect since May 1, 1980; those in Pennsylvania since July 22, 1982; those in Florida since October 1, 1983; and those in Washington since July 1, 1984.

The staff of the Minnesota Commission prepared a series of exhaustive impact evaluations; the most recent was published in 1984 and covered the first three years' experience (Knapp 1984a, 1984b). A series of reports from an independent analysis of Minnesota impact data has been published (Miethe and Moore 1985, 1987; Moore and Miethe 1986; Miethe 1987). The Pennsylvania Commission has published a series of statistical reports on sentencing in Pennsylvania (Pennsylvania Commission on Sentencing 1984, 1985, 1986a, 1987), and articles by members of its staff on impacts have been published (e.g., Kramer and Lubitz 1985), and unpublished impact assessments are available (Lubitz and Kempinen 1987). In addition, a number of papers have been presented at academic meetings (Kramer, Lubitz, and Kempinen 1985; Kramer and Scirica 1985). Washington has undertaken a major in-house evaluation from which a preliminary report on the first six months of 1985 became available in November 1985 (Washington State Sentencing Guidelines Commission 1985); a more comprehensive report on 1985 was released in December 1986 (Washington State Sentencing Guidelines Commission 1986); and a preliminary report on 1986 was released late in 1987 (Washington State Sentencing Guidelines Commission 1987). Sketchy reports are available from Florida (Holton 1987).

A number of questions can be asked about the impacts of sentencing guidelines on sentencing patterns. Did judges comply with guidelines, and to what extent? Were sentencing patterns under guidelines different from the patterns that existed before guidelines? Did sentences become more severe? Did disparities increase or decrease? What was the interaction between the guidelines and plea bargaining? Finally, were there important adverse effects on the operation of the courts— did trial rates increase, case processing times increase, or the appellate courts become inundated by sentence appeals?

The following sections discuss these questions in sequence. To anticipate the conclusions that can be drawn from the Minnesota, Washington, and Pennsylvania experiences:

1. All three guidelines systems achieved high compliance rates.

2. All three guidelines systems apparently succeeded in changing sentencing patterns.

3. The lengths of sentences received by imprisoned offenders increased in Pennsylvania and Minnesota (the early indications in Washington are that sentence lengths have been slightly reduced).

4. Sentencing disparities apparently decreased in Minnesota, Pennsylvania, and Washington during the early years of guidelines; in Minnesota there was slippage in the second, third, and fourth years.

5. Prosecutors in Minnesota have changed charging and bargaining practices in an effort to circumvent the guidelines, with some success, and there are indications that this may be happening in Pennyslvania and Washington.

6. In all three states, there were no significant increases in trial rates, nor in Minnesota and Pennsylvania did average case processing times increase; sentence appeals were filed in only 1 percent of cases in Minnesota.

The evaluation findings are relatively clear. What is less clear is what they mean. For example, high rates of compliance may mean that sentencing guidelines are successfully inducing judges and lawyers to defer to sentencing policies set by the sentencing commissions, or they may mean that judges and lawyers are identifying the sentences they wish imposed and are then assuring through plea bargains and charge dismissals that the defendant is convicted of an offense bearing a sentence acceptable to both sides. Similarly, an increase in sentence severity may result from promulgation of the guidelines, or it may result from other causes. As findings are reviewed below, an effort is made to identify alternate explanations for evaluation findings.

1. *Compliance Rates.* The Minnesota, Washington, and Pennsylvania guidelines achieved relatively high compliance rates, as did those in Florida. In the following discussion, a "dispositional departure" is a sentence to incarceration when the guidelines prescribe an "out" sen-

TABLE 5

Dispositional and Durational Departure Rates in Minnesota

Year	Total (%)	Up (%)	Down (%)	No. of Cases
Dispositional departures:				
1978*	19.4	12	7.4	4,369
1981	6.2	3.1	3.1	5,500
1982	7.0	3.4	3.6	6,066
1983	8.9	4.5	4.4	5,562
1984	9.9	...	...	...
Durational departures:				
1978*	...	...	...	...
1981	23.6	7.9	15.7	827
1982	20.4	6.6	13.8	1,127
1983	22.9	6.0	16.9	1,124

SOURCES.—Knapp 1982, p. 22, fig. 3; 1984, tables 2, 6, 8, 9, 13, 15; Miethe and Moore 1987, p. vii.

* Preguidelines.

tence or an "out" sentence when the guidelines prescribe incarceration.[5] A "durational departure" is a sentence for a term outside the applicable guideline range.

a) Minnesota. Compared with sentencing patterns in 1978, Minnesota sentencing patterns changed significantly after guidelines took effect and became more consistent. Minnesota's rate of dispositional departures increased slightly during the first four years of guidelines experience and departures were about evenly divided between upward and downward departures. Durational departure rates were stable; downward departures exceeded upward departures by two to one for each of the first four years of guidelines experience (Miethe and Moore 1987, pp. vii–viii). Table 5 shows dispositional departure rates during the first four years.

Dispositional departure rates increased steadily, from 6.2 percent of cases in 1981 to 9.9 percent in 1984. Projected dispositional departures under the guidelines, if they had been superimposed over 1978 sentences, would have been 19.4 percent, suggesting that the guidelines significantly increased the consistency of sentencing. Looked at the other way around, in the first four years of Minnesota's experience with

---

[5] For Minnesota, a caveat: "in" means state prison, "out" means no state prison, but judges may order up to twelve months incarceration in a local jail.

guidelines, the dispositional compliance rates were 93.8 percent, 93 percent, 91.1 percent, and 90.1 percent.

To some extent, the increased dispositional departure rates in 1982 and 1983 resulted from the anomaly that seventy-five defendants in 1982, 111 defendants in 1983, and eighty-four defendants in 1984 elected to go to prison rather than receive nonprison sentences (Miethe and Moore 1987, p. xiii). The Minnesota Supreme Court has ruled that in many cases these requests must be honored (*State v. Randolph*, 316 N.W.2d 508 [Minn. 1982]). These cases count as aggravated departures, and therefore inflate their numbers.

These compliance figures are less impressive than first appears. Minnesota has very low imprisonment rates for persons convicted of felonies. In 1978, before guidelines took effect, 20.4 percent of convicted felons received prison sentences. In 1981, imprisonment was both the presumptive and the actual disposition in 15.0 percent of cases. In 1982, imprisonment was the presumptive disposition in 18.7 percent of cases and the actual disposition in 18.6 percent of cases. By 1984, the imprisonment rate had crept up to 19.6 percent. Thus nonimprisonment is the presumptive sentence in 80–85 percent of felony cases each year, and it would take a very large shift toward greater severity in sentencing of persons convicted of less serious offenses to significantly alter dispositional compliance rates.

Durational departure rates are also shown in table 5. The only clear pattern is that mitigated departures regularly exceed aggravated departures by a ratio of two to one. No comparisons with preguidelines durational patterns are shown because the parole release decisions in 1978 were not easily compared with postguidelines sentencing decisions.

b) Pennsylvania. Table 6 shows Pennsylvania compliance and departure rates for 1983–86. Table 7 shows dispositional and durational departure rates for the same years. Approximately 6 percent of sentences are dispositional departures each year and 6–8 percent more are durational departures (as in Minnesota, mitigated departures greatly exceed aggravated departures). Compared with Minnesota dispositional departures of 6–10 percent of cases, and durational departures ranging from 20 to 22 percent, the Pennsylvania guidelines appear to have achieved much greater consistency than Minnesota's. These comparisons are highly misleading, however, and it is likely that the Minnesota guidelines achieved much higher levels of sentencing consistency. Moreover, for reasons explained below, the Minnesota and Pennsylvania data are not comparable.

TABLE 6

Guideline Compliance Patterns in Pennsylvania (%)

Year	Departure Down*	Mitigated Range	Standard	Aggravated Range	Departure Up
1983	12	5	80.5	1	1
1984	12	5.6	78.5	1.7	2
1985	12	5.3	78.5	1.7	2
1986	9	4.9	81.7	2.3	2

SOURCES.—Pennsylvania Commission on Sentencing 1984, fig. I, table 1; 1985, fig. G, table 6; 1986a, fig. G, table 5; 1987, fig. F, table 5.

NOTE.—Percentages do not total 100% due to rounding.

* Apparently includes both dispositional departures and durational departures downward; see note to table 7.

There are at least three reasons why Pennsylvania's guidelines have had less effect than appears. First, these departure rates appear lower than Minnesota's, but this may be because Pennsylvania's wide ranges allow enormous scope for variation without departures. For example, the combined guideline range in Pennsylvania for a person convicted of an aggravated robbery who had previously been convicted of a robbery would be nine to thirty-six months (Offense Level 6, Prior Record Score 3; mitigated range = 9–12 months, standard range = 12–29 months, aggravated range = 29–36 months). Under the Minnesota guidelines, the guideline range for a comparable offender would

TABLE 7

Departure Rates in Pennsylvania (%)

Year	Durational Departure Upward	Durational Departure Down	Dispositional Departure
1983	1	6	6
1984	2	5	6
1985	2	6	6
1986	2	4	5

SOURCES.—Pennsylvania Commission on Sentencing 1984, table 3; 1985, table 8; 1986a, table 7; 1987, table 7.

NOTE.—It appears from the Pennsylvania reports that most dispositional departures involve nonincarcerative dispositions for persons for whom incarceration is the presumptive sentence: the "departure down" reported in table 6 for each year appears to include both the "dispositional departures" and the "durational departures" for that year.

TABLE 8

Pennsylvania 1984 Compliance Data Disaggregated*

	N	Complete Conformity (%)	Dispositional Departure (%)	Duration (%)	
				Up	Down
All offenses	25,694	87.0†	6.0	2.0	5.0
Misdemeanors‡	11,168	97.0	1.25	.3	1.0
Felonies	14,526	79.4	9.6	3.3	8.1

SOURCE.—Pennsylvania Commission on Sentencing 1985, table 8.

* Because the source data are expressed as percentages, these disaggregations are not exact; nonetheless, if the source data are accurate, the disaggregation shown in this table should be a close approximation.

† Rows do not equal 100% due to rounding.

‡ Made up of the following offenses: "other misdemeanors," "crimes codes misdemeanors," "VUFA/unloaded firearms," "theft MI," "retail theft MI," "drug misdemeanor."

be thirty to thirty-four months (Offense Level 7, Criminal History Score 1).

Second, the Pennsylvania compliance rates are heavily influenced by high compliance rates for minor offenses. For example, of 25,694 sentences imposed in the one-year period covered by the Pennsylvania Commission's 1985 report (table 8), 6,987 of those cases, more than a quarter, fell in the category "crimes code misdemeanors," of which 97 percent resulted in sentences in the normal three-part guideline range (the normal guideline range is 0–6 months or 0–12 months for most misdemeanants); that single offense category therefore constitutes more than 25 percent of the statewide compliance with Pennsylvania's guidelines. Other misdemeanors totaling 4,181 sentences in 1984 experienced complete compliance rates ranging from 94 to 100 percent.

Taken together, the complete compliance rate (that is, neither a durational nor a dispositional departure) for all 11,168 reported misdemeanors was 97 percent. When felony and misdemeanor sentencing are disaggregated, as table 8 shows, the resulting complete compliance rate for felons is 79.4 percent, the dispositional departure rate is 9.6 percent, and the combined durational departure rate is 11.4 percent.

Further evidence of low real levels of compliance in Pennsylvania is shown in a recent article by the executive and associate directors of the Pennsylvania commission (Kramer and Lubitz 1985). Table 9, taken from that article, shows compliance rates in 1983 for selected offenses.

TABLE 9

Compliance with Guideline Sentences Imposed in 1983 for Selected Offenses

Offense	N	Comply (%)	Above (%)	Below (%)
Aggravated assault	574	70	0	30
Arson	95	64	1	35
Burglary	2,538	77	3	20
Criminal trespass	451	93	0	7
Drug felonies	872	80	2	18
Escape	99	40	0	60
Forgery	450	85	0	15
Involuntary deviate sexual intercourse	69	68	0	32
Rape	75	76	4	20
Retail theft	611	84	1	15
Robbery	1,020	83	5	12
Terroristic threats	130	92	0	8
Theft-felony	906	89	1	10
Weapons	454	81	1	18

SOURCE.—Kramer and Lubitz 1985, p. 490.

"Compliance" in table 9 means imposition of any sentence from within the combined mitigated, standard, and aggravated ranges.

The offenses set out in table 9 are generally felonies and therefore are comparable with the offenses, only felonies, that are affected by Minnesota's guidelines. Pennsylvania's level of compliance for felony sentences appears lower than Minnesota's even when the different widths of "compliant" guideline ranges are ignored. Compliance rates for aggravated assault, arson, burglary, drug felonies, rape, and robbery range from 64 percent to 83 percent.

Third, because of plea bargaining, even the weak evidence summarized above for compliance with Pennsylvania's guidelines may be overstated. Table 10, taken from the Pennsylvania Commission's 1983 and 1986 reports, shows guideline conformity rates for selected offenses.

The offenses shown are of sets of related offenses of variable severity, and they exhibit certain common features that appear in both the 1983 and the 1986 data.[6] Downward departure rates in 1983 are very high for persons convicted of the *most serious* offense of a class (aggravated

[6] I describe here only the 1983 data, but table 9 shows that 1986 data are comparable.

TABLE 10

Statewide Conformity in Pennsylvania in 1983 and 1986, Selected Offenses (%)

Offense	Standard Range		Aggravated Range		Mitigated Range		Departure Up		Departure Down	
	1983	1986	1983	1986	1983	1986	1983	1986	1983	1986
Aggravated assault:										
F2	36	47	4	5	12	12	2	3	46	33
F3	100	†	0	†	0	†	0	†	0	†
M1	70	71	1	2	10	8	0	1	19	18
Arson:										
F1	13	33	0	4	10	16	0	3	77	44
F2	62	48	0	8	11	10	5	1	22	33
Burglary:										
ogs* 7	39	40	3	4	25	18	3	9	29	29
ogs 6	49	56	3	4	14	13	4	5	31	22
ogs 5	78	77	2	4	5	5	2	3	12	11
Retail theft:										
F3	62	65	2	2	9	12	1	0	25	20
M1	91	96	0	0	4	1	0	0	5	2
Robbery:										
F1	48	59	6	7	10	10	15	11	25	12
F2	67	73	4	4	6	7	6	4	20	12
F3	85	87	1	3	4	3	2	2	17	5

SOURCES.—Pennsylvania Commission on Sentencing 1984, table 1; 1987, table 4.

* Offense gravity scale.

† 1986 data are not available.

assault—46 percent; arson—77 percent; burglary—29 percent; retail theft—25 percent; robbery—25 percent). However, persons convicted of the *least serious* version of the offense tend to be sentenced from within the standard range (aggravated assault—70 percent; arson—62 percent; burglary—78 percent; retail theft—91 percent; robbery—85 percent). These patterns support a number of hypotheses about variations in plea bargaining practices. In courts in which sentence bargaining is the norm, the parties may agree to conviction of the offense charged but with an understanding that the guideline sentence will be reduced substantially. This would explain the high downward departure rates for the most serious form of an offense. In charge bargaining courts, the parties may agree to conviction of a reduced charge and imposition of a sentence from within the standard range. This would explain high rates of sentences within the normal guidelines ranges for the least serious form of an offense. If these hypotheses are valid, one cannot conclude anything about compliance from the aggregate data. Whether these hypotheses are valid can be tested by participant observation research on plea bargaining in Pennsylvania. A recent analysis by the Pennsylvania Commission's staff found that there were significant increases under guidelines in the percentage of cases with dropped charges, the average number of charges dropped per case, and the percentage of cases with reduced charges, all of which is consistent with increased charge bargaining (Lubitz and Kempinen 1987); these conclusions are based on analyses of aggregate data, and the issue remains unresolved.

Table 10 shows how high compliance rates can be compatible with extensive plea bargaining. Critics of sentencing guidelines have suggested that greater predictability allows the prosecutor increased power (e.g., Alschuler 1978). Or, in jurisdictions in which plea bargaining is the norm, the specificity that accompanies determinate sentencing may allow bargaining to work backwards from the sentence to the offense. That is, counsel can agree on an appropriate sentence, locate it on the sentencing grid, and then reach agreement concerning the offense to which the defendant will plead guilty (there is evidence that something comparable sometimes happens under California's Determinate Sentencing Law: Casper, Brereton, and Neal 1983, p. 412).

c) Washington. Washington has relatively narrow guidelines, only one guideline range for each offense and offender, and a demanding standard for departures. Only 3.5 percent of sentences in 1985, the first full calendar year of guidelines experience, were "exceptional" sentences that satisfied the "substantial and compelling" test and therefore were "departures" (Washington State Sentencing Guidelines Commission 1986, table 5). Washington has, however, a special "first offender" provision (for persons convicted of a nonviolent, nonsexual offense who have no prior felony conviction); this option permits the judge to order a treatment-oriented sentence and jail time not to exceed ninety days in place of whatever sentence the guidelines might prescribe. The first offender provision applied to 22.7 percent of offenders in 1985, of whom about half benefited from the special provision; it is unclear how to factor these cases into compliance rates (1986, fig. 3).

d) Florida. Holton notes that "since the implementation date of October 1, 1983, guidelines recommended sentences have been imposed [in Florida] approximately 80 percent of the time. The current rate of compliance is 81.5 percent. . . . The reduction of unwarranted variation and disparity has become a reality in the vast majority of cases in the State of Florida" (Holton 1987, p. 4).

Unfortunately, the data do not support that conclusion. An 80 percent compliance rate is less impressive than may first appear, for several reasons. First, because of the width of the Florida ranges (3.5 to 7 years is a typical range), a large percentage of cases can be expected to fall within the guidelines by chance. Second, the guidelines cover all felonies and, in any jurisdiction, most first offenders and many offenders convicted of minor offenses will be presumed "out"; if, say, 70 percent of offenders are not subject to an incarcerative presumption, most of these will receive a nonincarcerative sentence, and the system will automatically have a "compliance rate" in the 60–70 percent range. Third, when Florida's 80 percent overall compliance rate is disaggregated by offense category, the picture changes. Although some offense categories, including property offenses (theft, forgery, fraud—87.5 percent) and weapon offenses (90.4 percent), have high compliance rates, other offense categories, including homicide (66.9 percent), sexual offenses (55.3 percent), and robbery (67.5 percent), exhibit much lower compliance rates.

2. *Changes in Sentencing Patterns.* The Minnesota, Washington, and Pennsylvania commissions all appear to have achieved their major policy goals concerning imprisonment patterns. Both the Minnesota and the Washington commissions decided, as a matter of policy, to attempt to change patterns of prison use by emphasizing the use of prison for persons convicted of violent offenses, including first offenders, and by de-emphasizing the use of imprisonment in nonviolent cases, including

those involving offenders with extensive criminal records. In Pennsylvania, the legislature directed that sentencing be made more severe when it rejected the first set of guidelines proposed by the commission, and the commission heeded that directive when it formulated the second set of guidelines.

In Minnesota, in the first year of experience with guidelines, 78 percent of offenders convicted of serious violent offenses and having a minor criminal record, or none at all, were imprisoned; that constituted a 73 percent increase over preguidelines practices. Conversely, of those convicted of minor property offenses and having moderate to extensive criminal records, only 15 percent were imprisoned under the sentencing guidelines during the first year; that constituted a 72 percent reduction. During the second, third, and fourth years, sentencing appeared to shift back toward traditional patterns. Imprisonment rates for violent offenders were higher than 1978 preguidelines levels in 1981 and 1982 but in 1984 fell below the 1978 level (Knapp 1984a, p. 31; Miethe and Moore 1987, p. x). By 1983, the imprisonment rate for low-severity property offenders was at almost the preguidelines level, but this may camouflage the guidelines' impact. A major reason for incarceration of such offenders was that they *requested* incarceration; the Minnesota Supreme Court has held that such requests must be honored. Some offenders requested incarceration because they were being imprisoned for another, more serious, offense and wanted the sentences to run concurrently. Other offenders, however, who constituted 4 percent of prison admissions in 1981 and 10 percent in 1983, apparently preferred incarceration because it appeared less onerous than an "out" sentence. Under anomalies in the Minnesota guidelines, some "out" sentences are potentially harsher than some "in" sentences. A person receiving a one-year prison term would, assuming "good time" was credited, be released in eight months. An "out" sentence might include twelve months in jail plus a lengthy term of probation with conditions, and, if probation were revoked, a state prison sentence of twelve to thirty months might be imposed. If the anomalies were eliminated so that this category of offenders did not request imprisonment, the imprisonment rate for low-severity property offenders in 1983 and 1984 might be little higher than the 1981 rate.

Washington also seems to have succeeded in altering sentencing patterns. In 1982, the preguideline comparison year chosen, 49 percent of persons convicted of violent offenses received prison sentences; in 1985, under the guidelines, 65 percent of persons convicted of violent offenses received prison sentences. Conversely, in 1982, 87 percent of persons convicted of nonviolent offenses received nonprison sentences; during 1985, the figure was 91 percent (Washington State Sentencing Commission 1986, fig. 1). The Washington data are cruder than Minnesota's, for they do not distinguish among either violent or nonviolent offenses in terms of their relative severity, but the pattern is clear. In both jurisdictions, during the first year's experience under guidelines, there were substantial shifts in the patterns of sentences imposed toward the direction contemplated by the creators of the guidelines.

The Pennsylvania guidelines were intended to increase sentencing severity for many offenses and appear to have achieved that goal. Table 11 shows, for persons convicted of selected offenses, percent incarcerated and mean minimum sentences for the years 1983 to 1986. In general, both the proportions imprisoned and the average sentences increased steadily. Pennsylvania is, however, an indeterminate sentencing state, and release dates are set by a parole board; consequently, the minimum sentence does not necessarily indicate actual average time served at release.

3. *Sentencing Severity.*   Sentencing severity appears to have increased in Minnesota and Pennsylvania and to have decreased in Washington after guidelines took effect. The Pennsylvania evaluations showed increases in sentencing severity in each of the first two years of experience with guidelines. The 1983 report concluded, "incarceration rates and incarceration lengths increased substantially over previous levels, especially for violent crimes" (Pennsylvania Commission on Sentencing 1984, p. i). The commission's conclusion in 1984 was that "sentencing severity for serious crimes increased over previous levels," for the second year (Pennsylvania Commission on Sentencing 1985, p. 1). By every measure shown in table 12, sentencing in Pennsylvania appears to have been more severe in 1984 than in 1983 but to have stabilized thereafter. Table 11 also shows increasing proportions of convicted offenders imprisoned and for increasing average minimum terms for selected serious offenses.

In Minnesota, also, sentencing severity appears to have increased during the first three years after implementation of the guidelines. During the first year, the average sentence imposed was 38.3 months, and the average projected actual incarceration (taking account of good time) was 25.5 months. Those figures increased in 1982 to forty-one months and 27.3 months and would likely have increased again in the

TABLE 11

Sentencing Severity in Pennsylvania, Selected Offenses, 1983–86

	1983		1984		1985		1986	
Offense	Percentage Incarcerated	Minimum Sentence*	Percentage Incarcerated	Minimum Sentence*	Percentage Incarcerated	Minimum Sentence*	Percentage Incarcerated	Minimum Sentence*
Aggravated assault (F2)	75	18.5	78	22.6	78	23.3	80	22.7
Burglary (1)	86	23.6	73	22.9	85	24.8	87	25.6
Burglary (2)	81	14.9	82	18.6	80	15.8	85	16.9
Burglary (3)	62	12.6	67	14.0	68	14.0	69	12.5
Rape	91	48.7	95	52.0	93	56.9	96	54.7
Robbery (F1)	93	39.6	96	44.3	94	44.3	95	46.3
Robbery (F2)	79	14.5	81	17.1	82	15.9	84	16.1
Robbery (F3)	62	10.2	69	12.0	66	10.9	72	10.6

SOURCE.—Pennsylvania Commission on Sentencing 1987, table 19.
* Months.

TABLE 12

Sentencing Severity in Pennsylvania in 1983–86

Year	Defendants Incarcerated (%)	Minimum Average Incarcerated	Maximum Average Incarcerated	Average Minimum Jail Sentence	Average Maximum Jail Sentence	Average Minimum Prison Sentence	Average Maximum Prison Sentence	Minimum Sentence in Excess of Five Years (%)
1983	55.0	12.1	33.4	6.4	20.5	24.4	61.5	3.3
1984	57.0	N.A.	N.A.	6.8	22.2	28.7	70.0	6.0
1985	56.6	14.4	39.0	6.4	21.2	28.6	71.7	6.0
1986	56.2	14.1	38.2	6.2	21.2	29.3	71.7	5.9

NOTE.—All times are given in months.
SOURCES.—Pennsylvania Commission on Sentencing 1984, p. 17; 1985, p. 22; 1986a, p. 25; 1987, p. 24.

third year but for a series of changes made by both the Minnesota legislature and the commission aimed at reducing sentence lengths (and prison overcrowding); the resulting figures for 1983 were 36.5 months and 24.3 months (Knapp 1984*a*, p. 30). By a different measure, however, Minnesota sentencing patterns showed steady increases in severity. The percentage of felony convictions resulting in prison sentences increased from 15 percent in 1981 to 18.6 percent in 1982, 20.5 percent in 1983, and 19.6 percent in 1984 (Miethe and Moore 1987, p. vii). In 1978, 20.4 percent of convicted felons received prison sentences, so the apparent increase in prison use between 1981 and 1984 may instead be a reversion to preguidelines levels.

The Washington evaluation of the first full calendar year of guidelines experience concluded in the aggregate that "persons sentenced under the Sentencing Reform Act in 1985 would serve less time in prison than those sentenced under the indeterminate sentencing system in 1982" (Washington State Sentencing Guidelines Commission 1986, p. 8). Unfortunately, these gross aggregate punishment comparisons are not especially enlightening. The percentage of violent offenders receiving prison sentences increased from 49 percent in 1982 to 65 percent in 1985, and the corresponding percentage of property offenders declined from 13 percent to 9 percent. This may mean that relatively less serious violent crimes received prison sentences in 1985, which would tend to reduce the average sentence severity. At the same time, in 1982, 20 percent of Washington felony convictions were for violent crimes; in 1985, only 14 percent were for violent crimes. It is not known whether this reflects changes in crime rates or changes in charging or plea bargaining.

Nothing can be said with confidence about sentence severity under Washington's guidelines without much greater disaggregation of the statistical analyses. The declining proportion of violent crime convictions and the increasing proportion of convicted violent offenders who receive prison sentences could have opposite effects on average severity. For many offenses, the percentages of offenders incarcerated changed significantly between 1982 and 1985, and it is impossible to know whether apparently reduced mean sentences result from imposition of prison sentences on persons who commit relatively less serious crimes or from the effects of the guidelines (Washington State Sentencing Guidelines Commission 1986, p. 49).

4. *Extent of Sentencing Disparities.*   In all three jurisdictions, there was evidence that sentencing became more consistent under guidelines than

before. In Minnesota, the 1984 evaluation concluded that "disparity in sentencing decreased under the sentencing guidelines. This reduction in disparity is indicated by increased sentence uniformity and proportionality. . . . Although sentencing practices were still more uniform and proportional in 1982 and 1983 than sentencing practices prior to the guidelines, there was less uniformity and proportionality in 1982 and 1983 than there was in 1981" (Knapp 1984*a*, pp. v–vi). A statistical analysis of the first eighteen months of guidelines experience in Minnesota similarly concluded that Minnesota "was largely successful in reducing preguideline disparities in those decisions that fall within the scope of the guidelines" (Miethe and Moore 1985, p. 360). On extension of their study to encompass four years of guidelines experience, Miethe and Moore conclude, "the decision to imprison has become far more uniform under the guidelines. Although there was a slight increase in grid variance over post-guideline periods (which indicates greater non-uniformity), the variances in the 'in/out' decision by 1984 still remained far below the pre-guideline level" (1987, p. ix). Miethe and Moore reached a similar conclusion about durational consistency.

One major weakness of the Minnesota guidelines is that they deal only with felony sentencing and then primarily with state prison sentences. Although the enabling legislation provided that "the commission may also establish appropriate sanctions for offenders for whom imprisonment is not proper . . . ", the commission elected not to do so. As a consequence, the guidelines created presumptions as to who goes to prison but provide no guidelines concerning sentencing of persons not receiving *state prison* sentences. Inasmuch as up to one year's *jail incarceration* may be imposed as a condition of probation, the absence of guidance could well have produced considerable disparity. Moreover, for those repetitive property offenders whom the commission preferred not receive prison sentences, jail remains an available option. The foreseeable confusion resulted: the commission's three-year evaluation concluded: "nonconformity of [jail] use is found for every racial and gender group, and there has been very little improvement in uniformity of jail use from 1978 to jail use in 1981, 1982, and 1983" (Knapp 1984*a*, p. 48).

The Washington guidelines appear to have reduced sentencing disparities. Because high compliance rates were obtained, it is likely that substantial consistency was achieved. The commission's evaluation for 1985 concluded, as to consistency in imposition of incarcerative sentences, "the Sentencing Reform Act has clearly increased consistency in the imprisonment decision" (1986, p. 7). The commission's evaluation also concluded that sentencing became more consistent when offenders' sentences were compared controlling for criminal history and the conviction offense. There was "a reduction of over 60 percent in sentence length variance" (1986, p. 9).

The Pennsylvania evidence is difficult to assess. The commission's evaluation of 1983 sentencing asserts: "it appears that Pennsylvania's guidelines are accomplishing their intended goal of reducing unwarranted disparity" (1984, p. i), and the 1984 evaluation notes, "sentences became more uniform throughout the state" (1985, p. i). These conclusions presumably are inferences drawn from high "conformity with guideline" rates. As these may, for reasons discussed above, be plea bargaining artifacts, it is not clear whether disparities have been reduced and, if so, by how much.

It is difficult to know how to assess Pennsylvania's shift. Less has been published about the Pennsylvania experience than about Minnesota. One of the goals of the Pennsylvania guidelines was to lessen differences in sentencing patterns between rural and urban courts. An analysis by the executive and research directors of the Pennsylvania Commission indicates much greater similarity in urban and rural sentencing patterns after guidelines than before (Kramer and Lubitz 1985, table 4).

5. *Plea Bargaining.* A former chairman of the Minnesota commission has written about the need for prosecutors to develop prosecutorial guidelines because of "the potential of the prosecutor to undermine the uniformity desired by the guidelines" (Rathke 1982, p. 271). Experience has validated that prediction, as is shown by direct evidence from Minnesota and indirect evidence from Pennsylvania and Washington.

The Minnesota evaluation investigated plea bargaining under guidelines in a number of ways. The overall conclusion was that, under guidelines, "[t]here were more charge negotiations and fewer sentence negotiations. There were more charge reductions that affected the severity level of the offense and an increase in the number of conviction offenses which affected the criminal history score of the offender" (Knapp 1984*a*, p. vi).

Table 13 shows the findings of the commission's study of conviction methods in eight counties for 1978 and the first two years under guidelines. Compared with 1978, the percentage of cases resolved by charge

TABLE 13

Method of Obtaining Conviction, Eight-County Area (%)

	1978	1981	1982
Trial	5.8	4.7	5.6
Straight plea	17.1	25.8	15.7
Charge negotiation	21.1	27.6	31.3
Sentence negotiation	34.3	23.4	25.7
Plea negotiation charge and			
sentence	21.7	18.5	21.6
Total	100.0	100.0	99.9

SOURCE.—Knapp 1984, table 27.
NOTE.—Percentages do not total 100% due to rounding.

negotiations in 1982 increased from 21.1 percent to 31.3 percent. The percentage of cases resolved by sentence negotiations fell from 34.3 percent in 1978 to 25.7 percent in 1982.[7]

An increase in charge bargaining should be no surprise. The Minnesota guidelines are based on the charge of conviction and, assuming the judge will impose a sentence from within the applicable guideline range, the sentencing ramifications of a "vertical" charge reduction are explicit and predictable. This is particularly true when the charge reduction moves the case across the "in/out" line from the area of presumptive prison sentences to the area of presumptive nonprison sentences. Compared with the preguidelines year of 1978, the percentage of cases in which there were charge reductions across offense severity levels in 1983 increased from 12 percent to 27 percent (Knapp 1984a, p. 78).

The increase in vertical charge bargaining is thus explicable in terms of case dispositions. A change in Minnesota "horizontal" charging and bargaining practices resulted from an effort by prosecutors to manipulate the guidelines (see Miethe and Moore 1987, p. xi). Many prosecutors apparently disagreed with the commission's policy decision to de-

---

[7] Miethe, using ordinary least squares regression analyses, concluded that "prosecutors' charging and plea bargaining practices remained fairly stable across pre- and post-guideline periods" (1987, p. 165). I am skeptical about that conclusion, largely because the patterns in table 13 seem so clear and so consistent with most people's intuitions about prosecutorial strategies. Miethe finds confirmation for his conclusions in the absence of evidence of socioeconomic "differentiation in the type of persons who receive charge and sentence concessions" under guidelines (1987, p. 173). Here too I am unconvinced, for I perceive no strong theoretical link between plea bargaining manipulations of guidelines and comparative disadvantage to the socioeconomic disadvantaged.

crease the use of state prison incarceration as a sanction for property offenses. Under the guidelines, an offender convicted of a minor property offense had to accumulate a substantial criminal record before prison became the presumptive sentence. In a deliberate effort to increase property offenders' criminal history scores, prosecutors required property offenders to plead guilty to multiple charges more often than in the past. Prior to guidelines, a person believed to have committed three burglaries might be convicted of one, which would yield a criminal history score of 1 when next he came before the court for sentencing. After the guidelines took effect, however, this same first-time offender might be required to plead guilty to three counts of burglary, which, the next time he came before a court for sentencing, would give him a criminal history score of 3. A Minnesota Supreme Court decision, *State v. Hernandez*, 311 N.W.2d 478 (Minn. 1981), exacerbated this problem when it held that multiple convictions on the same day could be taken into account; this meant that an offender who had no prior convictions before the day of sentencing, but who was convicted of six property offenses, could be treated as having five prior convictions when sentenced for the sixth offense. Prosecutors apparently intentionally attempted to undermine the commission's policies in this way, and the commission changed the criminal history scoring system to offset this prosecutorial tactic (Knapp 1984*a*, pp. 71–86, p. 31).

The survival of sentence negotiations may appear surprising, especially when the Minnesota Supreme Court has held that a sentence negotiation is not a "substantial and compelling reason" for departing from guidelines (*State v. Garcia*, 302 N.W.2d 643 [Minn. 1981]). Despite that prohibition, the single most common reason provided by judges for departures from guidelines is "pursuant to plea negotiations." Reconciling this pattern with the Supreme Court's decision is not difficult. In practice, such a case would come before the court only if one of the parties appealed the sentence imposed pursuant to the negotiation, and neither party is likely to do so. Although, as noted in table 13, the percentage of cases disposed by sentence negotiations fell from 34.3 percent in 1978 to 25.7 percent in 1982, the latter figure remains substantial. (Dale Parent, the first director of the Minnesota Commission, has informed me that these statistics are misleading because many of the sentence bargains concern sentences *within* the guidelines range, conditions of probation, or "bogus" bargains not to seek aggravation of the sentence.) In addition, because the Minnesota guidelines do not set presumptions for sentencing of the 80–85 percent

TABLE 14

Conviction Offenses by Seriousness Levels, 1982 and 1985 (%)

Level	FY 1982	Jan.–June 1985	Difference
XIV	.2	.1	− .1
XIII	.5	.3	− .2
XII	.3	.2	− .1
XI	.1	.2	+ .1
X	.9	.4	− .5
IX	5.6	3.6	−2.0
VIII	1.4	.6	− .8
VII	3.4	2.0	−1.4
VI	4.7	5.7	+1.0
V	.8	.7	− .1
IV	10.6	9.7	− .9
III	8.3	10.1	+1.8
II	34.5	33.3	−1.2
I	28.7	31.1	+2.4
Unranked	.0	1.9	+1.9
Total	100.0	99.9	...

SOURCE.—Washington State Sentencing Guidelines Commission 1985, p. 3.

NOTE.—Level XIV is the most serious category (aggravated murder). First-time offenders who commit a Level VI offense and above have a guideline prison term. Percentages do not equal 100% due to rounding.

of offenders who do not receive state prison sentences, there is plenty of legitimate scope for sentence bargaining about jail terms, probation conditions, and similar matters.

The evidence on plea bargaining under the Washington and Pennsylvania guidelines is much more ambiguous. As noted earlier, in discussion of table 10, the patterns of conviction offenses and sentencing outcomes in Pennsylvania suggest that plea bargaining has adapted to the guidelines.

In Washington, the initial evaluation report comparing sentencing outcomes for 1982 and the first six months of 1985 suggested that charge bargaining around the guidelines is playing a prominent role (Washington State Sentencing Guidelines Commission 1985). Table 14 shows the offense seriousness levels by conviction in Washington state during the two periods. There is an almost invariant shift downward in the percentages of cases disposed at each of severity levels 7–14, supporting an inference that many cases that would have been sentenced in 1982 at one level are being sentenced in 1985 at a lower level as a result of charge bargains. The increase in cases at level 6 (the presumptive prison sentence level) may indicate that, regardless of charge concessions, prosecutors in some cases insisted on pleas to charges calling for prison sentences. These analyses, however, are no more than inferences, and little more can be said until more exhaustive evaluations have been completed.

The later evaluation for the full 1985 calendar year revealed that the guilty plea and trial rates were virtually identical in 1982 and 1985 (1986, p. 39). However, the report notes a decline in the proportion of violent offenses from 18 percent in 1982 to 14 percent in 1985 and observes, "at this time, it is not known if this change reflects a decrease in the violent crime rate, an increase in the non-violent crime rate, a change in charging practices by prosecuting attorneys, or some other change" (1986, p. ix).

6. *Trial and Appeal Rates.*   Opponents of determinate sentencing and sentencing guidelines, especially judicial opponents, have often argued that determinate sentencing reduces the incentives for offenders to plead guilty. As a consequence, it is argued, offenders would insist on jury or bench trials, confident that their sentences would not be increased significantly were they convicted at trial in comparison with sentences following a guilty plea (Washington State Sentencing Guidelines Commission 1986, p. 39). If that hypothesis is sound, trial rates should increase in the sentencing guidelines jurisdictions.

In Washington, they were stable. In 1982, before guidelines, 90.1 percent of cases were disposed of by pleas, 7.8 percent by jury trials, and 2.1 percent by bench trials. During 1985, under guidelines, the plea rate remained 90.1 percent, the jury trial rate declined to 6.7 percent, and the bench trial rate increased slightly to 2.8 percent (Washington State Sentencing Guidelines Commission 1986, p. 39).

In Minnesota, in 1978, before guidelines, and in 1981 and 1982, under guidelines, the percentages of felony cases disposed of after trials, rather than by guilty pleas, were 5.8 percent, 4.7 percent, and 5.6 percent (Knapp 1984a, p. 72). In neither Washington nor Minnesota, notwithstanding their narrow sentencing guidelines, does the evidence suggest that large numbers of defendants chose to plead not guilty because of the lessened jeopardy they might feel concerning penalties that would be imposed after a conviction at a trial.

An analysis of Pennsylvania dispositions under guidelines found no significant changes in the rate of jury trials and no significant increases in case processing time (Lubitz and Kempinen 1987). Nor has the establishment of appellate sentence review resulted in flooded appellate dockets. While no data are available from Washington and Pennsylvania, fewer than 1 percent of Minnesota sentences have been appealed. As Kay Knapp's important treatise (Knapp 1985) demonstrates, the Minnesota appellate courts have taken sentence appeals seriously. The appeals courts had by 1985 decided more than 300 appeals, and in general have upheld the guidelines. They have established standards for departures and for the extent to which sentences can be increased in aggravated cases. Minnesota may become the first American jurisdiction to have a meaningful system of appellate sentence review.

IV. Statutory Determinate Sentencing

The Maine legislature abolished parole release in Maine in 1975 and thereby became the first state to replace an indeterminate sentencing system with a determinate sentencing system. "Determinate" sentencing means different things to different people (e.g., von Hirsch and Hanrahan 1981). "Indeterminate" sentencing systems were so called because an imprisoned offender's actual date for release from prison could not be known until it was set by the parole board. The length of a prison sentence would not be determined until it was over. By analogy, therefore, to many people, a "determinate" sentencing system is simply one in which parole has been abolished and, accordingly, the length of a prison sentence can be known, that is, "determined," at the time that it is imposed (given certain assumptions about the operation of good time laws). By that definition, at least ten states—California, Colorado, Connecticut, Illinois, Indiana, Maine, Minnesota, New Mexico, North Carolina, and Washington—have adopted determinate sentencing because they have abolished parole release for the vast majority of imprisoned offenders.

Determinate sentencing laws can be divided into three general categories.[8] First, Maine occupies a category in itself in that it abolished parole release but established no standards to govern judicial sentencing decisions. When parole release was abandoned, Maine adopted a new criminal code, based generally on the *Model Penal Code* (American Law Institute 1962). The *Model Penal Code* was drafted for use in indeterminate sentencing systems and divided all felonies into three classes and

---

[8] Mandatory sentencing laws might also be considered a form of determinate sentencing; see Appendix for a brief overview of evaluations of the impact of these laws.

specified no sentencing standards other than lengthy maximum authorized sentences for each felony class. What this combination of parole abolition and lengthy sentence maximums meant was that judges had no guidance for the sentences that they set. With parole abolished, only three mechanisms existed in Maine under the new statutes for review of arbitrary, disparate, or extremely long sentences. The first was a mechanism for petition for resentencing by the Department of Corrections. This procedure was declared unconstitutional by the Maine Supreme Court on the basis that the judge's power to resentence on petition violated the constitutional doctrine of Separation of Powers and intruded on the "commutation power expressly and exclusively granted by the state constitution to the Governor" (*Maine v. Hunter* [1982]). The second was the governor's commutation power, a power that is seldom exercised in Maine. The third is appellate sentence review, which, in Maine, as in most states, does not afford meaningful scrutiny to sentencing decisions.

The second category of determinate sentencing laws is represented by statutes in North Carolina and California that set out specific standards for sentences. This second group of determinate sentencing laws, in principle, is not substantially different from sentencing guidelines. The standards are simply set out in a statute enacted by a legislature rather than in presumptive guidelines developed by a sentencing commission. In practice, sentencing commission guidelines are much more specific and detailed than any statutory determinate sentencing law.

The third category of determinate sentencing laws, exemplified by states like Illinois, Indiana, and Arizona, specify only very general standards for sentencing. In Indiana, for example, the statutory sentencing range for Class B offenses is six to twenty years, and the range for Class A offenses is twenty to fifty years (Lagoy, Hussey, and Kramer 1978; Hussey and Lagoy 1983). These determinate sentencing laws, none of which has been subjected to a rigorous evaluation (assuming a rigorous evaluation of so nebulous a set of standards is a sensible thing to attempt), provide little more guidance to sentencing than is afforded by Maine's law or by indeterminate sentencing laws. The only evaluation of such a system known to me, of which a second part dealing with judicial sentencing decisions remains to be published, concluded: "the [Illinois] Act's efforts to structure the exercise of discretion by prosecutorial, judicial, and correctional officials in the bargaining for, imposing, and serving of criminal sentences have been systematically ignored, subverted, or invalidated" (Schuwerk 1984, p. 739).

A number of hypotheses have been offered about the operation of determinate sentencing laws: that they will be systematically manipulated by plea bargaining counsel; that they will reduce sentencing disparities because sentences will tend to cluster around the statutory standards; that trial rates will increase because the incentive to plead guilty will be removed by increased predictability about sentences to be imposed; that more "marginal" offenders will receive prison sentences because judges need no longer worry that the parole boards will keep them in prison for an unduly long period.

The impacts of determinate sentencing laws have been undramatic. Determinate sentencing laws shift discretion to judges and prosecutors; prosecutors have used their control over charging and plea bargaining to strengthen their influence in determining sentences imposed. However, criminal justice systems have readily absorbed determinate sentencing laws and, in general, trial rates have not increased and case processing delays have not become greater.

The move toward statutory determinate sentencing seems now to have ended, perhaps because ten years' experience suggests that presumptive sentencing guidelines developed by a sentencing commission are a much more effective means for establishing and enforcing comprehensive system-wide sentencing standards. No jurisdiction, to my knowledge, has adopted a statutory determinate sentencing law in the last few years. Many jurisdictions, including Louisiana, Maine, New York, Oregon, South Carolina, Tennessee, Wisconsin, and the federal system, have established sentencing commissions.

Our knowledge about the operation of determinate sentencing laws comes primarily from evaluation of their operation in three jurisdictions: California, Maine, and North Carolina.

A. California

The original California determinate sentencing law, often referred to as "DSL," took effect July 1, 1977, and has been more extensively evaluated than any other state's. The law has, at the time of writing, been in effect for more than ten years. Six years after the law took effect, the National Academy of Sciences Panel on Sentencing Research commissioned a paper summarizing the findings of the evaluation research. Because it would be difficult credibly to claim that changes in sentencing patterns or court processes after 1982 resulted from passage of the determinate sentencing law in 1976, rather than from political, social, or other changes, I here simply restate the findings of the National Academy of Sciences assessment:

> A procedural change as fundamental and complex as DSL has potential for widespread impact on the processing of criminal cases. In actual practice, however, we found relatively few changes that might be attributed to DSL:
>
> Judges largely complied with the requirements of the law when sentencing convicted defendants; the considerable discretion of the prosecutor in initial charging and later dismissal practices was not affected.
>
> There is no evidence of substantial changes in initial charging practices, at least for cases finally disposed of in superior court.
>
> Explicit bargaining over the length of prison terms was limited to those jurisdictions already engaged in extensive sentence bargaining.
>
> Enhancements and probation ineligibility provisions represented important bargaining chips for the prosecutor; these allegations were frequently dropped in return for defense agreements to prison terms.
>
> While there were no substantial changes in aggregate guilty plea rates, there is some evidence that early guilty pleas did increase after DSL.
>
> Prison use definitely increased after DSL; this increase was accompanied by apparent increasing imprisonment of less serious, marginal offenders. These increases in prison use, however, are best viewed as continuations of preexisting trends toward increased prison use in California and not as effects of DSL.
>
> Also consistent with preexisting trends, both mean and median prison terms to be served continued to decrease after DSL. There are also some indications of a decline in variation of sentences for the same convicted offense, although the range of sentences observed under DSL remains broad.
>
> The Adult Authority exercised an important role in controlling the size of prison populations through their administrative releasing function; without some similar "safety valve" release mechanism, California's prison population can be expected to increase dramatically as a result of increasing prison commitments and only marginal decreases in time served, particularly in view of legislative increases in prison terms. [Cohen and Tonry 1983, pp. 355–57; drawing upon Brewer, Beckett, and Holt 1980; Ku 1980; Lipson and Peterson 1980; Sparks 1981; Utz 1981; Casper, Brereton, and Neal 1982]

B. North Carolina

North Carolina's "Fair Sentencing Act" applies to felonies committed on or after July 1, 1981. It specifies a presumptive prison sentence for each felony and specifies aggravating and mitigating factors that judges must consider in setting sentences. The judges are required either to impose the presumptive term or to give reasons for doing otherwise (unless the term was imposed pursuant to a judge-approved plea bargain). The judge may in his discretion, without giving reasons, suspend prison terms with or without probation supervision, impose consecutive prison terms for multiple convictions, and grant special status to committed youthful offenders. The statute provided a right of sentence review of prison terms longer than the presumptive term and eliminated discretionary parole for most offenders.

An evaluation of the impacts of the North Carolina law was conducted by researchers at the Institute of Government of the University of North Carolina (Clarke et al. 1983; Clarke 1984, 1986, 1987). The researchers conducted extensive interviews with prosecutors, judges, and defense attorneys, and carried out statistical analyses of four different sources of data.

Overall, the researchers concluded that judges for the most part complied with the provisions of the law, that charge bargaining increased, that trial rates did not increase, but declined, that sentencing severity declined for many offenses, that sentencing disparities declined, and that prison populations were unlikely to increase as a result of passage of the law.

1. *Trial Court Dispositions.* Some North Carolina officials believed that the increased predictability of sentencing outcomes under the new law would remove the incentive to plead guilty and therefore increase trial rates. The evaluation's major empirical analysis, using data from twelve counties, showed that the percentage of dispositions resulting from jury trials declined from 7.7 percent of dispositions in 1979–80 before the law took effect to 4.0 percent in 1981–82 after the law took effect (Clarke 1987, p. 22). Because judges could impose a sentence other than the presumptive sentence in cases in which there was a sentence bargain, without giving reasons and without precipitating sentence appeals, some observers predicted that sentence bargaining would increase. In fact, sentence bargaining became less frequent under the new law (Clarke 1984, p. 146) and charge bargaining increased (Clarke 1987, p. 22).

2. *Trial Court Delay.* Some observers hypothesized that court de-

lays would increase under the new law, both because sentencing procedures would become more complicated and because increased certainty would reduce defendants' incentive to plead guilty. Instead, jury trial rates declined rather than increased and, perhaps partly as a result, "disposition times in trial court *decreased* in the twelve counties studied" (Clarke et al. 1983, p. 4).

3. *Severity and Variation in Sentencing.* Much as has happened with Minnesota's sentencing guidelines, the effects of North Carolina's sentencing law have weakened with the passage of time. The evaluators initially concluded that sentencing disparities were reduced and sentencing severity declined after implementation of the new law: "with regard to the length of active prison terms imposed for felonies, *sentencing became generally less severe after the FSA and also varied less*" (Clarke et al. 1983, p. 6). The reason for decreases in sentencing disparities among persons receiving prison sentences is relatively straightforward: "*The median active sentence length imposed under the FSA was equal to the presumptive prison term in most cases*" (Clarke et al. 1983, p. 6). This means that judges imposed the presumptive sentence in many cases, and as a result, disparities among people imprisoned for that offense decreased.

By the time the North Carolina law had been in effect for five years, much of its effect had worn off: "Comparison of the entire five years experience under the Felony Sentencing Act shows that the net effect of the FSA has been to reduce both the length of and the variation in felony sentences. . . . But the effects of the FSA seem to have 'worn off'. . . . By 1985–86, sentence lengths and variations appeared to be returning to their pre-FSA levels" (Clarke 1987, p. 10).

There was also a brief decrease after the new law took effect in the percentage of felons receiving supervised probation. For persons charged with felonies and convicted of *some* charge (half the time a misdemeanor), there was no increase in the likelihood of receiving an active prison sentence. "But for defendants convicted of felonies statewide, the Department of Corrections data indicated that the chance of receiving an active prison sentence (rather than supervised probation) increased from 55 percent in 1979 (pre-FSA) to 63 percent in 1981–82 (post-FSA)" (Clarke 1984, p. 148). The percentage of offenders receiving supervised probation fell from 40 percent to 32 percent in the first year of the new law; in the second and subsequent years, the rate returned to 40 percent (Clark 1987, p. 9).

Finally, the evaluators concluded that the FSA, by reducing time served in prison for felonies, contributed to a slowing in the growth of the prison population in the 1980s (Clarke 1987, p. 10). However, because many of the determinate sentencing law's effects appear to have been short-lived, Clarke is apprehensive that the growth of North Carolina's prison population will accelerate (Clarke 1987, p. 15).

4. *Summary.* The initial North Carolina findings strongly resemble California's: judges largely complied with the requirements of the law, and the median sentence imposed for felony offenders was the sentence specified in the statute; there were no substantial changes in charging practices; there were no substantial increases in trial rates or court delays; there was an increase in the proportion of convicted felons receiving prison sentences, offset to some extent by decreases in the average time to be served. Clarke (1984) concluded the earlier evaluation report with the words: "On balance, it is fair to conclude from this study that the FSA accomplished at least some of what it was intended to accomplish—and without creating the problems that critics predicted it would produce" (1984, p. 142). He concludes the five-year follow-up with a suggestion that North Carolina consider shifting to a sentencing commission guidelines approach (1987, p. 25).

C. Maine

There have been a series of evaluations of the Maine law (Kramer et al. 1978; Anspach 1981; Anspach, Lehman, and Kramer 1983). For a variety of reasons, largely having to do with Maine's small population and the resulting small numbers of cases for use in statistical comparisons, it is difficult to have much confidence in the findings of statistical analyses of sentencing practices (the reasons for this skepticism are set out in Cohen and Tonry 1983, pp. 429–35). The most substantial of the evaluations concluded:

> The 1976 sentencing reform had little impact on the type of sentences or the severity of sentence types given to offenders in Maine. For more serious felony offenders, split sentences increasingly replaced incarceration only sentences. However, since incarceration only sentences before 1976 were generally followed by parole supervision, it would be difficult to argue that post-reform split sentences (incarceration followed by probationary supervision) are significantly less severe.
> In essence, the increased use of split sentences, accelerated and reinforced by the reform, represents the development of a structured, judicially imposed, functional equivalent to parole.
> [Anspach, Lehman, and Kramer 1983, p. 65]

By 1986, split sentences had become the most commonly imposed sentences in Maine, and the system is often called "judicial parole."

The evaluators were unable to draw any further conclusions about the impact of the 1976 law on sentencing disparities:

> Overall, there is little indication that the reform had a substantial, systematic, or consistent effect on the criteria used in the decision as to the type of sentence to impose. Although there is clearly a great deal of variation in criteria used, there is no indication this variation is different either in magnitude or form before and after the reform. The reform has neither resulted in an overall increase in the consistency in the basis of decisions about sentence types, nor has it resulted in an overall increase in the predictability of sentence types. [Anspach, Lehman, and Kramer 1983, p. 103]

As to sentence length, however, the researchers concluded, "Overall, the consistency and predictability of sentence length decisions have decreased under the new sentencing structure" (Anspach, Lehman, and Kramer 1983, p. 108). This finding should come as no surprise given the absence from the Maine sentencing system of any standards for sentences.

Taken together, the evaluations in North Carolina and California suggest that judges—at least for a time—will attempt to impose sentences as directed by statutory presumptive sentencing laws, that neither trial rates nor court processing delays necessarily increase as sentencing outcomes become more predictable, and that greater consistency in sentences can be achieved.

V. Structuring Sentencing

To this point this essay has attempted to demonstrate that useful knowledge has accumulated about the effects of efforts to structure sentencing. Voluntary guidelines and many determinate sentencing laws are often simply ineffective. Mandatory sentencing is ham-fisted and has at least as many unfortunate unintended consequences as intended consequences. Some presumptive guidelines systems and some statutory determinate sentencing systems, by contrast, in broad terms seem capable of making sentencing fairer, more consistent, and more predictable.

This final section considers three sets of interrelated questions about future efforts to structure sentencing: What are the next generations of policy issues to be addressed? What have we learned about the processes of change and of acquisition of knowledge about change? And, much more speculatively, adverting to an issue raised in Section I, are efforts to structure sentencing important in their own right, and likely to endure and develop, or are they merely epiphenomenal surface indicators of underlying social perturbations?

A. Next Steps in Policy Formulation

The accomplishments of sentencing reform in Washington, Minnesota, and North Carolina are relative. Compared with a hypothetical comprehensive system of structured discretion in which decision standards are rational and consistent and decision makers are fully accountable, these initiatives are partial and porous. Compared, however, with the prevailing American practice before 1975 and with what then seemed possible, these initiatives have been remarkably effective. In the early days, policymakers purposely ducked some issues and interests that presented great difficulty. Now that it is clear that more modest aims can be realized, some of those discreetly deferred issues should be addressed.

1. *Plea Bargaining.*   Within hours, surely, of the first proposals for determinate sentencing, a skeptic must have pointed out that structured judicial discretion would shift power to prosecutors unless their discretions also were structured. In statutory systems like California's, or presumptive guidelines systems like Minnesota's, in which the presumptive sentence is based on the offense of conviction and some measure of prior criminal history, plea bargaining lawyers can determine the presumptive sentence by determining the conviction offense. In effect, charge bargaining can become plea bargaining. Frank Zimring (1977) and Albert Alschuler (1978) were writing about this problem soon after the shift to determinate sentencing began.

Policymakers, of course, were alert to this interaction between reduced judicial discretion and enhanced prosecutorial power but, for prudential reasons, chose to ignore it. With the exception of a few statutory limits on plea bargaining under mandatory sentencing laws, no statutory determinate sentencing law seriously addressed the problem of increased prosecutorial power. The sentencing commissions have not done much better. Minnesota basically ignored the problem; its only nod to plea bargaining was a somewhat obscure provision providing that "the exercise of constitutional rights by the defendant during the adjudication process" may not be asserted as the justification for departing from the guidelines. This was an effort to discourage systematic and punitive increases of sentences for defendents who refused to plead guilty and who were convicted after trial (Minnesota Sentencing Guidelines Commission 1980, Sec. II.D.03.1[e]). The Florida and Pennsylvania sentencing commissions ignored the problem altogether.

The Washington State commission had statutory authority to "devise recommended prosecuting standards in respect to charging of offenses and plea agreements" (title 9 R.C.W., Sec. 9.94A.040[2][b]), but adopted prosecutorial standards of considerable elasticity. The standard for charge bargains is that the conviction offense should "adequately describe the nature of defendant's conduct" (Boerner 1985, pp. I-34–I-36). Unfortunately, "adequately" is an ambiguous word and reasonable people can differ on whether a robbery is an armed robbery or a robbery or a theft or an assault and judges (and counsel) accordingly have considerable room to maneuver. That this ambiguity is real and not merely the invention of an overly skeptical academic analysis is shown by the Washington commission's deliberate choice of "adequately describes" over "adequately and accurately describes" as a means to preserve plea bargaining flexibility (Boerner 1985, p. I-36)

The U.S. Sentencing Commission had statutory authority to issue general policy statements concerning judicial authority "to accept or reject a plea agreement" (Sentencing Reform Act 1984, Sec. 994[a][2][E]), but it too ducked the issue by adopting loose standards for control of plea bargaining. The key conditions are, for charge bargains, that the "remaining charges *adequately* reflect the seriousness of the actual offense behavior" (my emphasis), and for sentence bargains, that "the agreed sentence departs from the applicable guideline range for justifiable reasons" (U.S. Sentencing Commission 1987*b*, Sec. 6B1.2). These standards, like Washington's, impose few constraints.

A number of approaches are available for controlling plea bargaining under determinate sentencing. There have been calls for explicit but limited guilty plea discounts (Gottfredson, Wilkins, and Hoffman 1978), charge reduction guidelines (Schulhofer 1980), and real offense sentencing (National Conference of Commissioners on Uniform State Laws 1979). This last is a proposal that sentencing be based on "actual offense behavior," or "the real offense," rather than the conviction offense; this is usually proposed as a way to undercut plea bargaining by basing sentencing not on the statutory offense to which the defendant pled guilty, which may be an artifact of plea bargaining, but on the offense itself. The most radical and comprehensive proposal for real offense sentencing to date appeared in the U.S. Sentencing Commission's (quickly abandoned) September 1986 set of proposed federal sentencing guidelines (see Tonry and Coffee 1987 for a discussion of the strengths and weaknesses of the various approaches).

Now that it is clear that some determinate sentencing systems can achieve many of their goals, there is no excuse for sentencing policymakers any longer to ignore plea bargaining. If sentencing in America is to become principled and consistent, the power of the prosecutor must be structured and limited just like that of the judge (and, where parole survives, the parole board).

2. *Jail and Misdemeanors.* It is time for sentencing reform to create standards and accountability for all sentences. This means that guidelines should govern all felony sentences, not merely prison sentences, and should also govern misdemeanor sentences. The Minnesota guidelines, for example, apply only to felonies, and set concrete standards only for the 15 to 20 percent of felony sentences for which prison is an appropriate sentence. The judges retain complete discretion over the 80 percent of prescriptive "out" sentences and can impose anything from nominal probation to twelve months jail for these offenses. Pennsylvania established guidelines for felony and misdemeanor sentences but, as discussed in Section III, the Pennsylvania guidelines are so broad and weak that they cannot be considered a serious attempt at a comprehensive system of structured discretion. The Washington State guidelines do set standards for sentences to jail and prison, but apply only to felony convictions.

Guidelines that set standards only for felony prison sentences will in most jurisdictions regulate sentences for only a minority of crimes. Guidelines that set standards for all felonies still regulate only a minority of crimes. Only when sentencing discretion is structured for both felonies and misdemeanors will a principled comprehensive sentencing system become possible.

3. *Nonprison Sentences.* No jurisdiction has as yet made a serious attempt to set standards for noncustodial sentences. Most jurisdictions, including all the statutory determinate sentencing states, and most presumptive guidelines systems, provide no guidance whatever to judges concerning nonincarcerative sentences. Washington State has established rules for interchangeability between short periods of incarceration and community service (e.g., one day of partial confinement or

eight hours of community service may be substituted for one day of total confinement to a maximum of thirty days), but that is all.

A number of proposals have been made for development of sentencing standards for all kinds of punishment (e.g., Minnesota Citizens Committee on Crime and Justice 1982; duPont 1986), but they have not been adopted anywhere. Some jurisdictions have been authorized to develop guidelines for nonincarcerative sentences, but have declined to do so. Minnesota's enabling legislation provided in Section 9(5)(2), for example, "the sentencing guidelines promulgated by the commission may also establish appropriate sanctions for offenders for whom imprisonment is not proper," including day fines, probation, community service, and other nonprison sanctions. The federal legislation granted similar authority to the U.S. Sentencing Commission.

Disparity and arbitrariness are likely to be greater for misdemeanors and less serious felonies than for serious felonies and, sooner or later, sentencing policymakers will attempt to structure sentencing discretion in all cases. There are difficult issues to be addressed. When, and to what extent, are nonprison punishments meaningfully equivalent to a prison sentence? How large a fine is equivalent to thirty days of community service or six months in jail? What principles ought to govern decisions among punishments or the relation between appropriate punishments and governing purposes at sentencing? These are challenging but not unsolvable questions, and seem difficult primarily because they appear novel. Someone must begin seriously to address and conscientiously to answer such questions if comprehensive, principled sentencing is ever to become more than a platitudinous undertaking in this country.

4. *A Systems Approach.* "Truth in policy making" helps. The American population of state and federal prisoners on December 31, 1986, reached 547,000 (Bureau of Justice Statistics 1987). Prisons in most states are overcrowded (e.g., Blumstein, in this volume), and that reality inevitably affects decision making in individual cases and policymaking in general. Policy-making that takes account of limited resources inevitably is more realistic, and likely to be more effective, than policy-making that ignores resource constraints. The Minnesota Sentencing Guidelines Commission, as noted earlier, construed an ambiguous statutory reference to correctional resources ("take into substantial consideration") (Laws of Minn. 1978, Chap. 723, Sec. 9[5][2]) as an absolute bar on adoption of guidelines that would increase prison popu-

lations beyond existing capacity. This forced the commission to make choices and meant that the policies they eventually adopted were realistic. The U.S. Sentencing Commission, by contrast, ignored statutory references to prison capacity and adopted guidelines so severe that they are likely to be circumvented widely. It takes no great insight to suppose that unrealistic standards are less likely to elicit respect and compliance than realistic standards. Minnesota showed (and Washington State repeated the demonstration) that acknowledgment of resource limits enriches policy-making; structured sentencing initiatives that ignore this lesson will suffer the consequences.

B. Learning about Change

A number of important things have been learned in the last decade about learning about change.

1. *Research Strategy.* In retrospect, much of the earliest research on sentencing changes was badly flawed. Sometimes the use of quasi-experimental research designs comparing outcomes in brief periods before and after the change made it hard to know whether apparent changes merely reflected preexisting changes or were otherwise misleading. Other times the use of sampling methods that looked only at felony cases fell prey to the sample selection problem and may not have recognized that the legal changes altered charging or indictment practices and as a consequence that the samples of cases before and after the change were not comparable. These problems are now well understood (see Blumstein et al. 1983) and the better, more recent, studies (e.g., Casper, Brereton, and Neal 1982) have addressed them.

2. *The Importance of Process.* It is both what is done, and how, that determines the effects of sentencing changes. It is odd that this lesson needs to be relearned again and again, in every realm of public policy. Both the history and the conventional wisdom of mandatory sentencing teach that the passage of a new law is not necessarily reason to predict that decision makers will comply with it. Susan Martin's description of the development of sentencing guidelines in Minnesota and Pennsylvania suggests that the explanations for the uncontroversial acceptance by the Minnesota legislature of the Minnesota guidelines and the rejection by the Pennsylvania legislature of the initial Pennsylvania guidelines can be found in their political strategies (1984). The Minnesota commission saw itself involved in an "open political process" in which potentially hostile groups were brought into the development process, won over, and thereby neutralized. The Pennsylvania commission was

much less effective in this regard and found itself with many opponents and few supporters when it faced the legislature.

Similarly, once a new system has been adopted, it cannot be self-executing. Judges, prosecutors, lawyers, and probation officers need to be trained, proselytized, and monitored. These unexciting tasks take time and money, but if new systems are to take hold, these matters of process must be addressed.

3. *Accumulation of Knowledge.* Knowledge about the effects of structured sentencing has accumulated almost too tidily. For example, research that showed the effectiveness of parole guidelines at reducing disparity (Gottfredon, Wilkins, and Hoffman 1978) was followed by research that showed the effectiveness of sentencing guidelines at reducing disparity (Knapp 1984a) which was followed by research that showed the effectiveness of bail guidelines at reducing disparity (Goldkamp and Gottfredson 1985). For another example, research that showed that sentence bargaining bans led to increased charge bargaining was followed by research that showed that charge bargaining bans led to increased sentence bargaining and was in turn followed by research showing that comprehensive plea bargaining bans can be effective (Cohen and Tonry 1983).

As the evidence has accumulated, it has become clear that it is possible to structure sentencing discretion and thereby to alter the patterns of decisions that are made. The care given to training, implementation, and monitoring is important. It matters whether an innovation is comprehensive or limited. It matters critically whether systems exist to police the compliance of decision makers with the applicable standards. All in all, though, we know how to develop, implement, and monitor systems of structured discretion, and if the will to achieve meaningful change is present, the knowledge is available to achieve it.

C. Change and Continuity

To this point, this concluding section has been positive. Now the skepticism. For all the evidence that thoughtful, ambitious, well-implemented sentencing changes can achieve many of their goals, there is also evidence that the sought-after changes are sometimes short-lived. In Minnesota, prosecutors apparently willfully attempted to defy policy decisions about limited use of imprisonment for property offenders. Over time, the proportion of convicted offenders receiving prison terms returned to preguideline levels. In North Carolina, after early indications of substantial impact on sentencing outcomes, similar reversions to preinnovation patterns occurred.

This pattern of reversion to prechange behavior can be understood in a number of ways. First, it can be seen as evidence that the structures and rules governing sentencing are epiphenomenal. The patterns of imposition of criminal punishments respond to deeper social forces than those that shape sentencing policy. Work by Nils Christie and Alfred Blumstein and Jacqueline Cohen (1973) on the stability of punishment suggests that each society has its own relatively stable level of punishment. If this is true, the structures and standards of sentencing may not much matter; whatever social forces determine the prevailing punishment levels will continue to do so, and changed structures will have at best only marginal effect. The evidence from California (Casper, Brereton, and Neal 1982) and North Carolina (Clarke 1987) concerning the extension of preexisting trends under new sentencing systems is consistent with this view.

Even if considerable credence is given to this structural account of punishment, however, important (and deeper) questions remain. For example, should human beings for epistemological reasons continue to wrestle with issues of principle and justice even if we conclude that the decisions we reach are unlikely in the long run to be important? My view is that we should continue to act as if resolution of normative questions of principle matters, even if we believe it does not, but these are issues for philosophers and are not pursued here further.

There is, second, a more optimistic account to be offered of reversion to preexisting practices. One inevitable problem confronting efforts to institutionalize legal and programmatic change is to maintain momentum under a second generation of leaders, after the inspired or charismatic innovators have moved on. A bureaucratic hardening of the arteries affects most programs, and there is no reason to believe that sentencing programs are immune from this malady. Once the heady days of innovation are past, especially after the early leaders have departed, any institution is challenged by lethargy, routinization, and increased subservience to the interests of program administrators. In the well-known effort to diminish reliance on institutionalization of juvenile offenders in Massachusetts, for example, a notion of institutionalized instability influenced the development of community alternatives to incarceration (Miller and Ohlin 1985). If this account applies to efforts to structure sentencing, the final conclusion to be drawn is positive: the effort to achieve meaningful long-term changes in punishment patterns through policy-making is not hopeless, merely difficult, and the key problem is to develop ways to ensure the maintenance, or continual recreation, of the reforming spirit (see, e.g., Clarke 1987; Knapp 1987; Miethe and Moore 1987).

Where the truth lies, I do not know. What I do know is that, if we believe in rationality, there is a substantial body of research on sentencing that suggests paths that can, with promise, be followed.

APPENDIX

Mandatory Sentencing Laws

Mandatory sentencing laws might also be considered a form of statutory determinate sentencing. The limitations of such laws are well known. Despite their political popularity, mandatory sentencing laws tend to be circumvented and to produce injustices in individual cases. Evaluations have demonstrated that police (Carlson 1982), judges (Heumann and Loftin 1979), and lawyers (Bynum 1982; Joint Committee on New York Drug Law Evaluation 1978) will alter their procedures in order to avoid application of mandatory sentencing laws in cases where they consider the required sentence to be unduly severe. Evaluations have also repeatedly shown that the probability that a person arrested will be imprisoned does not increase after passage of a mandatory sentencing law, but that those who are imprisoned often receive sentences of greater severity (Beha 1977; Joint Committee on New York Drug Law Evaluation 1978; Rossman et al. 1979; Carlson 1982; Pennsylvania Commission on Crime and Delinquency 1986).

These findings suggest that mandatory sentencing laws are not an especially effective way to achieve certainty and predictability in sentencing. To the extent that they prescribe sanctions more severe than lawyers and judges believe appropriate, they can be, and are, circumvented. For serious criminal charges, the mandatory sentencing laws are often redundant in that offenders are, in any case, likely to receive prison sentences longer than those mandated by statute. For less serious cases, mandatory sentencing laws tend to be arbitrary; they result either in increased rates of dismissal or diversion of some defendants to avoid application of the statute or occasionally result in sentencing of "marginal" offenders in ways that most parties involved consider unduly harsh. Thus the evidence simply does not demonstrate that mandatory sentences "work." For this reason, and because I have discussed this literature at length elsewhere (Cohen and Tonry 1983), nothing more is said here about mandatory sentencing.

REFERENCES

Alschuler, Albert W. 1978. "Sentencing Reform and Prosecutorial Power." *University of Pennsylvania Law Review* 126:550–77.

American Law Institute. 1962. *Model Penal Code (Proposed Official Draft)*. Philadelphia: American Law Institute.

Anspach, Donald F. 1981. "Crossroads of Justice: Problems with Determinate Sentencing in Maine—Interim Report." Unpublished manuscript. Portland: Department of Sociology, University of Southern Maine.

Anspach, Donald F., Peter H. Lehman, and John H. Kramer. 1983. "Maine Rejects Indeterminacy: A Case Study of Flat Sentencing and Parole Abolition." Unpublished document prepared for the National Institute of Justice. Portland: Department of Sociology, University of Southern Maine.

Beha, James A. II. 1977. "'And Nobody Can Get You Out:' The Impact of a Mandatory Prison Sentence for the Illegal Carrying of a Firearm on the Use of Firearms and on the Administration of Criminal Justice in Boston." *Boston University Law Review* 57:96–146 (Part I), 289–333 (Part II).

Blumstein, Alfred, and Jacqueline Cohen. 1973. "A Theory of the Stability of Punishment." *Journal of Criminal Law and Criminology* 64:198–206.

Blumstein, Alfred, Jacqueline Cohen, Susan E. Martin, and Michael Tonry, eds. 1983. *Research on Sentencing: The Search for Reform*, 2 vols. Washington, D.C.: National Academy Press.

Blumstein, Alfred, Jacqueline Cohen, and Daniel Nagin. 1978. *Deterrence and Incapacitation: Estimating the Effects of Criminal Sanctions on Crime Rates*. Washington D.C.: National Academy of Sciences.

Boerner, David. 1985. *Sentencing in Washington—A Legal Analysis of the Sentencing Reform Act of 1981*. Seattle: Butterworth.

Brewer, D., G. E. Beckett, and N. Holt. 1980. *Determinate Sentencing in California: The First Year's Experience*. Chino: California Department of Corrections.

Bureau of Justice Statistics. 1987. *Prisoners in 1986*. Bureau of Justice Statistics Bulletin No. NCJ-104864. Washington, D.C.: U.S. Government Printing Office.

Bynum, Timothy S. 1982. "Prosecutorial Discretion and the Implementation of a Legislative Mandate." In *Implementing Criminal Justice Policies*, edited by Merry Morash. Beverly Hills, Calif.: Sage.

Call, Jack E., David E. England, and Susette M. Talarico. 1983. "Abolition of Plea Bargaining in the Coast Guard." *Journal of Criminal Justice* 11:351–58.

Canadian Sentencing Commission. 1987. *Sentencing Reform: A Canadian Approach*. Ottawa: Canadian Government Publishing Centre.

Carlson, Kenneth. 1982. *Mandatory Sentencing: The Experience of Two States*. National Institute of Justice, U.S. Department of Justice. Washington, D.C.: U.S. Government Printing Office.

Carrow, Deborah M. 1984. "Judicial Sentencing Guidelines: Hazards of the Middle Ground." *Judicature* 68:161–71.

Carrow, Deborah M., Judith Feins, Beverly N. W. Lee, and Lois Olinger. 1985a. *Guidelines without Force: An Evaluation of the Multijurisdictional Sentencing Guidelines Field Test*. Cambridge, Mass.: Abt.

———. 1985b. *Guidelines without Force: An Evaluation of the Multijurisdictional Sentencing Guidelines Test, Technical Appendices.* Cambridge, Mass.: Abt.

Casper, Jonathan D., David Brereton, and David Neal. 1982. *The Implementation of the California Determinate Sentencing Law.* Washington, D.C.: U.S. Department of Justice.

———. 1983. "The California Determinate Sentence Law." *Criminal Law Bulletin* 19:405–33.

Church, Thomas, Jr. 1976. "'Plea' Bargains, Concessions, and the Courts: Analysis of a Quasi-Experiment." *Law and Society Review* 10:377–401.

Clarke, Stevens H. 1984. "North Carolina's Determinate Sentencing Legislation." *Judicature* 68:140–52.

———. 1986. *Indeterminate and Determinate Sentencing in North Carolina, 1973–85: Effects of Presumptive Sentencing Legislation: Preliminary Draft.* Chapel Hill: Institute of Government, University of North Carolina.

———. 1987. *Felony Sentencing in North Carolina 1976–1986: Effects of Presumptive Sentencing Legislation.* Chapel Hill: Institute of Government, University of North Carolina at Chapel Hill.

Clarke, Stevens H., Susan Turner Kurtz, Glenn F. Lang, Kenneth L. Parker, Elizabeth W. Rubinsky, and Donna J. Schleicher. 1983. *North Carolina's Determinate Sentencing Legislation: An Evaluation of the First Year's Experience.* Chapel Hill: Institute of Government, University of North Carolina at Chapel Hill.

Cohen, Jacqueline, and Joan Helland. 1982. "Methodology for Evaluating the Impact of Sentencing Guidelines." Unpublished paper. Pittsburgh: Urban Systems Institute, School of Urban and Public Affairs, Carnegie-Mellon University.

Cohen, Jacqueline, and Michael Tonry. 1983. "Sentencing Reforms and Their Impacts." In *Research on Sentencing: The Search for Reform*, vol. 2, edited by Alfred Blumstein, Jacqueline Cohen, Susan E. Martin, and Michael Tonry. Washington, D.C.: National Academy Press.

Criminal Courts Technical Assistance Project. 1980. *Overview of State and Local Sentencing Guidelines and Sentencing Research Activity.* Washington, D.C.: American University Law Institute.

duPont, Pete. 1986. "A Governor's Perspective on Sentencing." In *Crime and Punishment in Modern America*, edited by Patrick B. McGuigan and Jon S. Pascale. Washington, D.C.: Free Congress and Research Foundation.

Frankel, Marvin E. 1972. *Criminal Sentences: Law without Order.* New York: Hill & Wang.

Goldkamp, John S., and Michael R. Gottfredson. 1985. *Policy Guidelines for Bail: An Experiment in Court Reform.* Philadelphia: Temple University.

Gottfredson, Don M., Leslie T. Wilkins, and Peter B. Hoffman. 1978. *Guidelines for Parole and Sentencing.* Lexington, Mass.: Lexington Books.

Heumann, Milton, and Colin Loftin. 1979. "Mandatory Sentencing and the Abolition of Plea Bargaining: The Michigan Felony Firearm Statute." *Law and Society Review* 13:393–430.

Holton, Leonard. 1987. "An Overview of Sentencing Guidelines in Florida."

Unpublished manuscript. Tallahassee: Florida Sentencing Guidelines Commission.

Hussey, Frederick A., and Stephen P. Lagoy. 1983. "The Determinate Sentence and Its Impact on Parole." *Criminal Law Bulletin* 1983:101–30.

Joint Committee on New York Drug Law Evaluation. 1978. *The Nation's Toughest Drug Law: Evaluating the New York Experience.* A project of the Association of the Bar of the City of New York and the Drug Abuse Council, Inc. Washington, D.C.: U.S. Government Printing Office.

Knapp, Kay A. 1984a. *The Impact of the Minnesota Sentencing Guidelines—Three Year Evaluation.* St. Paul: Minnesota Sentencing Guidelines Commission.

———. 1984b. "What Sentencing Reform in Minnesota Has and Has Not Accomplished." *Judicature* 68:181–89.

———. 1985. *Minnesota Sentencing Guidelines and Commentary Annotated.* St. Paul: Minnesota CLE Press.

———. 1987. "Implementation of the Minnesota Guidelines: Can the Innovative Spirit Be Preserved?" In *The Sentencing Commission and Its Guidelines*, by Andrew von Hirsch, Kay A. Knapp, and Michael Tonry. Boston: Northeastern University Press.

Kramer, John H., Frederick A. Hussey, Stephen P. Lagoy, Dan Katkin, and C. Vance McLaughlin. 1978. *Assessing the Impact of Determinate Sentencing and Parole Abolition in Maine.* Report to the Law Enforcement Assistance Administration. Portland: Department of Sociology, University of Southern Maine.

Kramer, John H., and Robin L. Lubitz. 1985. "Pennsylvania's Sentencing Reform: The Impact of Commission-established Guidelines." *Crime and Delinquency* 31:481–500.

Kramer, John H., Robin L. Lubitz, and Cynthia A. Kempinen. 1985. "Sentencing Guidelines: A Quantitative Comparison of Sentencing Policy in Minnesota, Pennsylvania and Washington." Paper presented at the annual meeting of the American Society of Criminology, San Diego, November.

Kramer, John H., and Anthony J. Scirica. 1985. "Complex Policy Choices: The Pennsylvania Commission on Sentencing." Paper presented at the annual meeting of the Academy of Criminal Justice Sciences, Las Vegas, April.

Kress, Jack M. 1980. *Prescription for Justice: The Theory and Practice of Sentencing Guidelines.* Cambridge, Mass.: Ballinger.

Ku, R. 1980. *American Prisons and Jails.* Vol. 4, *Case Studies of New Legislation Governing Sentencing and Release.* Washington, D.C.: National Institute of Justice.

Lagoy, Stephen P., Frederick A. Hussey, and John H. Kramer. 1978. "A Comparative Assessment of Determinate Sentencing in the Four Pioneer States." *Crime and Delinquency* 24:385–400.

Lipson, Albert J., and Mark A. Peterson. 1980. *California Justice under Determinate Sentencing: A Review and Agenda for Research.* Santa Monica, Calif.: Rand Corp.

Loftin, Colin, and David McDowall. 1981. "'One with a Gun Gets You Two':

Mandatory Sentencing and Firearms Violence in Detroit." *Annals of the American Academy of Political and Social Science* 455:150.

———. 1984. "The Deterrent Effects of the Florida Felony Firearm Law." *Journal of Criminal Law and Criminology* 75:250–59.

Loftin, Colin, Milton Heumann, and David McDowall. 1983. "Mandatory Sentencing and Firearms Violence: Evaluating an Alternative to Gun Control." *Law and Society Review* 17:287–318.

Lubitz, Robin L., and Cynthia A. Kempinen. 1987. *The Impact of Pennsylvania's Sentencing Guidelines: An Analysis of System Adjustments to Sentencing Reform.* State College: Pennsylvania Commission on Sentencing.

Martin, Susan. 1984. "Interests and Politics in Sentencing Reform: The Development of Sentencing Guidelines in Pennsylvania and Minnesota." *Villanova Law Review* 29:21–113.

McCloskey, John P. 1985. "The Effectiveness of Independent Sentencing Commission Guidelines: An Analysis of Appellate Court Decisions in Two Jurisdictions." Paper presented at the annual meeting of the American Society of Criminology, San Diego, November.

Messinger, Sheldon, and Phillip Johnson. 1978. "California's Determinate Sentence Laws." In *Determinate Sentencing: Reform or Regression.* Washington, D.C.: U.S. Government Printing Office.

Miethe, Terance D. 1987. "Charging and Plea Bargaining Practices under Determinate Sentencing: An Investigation of the Hydraulic Displacement of Discretion." *Journal of Criminal Law and Criminology* 78:155–76.

Miethe, Terance D., and Charles A. Moore. 1985. "Socioeconomic Disparities under Determinate Sentencing Systems: A Comparison of Preguideline and Postguideline Practices in Minnesota." *Criminology* 23:337–63.

———. 1987. *Evaluation of Minnesota's Felony Sentencing Guidelines.* Report to the National Institute of Justice, Washington, D.C.

Miller, Alden, and Lloyd Ohlin. 1985. *Delinquency and Community.* Beverly Hills, Calif.: Sage.

Minnesota Sentencing Guidelines Commission. 1980. *Report to the Legislature—1980.* St. Paul: Minnesota Sentencing Guidelines Commission.

Moore, Charles A., and Terance D. Miethe. 1986. "Regulated and Unregulated Sentencing Decisions: An Analysis of First-Year Practices under Minnesota's Felony Sentencing Guidelines." *Law and Society Review* 20:253–77.

National Conference of Commissioners on Uniform State Laws. 1979. *Model Sentencing and Corrections Act.* Chicago: National Conference of Commissioners on Uniform State Laws.

New York State Committee on Sentencing Guidelines. 1985. *Determinate Sentencing Report and Recommendations.* Albany: New York State Committee on Sentencing Guidelines.

Parent, Dale. 1988. *Structuring Sentencing Discretion: The Evolution of Minnesota's Sentencing Guidelines.* Stoneham, Mass.: Butterworth.

Pennsylvania Commission on Crime and Delinquency. 1986. *The Effects of Five-Year Mandatory Sentencing in Pennsylvania.* Harrisburg: Pennsylvania Commission on Crime and Delinquency.

336   Michael Tonry

Pennsylvania Commission on Sentencing. 1981. *Pennsylvania Bulletin.* January 24, 1981, pp. 463–76.

———. 1984. *1983 Report: Sentencing in Pennsylvania.* State College: Pennsylvania Commission on Sentencing.

———. 1985. *1984 Report: Sentencing in Pennsylvania.* State College: Pennsylvania Commission on Sentencing.

———. 1986a. *1985 Annual Report.* State College: Pennsylvania Commission on Sentencing.

———. 1986b. *Sentencing Guidelines Implementation Manual.* State College: Pennsylvania Commission on Sentencing.

———. 1987. *1986–87 Annual Report.* State College: Pennsylvania Commission on Sentencing.

Phillips, H. J. 1984. *Final Report of the Maine Sentencing Guidelines Commission.* Report Submitted to the 111th Maine Legislature, Augusta, Maine.

Pierce, Glen L., and William J. Bowers. 1981. "The Bartley-Fox Gun Law's Short-Term Impact on Crime in Boston." *Annals of the American Academy of Political and Social Science* 455:120–32.

Rathke, Stephen C. 1982. "Plea Negotiating under the Sentencing Guidelines." *Hamline Law Review* 5:271–91.

Rich, William D., L. Paul Sutton, Todd D. Clear, and Michael J. Saks. 1982. *Sentencing by Mathematics: An Evaluation of the Early Attempts to Develop Sentencing Guidelines.* Williamsburg, Va.: National Center for State Courts.

Rossman, David, Paul Froyd, Glen L. Pierce, John McDevitt, and William J. Bowers. 1979. *The Impact of the Mandatory Gun Law in Massachusetts.* National Institute of Law Enforcement and Criminal Justice, Law Enforcement Assistance Administration, U.S. Department of Justice. Washington, D.C.: U.S. Government Printing Office.

Schulhofer, Stephen. 1980. "Sentencing Reform and Prosecutorial Power." *University of Pennsylvania Law Review* 126:550–77.

Schuwerk, Robert P. 1984. "Illinois' Experience with Determinate Sentencing: A Critical Reappraisal, Part 1: Efforts to Structure the Exercise of Discretion in Bargaining for, Imposing, and Serving Criminal Sentences." *DePaul Law Review* 33:631–739.

Shane-DuBow, Sandra, Alice P. Brown, and Erik Olsen. 1985. *Sentencing Reform in the United States: History, Content, and Effect.* Washington, D.C.: U.S. Government Printing Office.

Sparks, Richard S. 1981. "Sentencing Before and After DSL: Some Statistical Findings." In *Report on Strategies for Determinate Sentencing.* Unpublished document prepared for the National Institute of Justice, U.S. Department of Justice. Washington, D.C.

———. 1983. "The Construction of Sentencing Guidelines: A Methodological Critique." In *Research on Sentencing: The Search for Reform*, vol. 2, edited by Alfred Blumstein, Jacqueline Cohen, Susan Martin, and Michael Tonry. Washington, D.C.: National Academy Press.

Sparks, Richard F., and Bridget A. Stecher. 1979. "The New Jersey Sentencing Guidelines: An Unauthorized Analysis." Paper presented at the annual meeting of the American Society of Criminology, Philadelphia, November.

Sparks, Richard F., Bridget A. Stecher, Jay Albanese, and Peggy L. Shelly. 1982. *Stumbling toward Justice: Some Overlooked Research and Policy Questions about Statewide Sentencing Guidelines.* Report to the National Institute of Justice, U.S. Department of Justice, Washington, D.C.

Tonry, Michael. 1987. *Sentencing Reform Impacts.* National Institute of Justice, U.S. Department of Justice. Washington, D.C.: U.S. Government Printing Office.

Tonry, Michael, and John C. Coffee, Jr. 1987. "Enforcing Sentencing Guidelines: Plea Bargaining and Review Mechanisms." In *The Sentencing Commission and Its Guidelines*, by Andrew von Hirsch, Kay A. Knapp, and Michael Tonry. Boston: Northeastern University Press.

U.S. Sentencing Commission. 1986. *Sentencing Guidelines, September 1986—Preliminary Draft.* Washington, D.C.: U.S. Sentencing Commission.

———. 1987a. *Revised Draft Sentencing Guidelines, January 1987.* Washington, D.C.: U.S. Sentencing Commission.

———. 1987b. *Sentencing Guidelines and Policy Statements, April 13, 1987.* Washington, D.C.: U.S. Government Printing Office.

Utz, P. 1981. "Determinate Sentencing in Two California Courts." In *Report on Strategies for Determinate Sentencing.* Unpublished document prepared for the National Institute of Justice, U.S. Department of Justice, Washington, D.C.

von Hirsch, Andrew, and Kathleen Hanrahan. 1981. "Determinate Penalty Systems in America: An Overview." *Crime and Delinquency* 27:289–316.

von Hirsch, Andrew, Kay Knapp, and Michael Tonry. 1987. *The Sentencing Commission and Its Guidelines.* Boston: Northeastern University Press.

Washington State Sentencing Guidelines Commission. 1983. *Sentencing Guidelines Commission: Report to the Legislature.* Olympia: Washington State Sentencing Guidelines Commission.

———. 1985. *Sentencing Practices under the Sentencing Reform Act: A Preliminary Report.* Olympia: Washington State Sentencing Guidelines Commission.

———. 1986. *Preliminary Evaluation of Washington State's Sentencing Reform Act.* Olympia: Washington State Sentencing Guidelines Commission.

———. 1987. *Preliminary Statistical Summary of 1986 Sentencing Data.* Olympia: Washington State Sentencing Guidelines Commission.

Wilkins, Leslie T., Jack M. Kress, Don M. Gottfredson, Joseph C. Calpin, and Arthur M. Gelman. 1978. *Sentencing Guidelines: Structuring Judicial Discretion—Report on the Feasibility Study.* Washington, D.C.: U.S. Department of Justice.

Zeisel, Hans, and Shari Diamond. 1977. "Search for Sentencing Equity: Sentence Review in Massachusetts and Connecticut." *American Bar Foundation Research Journal* 4:881–940.

Zimring, Franklin E. 1977. "Making the Punishment Fit the Crime: A Consumer's Guide to Sentencing Reform." *Hastings Center Report* 6(6):13–21.

Author Index—Volumes 1–10*

Baldwin, J. (1):29; (2):269
Bayley, D. H. (1):109; (10):1
Berk, R. A. (9):183
Biles, D. (5):235
Bittner, E. (1):239
Blumstein, A. (6):187; (10):231
Bondeson, U. (6):237
Bottoms, A. E. (8):101
Brennan, T. (9):201, 323
Bursik, Jr., R. J. (8):35

Clarke, R. V. (4):225; (6):147;
  (10):79
Cohen, J. (5):1
Cook, P. J. (2):211; (4):49; (7):1
Cornish, D. B. (6):147
Croft, J. (5):265

Doob, A. N. (5):253

Farrington, D. P. (1):289; (4):257;
  (6):187; (7):189; (9):53

Gaes, G. G. (6):95
Glaser, D. (1):203; (9):249
Goldkamp, J. S. (9):103
Gottfredson, D. M. (9):1
Gottfredson, M. R. (7):251
Gottfredson, S. D. (8):387; (9):21
Greenwood, P. W. (7):151
Gurr, T. R. (3):295

Hagan, J. (4):91
Hawkins, G. (5):85
Hay, D. (2):45

Ignatieff, M. (3):153

Jacobs, J. B. (1):1; (2):429; (10):171
Johnson, P. E. (6):221
Junger-Tas, J. (5):281

Kaiser, G. (5):297
Kleiman, M. A. R. (7):289
Klein, M. W. (1):145
Kobrin, S. (8):67

Lane, R. (2):1
Loeber, R. (7):29
Loftus, E. F. (3):105

Mayhew, P. (10):79
McConville, M. (2):269
McDonald, S. C. (8):163
McGahey, R. M. (8):231
Mednick, S. A. (2):85
Mennel, R. M. (4):191
Miller, M. (6):1
Moitra, S. (6):187
Monahan, J. (4):145
Morris, N. (6):1

Nagel, I. H. (4):91

* The number in parentheses indicates the volume in which the author's essay is published.

Orne, M. T. (3):61

Pease, K. (6):51
Petersilia, J. (2):321; (9):151

Rafter, N. H. (5):129
Reiss, Jr., A. J. (8):1; (10):117
Reuter, P. (7):289
Richards, D. A. J. (3):247
Rumbaut, R. G. (1):239

Sampson, R. J. (8):271
Schuerman, L. (8):67
Sechrest, L. (9):293
Shearing, C. D. (3):193
Sherman, L. W. (8):343
Skogan, W. G. (8):203; (10):39
Skolnick, J. H. (10):1
Smith, D. A. (8):313

Snare, A. (6):237
Sparks, R. F. (2):159; (3):1
Steadman, H. J. (4):145
Stenning, P. C. (3):193
Stouthamer-Loeber, M. (7):29

Taylor, R. B. (8):387
Toby, J. (4):1
Tonry, M. (9):367; (10):267
Turner, S. (9):151

Volavka, J. (2):85

Weigend, T. (2):381
West, D. J. (5):183
Wiles, P. (8):101

Zimring, F. E. (1):67

Title Index—Volumes 1–10*

Age and Crime (7):189

American Youth Violence: Issues and Trends (1):67

Attitudes and Policies toward Juvenile Delinquency in the United States: A Historiographical Review (4):191

Biology and Crime (2):85

The British Gas Suicide Story and Its Criminological Implications (10):79

Causal Inference as a Prediction Problem (9):183

Changing Conceptions of the Police Role: A Sociological Review (1):239

Classification: An Overview of Selected Methodological Issues (9):201

Classification for Control in Jails and Prisons (9):323

Classification for Risk (9):249

Classification for Treatment (9):293

Co-offending and Criminal Careers (10):117

Community Careers in Crime (8):67

Community Organizations and Crime (10):39

Community Service Orders (6):51

Continental Cures for American Ailments: European Criminal Procedure as a Model for Law Reform (2):381

Crime and Justice in Eighteenth- and Nineteenth-Century England (2):45

Crime and Mental Disorder: An Epidemiological Approach (4):145

Crime in Cities: The Effects of Formal and Informal Social Control (8):271

Criminal Career Research: A Review of Recent Evidence (2):321

Criminal Juries (2):269

Criminological Research in Scandinavia (6):237

A Critique of Marxist Criminology (2):159

Deinstitutionalization and Diversion of Juvenile Offenders: A Litany of Impediments (1):145

Delinquency Careers: Innocents, Desisters, and Persisters (6):187

The Demand and Supply of Criminal Opportunities (7):1

Differences in Criminal Behavior and Court Responses among Juvenile and Young Adult Defendants (7):151

* The number in parentheses indicates the volume in which the essay is published.

Does Gentrification Affect Crime Rates? (8):163

Ecological and Areal Studies in Great Britain and the United States (1):29
Ecological Stability and the Dynamics of Delinquency (8):35
Economic Conditions, Neighborhood Organization, and Urban Crime (8):231
The Effects of Overcrowding in Prison (6):95
Environmental Design, Crime, and Prevention: An Examination of Community Dynamics (8):387
Eyewitness Testimony: Psychological Research and Legal Thought (3):105

Family Factors as Correlates and Predictors of Juvenile Conduct Problems and Delinquency (7):29
Fear of Crime and Neighborhood Change (8):203

Gender and Crime: Offense Patterns and Criminal Court Sanctions (4):91
Guideline-based Justice: Prediction and Racial Minorities (9):151

Historical Trends in Violent Crimes: A Critical Review of the Evidence (3):295
Housing Tenure and Residential Community Crime Careers in Britain (8):101

Incapacitation as a Strategy for Crime Control: Possibilities and Pitfalls (5):1
The Influence of Gun Availability on Violent Crime Patterns (4):49

The Law and Criminology of Drunk Driving (10):171

Longitudinal Research on Crime and Delinquency (1):289

Modeling Offenders' Decisions: A Framework for Research and Policy (6):147
Modern Private Security: Its Growth and Implications (3):193

The Neighborhood Context of Police Behavior (8):313

The Organization of Criminological Research: Australia (5):235
The Organization of Criminological Research: Canada (5):253
The Organization of Criminological Research: Federal Republic of Germany (5):297
The Organization of Criminological Research: Great Britain and the Council of Europe (5):265
The Organization of Criminological Research: Netherlands (5):281

Police Function, Structure, and Control in Western Europe and North America: Comparative and Historical Studies (1):109
Policing Communities; What Works? (8):343
Predicting Individual Crime Rates (9):53
Prediction: An Overview of Selected Methodological Issues (9):21
Prediction and Classification in Criminal Justice Decision Making (9):1
Prediction and Classification: Legal and Ethical Issues (9):367
Prediction in Criminal Justice Policy Development (9):103
Predictions of Dangerousness (6):1
Prison Labor and Prison Industries (5):85
Prison Populations: A System Out of Control? (10):231

The Prisoners' Rights Movement
and Its Impacts, 1960–80 (2):429
Prisons for Women, 1790–1980
(5):129

Race Relations and the Prisoner
Subculture (1):1
Randomized Experiments on Crime
and Justice (4):257
Research in Criminal Deterrence:
Laying the Groundwork for the
Second Decade (2):211
A Review of Crime-Causation
Theory and Its Application
(1):203
Rights, Utility, and Crime (3):247
Risks and Prices: An Economic
Analysis of Drug Enforcement
(7):289

Sex Offenses and Offending (5):183
Situational Crime Prevention: Its
Theoretical Basis and Practical
Scope (4):225

State, Civil Society, and Total
Institutions: A Critique of Recent
Social Histories of Punishment
(3):153
Structuring Sentencing (10):267
Substantive Contributions of
Victimization Surveys (7):251
Surveys of Victimization—an
Optimistic Assessment (3):1

Theme and Variation in Community
Policing (10):1
The Turnabout in the Insanity
Defense (6):221

Urban Police and Crime in
Nineteenth-Century America (2):1
Use and Misuse of Hypnosis in
Court (3):61

Violence in School (4):1

Why Are Communities Important in
Understanding Crime? (8):1